INDIA AFTER NAXALBARI

INDIA AFTER NAXALBARI

Unfinished History

Bernard D'Mello

MONTHLY REVIEW PRESS

New York

Library of Congress Cataloging-in-Publication Data
available from the publisher

ISBN: 978-158367-706-3 (paper)
ISBN: 978-158367-707-0 (cloth)

MONTHLY REVIEW PRESS, NEW YORK
monthlyreview.org

Typeset in Minion Pro

5 4 3 2 1

Contents

Dedicated to the memory of

ANURADHA GHANDY (1954–2008)
She led the struggle for bread and roses, the fight for a richer and fuller life for all

NIRMAL KUMAR CHANDRA (1936–2014)
One of India's finest radical economists, whose aspirations lay beyond the limits of "acceptable scholarship"

P. A. SEBASTIAN (1938–2015)
Indefatigable lawyer–crusader for democratic rights, pioneer of Russell Tribunals in India

Acknowledgments

As I write these words of gratitude, I am filled with sadness upon hearing about the passing away of comrade Vikas (Arvind was his other alias), a politburo member of the Communist Party of India (Maoist). In the mid-1980s, as a journalist associated with the Kolkata-based radical-left weekly, *Frontier*, on a visit to the countryside of the district of Gaya in the State of Bihar, I first met Vikas, who was then a prominent leader of the Mazdoor Kisan Sangram Samiti (worker–peasant militant struggle association), and the Communist Party of India (Marxist–Leninist) (Party Unity), one of the predecessors of the CPI (Maoist). Vikas related to the poor and land-less peasants in an utterly egalitarian and democratic manner; he seemed to have earned their affection, loyalty, and respect by his deeds.

On this trip, when I was leaving a village on my way to the next one, an elderly man under the care of his grandson insisted on accompanying us (me, a *Frontier* companion, and our local guide) right to the outskirts of his village. When the time came to say our goodbyes and *Lal Salaams* (Red Salutes), I told him that he should not have taken all this effort to come so far with us. To which he replied: "You have come all the way from Kolkata to learn about us, our lives, our struggles, and our concerns. You care about us."

I never forgot Vikas or what this peasant-comrade told me, and was inspired, much later, when I felt adequately intellectually equipped, to write the essay "What Is Maoism?." And now, I've penned this book. Hundreds of millions of people have been the victims of Indian capitalism's irrationality, brutality, and inhumanity, and it is the actions of those who could not remain unmoved and were compelled to revolt that have motivated me to write this book. But as I write these words of a sense of obligation, I record with sorrow the death of Ashok Mitra, my favorite columnist, whose weekly columns, taken together, constitute what I have called a Guernica of political prose, so full of life, of anger and indignation, as well as empathy and compassion. He had given me some sound advice on finishing what I had begun, this book, and looked forward to the end product, but now he's no more.

The New York-based independent socialist magazine, *Monthly Review* has, over the years, been an essential part of my education, and it's wonderful that Monthly Review Press is publishing this book. The Marxist intellectual "underworld" in India has proved to be one of the best circles for my political education—Samar Sen, Timir Basu, P. A. Sebastian, Sumanta Banerjee, C. V. Subba Rao, K. Balagopal, Tilak Dasgupta, Ajit Roy, Sudesh Vaid, Gautam Navlakha, and Rajani X. Desai come to mind at first thought. Besides the ones I mention, there have also been left-party activists, feminists, ecologists, Dalits, oppressed nationalists, democratic rights' campaigners, and pacifists, from whose insights, probing questions, and criticism I have learned a great deal. I was very fond of my thesis supervisor, the radical economist Nirmal Kumar Chandra, who later became a good friend and encouraged me on the unconventional path I took, which has eventually led to this book. And, I cannot forget my first editor, Samar Sen (Shômor babu), founder-editor of *Frontier*, celebrated post-Tagorean Bengali poet, who encouraged me to widen my intellectual repertoire.

Initial versions of what became chapters 6 and 9 first appeared in the *Economic & Political Weekly* (*EPW*), whose then editor C. Rammanohar Reddy's comments and suggestions helped improve both form and content. The preliminary text of chapter 9 was in the form of notes that I had prepared for a Sheikh Abdul Rawoof memorial lecture I delivered at Thrissur (in Kerala) in March 2014. I presented an embryonic version of chapter 8 at a seminar organized by the Committee for the Protection of Democratic Rights in Nagpur, and in a lecture organized by students of the Radical Study Circle, Tata Institute of Social Sciences (TISS), Mumbai, both in 2015. Parts of chapter 10 were presented as part of the first Randhir Singh memorial lecture I was invited to deliver at New Delhi in January 2017.

Chapters 1, 4, and 7 first took shape in a series of lectures I gave on the Maoist movement in India for a postgraduate course on "State, Democracy, and Conflicts in India," taught by Professor Farrukh Faheem at the TISS. I also benefitted from a conference on "Marxist Revolutionary Movements across the World" at the University of Oxford in July 2011, organized by professors Alpa Shah and Stephen Feuchtwang, where I presented a paper on the Maoist movement in India. The Monthly Review Foundation's former online magazine, *MRZine*, with Yoshie Furuhashi as editor, and the Bengali "small magazine," *Aneek*, with the late Dipankar Chakrabarty as editor, were open to my ideas and analyses presented in occasional journalistic pieces, which, taken together, made the penning of chapter 7 a lot easier than it would otherwise have been.

I thank Subhas Aikat of the Kharagpur-based Cornerstone Publications; Rajani Desai and Girish Srinivasan of the Mumbai-based Research Unit for Political Economy; Alpa Shah, Swapna Banerjee-Guha, Ajmal Khan, and Arup Sen for readily responding to my requests to locate and send me certain essential books and papers. The construction of the maps I owe to my *EPW* colleague, Abhishek Shaw, and I am grateful to him for devoting precious hours to the task. For the photograph of Maoist guerrillas on the march that graces the book's cover, Monthly Review Press and I are obligated to the well-known documentary filmmaker Sanjay Kak.

The writing of this book put an unintended additional load on my *EPW* colleagues, for I was on leave from my job for a year and a half. I express my sense of obligation to them.

I am grateful to John Mage for reading a first draft of the entire manuscript. His classical approach to Marxist analyses, his queries, his pointing me to errors, his encouragement. John, I needed the kind of gentle assurance and guidance you provided with regard to my ways of looking at and thinking about the subject matter of this book. Uma and Anand Chakravarti's helpful comments on a draft of the Appendix on Caste were valuable. Swapna Banerjee-Guha's reactions to a draft of chapter 1 gave me the confidence I needed to plod on, for she had been what social anthropologists call a "participant observer" in Kolkata in the course of "Spring Thunder," Phase I. Stephen Rego, who copyedited the entire manuscript, actually did much more than that—his observations on chapters 1, 4, and 7 have enriched both form *and* content. Michael D. Yates, Director, Monthly Review Press, read the entire manuscript after it had been copy-edited, and helpfully pointed to transatlantic differences with regard to commas and much else that both Stephen and I had overlooked. Michael's words, "I enjoyed reading your book and learned a great deal from it," mean a lot to me. Thank you, Michael.

I must record a big thank-you to Martin Paddio and Susie Day at Monthly Review Press; and to K. K. Saxena, publisher, Aakar Books, Delhi; for all it takes to reach out to readers and keep the enterprise going.

Finally, words would never suffice to express my gratitude to ma and pa, Jean Florence Abrahams and Charles Francis D'Mello, working-class parents who raised me; to Pauline Menezes, my partner, who has stood by me through my darkest nights, kept me from the brink of the abyss. And, to our son Samar and daughter Vera, I am now in debt to the tune of five holidays in the hills and by the riverside.

—BERNARD D'MELLO
Mumbai, May 1, 2018

Introduction

Alongside China, India has been hailed as one of the world's most significant "emerging" economies/markets. But one might well ask: in what way has India been "emerging"? Open to the expansion of Northern multinational capital that is driven to exploit "global labor arbitrage" opportunities? Open to international financial capital in its perennial hunt for capital gains? Unlike India, it is China, with huge current account surpluses on its balance of payments, deriving mainly from export of manufactured goods, which has proved capable of setting the terms of its "economic openness" and successfully directing the accumulation process to its own national development. While China has been open to capital exploiting the global labor arbitrage opportunity it offers in the production of manufactured goods for export to Northern markets, India has been offering the same in Information Technology (IT)-enabled services. India's international competitiveness in IT–enabled services derives from the fact that the value created by its IT workers is a multiple of what they are paid, and much of the surplus value is captured through exchange by the Northern clients of the Indian IT–enabled service-providing firms.

But despite being a successful exporter of IT–enabled services, India continues to systematically run a deficit on the current account of its balance of payments. And it has been dependent mainly on inflows of speculative capital to finance that deficit. Its foreign exchange reserves have been built up mainly because net capital inflows have been exceeding the current account deficits. India's fiscal, monetary, and financial policies are significantly tailored to entice international financial capital and retain it, for a steady depletion of the foreign exchange reserves could possibly set off a capital flight by financial speculators, leading to quick disappearance of these reserves. After all, it doesn't take much Northern money to push up stock-market prices, nor will it take much to generate a capital flight and a sudden collapse of those prices. The "emerging" Indian stock market can suddenly turn into a "submerging" one.

At $2,088.5 billion and $1,590 in 2015, India's gross national income (GNI)—total domestic and foreign value-added claimed by residents—and GNI per capita are merely one-fifth of China's. Moreover, India's monstrous income inequality is worse than China's. The proportion of India's population below an international poverty line of $3.10 a day in 2011 was 68.0 percent (more than Bangladesh's 63.0 percent figure) while the same was only 19.1 percent in China. In 2015, India's under-five mortality rate (per 1,000 live births) and maternal mortality rate (per 100,000 live births) were 48 and 174, respectively, compared to China's 11 and 27, respectively.

The percentage of children under age five who are stunted—a largely irreversible outcome of inadequate nutrition and repeated bouts of infection during the first 1,000 days of a child's life—is 38.7 percent in India (higher than Bangladesh's 36.4 percent figure) compared to 9.4 percent in China.[1] Mother India, "Yours is a sadness that / fails to comfort the children crawling over / your barren breasts," the radical Telugu poet Cherabanda Raju would have lamented. Indeed, the percentages of India's urban and rural populations not even able to access the minimum calorie norms of 2,100 and 2,200 calories per person per day, 65 percent and 68 percent, respectively, in 2011–12, is indicative of mass hunger. The corresponding figures in 1993–94 were 57 percent and 58.5 percent, respectively, and so there is *growing* mass hunger.[2] To give meaning to the above-mentioned development indicators in a world context, one must emphasize that in 2011, as much as 17.5 percent of the world's population resided in India, and 19.4 percent in China.

One can go on, but the sharp differences between India and China on key indicators of development is there for all to see, and one begins to feel India's misery. India remains among the most poverty-stricken countries of the world, with most of its population still inadequately fed, miserably clothed, wretchedly housed, poorly educated, and without access to decent medical care. Its *deeply oppressive and exploitative social order is crying out for revolutionary change.*

I am, however, not going to say that China did this and that, which India did not do. India gained political independence in 1947; China accomplished a popular, national, anti-semi-feudal, anti-imperialist revolution in 1949. This as a result of a protracted class struggle from 1927 to 1949 led by the Chinese Communist Party, independently of Chinese big business. This revolution succeeded in changing the class structure and social institutions to create a distinctively egalitarian society. But China's post-Mao leadership, from the late 1970s onward, steering the same non-capitalist state, gradually, one step leading on to the other, worked to bring back capitalism in the economy, leading to an appalling maldistribution of income. With an extensive revolutionary history, however, revolutionary consciousness and motivation is unlikely to just fade away. New waves of revolution are likely to come again.

Even as the Chinese and the Indians have been making their own history, they have not been able to, indeed, cannot make it as they please. The revolutionary process has been developing unevenly and more slowly in India, thwarted by its inevitable accompaniment, counterrevolution, whose principal base has been in the "overdeveloped" Indian state. India's unfinished revolution has, nevertheless, been gathering strength and augmenting its forces against the counterrevolution. However, more recently, a major section of the latter, with a fascist ideology and a powerful, reactionary mass movement backing it, has gone on an offensive against the forces of liberal-political democracy *and* the left, this by using a mix of electoral politics and illegal violence to advance its goal of instituting a Hindu *Rashtra* (nation). To be able to write wisely about India's present, one needs to know where India is going, for which viewing "the present as history" is a must. To understand India, it is essential to get to the roots of the poverty, the misery, the degradation, and the injustice that the majority of its people suffer. And importantly, one must comprehend, recognize, and empathize with the struggles, the unrest, and the ideas emanating from the exploitation, the oppression, and the domination that often become unbearable.

Chapter 1, titled "Naxalite! 'Spring Thunder,' Phase I," begins with an account of a revolutionary armed peasant uprising in 1967 in Naxalbari, at the foot of the Himalayas. I view this rebellion as part and parcel of a (then) contemporary, worldwide impulse among radicals embracing the spirit of revolutionary humanism. It was this revolutionary struggle that inspired the creation of the Communist Party of India (Marxist–Leninist) in 1969. The uprising at Naxalbari stimulated insurrections in other parts of the country, and so, when Charu Mazumdar, the leader of what became the Naxalite movement, predicted in the fall of 1967 that "Naxalbari . . . will never die," he was saying something about the ability of his followers to survive, continue, and expand the movement in the face of ruthless repression let loose by the Indian state. Naxalbari came to stand for the road to revolution in India, and the term "Naxalite" found a place in the lexicon of world revolution.

In chapter 2, titled "'1968' India as History," I try to understand the "1968" decade—a world historic turning-point—in India where, too, revolutionary humanism came to the fore but was sought to be extinguished by extraordinary state repression. I touch upon a number of social movements

besides the Naxalite revolutionary uprising—the civil liberties and democratic rights movement; the "Chipko" ecological movement; the Dalit
Panther Movement of India's Untouchables, inspired by America's Black
Panthers; the evolution of the women's movements; militant movements of
workers; and so on.

The "1968" decade was marked by brutal state repression, with the
unleashing of political barbarism in a setting of unabated colonial policy.
In many respects, independent India has failed to make a break from its
colonial past. The '68ers of the various social movements and the Naxalite
insurgency drew their inspiration from the democratic and anti-imperialist
proclivities of the many peasant uprisings before and after 1885, the year
the Indian National Congress party was founded. That party, supported by
Indian big business, led the national movement for independence, successfully disguising what was a class project as *the* national project.

I view the longer process, from colonial times to the present, in terms
of a series of rebellions for justice and well-being by ordinary people that
incurred the wrath of the state and were crushed by brutal repression. What
followed was reform, with laws to that effect, accompanied by encouragement of a reformist strand among the political elite. The latter's dependability
was gauged by the extent to which it went in condemning the rebels/revo-
lutionaries and expressing faith in the establishment's will to bring about
gradual, progressive change. Opportunist to the core, the political elite took
advantage of the persistence of militant struggles to enhance its own bargaining power vis-à-vis the ruling classes. Its omissions and commissions
guaranteed the failure or the falsity of progressive reform, and rebellions
recurred, in newer forms, like the many Naxalbaris in three phases over the
last fifty years. In different ways and in changed contexts, India's "1968" is
still with us, in the questions it raised about the future, and in its quest for an
egalitarian, democratic India.

Chapter 2 takes a "voluntarist" view of "the present as history," focusing
on the determination and the will power of the protagonists, inspired by
their respective collective memories of India's modern past. In sharp contrast, chapter 3, titled "Unequal Development and Evolution of the Ruling
Bloc," takes a "determinist" view of "the present as history," focusing on the
ways in which history and the given conditions existing on the ground have
determined what has been happening. Neither approach is radical enough
without the other. The two, the "voluntarist" and the "determinist," have to
be intelligently synthesized to gain a fuller understanding of "the present as
history."

Chapter 3 tries to throw light on the principal characteristics of India's
underdeveloped capitalism and the process of dependent and unequal

development, steered, during the last six to seven decades, by an Indian big business–state–multinational capitalist ruling bloc. The chapter traces the evolution of India from a petty-commodity, tribute-paying social formation in the seventeenth century to Company–State Raj (rule) and the switch from "Old" to "New" colonialism in the nineteenth century, metamorphosing gradually into imperialist domination in the Leninist sense as that century drew to a close. The process leads on to a blossoming of Indian big business during the two wars and the inter-war period in the twentieth century. Following political independence in 1947, an ambivalent, integrated industrial development unfolds, especially from 1957 onward, leading on to the present twenty-first-century high-point of Indian big business, the multinationals, and Northern speculative financial capital in command, together shaping economic outcomes.

The colonial state was "overdeveloped" in relation to the economic base in terms of its powers of control and regulation, and the bureaucracy, the military, and the polity in independent India had a vested interest in continuity rather than change on this score. So also the services sector of the colonial economy relative to the physical commodity–producing sectors, even though, at independence, the primary sector remained dominant in terms of its contribution to India's gross domestic product and livelihoods. But, it was a matter of time, in independent India, when a bloated services sector relative to the primary and secondary sectors would become a systemic necessity, essential for the realization of the surplus generated in the latter sectors. This was because vast numbers of people got left out of the development that was supposed to accompany the growth of modern industry and there was no way by which agriculture could have ever reabsorbed them. The historical roots of both the contemporary huge reserve army of labor relative to the active army of wage labor and the huge mass of petty-commodity producers of goods and services as part of this labor reserve must be located in "the drain" of part of the surplus of the economy—siphoning this out without any quid pro quo—and in the process of de-proto-industrialization during the colonial period.

Chapter 4, titled "Naxalite! 'Spring Thunder,' Phase II," basically shows how a significant section of the Naxalites, in the period 1978–2003, take Mao's dictum that a people's war "can be waged only by mobilizing the masses and relying on them" seriously in their practice. They build a worker–peasant alliance. They set up women's organizations and link them with the peasants' and workers' organizations so that both men and women get joint titles to the occupied lands that are distributed among poor and landless labor households. They assign great importance to the caste question, for caste defines the culture of exploitation in the Indian countryside. And, they build village militias and armed guerrilla squads, which gradually coalesce into a people's guerrilla army in the face of full-scale counterinsurgency operations launched by the Indian state.

Chapter 5, titled "India's '1989'—'Financial Aristocracy' and Government à Bon Marché," covers the "1989" period—another world historic turning-point—in India, a sharp reactionary counterpoint to "1968," leading to monstrous income and wealth inequality and the emergence of a financial aristocracy. The latter gets its additional wealth more from pocketing the already available wealth of others, including public/state wealth, than from the appropriation of surplus value (and the surplus product) in production. Poor peasants and tribal forest dwellers, their habitats and environments violently and catastrophically uprooted in the course of capitalist growth of modern industry and infrastructure, have been left with no alternative but to either passively accept their relegation to irrelevance or to actively resist.

Rosa Luxemburg defined imperialism as "the political expression of the accumulation of capital in its competitive struggle for what remains still open for the non-capitalist environment"[3] within a capitalist country's own borders and beyond, through militarism and war. In this respect, one senses continuity vis-à-vis the colonial period, evident in the ongoing penetration of Indian big business and the MNCs into the tribal areas of central and eastern India, and the Indian state's engagement in a "war against its own people" as part of the land, mineral, and other natural-resource grabs over there.

I try to throw light on the state's handover of scarce natural-resource and other public assets cheap to Indian big business and multinationals, assets that are then commoditized, and become the source of capital gains. I attempt to unravel, in the specific context of the natural-resource grabs in the tribal areas of central and eastern India, what drives the economic process, and brings on the unbridled greed of the financial aristocracy, the political violence, the contests for political power, the fraud, the looting, the incapacity to recognize the value of older, nature-revering cultures, and the resistance of the victims, led by the Maoists. In short, I endeavor to understand what brings on the "imperialist" onslaught—in Rosa Luxemburg's sense of the term—of the Indian state and big business, within India's own borders, against their own people.

Chapter 6, titled "'The Near and the Far'—India's Rotten Liberal–Political Democracy," argues that capitalism in India is incompatible with liberal-political democracy if the latter is understood as governance in accordance with the will of the people. Liberal-political democracy is, however, seldom viewed in this way. Rather, and correctly, it is identified with free competition among two or more political parties for votes and political office, the counterpart of free competition for profits in capitalism's economic sphere. But, just as, in reality, oligopoly and market power rule in the economic sphere, so, in the political realm, the party that commands the most money and naked power is most likely to be voted into office.

Political rights are invariably violated in situations where bourgeois private property rights are threatened. India's liberal-political democracy requires the violence of the oppressed to be pressurized to deliver justice. The main reason why India's liberal-political democracy is rotten is because the process of capitalist development from colonial times to the present has essentially been a conservative modernization from above. And the caste system and discrimination on the basis of ethnicity, nationality, and religion have, so far, inhibited any stable, long-lasting unity of the oppressed and the exploited aimed at progressive modernization from below. This shackling of modernization from below, accompanied by severe state repression when a section of the oppressed unite and resist, has, so far, worked to deny the Maoist revolutionary movement, and indeed all progressive movements, evolution in accordance with their inner logic.

In chapter 7, titled "Maoist! 'Spring Thunder,' Phase III," I look at the Maoist revolutionary movement in the period 2004–2013, now with a significant guerrilla army in place, but yet grappling with the predicament of not being able to develop in accordance with its inner logic. The revolutionary movement suffers a major setback in the province of Andhra Pradesh (now split up into Telangana and Andhra Pradesh) when the ongoing counterinsurgency operations of the state manage to "hunt down" many of the main Maoist leaders. But the movement proves resilient in the Bastar region of Chhattisgarh province despite the unleashing of a state-backed, state-armed private vigilante force, and later, a centrally-coordinated, massive deployment of central and provincial armed police forces, that came to be known as "Operation Green Hunt." A very promising spread of the revolutionary movement in parts of Jangalmahal—the tribal blocks in West Midnapore, Purulia, and Bankura districts in the province of West Bengal—however, suffers defeat. At the heart of phase III of the Maoist revolutionary movement is unrelenting resistance to "imperialism," the latter, as understood in Rosa Luxemburg's sense of the term. I round off my presentation of fifty years of the Naxalite/Maoist movement with an explanation of the persistence of revolutionary mobilization and my understanding of where the movement is going.

Chapter 8, titled "'Rotten at the Heart'—the 'Secular State,'" deals with the abysmal failure of the Indian state to abide by its duty to safeguard individual and corporate "freedom of religion," to treat individuals as citizens with human rights irrespective of their religious affiliations, to not identify itself with any particular religion, and to not promote or interfere with any religion, thus separating itself from religion. I look at three major communal-hate pogroms, Delhi 1984, Bombay 1993, and Gujarat 2002, to pinpoint three grave "omissions and commissions" of the executive of the Indian state. One, powerful sections of the executive of the Indian state encouraged its law-and-order machinery to turn a blind eye to the terrible mass crimes that were being committed under its very nose. Two, they considered the perpetrators of these crimes to be "patriots" and those who wanted to bring these xenophobic liquidators to book as "betrayers of the nation." Three, they demanded of the public prosecutors and the investigative agencies that they protect the "patriots" accused of committing the terrible crimes. I also focus attention on the fact that the country's two major national political parties, the Congress party and the Bharatiya Janata Party, acted in a manner prejudicial to interreligious harmony, and engaged in unlawful activity with the intent of causing harm to particular religious communities.

Chapter 9, titled "'Little Man, What Now?'—In the Wake of Semi-Fascist and Sub-Imperialist Tendencies," discerns a semi-fascist regime in the making following the assumption into office of Narendra Modi as prime minister in 2014. I also trace the emergence of India as a nascent sub-imperialist power. In trying to conceptualize semi-fascism, I search for clues from historical fascism, even as I caution against permanently fixing the meaning of fascism based on its historical forms in Germany and Italy. Semi-fascism in the making in India encompasses an "authoritarian-democratic" regime and a sub-imperialist power, with the regime maintaining a close nexus with big business, nurturing and supporting the Hindutva-nationalist movement to the extent of being complicit in its criminal acts, and insisting on controlling its "necessary" enemies through the use of terror.

My conceptualization of sub-imperialism draws from the ideas of the Brazilian radical scholar Ruy Mauro Marini. I emphasize India's strategic alliance as a junior partner with U.S. imperialism, but with the privilege of prior consultation with Washington in matters of common concern in South Asia. I draw attention to the global face of Indian big business with its own multinational companies; state-led infrastructure projects in South Asia; super-exploitation of those who produce the surplus value and the surplus product; and the escalation of militarism with Washington as New Delhi's "Major Defense Partner." I emphasize the regional geopolitical–military dimension of Indian sub-imperialism. I also draw attention to the importance of the notions of *Akhand Bharat*—undivided India, geographically as it existed prior to Partition in 1947—and "Greater India" in defining the nation's geographical borders and ideological frontiers, respectively. I suggest that India's semi-peripheral status and its sub-imperialism are conducive to semi-fascism. And I include as an integral part of this sub-imperialism, the teaming up of the Indian state and big business, Indian and multinational, driven by the dynamic of "accumulation by dispossession," to advance their power, their influence, and their mutual interests in the "non-capitalist areas"[4] within the country, where all this is utterly disruptive and traumatic for the victims who are left with no other option but to uncompromisingly resist.

Where then is India going? Will what remains of India's continuing "1968" bring twenty-first-century "New Democracy" to the collective agenda? Or will the ongoing regression of "1989" lead the way to full-blown semi-fascism and sub-imperialism?

Chapter 10, "History, Memory, and Dreams—Reimagining 'New Democracy,'" as its title indicates, senses the need to re-imagine and state up-front what kind of "New Democracy" the united front against the sub-imperialist-capitalist order needs to institute upon coming to power in the course of a national, popular, democratic, anti-imperialist, anti-semi-feudal revolution in India. The sub-imperialist-capitalist order and present-day Indian society have proved to be totally incompatible with democracy when the latter is understood in terms of its basic principles and aspirations—liberty, equality, and comradeship (fraternity is not the appropriate word now).

While keeping in place its historic legacy, "New Democracy" needs to be re-imagined as part of a truly democratic, human needs–based "political transition period" on the long road to a communitarian basis for socialism. Taking the perspective of the "small voices" of "the present as history," and in empathy with those voices, I relook at the classic peasant question and the agenda of radical land reform and conceptualize the contemporary peasant question in terms of a series of peasant questions. I also stress the need for an interim program to first win the political battle against Hindutva-nationalism and semi-fascism.

But, more importantly, and in the light of the core political question that I pose in this book, *semi-peripheral underdevelopment or revolution*, I re-imagine the revolutionary horizon of India's Maoists, hoping that my scholarly doggedness and their political efforts might converge. Seventy years have gone by since India's independence, and my analysis (and conviction) is that capitalist development will not be able to overcome underdevelopment—mass poverty, misery, and degradation stemming from super-exploitation, oppression, and domination; technological backwardness; and economic dependence. Behind the affluence and luxury of the few lies the poverty and misery of the many. Behind the apparent civilization of the few lies the degradation of the many. From the latter half of the 1950s onward, the process of unequal development has led to a transition from peripheral underdevelopment to semi-peripheral underdevelopment. This is evident in the greatly enhanced power of the Indian state and the burgeoning wealth of Indian big business, but with the extreme backwardness of the periphery remaining in large parts of the country. There are definite limits to development in a semi-peripheral underdeveloped country like India, its sub-imperialism notwithstanding.

I'd like to say a few words about my analytical approach to the subject matter of the book. When I started work on the book I was not sure of the most fruitful approach, so I indulged in a bit of trial and error, and retained what I thought best. Reality, I was convinced, is fluid and ever-changing, and so one's definitions, concepts, and framework must be open-ended and capable of being adapted and applied in different contexts and periods. It is hardly the case that the political and ideological superstructure is always tightly circumscribed by the economic base. One must be open to empirical evidence. In this light, I sense that in an underdeveloped capitalist system like that of India's, the economic structure is not as much the autonomous sub-system it usually is in a developed capitalist system. But, of course, I view India as part of the capitalist world-system, operating within the framework and constraints of that system. And I am convinced that the truth of the "center" is, more often than not, revealed in the "periphery" and "semi-periphery" of the capitalist world-system.

In a country like India, politics dominates over economics more than in the developed capitalist countries. This is because—as Joan Robinson and John Eatwell put it in a heterodox economics textbook, *An Introduction to Modern Economics*—economic policy has been involved with the type of society that is emerging. "Is development intended to aim primarily at feeding the people and overcoming the grossest misery, or is it primarily to make room for a prosperous middle class, or to defend the privileges of [capital and] landed property?"[5] I came to studying economics after an exposure to science and engineering, and found the division of labor and the specializations in the social sciences a hindrance and detrimental to attaining a comprehensive understanding of the problems I sought to investigate. To be meaningful, social analysis must not partition real-world phenomena into separate economic, political, and sociological domains.

My approach in this book is interdisciplinary, with a historical perspective throughout, and I focus on the class struggle, even as I try not to lose sight of caste, which, with the persistence of its very slowly moving structure over the *longue durée*, continues to significantly define the culture of exploitation and oppression in India. This book draws on existing knowledge and analysis from "the library" and "the field," and puts them together in new and different ways, to raise questions and offer some conclusions which, hopefully, might help other writers to advance their own researches on India. If there are a few rich insights, these eye-openers might inevitably be accompanied by strands of incredible blindness. My intellectual debts will be found in the text and the endnotes, but, as regards the conceptual and analytical framework, I must mention, in particular, the influence of Samir Amin, Hamza Alavi, Ranajit Guha, Nirmal K. Chandra, Paul A. Baran, Paul M. Sweezy, Harry Magdoff, Ruy Mauro Marini, Immanuel Wallerstein, Barrington Moore, Jr., Rosa Luxemburg, Karl Marx, and Mao Zedong. At the heart of this book is a comprehension of "the present as history"—the way Paul M Sweezy understood this important intellectual task—for the present is still at hand and so we have the power to shape it and influence its outcome.

Without the Naxalite/Maoist insurgency and the other progressive movements that were kindled in the '68 period, capitalism in India would have by now turned barbaric. Revolution didn't happen but it forced reform; one can think of what it takes to grab a chunk of meat from the mouth of a tiger. A word or two about the spirit of the revolutionaries is then called for. They have been the architects of the revolutionary process that has being developing, albeit slowly and unevenly. I have, metaphorically, put myself in their shoes to feel their rage, fury, revulsion, and moral indignation directed against the powers-that-be, their empathy and compassion toward the oppressed, both in the face of the terror and the inhumanity of the counterrevolution . . . A refusal to remain silent and unmoved in the face of the myriad injustices and indignities the poor are made to suffer . . . The fetters of intuitive self-preservation thrown to the winds . . . Ready to fight on in the face of impossible odds . . . There's always the satisfaction of having fought courageously and conscientiously for a better world. India's underdevelopment is guaranteed to bring such people back into the political arena; stubborn individuals, they'll constantly be reborn; indeed, some of them might just refuse to die. They're bent upon doing what they promise to do—their deeds in harmony with their words. I take recourse to citing stanzas of Naxalite poetry to convey the feelings and emotions.

But as regards the Maoist strategy of "protracted people's war," the hard reality on this score is that all they have after fifty years is a relatively small guerrilla army of the poor, operating on the margins of Indian society. So they need to take serious stock of the impasse of this strategy when the movement is confronted with India's overdeveloped state, particularly the state's repressive apparatus, which is backed by a coercive legal structure and is endorsed by a colonial value system. The Indian state has been aggressively working to wipe out the movement by all available means, fair or foul, violating with impunity Common Article 3 of the Geneva Conventions and

Protocol II, relating to non-international armed conflict, and even conventional civil and political rights. The cycle of repression, resistance, and
further repression seems endless.

I nevertheless grasp the significance of the Maoist movement, and provide both a romantic eulogy and a critical analysis of it. This anti-systemic
movement has been holding the Indian banner for a relatively egalitarian and
a relatively democratic world high over a fairly long period. Viewed historically in terms of its antecedents from the mid-nineteenth century onward,
even though it has been defeated many times, it has, nevertheless, always
made a comeback and never given up the fight. Its more recent record has
however been blurred and smeared by what can only be described as a hys-
terical form of anti-Maoism. Hopefully, India's unfinished history might just
set that record straight. On my part, I refuse to sit on the fence and observe
both sides dispassionately. Warts and all, one needs to combine partisanship
with scrupulously temperate observation. I remain critically optimistic.

— 1 —

Naxalite! "Spring Thunder,"
Phase I

... [W]hen my child
Returns from school,
And not finding the name of the village
In his geography map,
Asks me
Why it is not there,
I am frightened
And remain silent.
But I know
This simple word
Of four syllables
Is not just the name of a village,
But the name of the whole country.
—AN EXCERPT FROM "THE NAME OF A VILLAGE,"
A HINDI POEM BY KUMAR VIKAL[1]

Tomar bari, aamar bari, Naxalbari, Naxalbari.
Tomar naam, aamar naam, Vietnam, Vietnam.

The name of the "village" was Naxalbari, situated at the foot of the Himalayas in the Darjeeling area of north Bengal, bordering Nepal to the west, Sikkim and Bhutan to the north, East Pakistan (now, Bangladesh) to the south. Naxalbari, Kharibari, Phansidewa and parts of the Siliguri police-station jurisdiction are where it all began in March 1967, and Naxalbari came to stand for this whole area. (Map 1 will be of help throughout this chapter; see pages 24 and 25.) Indeed, there was a time when conservative parents didn't want to send their sons/daughters to Kolkata's elite Presidency College for fear that—like the group of rebel-students

Map 1: Political Geography: "Spring Thunder," Phase I (1967–75)

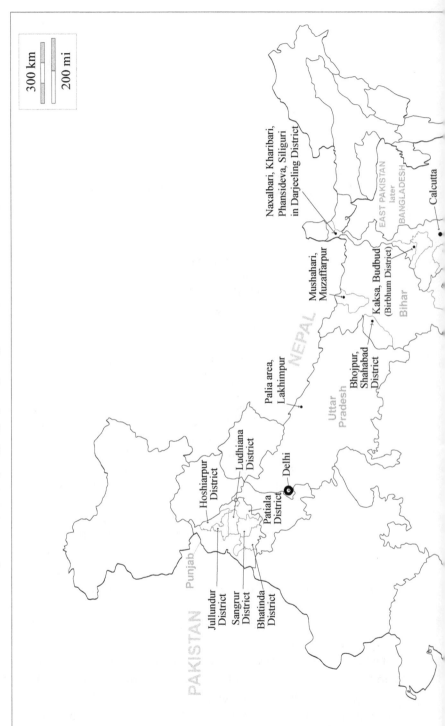

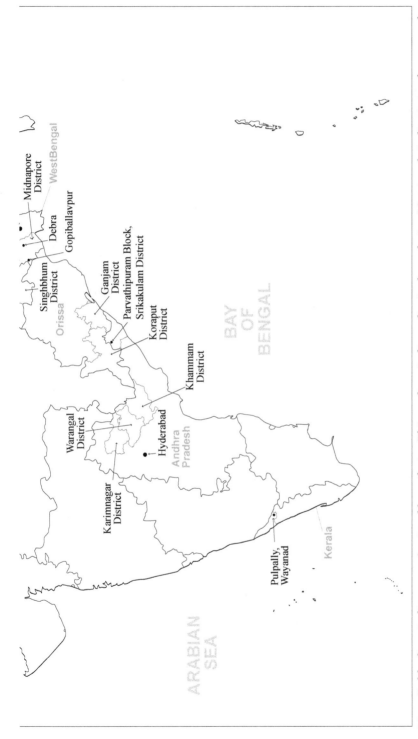

Note: Bolder lines indicate state/national boundaries. Thinner lines indicate district boundaries. Map is only indicative and not to scale.

Source: Map adapted from www.d-maps.com using information in Census of India.

who came to be known as the "Presidency Consolidation"—they might be "indoctrinated" by the "Naxalites," Maoist revolutionaries who were given that *naam* (name) from the village where the movement came into being. Indeed, the term *Naxalite* came to symbolize "any assault upon the assumptions and institutions that support the established order in India," and soon found "a place in the vocabulary of world revolution."[2]

The '68 generation had arrived, so to say, with the Cultural Revolution in China; the "Prague Spring" (that provoked the Soviet invasion) in Czechoslovakia; the Naxalbari uprising in India; a regenerated communist party and its New People's Army in the Philippines; *soixante-huitards* that were against the French establishment *and* the PCF (the French Communist Party); the German SDS (socialist German student league) that took on the West German establishment and the SPD (the German social-democratic party); the Civil Rights movement, fountainhead of the Black Panther Party, and the anti-(Vietnam) War movement in the United States; unprecedented student unrest, guerrilla war in the state of Guerrero, a militant labor movement, and land occupations by impoverished peasants, in Mexico, all pitted against the ruling establishment, the PRI (Institutional Revolutionary Party), entrenched in power for decades. Revolutionary humanism was in the air; political expediency evoked derision; Paul Baran and Paul Sweezy's *Monopoly Capital* exposed the Affluent Society for the delusion that it was; and youth, in political ferment, began to perceive the established (establishment?) left as having stripped Marxism of its revolutionary essence. Naxalbari was part and parcel of a (then) contemporary, worldwide impulse among radicals, young and not-so-young, embracing the spirit of revolutionary humanism.

But, today, all that remains of Naxalbari, in insurgent geography, is a memorial column erected by the Communist Party of India (Marxist-Leninist), the CPI(ML), in honor of the eleven who were killed in the police firing on May 25, 1967—seven women, Dhaneswari Devi, Simaswari Mullick, Nayaneswari Mullick, Surubala Burman, Sonamati Singh, Fulmati Devi, and Samsari Saibani; two men, Gaudrau Saibani and Kharsingh Mullick; and "two children," actually infants, whose names have not been inscribed. And, of course, there are the busts of Lenin, Stalin, Mao, and Charu Mazumdar, the latter, the Naxalite movement's "ideologue" and leader in its first phase. But even as the Indian Establishment made sure that the Naxal way of life was obliterated from Naxalbari, the name acquired a symbolic meaning. It came to stand for the road to revolution in India.

The ramifications of what happened at Naxalbari, what the poor peasants' armed struggle over there triggered, have not yet been fully deciphered. The Naxalbari armed struggle began in March 1967; by the end of July of that year, it was crushed. But, soon thereafter, in the autumn, Charu Mazumdar, who subsequently became the CPI(ML)'s General Secretary, said: ". . . hundreds of Naxalbaris are smoldering in India. . . . Naxalbari has not died and will never die."[3] Certainly, he was not daydreaming, for the power of memory and the dreams unleashed a powerful dynamic of resistance that, ever since, has alarmed the Indian ruling classes and the political establishment. Indeed, an editorial in the Chinese Communist Party's *People's Daily* on July 5, 1967, hailing the creation of the "red area of rural revolutionary armed struggle" in Naxalbari as "Spring Thunder over India," called it a "development of tremendous significance for the Indian people's revolutionary struggle."[4]

In 2017, the fiftieth year of the Naxalite movement in India, Charu Mazumdar's statement seems almost prescient. In 1968, an ongoing struggle in Srikakulam led by two schoolteachers, Vempatapu Satyanarayana, popularly known as "Gappa Guru"—who had married and settled among the tribes—and Adibhatla Kailasam, and organized under the Ryotanga Sangrama Samiti (peasant struggle committee) with guerrilla squads in self-defense, had mobilized "almost the entire tribal population in the Srikakulam Agency Area."[5] And Warangal, Khammam, Mushahari, Bhojpur, Debra–Gopiballavpur, Kanksa–Budbud, Ganjam–Koraput, Lakhimpur, and other "prairie fires" were not far behind. The origins of the CPI (Maoist), reckoned by the political establishment in July 2006, in the then Prime Minister Manmohan Singh's words at a conference in New Delhi, as India's "single biggest internal security challenge," must be traced to its roots. After all, the Maoist armed struggle in India, alongside the one in the Philippines, is one of the world's longest surviving peasant insurgencies.

WHERE IT ALL BEGAN

In March 1967, in the "semi-feudal" setting of Naxalbari, tribal peasants organized into peasant committees under the leadership of a revolutionary group within the CPI(Marxist)—CPM hereinafter—one of the main two of India's parliamentary communist parties,[6] and with rudimentary militias armed with traditional weapons, undertook a political program of anti-landlordism involving the burning of land records, cancellation of debts, the passing of death sentences on oppressive landlords, and the looting of landlords' guns. By May of the same year, the rebels established certain strongholds, Hatighisha (in Naxalbari), Buraganj (in Kharibari), and Chowpukhuria (in Phansidewa), where they were in control. But by the end of July, the movement collapsed under the pressure of a major armed-police action.

Be that as it may, in the Maoist view, Charu Mazumdar had not merely rebelled against the "revisionism" (stripping Marxism of its revolutionary essence) of the CPM in his writings—"Eight Documents" penned between January 1965 and April 1967[7]—but had also given a bold call for armed struggle in the rural countryside, and his followers in Naxalbari had heeded this appeal. The West Bengal state assembly elections were held in February 1967, and in keeping with Charu Mazumdar's suggestion that the revolutionaries should take advantage of the polls to propagate their politics, they took the benefit of the period of electoral campaigning to raise the political consciousness of the poor peasants, mainly Santhals, Oraons, and Rajbanshis, and the tea-garden workers, also tribal persons who had migrated largely from areas now part of the province of Jharkhand.

A Siliguri sub-division peasant convention and rally in mid-March 1967 swelled the ranks of the Krishak Samiti (peasant organization), which now began to prevent police from entering those villages that were considered strongholds. Any such attempt by the police led "thousands of armed peasants" accompanied by "hundreds of workers from the tea-plantations," to foil the endeavor. "On many occasions, the police were forced to retreat. Women also played a glorious role in the revolt. . . . In hundreds or more, the peasants raided the houses of several landlords, seized all their possessions and snatched their guns. They held open trials of some landlords and punished a few of them. It was only in a case like that of Nagen Roychoudhuri, a notorious landlord who fired on the peasants injuring some of them, that death sentence was awarded at an open trial and was carried out. The line adopted at Naxalbari was not to annihilate landlords physically but to wage a struggle to abolish the feudal order."

"The peasants formed small groups of armed units and peasant committees which also functioned as armed defense groups. Between the end of March and the end of April (1967) almost all the villages were organized."[8] The peasants resolved that after establishing the rule of the peasant committees in the villages, they would take possession of all land that was not owned and tilled by the peasantry and redistribute it. They did not seem to have reckoned what they would do when the armed forces of the state came to defend landlordism. On May 23, when a large police party tried to enter a village to make some arrests and the peasants resisted, a police officer was hit by arrows and he succumbed to his injuries in hospital. The police retreated but came back on May 25 in larger numbers and fired upon a group of mostly women and children when the men-folk were away, killing the eleven whom the martyrs' memorial column honors.

The Naxalbari peasants were actually doing what the leadership of the West Bengal Krishak Sabha, controlled by the CPM, had been recommending when the party was not in office. But, now, they were advised by the same leaders, in office as part of a United Front government, to abandon their armed struggle and depend on the state machinery to settle the land question, the same state bureaucracy that had been hand-in-league with the landlords. They were even warned (threatened?) that if they didn't give up political violence by such and such date, the police would deal harshly with them.

And, this the United Front government carried out—"Operation Crossbow" was unleashed from July 12 onward. "The entire area . . . was encircled by armed police and thousands of paramilitary forces. Police camps were set up in the villages. Constant patrolling of the area by armed men was carried out. The order to shoot Kanu Sanyal at sight was issued. Seventeen persons, including women and children, were killed. More than a thousand warrants of arrest were issued and hundreds of peasants were arrested."[9] According to a then superintendent of police, Darjeeling, "a powerful Army detachment was standing by on the fringe of the disturbed area."[10] Indeed, even after the operation was successfully accomplished, thousands of armed police remained in the Naxalbari area, even until 1969. Perhaps what unnerved the Establishment was the "very remarkable" coming together of the tea-plantation workers and the peasants, for on many an occasion, the peasants and the plantation workers, both essentially armed with their traditional weapons, "together forced the police to beat a retreat."[11]

But, despite such high points, the Naxalbari uprising, unable to take on the might of the repressive apparatus of the state, met quick defeat. The local leaders of the movement—Kanu Sanyal, Khokan Mazumdar, Jangal Santhal, Kadam Mullick, and Babulal Biswakarma—did not initiate the building of armed guerrilla squads nor did they establish a "powerful mass base," as Sanyal later wrote in self-criticism. So they could not maintain their strongholds, even temporarily. The consequences of the uprising were, however, far-reaching. The rural poor in other parts of the country were inspired to undertake militant struggles. As Sumanta Banerjee, who has penned one of the most moving and authentic accounts of Naxalbari and what happened in its aftermath, put it: "It was like the premeditated throw of a pebble bringing forth a series of ripples in the water. . . . The world of landless laborers and poor peasants . . . leapt to life, illuminated with a fierce light that showed the raw deal meted out to them behind all the sanctimonious gibberish of 'land reforms' during the last 20 years. . . . [Indeed, in keeping with the gravity of the situation, in November 1969] the then Union Home Minister, Y. B. Chavan warned that 'green revolution' may not remain green for long. . . . A general belief in armed revolution as the only way to get rid of the country's ills was in the air, and the possibility of its drawing near was suggested by the Naxalbari uprising."[12] And, as the other authoritative, independent account of the movement, that of Manoranjan Mohanty, put it: ". . . the Naxalbari revolt became a turning point in the history of Independent India by challenging the political system as a whole and the prevailing orientation of the Indian Communist movement in particular."[13]

Be that as it may, with defeat right at the time of the launch of the strategy of area-wise seizure of power staring the Maoist leadership in the face, the intent, the area-wise seizure, was glossed over by sympathizers, and the movement was depicted as one intending mere land redistribution. Nevertheless, "revisionism" came under severe attack, especially in West Bengal and Andhra Pradesh, where the Naxalite movement first established some strongholds, for the rebellion exposed the parliamentary left's, in particular the CPM's, politics of running with the hare and hunting with the hounds. The armed police that suppressed the peasant uprising at Naxalbari in 1967 were under orders from a coalition government of which the CPM was a prominent partner. The positive fallout was, however, the fact that some CPM members were deeply moved by Naxalbari. They posed the question as to why the party, even as it swore by "people's democratic revolution," refused to make any preparations—ideological, political, organizational and military—whatsoever to bring it about.

But instead of bridging the gap between the party's stated revolutionary intention and its actual "revisionist" practice, the CPM leadership threw the rebels out of the party. Operation Expulsion involved not only the purging of Charu Mazumdar, Kanu Sanyal, and the other local leaders of the Naxalbari uprising, but also Sushital Roy Chowdhury, a member of the West Bengal State Committee of the CPM, as well as the removal of other prominent party members such as Saroj Dutta, Parimal Dasgupta, and Pramod Sengupta who supported the Naxalbari uprising. At one point, the State Secretary of the CPM, Pramod Dasgupta, even branded the Naxalites as CIA agents! But for these comrades, dismissal from the CPM was a badge of honor. As Suniti Kumar Ghosh, de facto editor of what became the CPI(ML)'s central organ, *Liberation*, from November 1967 up to April 1972, put it: "Naxalbari [had] restored to the communist movement in India its soul."[14]

Indeed, a glimpse of the political life of one of the local leaders of the Naxalbari uprising, Babulal Biswakarma (Biswakarmakar), gives a sense of their identification with and commitment to the cause. Born in 1938 in a landless-peasant family, at the age of fifteen he took part in a demonstration of sharecroppers against a landlord-cum-moneylender charging even more than the going usurious rate of interest, and was injured and arrested. At seventeen, he became a full-time organizer in the CPI's Krishak Samiti in Phansidewa, and the very next year, a full-fledged member of the party. In 1967 he was a leading figure in the Naxalbari uprising, faced solitary confinement in jail and expulsion from the CPM, but as soon he was released on bail, he jumped bail and went underground to reorganize the Naxalbari armed struggle. What is generally recalled is the four-hour gun battle at midnight in the Naxalbari area on September 7, 1968, with a large posse of armed policemen, in which Babulal Biswakarma, unmindful of his own safety, made it possible for his comrades to move away but was riddled with bullets soon thereafter.[15]

SRIKAKULAM—GUERRILLA WARFARE TAKES HOLD

This was the spirit of Naxalbari, and it spread and struck in another ongoing, deep-rooted tribal-peasant struggle in the Agency area—parts of Parvathipuram and other taluks in the Eastern Ghats—of the then Srikakulam district in northeastern Andhra Pradesh. Organized by communist school teachers Vempatapu Satyanarayana and Adibhatla Kailasam, the Girijan Sangam (hill people's association) led several militant struggles in the 1960s. These fights were for the restoration of Girijan lands grabbed by merchant-moneylenders who had thereby become landlords. The Sangam also fought for the distribution of cultivable *banjar* (forest) lands, abolition of debt-peonage, fair prices for minor forest produce collected by the tribes, lifting of the prohibition on the use of forest timber by the Girijans, and Agency autonomy under local tribal governance. Indeed, the land grabbing from tribal people, which was illegal as per the Agency Tracts Interest and Land Transfer Act of 1917, further buttressed by the Andhra Pradesh Land Transfer Regulation of 1959, must be kept in mind.

With the split in the CPI in 1964, the leaders of the Sangam pitched their tents with the CPM. But, in the wake of Naxalbari in May 1967, the mass movement against exploitation and oppression by landlords, moneylenders, merchants, forest and revenue officials, and the police acquired a new resolve. The police also stepped up patrolling when the landlords sought enhanced protection. Following clashes, Section 144 of the Criminal Procedure Code, namely, unlawful assembly, was declared in late July. It was in this setting that two peasants were shot dead by the agents of the landlords on October 31, 1967 in Levidi (in the Parvathipuram block) and by early 1968 special police camps dotted the area and an armed police offensive began, accompanied by mass arrests.

In September 1968, a court acquitted the accused in the Levidi case, confirming the reasoning of the tribes that, besides the police, the legal system too was on the side of the landlords. The Girijans had a tradition of militancy. In the adjoining Agency area, from 1922 to 1924, under the leadership of the legendary Alluri Sitaramaraju, they had waged a guerrilla war against British colonialism and local oppressors,[16] and now they were geared up for it once more. The crucial factors here were not only the nature of the economic exploitation, social oppression, political domination, and the brutal state repression, but the volition and the reasoning of the tribal peasants, their political and social consciousness that motivated the armed resistance and the struggle for a just order that they were keen to embark upon. So, the Srikakulam district committee of communist revolutionaries, which supported the struggle led by the Sangam, decided to take the Naxalbari road.

In consultation with Charu Mazumdar in October 1968, they opted for an armed struggle and set up the Ryotanga Sangrama Samiti as an organ for the seizure of political power in the villages. Incidents like the November 25, 1968 raiding of the premises of the notorious landlord-cum-moneylender Teegala Narasimhulu, taking possession of hoarded paddy and other food grains, and seizing promissory notes and other legal records related to the debts the peasants had incurred over the years were emblematic of the radical politics of anti-landlordism that was brought into play.

It was in this setting that Charu Mazumdar's controversial tactic of "annihilation of class enemies" was applied, which was to generate a lot of differences regarding the question of tactics among the revolutionaries. But unlike Naxalbari, in Srikakulam, guerrilla squads were in operation in "strategic defense" and the movement was extended to the forests of the adjoining Koraput and Ganjam districts in the province of Orissa (Odisha since 2011).[17] The landlords had fled, the guerrilla squads and local militias were protecting the villages, and the Ryotanga Sangrama Samiti was in power and about to undertake land redistribution. Charu Mazumdar visited the area in March 1969 with high hopes that Srikakulam would emerge as "India's Yenan."[18]

Indeed, red political power did emerge; for a brief period, in around 300 of the 518 villages in the Agency area of Srikakulam, no forest or revenue official or *panchayat* (village council) person dared step in to claim any authority. The area was administered by the Ryotanga Sangrama Samiti, which had replaced the Girijan Sangam, and the *praja* (people's) courts were the legitimate judicial authority. The guerrilla squads not only defended the villages but also sought to resolve the people's problems, organize them, propagate revolutionary politics, and set up village defense squads. The Ryotanga Sangrama Samiti set up *praja* courts and the guerrillas conducted raids "directed against big landlords, moneylenders, police informers, and sometimes police camps."[19]

State repression inevitably followed, including "encounters" (extra-judicial killings). In October 1969, a 12,000-strong armed contingent of the Central Reserve Police Force encircled the zone where red political power prevailed and launched a brutal offensive. In retrospect, one might then say that the "encountering" of the brilliant young communist Panchadri Krishnamurthy, who had joined the Srikakulam guerrillas, and six of his comrades on May 27, 1969, was a precursor to a pattern of cold-blooded murders that were to become part and parcel of the "standard practice" of counterinsurgency.[20] In June 1969 the Agency parts of the district of Srikakulam were declared a "disturbed area" under the Andhra Pradesh Suppression of Disturbances Act, 1948. The guerrillas and the village defense squads, nevertheless, faced up to the huge "encirclement and suppression" campaign of the armed police that began in October 1969.

Tragically, however, some of the leading comrades, such as Nirmala Krishnamurthy, Panchadri Krishnamurthy's wife, who joined the Srikakulam guerrillas after her husband was "encountered," and Subbarao Panigrahi, the people's guerrilla-poet, were killed by the police in December 1969 in what were calculated murders. The two school teachers, Vempatapu Satyanarayana and Adibhatla Kailasam—who had joined the CPI(ML)—were captured and murdered on the night of July 10–11, 1970, marking the tragic beginning of the end of the movement in Srikakulam.

MANY NAXALBARIS

But besides Srikakulam, there were many other political eruptions in the wake of Naxalbari, in

- some of the northern Telangana districts, like Khammam, Warangal and Karimnagar, of Andhra Pradesh during 1969–71, organized independently by the CPI(ML) and the Andhra Pradesh Coordination Committee of Communist Revolutionaries, the latter led by Tarimela Nagi Reddy, Chandra Pulla Reddy, D. Venkateswara Rao, and Kolla Venkaiah;
- parts of Ganjam and Koraput districts of Orissa adjoining the areas of the Srikakulam movement;
- Mushahari block in Muzaffarpur district of Bihar in 1968–69;
- the Palia area in Lakhimpur-Kheri district of Uttar Pradesh in 1968–1970;
- Pulpally in the then Wayanad block of Kerala in 1968–69;
- Debra and Gopiballavpur in Midnapore district in 1969–70 and in Birbhum in 1970–71, both in West Bengal;
- some of the villages of Bhatinda, Hoshiarpur, Jalandhar, Ludhiana, Patiala, and Sangrur in Punjab during 1970 and 1971;
- Kanksa and Budbud in Burdwan district at the border with the Birbhum district of West Bengal between the early 1970s and 1974, led by Kanhai

Chatterjee, Amulya Sen, and Chandrashekar Das (they were the founders of what became the Maoist Communist Centre);

- the Bhojpur area in the then Shahabad district of Bihar between 1971
  and 1975;
- the upsurge of youth in Kolkata and other cities and towns of West
  Bengal in 1970–71, which came into the limelight for vandalizing the
  pictures and statues of political/cultural icons such as M. K. Gandhi, the
  preeminent leader of India's independence movement, Rammohun Roy,
  founder of the socio-religious reformist Brahmo Sabha movement in the
  late 1820s, Ishwar Chandra Vidyasagar, a key figure of the 19th century
  "Bengal Renaissance," and Vivekananda, best known for introducing
  Hinduism at the "Parliament of the World's Religions" in Chicago in
  1893;[21]
- the struggles of political prisoners in various jails in Andhra Pradesh,
  Bihar, and West Bengal.

The Birbhum armed struggle was one of the most significant that the
CPI(ML) led, so much so that the Indian Army was deployed in every
thana (police-station jurisdiction) of the area of struggle to crush it. In general, the ruthless offensive knew no bounds. The revolt of youth in Kolkata
and other cities and towns of West Bengal in 1970–71 was followed by the
massacre of more than a hundred young persons with CPI(ML) leanings
in Baranagar-Kashipur (north Kolkata) on August 12–13, 1971. This took
place soon after the proclamation of President's Rule in West Bengal in late
June 1971, with the aristocratic, wealthy barrister and Congress Party politician Siddhartha Shankar Ray exercising presidential power in the state.
Using hired hoodlums, euphemistically called "resistance groups," the
police went on a rampage, searching house-to-house to ferret out youth
suspected of CPI(ML) affiliation or simply party sympathizers, block-
ing all escape routes, rounding up and killing them in a most brutal and
cruel manner. Indeed, an elderly man was doused with petrol and burnt
alive because he didn't inform the killers of the whereabouts of his alleged
Naxalite nephew; and the hoodlums chopped off the hand of a school girl
in her teens just because she said she didn't know the whereabouts of her
brother. The bodies of the slaughtered were dumped in a nearby canal. And
then, the very next day, August 14, S.S. Ray visited the scene of the massacre, shown around the place, as one who was deeply concerned at what
happened, "by the killers themselves"![22]

Ray's right-hand man was Ranjit Gupta, then Inspector General of Police,
West Bengal, who devised the counterrevolutionary tactic of "polluting the
ocean." He created "secret squads who killed small businessmen, robbed

ferries, and bumped off a variety of individuals with a police carte blanche, if they were strict about shouting Naxalite slogans while acting."[23] And, of course, there were the "encounter" killings in which the cowardly cops aimed their guns at Naxalites precisely when they knew the latter couldn't shoot back, and then turned the victims into criminals. In his *Calcutta Diary*, the distinguished economist, political activist, writer, and columnist, Ashok Mitra, has this to say about the "encounter" deaths: "corpses are incapable of issuing rejoinders. . . . The corpse . . . [is] given an unsavory name . . . [extremist] . . . retroactive justification of trigger happiness. [From the second quarter of 1970 onward, the police assumed] summary powers to hunt down and kill 'undesirable' elements . . . point-blank killing . . . The British might have caviled at this 'something', but not us . . . You must not turn into a dreamer of extravagant dreams . . . [sacrifice] everything so that a new society could emerge . . . [For those who do, the powers-that-be have decided] that [such folks must be] shot like dogs under the canopy of the open sky in concocted encounters with the police."[24]

The Bengali woman of letters and political activist Mahasweta Devi's *Hajar Churashir Maa* (No. 1084's Mother) was written around the same time when Ashok Mitra penned those words. Translated into English by Samik Bandopadhyay, and later adapted to Hindi cinema by Govind Nihalani in *Hazaar Chaurasi Ki Maa*, the novel tells the story of Brati, unearthed by his apolitical mother, Sujata Chatterjee, in her quest to know her martyred Naxalite son. She had not known the true Brati ever when he was alive, but now she is determined to know what he stood for, more so in the face of the Chatterjee family's, and especially her husband Dibyanath's systematic denial of Brati and his politics. Brati was a Naxalite, and for the "crime" of being one, the Indian state reduced him to dead body number 1084. In Mahasweta Devi's novel, Sujata, the upper middle-class working woman, oppressed at home by her husband, finds solace in her son's comrade-and-lover Nandini, and in Brati's dead comrade Somu's mother, who belongs to the wretched of the Indian earth whose cause the Naxalites stood for.

BHOJPUR—THE WRETCHED STAND UP

The very mention of the damned of the Indian earth, however, reminds one of the movement in Bhojpur, which was greatly influenced by Charu Mazumdar's ideas about taking the struggle from armed resistance to armed offensive—annihilation of class enemies, especially the most notorious landlords, attacks on police camps and on troops on the move, and attempts to carve out liberated zones. Bhojpur, particularly its southern

part, is irrigated by the river Sone, and it thus became a "green revolution"
area, where *Dalit* (literally oppressed, used to depict India's "untouchables"
who were "outside" the caste hierarchy)[25] landless laborers, either casual or
bonded (through indebtedness), toiled at extremely low wages and suffered
a denial of basic human dignity—their wives and daughters constantly subjected to sexual tyranny—in the fields and other domains of the upper-caste
landlords, Rajputs and Bhumihars.

The latter wielded not only economic but also political power, their
links with the state apparatus underwriting such coercive dominance. Their
upper-caste status not only assured them access to the means of production
that the green-revolution techniques required but also structured the relations of production vis-à-vis the Dalit landless laborers. In such a milieu, it
was taken for granted that "unfree labor" would coexist with the landlords'
capitalistic drive for profit maximization. So full of themselves, the upper-
caste landlords even took liberties with middle-class *Shudra jati* (the fourth
social category within the caste hierarchy)[26] persons, with not infrequent
assaults on their sense of dignity. In what seemed an irremediable situation,
it was the ingenuity of the CPI(ML) that perceived a way out, by bringing
the landless laborers and these oppressed sections of the middle class/castes
onto a common political platform.[27]

A series of annihilations of the most hated landlords and their merce-
naries and snatching of arms marked the launch of the Bhojpur movement
in February 1971. What a unique blend of leaders it had—Jagdish Mahato,
a former school teacher; Rameshwar Ahir, a former dacoit (a member of a
band of armed robbers) who turned to Maoism while in prison; Ramayan
Chamar and his nephew Jwahar, both Dalits; Ganeshi Dusadh, also a Dalit,
the son of a bonded landless peasant; and Subroto Dutta, a Maoist intellectual who became the ideologue of the movement, known as "Jwahar"
to his followers. The coming together of an upper-caste Maoist intellectual, a socially oppressed middle-class radical, a poor/middle peasant of
an oppressed shudra caste, and persons who came from the wretched of
the Indian earth (Dalits)—that is what Sujata must have grasped about the
movement of which her dead son Brati was a part, when she met his dead
comrade Somu's mother, in *Hajar Churashir Maa*. And ex-army personnel from the shudra-jati, middle-peasants, helped train the members of the
armed squads, something lacking elsewhere in the Naxalite movement.

The biographies of some of the leaders of this movement might give us a
hint about the making of Naxalite revolutionaries in India. Jagdish Mahato,
the son of a peasant of Ekwari village in the Sahar block of Bhojpur, was
a science teacher at a school in the town of Arrah. In the 1967 elections,
on polling day, having campaigned vigorously for the CPI candidate, he

resisted in the face of a concerted rigging of the vote for the candidate who was sponsored by the landlords, was brutally assaulted, and had to be hospitalized for the next five months. He then organized a wage strike of the landless laborers, started publishing a periodical to propagate the ideas of the sole Dalit-architect of India's Constitution, B. R. Ambedkar, but nothing seemed to have come of his political interventions until he gave up his job as a teacher and became a full-time Naxalite with comrades like Rameshwar Ahir.

One day in 1971 the "Master"—that is what Jagdish Mahato came to be called—in conversation with one of his former colleagues of the Arrah school, said: "I know . . . that I am going to die one of these days. But I will die partly satisfied. For one change that our movement has brought about is that the landlords do not dare now to touch the women of the poor. And that is not a small change." Reportedly, the Master would prevail upon his Dalit followers to go forth to "force [their] acceptability as human beings." His practical lesson was: "This is a gun, the weapon of subjugation. Hold it straight, [and] go and deliver justice."[28]

That was the "Master." His close comrade, Rameshwar Ahir, also one of the founders of the Bhojpur movement, was the son of a poor peasant. Rameshwar was driven by upper-caste persecution to join a gang of dacoits, but while in jail he was influenced by Naxalite co-prisoners, and he joined the movement upon his release from prison. And one can never forget Ganeshi Dusadh, the son of a bonded landless peasant from Chauri village in the Sahar block. He was an outstanding guerrilla fighter under whose leadership the CPI(ML) guerrillas annihilated several notorious landlords and moneylenders, confiscated their lands, organized the peasants to sow those fields, sniper attacked government troops, and seized and distributed the food grains of big traders. Indeed, for six months, Chauri remained under the control of a revolutionary committee. But, on May 6, 1973, a posse of armed policemen entered the village and a twelve-hour battle ensued, with the guerrillas and the villagers on one side, the police and the landlords' henchmen on the other, in which, among others on both sides, Ganeshi was killed.[29]

Was it worth it, what Ganeshi Dusadh did? He and his comrades rose up; they risked everything. Why? Well, the truth is that a Dalit could be beaten, raped, or killed at the whim of an upper-caste landlord and virtually nothing would be done about it. The coming of age to political consciousness of the Dalits brought on more severe repression by the ruling upper caste-class combined against them. In Kilvenmani, a village in Thanjavur district of Tamil Nadu, forty-four Dalits—men, women and children—were forcibly herded into a hut and burned to death by hired hoodlums of the landlords on the night of December 24, 1968, because they struck work for higher wages. Predictably, the landlords who organized the massacre were exonerated by the courts for lack of evidence. What would anyone born into such a life have done? Who would blame the victims if they took up guns to deliver justice?

The "ideologue" of the Bhojpur movement, Subroto Dutta, known as "Jwahar" among the peasants, became general secretary of a reconstituted CPI(ML), operating in Bhojpur, in 1974. An "ardent follower of Charu Mazumdar"—as Sumanta Banerjee calls him—Jwahar "sharpened the party's military line," stressing "the need for building up a standing force," this in order to "forestall the 'encirclement and suppression' of guerrilla bases by the military, by attacking [the enemy's troops] . . . when they were on their way to the bases." Recruits to the Indian army from the oppressed castes, when they came home, found their fellow folk rising in revolt against landlordism, and many of them left the army to join the guerrillas. But with the declaration of the State of Emergency in June 1975, and the launching of "Operation Thunder" to liquidate the Naxalites and smash their strongholds, Jwahar was killed on November 25, 1975, when the police raided his hideout in a Bhojpur village.[30] In a sense, this marked the end of the first phase of the Naxalite movement. For with the passing of Jwahar, the CPI(ML)(Liberation), with Vinod Mishra as its new general secretary, was not inclined to follow the path of "protracted people's war" that leaders like Jagdish "Master," Rameshwar Ahir, Ganeshi Dusadh, and Jwahar had embarked upon. Mind you, it was not merely the Maoist consciousness of Subroto Dutta "Jwahar" that gave the Bhojpur uprising its revolutionary character; this essential quality was shaped by the actions and deeds of persons like Ganeshi Dusadh and Rameshwar Ahir.

"DOING IS ITSELF LEARNING"

What then of this phase of the Naxalite movement? April-May 1969 witnessed the birth of the CPI(ML)—the significance of the fact that it was the revolutionary struggle which created this political party must be emphasized. But inexplicably, though the program of the Party envisaged a worker–peasant alliance, the Party organization had not been built among the urban proletariat. As Asit Sen, who presided over the May-Day rally that made the public announcement of the formation of the Party, was to put it: "The working class . . . is still completely isolated from the present armed struggle."[31] Serious debate, however, didn't get a chance as bitter internal divisions and state repression did the movement in. By 1972, after the arrest, and later death, upon denial of proper medical treatment, of Charu Mazumdar in police custody on July 27, the CPI(ML) disintegrated.

Having gotten India's most wanted radical, the establishment must surely have heaved a sigh of great relief.

Charu Mazumdar "often failed to give the correct lead," but "his ideas still live on." When he claimed in the autumn of 1967 in the immediate aftermath of the defeat at Naxalbari that "Naxalbari has not died and will never die," he was saying something "about the ability of his followers to survive, continue and expand their movement in the face of the most ruthless repression launched by the Indian state." Born in a landlord family in Siliguri, Charu Mazumdar gave up his studies for the Intermediate examination and became a full-timer in the then outlawed CPI in the late 1930s in the party's Kisan Sabha (peasant front) and took a leading part in Jalpaiguri in the Tebhaga movement in undivided, mainly north, Bengal in 1946 to enforce the demand of the *bargadars* (sharecroppers) for a reduction in the rent paid to the *jotedars* (landlords) from half to one-third of the crop.

Embracing Mao's thought as early as 1948, he was well known in the CPI in Jalpaiguri and Siliguri for the anti-"revisionist" positions he took. Going against the tide of national chauvinism in the wake of India's China war in 1962, he was imprisoned for his views but stood his ground even after his defeat as a CPI candidate in a 1963 by-election for the Siliguri seat of the West Bengal State Assembly. When the party split in 1964, he joined the CPM as a Maoist in its ranks, but was censured the very next year when the first of his "Eight Documents" appeared. For him, the real fight against "revisionism" would begin when the poor and landless peasantry took the revolutionary road.

It was, however, only later that a fervent follower of Charu Mazumdar, Kondapalli Seetharamaiah (KS), would advance this political agenda. KS's efforts—relentless groundwork—eventually led to the formation of the CPI(ML)(People's War)—CPI(ML)(PW), on April 22, 1980. He and his close comrades made a major contribution to keeping alive the politics of the area-wise seizure of political power and the armed agrarian revolution following Charu Mazumdar's death and the subsequent disintegration of the original CPI(ML). They also tried to overcome the sectarian tendencies and adventurist tactics that had befallen the Party led by Mazumdar. KS (1915–2002)[32] was a veteran of the Telangana armed peasant struggle of the 1940s, who led a CPI unit in the fight against a minor zamindari at the border of Krishna and Nalgonda districts. Early on, he was recognized for his organizational abilities, especially in taking the Party to the masses (implementing the mass line). Later, inspired by the Cultural Revolution in 1966, he began organizing students in Warangal, establishing a strong base in the Regional Engineering College there.

Following Naxalbari, KS propagated the Charu Mazumdar line, became

a member of the Andhra State Committee of the CPI(ML) upon the formation of that Party, and coordinated with the Srikakulam unit. He played a
leading role in the collective learning from the defeat of the movement in
Srikakulam and in the review that diagnosed the basic lacuna of that struggle
in its failure to implement the mass line. Indeed, KS had a big hand, along
with the Digambara (naked), Thirugubati (revolt), and Pygambara (prophetic) poets, in the formation of the Revolutionary Writers' Association
(Viplava Rachayitala Sangham in Telugu, Virasam, in short) in 1970 and
the Jana Natya Mandali, along with radical cultural activists Narasingha
Rao and Gaddar, inspired by the songs of Subbrao Panigrahi,[33] in 1972. He
also nurtured the Radical Students' Union in 1974 and its "go to the village" campaigns that spawned many a professional revolutionary, and the
Radical Youth League in May 1975, just before the declaration of the State
of Emergency when all civil liberties and democratic rights were suspended.

For KS, "annihilation of class enemies" was only one form of struggle,
one tactic among others.[34] Indeed, the collective review conducted by KS
and his close associates in Andhra Pradesh culminated in the formulation
of a fresh tactical line called "Road to Revolution," whose first seeds began to
sprout in the peasant movement in Karimnagar and Adilabad districts soon
after the Emergency was lifted.[35] A legend in the period 1970–87, so his followers would say, KS inspired radical Telugu youth right from 1966 and had
a major role in building the CPI(ML)(PW) from scratch.

He played a stellar role in the creation of a gateway to "Spring Thunder,"
Phase II, which we examine in chapter 4. It is time then to touch upon the
essence of the Maoist strategy that the CPI(ML)(PW) intended to implement.
Although there were bitter differences over tactics, there was a remarkable
unanimity about the revolutionary strategy the original CPI(ML) chose, which
was that of the Chinese Revolution. Lin Biao, in his 1965 pamphlet, "Long
Live the Victory of People's War!," had famously summed up the essence of
this strategy of protracted people's war (PPW) in the following words: "To
rely on the peasants, build rural base areas, and use the countryside to encircle and finally capture the cities—such was the way to victory in the Chinese
revolution," which "broke out in a semi-colonial and semi-feudal country."[36]
Likewise, in the CPI(ML)'s view, India was also then a semi-colonial and
semi-feudal country, with the big landlords and the comprador-bureaucrat
capitalists the ruling classes. The main instrument of the PPW must be the
people's army, which had to be built on the political base of the Party. That
army had to master the art of guerrilla warfare and apply tactics flexible
enough to adapt to every twist and turn in the war and in keeping with the
movement's resources and the principle of self-reliance. The revolution had to
begin with a "New Democratic" stage, led by the workers in a worker–peasant

alliance, and would only transit to the socialist stage upon taking power at the national level. So, it was to be a "revolution by stages" *and* an "uninterrupted revolution." In the New Democratic stage, not only was the peasant question extremely important, but, as Lin Biao had reiterated, the "countryside, and the countryside alone, can provide the broad areas in which the revolutionaries can manoeuvre freely . . . [and] provide the revolutionary bases from which [they] . . . can go forward to final victory."[37]

In practice, however, the "adventurist" tactical line had led to defeat, the main reasons for which were the following:

- Rash optimism and neglect of the long, hard and patient underground organizational work that should have preceded the launch of armed struggle;
- Absence of an organization among the urban proletariat, though the Party had envisaged a worker–peasant alliance;
- Neglect of military requirements;
- Failure to integrate the "mass line" ("from the masses, to the masses") and mass organizations as necessary complements to armed struggle;
- Assigning of an undue importance to the tactic of "annihilation of class enemies," making it doubly difficult to undertake the kind of political work that was essential for the expansion of the movement;
- Gross underestimation of the retaliatory power of the Indian state, which turned out to be the most monstrous repression unleashed on a political movement in post-Independence India;
- No democratic means to resolve internal contentions over tactics, given that there was a remarkable intra-party consensus over strategy; and
- Inexplicable isolation of the students—youth, more generally—in the urban areas from the struggles of the urban working class.

A revolutionary war, nevertheless, as Mao put it, was "not a matter of first learning and then doing, but doing and then learning, for doing is itself learning."[38] Those who didn't learn from what they had done, were wiped out; those who learned from what they had done, recovered and lived to fight another day, and they have persevered right to this day, but their numbers are still very small compared to the size of this country.

In this account of the movement in its first phase, the focus has been on the armed struggles, not on the process of party formation and organizational matters. The latter began with a Coordination Committee of Communist Revolutionaries within the CPM, composed of Naxalites who wanted to give up the parliamentary path. This was followed by the formation of an All-India Coordination Committee of Communist Revolutionaries after severing all links with CPM. Despite internal differences, the process culminated in the formation of the CPI(ML) on April 22, 1969, and the first Party Congress in May 1970. In all these, there were significant internal differences. Frankly, in the absence of an archive, as regards such differences, and too many unknowns and unknowables, it may be better to refrain from comment.

INSURGENT POETRY

Instead, there is a need to bring to the fore the political good and the political evil in Indian society, for invariably, both have been obscured. The good, by the false or unwarranted accusations made against uncompromising left politics and against anyone who questions the assumptions and institutions that support the established order in India. The evil, effectively hidden by the claim that the Indian state is simply upholding "law and order" in the face of the violence of the Naxalites, deemed to be a "cancerous growth on the body of (Indian) democracy." That the most vulnerable sections of the people, Dalits and *adivasis* (tribal or aboriginal),[39] and those who couldn't remain unmoved at their plight and thus took up their cause, were subjected to the worst of the state's and the landlords' terror-with-a-vengeance, and that this could happen in a liberal-political democracy, no matter how reactionary, is hard to believe.

A lot can be gained by listening to the voices of some of the poets who came on the scene in the wake of Naxalbari, the Telugu verse writer Cherabanda Raju, for instance. One of the sympathizers of the Srikakulam armed struggle, Cherabanda Raju played a part in the formation of Virasam, the Revolutionary Writers' Association, and was charge-sheeted in the Secunderabad Conspiracy Case, instituted in May 1974, against the poets of Virasam. Believe it or not, this conspiracy case involved poets and their poetry, on the ground that they believed in violence and hence were subject to the normal course of criminal law. In the following, Cherabanda Raju conveys the shattering of the hopes that one had at the time of Independence, in a "bitter-sad tribute paid to Mother India":[40]

Oh my dear motherland!
. . .
Yours is a beauty that
pawns its parts in the world market-place.
Yours is a youth that
sleeps in the ecstasy of a rich man's embrace.
. . .
Yours is a sadness that

> fails to comfort the children crawling over
> your barren breasts.
>
> . . .
>
> Mother India,
> What is your destiny?

In another poem, written from jail, Cherbanda Raju, again:[41]

> Instead of removing
> the filth I hate to see
> they try to pluck out my eyes.
>
> . . .
>
> My voice is a crime,
> my thoughts anarchy,
> because
> I do not sing their tunes,
> I do not carry them on my shoulders.
>
> . . .
>
> Prisoner I may be
> but not a slave.
> Though battered and broken
> like a wave of the sea
> I will be born
> again and again.

And, Cherabanda Raju, once more, in red salute to the two peasants, Gunal Kista Gowd and Jangam Bhoomaiah, radical political activists who were charged with the annihilation of landlords in Adilabad district of Andhra Pradesh in 1970, sentenced to death, and executed on December 1, 1975 during the State of Emergency when lawyers defending the accused were also under detention:[42]

> . . .
>
> The gallows are trembling,
> unable to take away your breath.
> This edifice cannot stand any longer
> after robbing you of your life.
>
> . . .

Kista Gowd and Bhoomaiah were political prisoners, a category recognized by the leaders of India's freedom struggle in colonial times, but now, in Independent India, the law treated them as common criminals. It must be mentioned that Kista Gowd and Bhoomaiah did not consider their actions as criminal; they acted destructively but justly, nevertheless, to invert the old social order; this, publicly and collectively, and in solidarity with the oppressed. Had they not been Naxalites, subject to the worst kind of political prejudice, they would not have been victims of the Indian state's terror, for they had acted in the manner that they did "because they were appalled by the injustice of the massive suffering and suppression of the poor and they wanted to shock and shake the custodians of the *status quo*."[43] Indeed, on the eve of their execution, both of them "donated their eyes for transplantation for the needy. They said: 'Our eyes could not see the victory of the revolution. But those who will receive our eyes will surely watch that victory.'"[44]

There was an incident during the Non-Cooperation Movement against British colonialism—large-scale civil disobedience in 1920–22 led by M. K. Gandhi for the grant of "Swaraj" (self-government)—in Chauri Chaura in Gorakhpur district of eastern United Provinces on February 5, 1922, in which peasants, when at least two of their comrades were killed in police firing, set a police station on fire, which caused the death of twenty-two (some reports say twenty-three) policemen. This led Gandhi to withdraw the whole civil disobedience struggle, with the peasants condemned as "murderers" and traitors, the latter because they had broken their vow of non-violence, which was Gandhi's precondition for their participation. As many as nineteen persons were hanged in July 1923, including some of the leaders—Nazar Ali, Lal Mohammad, and Bhagwan Ahir—and there were many life sentences. The Congress government in the United Provinces, which assumed office in 1938, did not even bother about the pitiable conditions of the persons suffering life sentences or their near and dear ones; the lifers had to wait till 1942–43 to get released. And, to add insult to injury, after Indian independence, the Chauri Chaura militants were initially not even recognized as freedom fighters, and thus not entitled to pensions. Nevertheless, Chauri Chaura was a turning point in the nationalist movement for independence, for it inspired revolutionaries like Bhagat Singh and his comrades, and many others.[45]

Bhagat Singh (1907–1931) "is to South Asia what Che Guevara is to Latin America," an iconic figure of the radical left tradition. In a trial by a special tribunal which chose to violate basic principles of law and criminal procedure for colonial-political ends, he was convicted of the charge of assassinating an assistant superintendent of police, John Saunders, in 1928.[46] Singh (along with his comrades Sukhdev and Rajguru) was executed in Lahore (now in Pakistan) on March 23, 1931. Having come from the revolutionary strand of India's struggle for independence, the elite nationalist leadership, Gandhi and Jawaharlal Nehru, remained ambivalent about him, and nationalist historiography has marginalized his political contribution. The substitution of the slogan "Vande Mataram!" (Salutations to Mother India!) with the rallying cries "Inquilab Zindabad!" (Long Live the Revolution!), "Samrajyawad Ka Nash Ho!" (Death to Imperialism!), for which Bhagat Singh is credited, was alien to the political sense of the elite nationalists.

Clearly, Bhagat Singh had truly made the transition from the Hindustan Republican Association to the Hindustan Socialist Republican Association. He really hit the nail on the head when he wrote—and in this, he has proved prophetic—in a communication to young political workers on February 2, 1931, at a time the Congress Party was contemplating a compromise with the British government: "[W]hat difference does it make to them [workers and peasants] whether Lord Reading is the head of the Indian government or Sir Purshottamdas Thakurdas? What difference for a peasant if Sir Tej Bahadur Sapru replaces Lord Irwin!"[47] In the adoption of the hunger strike as a political weapon, he and his comrades took inspiration from their Irish counterparts, progenitors of this political tactic. Indeed, Jatin Das (1904–29), one of Bhagat Singh's comrades, died on September 13, 1929, after a sixty-three-day hunger strike in Lahore jail, and civil liberties and democratic rights activists and the Naxalites, in and outside the walls of prisons, to this day, commemorate that day as political prisoners' day.[48] It must be said that, unlike the parliamentary communist left, the Naxalites embraced the revolutionary traditions of the Ghadarites (we will come to them in chapter 2)—whom the colonial state treated viciously in the first Lahore Conspiracy Case, initiated in 1915—Bhagat Singh and his comrades, and even groups like the Anushilan Samiti that advocated "revolutionary terror" to end British rule in India.

"Naxalbari exploded many a myth and restored faith in the courage and character of the revolutionary left in India. . . . [T]he very problems they [the Naxalites] raised and tried to solve in a hurry had never been raised with such force of sincerity before or after Telangana. That is their achievement."[49] That was how the post-Tagorean poet and editor of the radical weekly *Frontier*, Samar Sen, summed it all up. Dedication and devotion of a high order, one might add, and immense perseverance, because of which, in Suniti Kumar Ghosh's words, "Naxalbari held out a promise—the promise of the liberation of . . . [the Indian] people from oppression and exploitation. [But] (t)hat promise is yet to be fulfilled."[50]

"ORDINARY PEOPLE IN EXTRAORDINARY CIRCUMSTANCES"

Neither the lives of the individuals who came to the fore in "Spring Thunder," Phase I, who have been profiled here, nor their "present as history," can be understood without comprehending both. The powers-that-be regarded these ordinary people as the greatest danger to India's liberal-political democracy and did what was expected of them to preserve the set-up. Given the positions of the Ranjit Guptas or the S.S. Rays, or indeed, the then prime minister Indira Gandhi, in the institutional structure of the system, it does not seem possible that they could have been sensitized to the consequences of their actions, although, five decades on, those repercussions are still unfolding. This narrative has tried to understand "Spring Thunder," Phase I ,from the perceptions of the revolutionary participants themselves, to figure out the motives and actions of the tribal- and Dalit-peasant protagonists.

Yes, there is a political intent to what I am doing but this does not mean that I cannot do it objectively. Certainly, my politics has shaped what I have written; my own experience and political participation in Indian society has influenced what I have penned. I detest the condescension of many Indian Marxists to the Naxalites, as if the Naxalites have been ignorant of Marxism, as if their politics had been nothing but "petty-bourgeois left adventurist," and that what they needed, metaphorically speaking, was an appointment with these Marxist intellectuals to provide them with good theory, which will then, in turn, lead to "correct" practice! Sheer arrogance, this treatment of ordinary people almost as things. I can sense the manner of their contemptuous scorn when they read what I have written, as if writing with deeply felt emotions is always bereft of objectivity.

Pray, how can anger and indignation, empathy and compassion, this in the face of terror and inhumanity, be considered out of place? Are not passion and rage the stuff that drives revolutionaries to make them what they are? Aren't all revolutionaries emotionally charged with fury, revulsion, and moral indignation against the powers-that-be? Isn't it the case that they cannot but raise objections and thus refuse to remain silent in the face of the myriad injustices and indignities that the poor are made to suffer, no matter the cost to themselves? Aren't revolutionary moments precisely those when the fetters of intuitive self-preservation are thrown to the winds? Why obfuscate such matters? I am writing about "ordinary people . . . in extraordinary circumstances," just like Sumanta Banerjee did, and I have strong opinions of the Naxalites who brought some of those ordinary people together in what became their joint radical political project. Perhaps my opinion has been shaped by the manner of the Maoist intellectuals I have known and trust, mainly those from the civil liberties and democratic rights struggle—here one comes across communists who are radical-democratic *and* libertarian, both qualities Marx associated with the word *communist*.

The Naxalites have been people with a revolutionary Marxist commitment; their politics has been the expression of their hopes for a better world.

They have had a sense of shared interests among themselves, and against the Indian state and ruling classes; they developed a revolutionary consciousness that has been radical-democratic, and this awareness has come from their own values and experience, in the course of their struggles, as they, mostly, lost against the repression and anti-democratic ethos of the Indian state and ruling classes. It was the fusion of the revolutionary romanticism of revolting middle-class youth with the class consciousness of toiling poor peasants and landless laborers that made "Spring Thunder," Phase I, what it was—both, the rebel youth and the poor peasants/landless laborers, could not have been made solely by the "vanguard" that came out of the CPM.

That vanguard as well as the rebel youth, both of whom had given up the comforts, the safety, and the privileges that came from their middle-class social origins, chose to pitch their lot with the deprived peasants and laborers; they took up the revolutionary cause, and thus risked their very lives. Unlike the leaders and cadre of the parliamentary left parties, they were hounded by the repressive apparatus of the Indian state; many of them remained in detention without trial for years, brutally tortured in police interrogation cells; some of them were cold-bloodedly assassinated in the forests of Srikakulam or "shot like dogs under the canopy of the open sky" on the Kolkata *maidan*, like the communist poet and leader of the West Bengal unit of the CPI(ML) Saroj Dutta was, on the midnight of August 4/5, 1971.

Despite the positive resolve of the leaders and the resolute support that they got in some of the areas of armed struggle, the Naxalites erred, both in the adoption of appropriate tactics and in correctly responding to the course of events. But what of the existing conditions on the ground and the context, what of the then "present as history"? What was new in India in the decade of the mid-1960s to the mid-1970s and what was part of the longer process? It is time to turn then to "'1968' India as History." One aspect that needs to be kept in mind, though, about "Spring Thunder," Phase I, while looking at India after Naxalbari, can be stated thus: In the failure of armed struggle and mass mobilization to come together, in the inability of the developing class consciousness and evolving revolutionary romanticism to find a common cultural home,[51] something was lost. What and how much, I really cannot say for sure, but certainly, the Indian people and the Naxalite movement were among the losers. Basically, the process of democratization lost what would have possibly been one of its most imaginative allies. Charu Mazumdar had encouraged urban youth, especially students— revolutionary romantics—joining the revolutionary movement to go to the countryside and "integrate with workers and poor and landless peasants,"[52] learning from them and teaching them, and in the process build a common cultural home. But this was not to be, at least during "Spring Thunder,"

Phase I. The process had, however, begun, for instance, in Srikakulam with the guerrilla-poet Subbarao Panigrahi's attempts to reach out to people through their own cultural forms. Some of these youngsters, not within the gaze of the "Stalinist" leaders, and hence not constricted by the fiat of the Party, could allow their creative energies and those of the poor peasants and landless laborers to unfold. Both could then emerge as historical persons, responsible for their actions.

Marx famously expressed the thought that people, in the process of changing the world, at the same time change themselves. The poor and landless peasants—from tribal, Dalit or lower caste social backgrounds—made an attempt to overthrow their oppressors and change the class structure and institutions of Indian society. In undertaking these tasks, alongside middle-class, romantic revolutionaries in the making, their own conceptions of Indian society had begun to evolve, so also their values, their needs, their abilities, their aspirations. But abrupt defeat cut all of these short. Marx also famously said that human beings make their own history, but he was quick to add that they cannot and will not be allowed to do so in the manner of their own choosing. Nevertheless, "Spring Thunder," Phase I, was an indication, a portent, of a section of the Indian people reemerging, gathering strength once again, augmenting their forces to engage in a struggle that was going to be protracted, hard, and cruel over the years to follow.

2

"1968" India as History

This stain-covered daybreak, this night-bitten dawn,
This is not that dawn of which there was expectation;
This is not that dawn with longing for which
The friends set out, (convinced) that somewhere
          they would be met with,
Somewhere must be the stars' last halting-place,
Somewhere the verge of night's slow-washing tide,
Somewhere an anchorage for the ship of heartache.
          —FAIZ AHMED FAIZ, "DAWN OF FREEDOM,"
                    AUGUST 1947, TRANSLATED BY
                    VICTOR G. KIERNAN.[1]

The keepers of the past cannot be the builders of the future.
          —PAUL A. BARAN, "ON THE POLITICAL ECONOMY OF
                    BACKWARDNESS," 1952[2]

The extremes of violent state repression of the Naxalite movement in its first phase suggest that the colonial state, especially its repressive apparatus, remained firmly embedded in its successor in independent India. Independence in 1947 was, above all, a mere transfer of power. The threat to liberal-political democracy was from the establishment and the ruling classes, not from the Naxalite movement. "1968" India—when the spirit of revolutionary humanism came to the fore but was striven to be extinguished by extraordinary state repression—must, however, be grasped, and this can best be done by comprehending it as history. Certainly, those times, from the latter half of the 1960s right through the 1970s, have long passed, so nobody can influence their shape and outcome, but they are still breathing as history, and with an idea of where India has gone since then, it is possible to write more wisely about them. It would be more difficult to write wisely about India in the present, because for that it would be necessary to figure out where India is proceeding. This would be the challenge in this book, to sense where India is making its way so that one can write wisely about its present and thereby possibly be of some help to a collective socialist endeavor to influence its shape and outcome. As Paul Sweezy wrote in the preface to his book, *The Present as History:*[3]

> Everyone knows that the present will someday be history. I believe that the most important task of the social scientist is to try and comprehend it as history now, while it is still the present and while we still have the power to influence its shape and outcome.

Like the present, "1968" India is an historical problem. It can be understood by making use of history. The Indian establishment, the ruling classes, the wretched of the Indian earth, and those who couldn't remain unmoved by what was happening, all of them did what they did, not merely because they were compelled by history, the unique conditions existing on the ground at the time, and the context, to do what they did. History and the existing conditions and context certainly determined the range of possible outcomes, but the actual outcome was the result of the respective moves of the principal opponents and how each of them responded to the course of events then unfolding.

In sharp contrast to such an approach, the historian and writer Ramachandra Guha, in his account of the history of India as an independent nation, explains what happened by attributing much of it to the volitions and the personalities of key figures in the establishment. For instance, Jawaharlal Nehru, independent India's first prime minister, is depicted as an authentic liberal who, more than any other personality at the helm until his death in 1964, is said to have shaped the "democratic" foundations of the Indian political system. All was supposedly more-or-less well with Indian democracy until an authoritarian personality, Mrs. Indira Gandhi, took office as India's third prime minister. She is said to have ultimately let down "the world's largest democracy," indeed, even subverting it from June 26, 1975, to January 18, 1977, during the Emergency,[4] but "government by the people" bounced back into shape soon after![5]

Guha, nevertheless, is restrained; some other liberal writers really go overboard, for instance, Salman Rushdie, in his novel *Midnight's Children*, pillorying Mrs. Gandhi as the witch-like Widow "responsible for everything that's wrong in India." Her son Sanjay, who is depicted as a villain called "Labia Lips," accuses his mother of having caused his father's death by "cruelly and selfishly neglecting him." The case of Rushdie assumes relevance because he has claimed that *Midnight's Children* is "'imaginatively true,'" "actually about history and the ways in which memory recovers and recreates the past." Of course, a post-modernist narrative claiming to be "imaginatively true," without a shred of corroboration, accusing Mrs. Gandhi of being responsible for her husband's death, this by making up what her son is claimed to have charged her with, is all part of a larger plot to depict her as the culprit responsible for the mess that India was in.[6] As the eminent historian Ranajit Guha said, more generally, of the liberal critics of Mrs. Gandhi at the time—they even engaged in "character-assassination in order to cover up their own failure to understand and explain the Emergency," peddling "the myth that all had been well with Indian democracy until an authoritarian personality subverted it on 26 June 1975."[7]

The Emergency—when the Opposition was jailed, the press gagged, the constitution emasculated, and elections suspended—is widely regarded as an exception in India's otherwise excellent "democratic record." Liberals apart, even influential left historians, Professor Bipan Chandra, for example, bought this story. What was essentially a class project—the Gandhi-Nehru-supported-by-the-big-bourgeoisie-led national movement (Chandra characterizes it as a "bourgeois democratic movement")—was depicted as *the* national project, never mind the democratic and anti-colonial proclivities of the many autonomous peasant uprisings before and after 1885 that were also part of the independence struggle. To this left historian, the "bourgeois democratic movement," led by Gandhi and his protégé Nehru and supported by the Indian bourgeoisie, was all that mattered, for the capitalist class, he claims, was independent, anti-imperialist, very modern and liberal, and it was these characteristics that, over time, shaped the political culture and economy of independent India.[8] Indeed, for the period after the transfer of power, even when it had become evident that the socioeconomic and state structures of the past had remained largely intact, Professors Bipan Chandra, and his former students turned colleagues, Mridula Mukherjee and Aditya Mukherjee, remained captivated by what they identified as the progressive sections of the bourgeoisie, and with Nehru and the Nehruvian model of development. Their largely uncritical glorification, bordering on hero worship, of Nehru makes it difficult for the discerning reader to distinguish them from conventional Congress nationalist historians.[9]

Clearly a section of left intellectuals was deceived by the then establishment's marketing (dressing up) of what was in fact a class project as *the* national project. The world looks very different when one examines it from below. "1968" India was packed with contradictions that came into the open in the political struggles of the underdogs to resolve them and in the severe repression of those campaigns by the Indian state.

I came of political age at this time, and so I don't think I can be dispassionate in my analyses of them. But I will try to throw some light on the main social issues of the time, making no pretense to comprehensiveness. Essentially, there are two distinct parts to what I am about to deal with, one, the various fountainheads of resistance and struggle, and two, the sources of the repression. The two cannot but be viewed in interaction with each other, for both are embedded in the history I am setting out. The distinction might however prove fruitful to grasp right at the start. I will try to explain important developments, and figure out the social forces of the past from which they emerged. I believe that if one looks reality in the face, the chances of adequately explaining it are better. For instance, that the principal architect of the Emergency, Mrs. Gandhi, could come back to power, in 1980, in a matter of three years, indeed, legitimately via a massive popular mandate, when in 1977 her opponents triumphantly rode into office on the back of public indignation against her Emergency, says something important about the shallow democratic consciousness of the Indian establishment and ruling classes.

THE CHARACTER OF THE ESTABLISHMENT

The declaration of the state of Emergency in June 1975 brought, as one commentator put it,

> 19 months of terror during which there were wholesale arrests without any redress; all conceivable opponents of the regime were jailed; prison conditions became more savage still; many more 'ordinary' prisoners were chained, assaulted, maimed; some vanished, and not even their corpses were found.[10] 'Black laws' were passed; men of all ages, young and old, in towns and villages were forcibly sterilized; without warning, strong-arm squads marched into urban bustees, demolished homes, shops and workshops, pushed the people into trucks and deported them to distant barren sites. At the same time, strikes and meetings were banned; . . . wages were effectively cut and bonuses withdrawn. . . . And none of this was allowed to be reported; press censorship and a strict monopoly of official news manufacture were imposed.[11]

And, as another narrator, with an emphasis on the economy put it,

> rapid industrial growth, increasing exports and foreign investment, and benefits for urban bourgeois classes and rural agricultural

entrepreneurs, with the costs being paid by a repressed industrial laboring class, an urban lumpenproletariat and the lower echelons of the peasantry and landless agricultural workers in the country-side, all kept firmly in tow through an increasingly powerful police establishment . . . , with the whole process enveloped in continual gasconades of leftist rhetoric from a rightist central government.[12]

It must be stressed that all these happenings were in keeping with the class character of a regime that permitted capital untrammeled power over labor. At the time, J. R. D. Tata, board chairman of one of India's top large business houses, told a U.S. journalist that "things had gone too far. You can't imagine what we've been through here—strikes, boycotts, demonstrations. Why, there were days I couldn't walk out of my office into the street. The parliamentary system is not suited to our needs."[13]

The substance of the state repression was, however, in place even before the declaration of the Emergency; the latter only greatly enhanced the degree of it. Consider the ordeal of Primila Lewis, a '68er, who along with her British husband, then the head of the Indian branch of Oxford University Press, had rented a farmhouse in the Mehrauli *tehsil* (an administrative subdivision of the district) just south of New Delhi in 1971, much before the Emergency began. There, she was to find, much to her dismay, that her neighbors, pillars of the establishment, high-level diplomats, senior bureaucrats and military officers, top industrialists and politicians, including Prime Minister Indira Gandhi herself, were provided land and other facilities for their "model farms" dirt cheap by the Delhi Development Authority. They were, in effect, absentee landlords who practiced a modern-day version of slavery in the treatment of their farm-workers. All the labor laws on the statute, including the Minimum Wages Act, were being violated with impunity. Impelled by a sense of natural justice, and with courage, Primila helped organize the Mehrauli Agricultural Workers' Union.[14]

A mere suggestion that the "modern" gentry implement the provisions of labor law on their farms was enough of a provocation, for none of these modern-day slave owners seemed to have an iota of democratic conscious-ness. Did the wretched low-caste, migrant farm-workers, driven by poverty from their villages in Bihar and eastern Uttar Pradesh, have any rights at all? The union, the "modern" gentry decided, had to be stamped out, not a difficult task, given the fact that the government, through the police, the bureaucracy and the judiciary as its handmaidens, had no commitment to implement the law that it had itself enacted. As for Primila, having unequiv-ocally declared that she was on the side of the farm-workers, she was to be treated just like the laborers she had helped organize, with an added dose of personal vendetta for disowning her own class, for becoming, what the establishment deemed, a "Naxalite."

Strictly speaking, a Naxalite is one who has been part of an organized armed struggle not merely to overthrow the established government and regime but also to upturn the existing class-caste structure, to bring about a "New Democratic" revolution. But, in the prevailing context of rebellion, even a left-winger who was part of a collective endeavor that challenged the prevailing political authority with a view to overthrowing the existing government, or indeed, even one who took on the existing political authority without any intention of replacing it, was also deemed a "Naxalite," if s/he proved sufficiently sincere, courageous, and uncompromising. Like Primila, and mattering little whether they were deemed Naxalites or not, there were thousands of such '68ers in the India of those times.

HUG THE TREES, SAVE THE VALLEY

The '68ers include even those "crusading Gandhians" and "ecological Marxists" whom the ecologist Madhav Gadgil and the social historian Ramachandra Guha associate with "that most celebrated of 'forest conflicts,' indeed, 'ecological conflicts,' the Chipko (Hug the Trees) movement that began in April 1973."[15] Guha's *The Unquiet Woods: Ecological Change and Peasant Resistance in the Himalaya*, first published in 1989, views the Chipko Movement in a broader historical perspective, locating its historical roots in the forest policy of the colonial period, designed to meet the demand for teak wood for shipbuilding and railway tracks. This policy led to deep, widespread resentment in the wake of violation of the customary rights of the peasants to the forests, and concomitant peasant struggles, provoked, to a significant extent, by such usurpation and alienation. In the Kumaun and Tehri Garhwal areas of Uttarakhand in the central foothills of the Himalayas, the Chipko movement's links with the earlier struggles against enclosure of the forests essentially derived from a basic continuity of the National Forest Policy of 1952 with its counterpart of 1894. Guha, however, makes no mention of the extensive strategic network of roads that was put in place in Uttarakhand after India's 1962 China war, which surely made the region more accessible for resource extraction. Chipko nevertheless captured metaphorically, and indeed, quite imaginatively, the image of protesting women hindering commercial logging by thrusting themselves between the trees and the logger's saws.

What is also interesting in Guha's account is his contrast of the three strands of the movement, the ones separately led by two Gandhians, Sunderlal Bahuguna and Chandi Prasad Bhatt, with the latter stressing reforestation of barren hillsides and the setting up of micro-hydel (hydroelectric) projects. There was also the Marxist-oriented Uttarakhand Sangharsh Vahini (USV), the movement's third strand, emphasizing that the human–nature relationship can only be transfigured into one which is ecologically harmonious if human relationships are transformed from exploitative to egalitarian associations. Among the prominent USV activists were the historian Shekhar Pathak, left-wing lawyers Shamsher Singh Bist and P. C. Tewari, and the Dalit student leader Pradeep Tamta. These activists differed from the Gandhians in some respects. They hailed from Kumaun, not Garhwal; they came from the student movement, not the Sarvodaya movement; and unlike the Gandhians, they were actively involved in the movement for a separate hill state, this to overcome decades of "over-exploitation" by the plains. Nevertheless, they had enormous respect for the Gandhians, particularly for Chandi Prasad Bhatt, and in their own activities, they eschewed violence. In the 1970s they organized struggles against deforestation, targeting forest contractors and the state, while in the 1980s, they led a major campaign against alcoholism, focusing on violence against women by drunken men.[16]

Chipko and an earlier *satyagraha* (non-violent resistance) in the early 1920s at Mulshi (close to Pune in the Sahyadri hills in Maharashtra)—where the business house of the Tatas had proposed to construct a series of dams— may be said to have inspired the activists of the environmental movements and campaigns of the "1968" period and beyond. Considering the 1970s, and part of the 80s when the spirit of "1968" was still alive, and eschewing comprehensiveness, the following are some of the better known ecological movements/campaigns:

- the campaign to "Save Silent Valley," a tropical forest in Palakkad district of Kerala, which began in 1973, in the wake of a planned hydroelectric project there, and in which the Kerala Sastra Sahitya Parishad took an active part;
- the movement to "save the Bhagirathi" and stop the proposed Tehri Baandh (dam) project on that river in the Garhwal Himalaya in Uttarakhand;
- the movement to save the Narmada led by the Narmada Ghati Navnirman Samiti (Narmada Valley reawakening committee) in Madhya Pradesh and the Narmada Ghati Dharangrasth Samiti (committee for the dam-affected people of the Narmada Valley) in Maharashtra, which became the Narmada Bachao Andolan, as also, initially, the struggle led by the Chhatra Yuva Sangharsh Vahini (student-youth struggle forum) in Gujarat, where the terminal dam, the Sardar Sarovar, was to come up, entailing the submersion of a number of villages there;

- the movement to protect the forests and safeguard tribal livelihoods in the wake of planned mining of bauxite deposits in the forested Gandhamardhan Hills in Balangir and Sambalpur districts in Orissa (Odisha from 2011); and,
- peasant and fisher folk opposition to the setting up of a missile test range in the Baliapal-Bhograi area in Baleshwar district of Orissa.

Preceding the development projects underlying these ecological movements, there were the large dam projects of the 1950s: the Bhakra Nangal Project on the Sutlej River in the Himachal region; the Damodar River Valley Project spread over parts of Jharkhand and West Bengal; the Hirakud Dam, near Sambalpur in Orissa, on the Mahanadi River; and the Nagarjunasagar Project on the Krishna River where it formed the boundary between the Nalgonda and Krishna districts in the then Andhra region. These were all designated the "temples of modern India" in Jawaharlal Nehru's proclamations. Their victims, thousands of poor households displaced along with loss of their livelihoods, and without any resettlement and rehabilitation worth the name, were made to suffer all this adversity in the "national interest." Identifying these victims and placing them alongside the principal beneficiaries of these projects gives a solid clue to the nature of the ruling classes and their political representatives in the Congress Party of those times. Ecological conflicts were a long time coming in independent India, and it was "1968" that brought them on the political agenda, with *Satyagraha* once more a significant part of the political lexicon of protest.

The forms of protest under the rubric of *Satyagraha* in almost all the campaigns/movements resisting environmental degradation have been the *pradarshan*, a collective show of strength of the likely victims; the *dharna* (a sit-down strike) attempting to stop work on the project; the *gherao*, involving the surrounding of an official and heckling him/her until the person is forced to accede to the demands or the police intervenes and rescues him/her; *raasta roko* (road blockade), which disrupts transportation channels; the *jail bharo* (fill the jails), in which the protestors court arrest by breaking a law that in times of unrest prohibits large gatherings; and the *bhook hartal* (hunger strike), in which a charismatic figure undertakes a "fast-unto-death" to compel the authorities to yield to campaign demands.[17] These six protest forms didn't originate in Gandhi's *Satyagraha,* and neither were they the main instruments of protest only in the environmental conflicts. Widely undertaken by the left in the struggles of workers, they proved efficacious only when they threatened to precipitate a (local) crisis of the state, which is what radical mass protest managed to do, even when it adopted some of these non-violent forms, only to bring on violent suppression by the state.

"NOTION OF WITNESS"

In India, violence and non-violence are usually contrasted as mutually exclusive Marxist and Gandhian ways of confronting oppression. This is far from the truth. At the heart of all radical political activity is organizing and convincing people, not only of the need to fight against oppression, but of the need for a new society free of oppression. Most of this political activity involves, among other essential attributes, non-violent defiance, albeit in a more committed manner. At the heart of the philosophy of non-violent resistance is the "notion of witness." A small number of highly committed persons, by force of example, involving a great deal of sacrifice, and taking huge risks, teach a large number of people and, in the process, change the political consciousness of these people and win them over in the collective struggle for freedom and justice.

But just like the colonial state perceived the just peasant uprisings of the nineteenth century as pathologies—disease metaphors (contagion, contamination) were common and the insurgencies were deemed criminal—so also the independent Indian state viewed the Naxalite movement. A radical '68er, Mary Tyler—a British schoolteacher who was arrested in 1970 in Singhbhum district of Bihar and spent five years in prison as an "undertrial," the charges against her never proven in court—consigns the criminal imputations to the historical dustbin when she movingly articulates the political core of being a Naxalite:[18]

> Amalendu's crime, Kalpana's crime, is the crime of all those who cannot remain unmoved and inactive in an India where a child crawls in the dust with a begging bowl; where a poor girl can be sold as a rich man's plaything; where an old woman must half-starve in order to buy social acceptance from the powers-that-be in her village; where countless people die of sheer neglect; where many are hungry while food is hoarded for profit; where usurers and tricksters extort the fruits of labour from those who do the work; where the honest suffer while the villainous prosper; where justice is the exception and injustice is the rule; and where the total physical and mental energy of millions of people is spent on the struggle for mere survival. It is the crime of those who know that a radical change is necessary, so that the skill, creativity, ingenuity and diligence of the Indian people can be given full scope to work in building a different kind of India, a truly independent India, a better India.

More generally, "1968" and its political "children," the '68ers, are metaphors that stand for a period and its rebels when there was what Trotsky might have called a "crisis in the affairs of the ruling order"—serious division within the ranks of the dominant classes over major strategic policies, and massive reverberations, including Spring Thunder, from the exploited and the oppressed. Sadly, soldiers of the Indian Army and ordinary cops of the paramilitary and armed police continued to take and carry out orders that directed them to use force against the rebels. But even though, overwhelmingly, the means of coercion remained firmly in the hands of the duly constituted authorities of the Indian state, the whiff of revolution nevertheless lingered in the air.

Consider the early political set of circumstances affecting Sushil Roy, later in his life a politburo member of the CPI(Maoist), who, after being incarcerated and treated callously in jail for almost a decade, passed away in July 2014 at the age of 76. Active in the communist movement since the early 1960s, Roy joined the CPM in 1964 after the split in the CPI, energetic in the working-class front, and hoping that the new party would take the revolutionary road. The mid-1960s were years of successive droughts, severe shortages of food-grains and other necessities such as edible oil and kerosene, high inflation in the midst of industrial stagnation, with declining real wages only partially and belatedly compensated if one worked in a factory in which the workers had an effective union.

Roy participated in the 1966 food uprising, in the pitched battles with the police in Kolkata and its suburbs, when hunger stalked the land, and in the "street fights" of the '68 period. Those tumultuous years were also the times of "*Tomaar naam, Aamar naam,* Vietnam, Vietnam," the expression of wholehearted solidarity with the people of Vietnam in their struggle against U.S. imperialism. Indeed, one of the first acts of the CPM when it came to power in a coalition government with the Bangla Congress and other parties in March 1967 was to rename Harrington Road in what was then Calcutta after the Vietnamese communist revolutionary leader Ho Chi Minh, thereby changing the address of the United States Consulate there to 7 Ho Chi Minh Sarani! But then Naxalbari happened in May 1967, only to be crushed by the repressive apparatus of the state, as we have seen in the previous chapter, exposing the parliamentary left's, especially the CPM's, politics of running with the hare and hunting with the hounds. It led to a rejection by the revolutionary left of the cultural, moral, and political values that the establishment left had imbibed, since 1951, from the dominant classes.

Sushil Roy was deeply moved by the Spring Thunder of Naxalbari, even hailing its line— "Naxalbari Ek Hi Raasta" (Naxalbari is the only way). At a general body meeting where the CPM bosses were in command, he asked why the party, even as it has made "people's democratic revolution" its "word of worship," refused to make any preparations—ideological, political, organizational, and military—to bring it about. A founding politburo member of the CPM, chairing that meeting, was said to be so annoyed that he asked Roy to get out. For the latter, this was a blessing in disguise, for the episode marked a new beginning. Roy went on to become a professional revolutionary, joining Dakshin Desh, the precursor of the Maoist Communist Centre.

Roy was a communist, but more generally, communist or not, '68ers looked forward to a society wherein the basic needs of everyone for food, clothing, and shelter, potable water and sanitation, healthcare, education, and cultural enjoyment would be met. It was clear to them that all these needs could be fulfilled with Indian society's inherent strengths, resources, and capacities; the creativity, ingenuity, and productivity of common people. To begin with, the movement would have to take on the establishment and the ruling classes, which were the greatest hindrance to such a process of development. The '68ers dreamt of a just and humane society, but what distinguished the Naxalites among them was not only that they had a strategic goal for the long haul—New Democracy leading on to socialism—but that they were organizing the wretched of the Indian earth to achieve that goal, for they believed very seriously in their dream. And Dalits, defined more inclusively, were at the core of this damned of the Indian earth.

BLACK PANTHERS, DALIT PANTHERS

In 1972, in the wake of two widely publicized outrages against Scheduled Caste persons—the official caste designation of the Ati-Shudra Dalits—in the state of Maharashtra, the Marathi Dalit–Buddhist writer Raja Dhale, bitterly condemning the social order that was responsible for such atrocities, went on to characterize the 25th jubilee of independence as a black anniversary.[19] Predictably, the caste-Hindu establishment castigated Dhale as an anti-national and demanded that the government take action against him for "showing disrespect to the national flag." The Dalit poet Namdeo Dhasal forcefully came to Dhale's defense in an interview published in the Marathi daily, *Navakal*: "Is a national emblem like a flag more valuable than human beings? In a society as ridden with discrimination and divisions as Indian society is, what is the significance of a common national emblem?"[20]

Earlier that year, in May, the militant Dalit protest organization and movement, Dalit Panthers, was founded by Namdeo Dhasal and the poet/writer J. V. Pawar. Dhasal's defense of Dhale led the latter to join the Panthers. The Dalit Panthers were inspired by the African-American Black Panther Party. The latter, founded in October 1966 in Oakland, California, played an important part in the black liberation struggle, this despite the dirty tactics of the U.S. Federal Bureau of Investigation that did them in. Dhasal issued a Manifesto of the Dalit Panthers,[21] which defined Dalits as

> (m)embers of scheduled castes and tribes, neo-Buddhists, the work-ing people, the landless and poor peasants, women and all those who are being exploited politically, economically and in the name of reli-gion . . . [and identified its friends as] (r)evolutionary parties set to break down the caste system and class rule. [These are] (l)eft parties that are left in the true sense. . . . [Well aware of the consequences, the Manifesto unambiguously states that] (t)he struggle for the emanci-pation of the dalits needs a complete revolution . . . [and as part of its program, it is clear that] dalits must live, not outside the village in a separate settlement, but in the village itself.

Left radicalism was in the political DNA of some of the young Dalit writ-ers and poets, mixed as this was with anger and disgust at the opportunistic tactics of the mainstream Dalit politicians of the Republican Party of India (RPI), co-opted as they were by the Congress Party. The mainstream com-munist parties, the CPI and the CPM, seemed to have failed to sense the deep frustration of the Dalits, this most deeply socially oppressed section of Indian society. Indeed, liberal-political democracy in a country like India, without the abolition of the caste system, and thus without a polity of equal citizens in a "fraternity" (comradeship) of the people, has been rotten. The bitterness and resentment that the "semi-feudal" caste order aroused in its inflamed victims found expression in the militant protests of tens of thou-sands of volatile Dalits, a potential reservoir for radical change. The Panthers' successful call for the boycott of a by-election to the Lok Sabha (the lower house of Parliament) from the constituency of Central Bombay in January 1974 unnerved the political establishment. The RPI leadership, on its part, resolved to crush the Panthers wherever they were, its task made easier by the Congress government-directed police force that mercilessly suppressed militant Panther protest with brute force.[22]

The harsh, yet candid, social realism of Namdeo Dhasal's poems, in unembellished form, are an expression of the feelings of this most oppressed and downtrodden section of Indian society. Here is an excerpt.[23]

Dog, leashed dog,
He howls and barks from time to time.
This is his constitutional right.
He lives on stale crumbs.
His mind is calloused with enduring injustice.

If at a rebellious moment it becomes unbearable
And he jerks at his leash, tries to break his chain,
Then he is shot.
—NAMDEO DHASAL, excerpt from "Song of the Republic and the
Dog," translated by Vidya Dixit, Gail Omvedt, Jayant Karve,
Eleanor Zelliot, and Bharat Patankar

Article 17 of the Indian Constitution states: "Untouchability is abolished and its practice in any form is forbidden. The enforcement of any disability arising out of Untouchability shall be an offence punishable in accordance with law." The intent of Dr. B. R. Ambedkar, who was the chairperson of the drafting committee of the constitution, which came into effect on January 26, 1950, was to put an end to Untouchability, but the Establishment's cultivated amnesia about this proviso brushed aside his "liberty, equality, fraternity" ideals. Potable water from the common wells in villages has been denied to the former Untouchables; restaurants refuse to serve them food in the cutlery meant for everyone else; they have been denied entry into temples; their representatives, if any, in the village panchayats have been made to sit separately from the rest; largely, Scheduled-Caste households have been made to live outside the boundaries of the village proper, in separate settlements; indeed, even in Mumbai, the country's most bourgeois metropolitan city, there have been separate Scheduled Caste residential pockets, Maharwadas, Mangwadas, and Golpithas. Moreover, Scheduled Caste children were discriminated against in the schools; and bonded and other forms of forced labor have continued to prevail.[24]

In 1969, the Elayaperumal Committee Report testified to these and other discriminatory caste-Hindu practices, but even the Prime Minister, Mrs. Gandhi, who swore by the Nehruvian "socialistic pattern of society," ignored its findings, and the report gathered dust in filing cabinets. And worse, in Kilvenmani, a village in Thanjavur district of Tamil Nadu, forty-four Dalits—men, women, some with infants, and children—were forcibly herded into a hut and burned to death by hired hoodlums of the landlords on the night of December 24, 1968, because they had struck work for higher wages. The memory of it, the inhumanity, the cruelty, moves one to tears.

The Panthers came on the Maharashtrian scene with great force and promise, but then, in the face of severe repression, and disputes over the uneasy marriage of the ideas of Ambedkar and Marx, split into factions, two in 1974 itself, barely surviving, with one foot in the grave.[25] Far off, in the state of Bihar, the Naxalite movement had forced the state's politicians to reconsider agrarian reforms, but the upper-caste landlords, riding high in the aftermath of the crushing of that movement, were in no mood to cede ground to the downtrodden. State propaganda that grossly exaggerated the achievements of Mrs. Gandhi's 20-point program during the Emergency had, however, created a stir among the underdogs, enhancing expectations of debt redemption, occupancy rights of sharecroppers, and higher wages for landless laborers in rural Bihar. Moreover, the Naxalite movement, crushed though it was by then, had emboldened the oppressed.

This brought on landlord retaliation in the aftermath of the Emergency and the coming of the Janata Party to power in the March 1977 general elections. Perceiving the Congress Party to have failed them, the landlords, who generally managed the "vote banks," had switched sides. A spate of atrocities against Scheduled Caste and Other Backward Class (that is, backward caste) landless laborers and poor peasants followed, the socioeconomic identity of the victims confirming the Panthers' inclusive characterization of the oppressed and the downtrodden as Dalits, including women.

OFF THE GROUND—WOMEN'S MOVEMENTS

"1968" also witnessed women's solidarity irrespective of caste or class, and I need to mention the militancy of middle-class women in the wake of the Mathura rape case that sparked off autonomous women's movements in independent India. Two policemen had raped a young, unlettered, poor tribal girl, who worked as a domestic help, on the night of March 26, 1972, inside a police station in Chandrapur district of Maharashtra, but the accused were acquitted by the Supreme Court. The SC judgment, *Tuka Ram and another vs. State of Maharashtra*, dated 15 September 1978, reversed the decision of the Nagpur Bench of the Bombay High Court on the grounds that Mathura had raised no alarm, and further, that there were no visible marks of injury on her person, suggesting that she had passively consented to sexual intercourse, and such consent was not vitiated by fear of death or hurt.

Thus, according to the Supreme Court, relying on Section 375(c) of the Indian Penal Code, Mathura was not raped. One might ask, a "forlorn young girl . . . from a poor, humble background and [with] hardly any education . . . [i]n the dead hours of the night . . . in a police station . . . forbiddingly fearsome . . . stupefied and stunned . . . [could] her passive submission, even if such was the case, . . . amount to consent either in fact or in law"?[26] For the first time women mobilized across the lines of class, caste, and political affiliation—in a public outcry and widespread protests, which forced amendments to various sections related to Indian rape law. The latter was by then more than a century old, desperately crying out for amendments in the light of past experience with its working. The campaign against rape, and, more generally, against women's oppression and patriarchy, brought a number of women's rights advocates and women's organizations to the fore across the country.

LIMITS OF WORKER MILITANCY

Such budding comradeship among women apart, "1968" didn't bring forth any across-the-board "fraternity" (comradeship) of the exploited that could have relieved the distress of the working class. The year 1973–74 was unbearable. This was when the prices of food-grains, edible oil and kerosene, the most basic of commodities in the consumption basket of workers, hit the roof. The twenty-day strike in the Indian Railways that began on May 8, 1974, was historic in more ways than one. The Indian Railways was the country's largest employer, and the strike encompassed the entire rail network, affecting the very "lifeline" of the Indian economy. The strike thus raised the anxiety levels of Indian big business and, consequently, brought on massive state retaliation. The army and the paramilitary forces were deployed on a war footing; 15,000 union-activist workers were served dismissal notices; 50,000 participants were arrested. The Defence of India Rules (DIR) of 1971 (framed under the Defence of India Act, 1971) and the Maintenance of Internal Security Act (MISA), otherwise meant to be applied in the event of an external national threat, were put into operation by the state against its own citizens.[27]

Unlike in the past, the railway workers, especially those who had organized themselves independently in the "category" (some of them craft) unions, like the locomotive workers, had begun to militantly challenge the "status quo in the Indian Railways' system of industrial relations," epitomized by the accommodating attitude of the two main (recognized) unions—the Congress Party–controlled National Federation of Indian Railwaymen and, to a lesser extent, the "socialist"-steered All-India Railwaymen's Federation (AIRF). These apex unions had, over the last two decades, been thoroughly co-opted by railroad management.[28]

So, it was the railway workers themselves, in the face of grievances that remained poorly addressed over two decades, who became the "conscious agents of their own interests," thereby creating the momentum for the strike that the AIRF had to lead, to restore its credibility among the workers. What made the strike almost historic was the fact that the railway workers took it upon themselves and showed their potential to "break the bounds of the kind of token action beloved of the institutionalized social-democratic labor movement." The latter, it should be noted, was led by a union structure and supported by parties that ideally wanted a "monopoly on negotiating the terms of labour's contract with capital."

Though the strike was historic, the workers couldn't break this structure, the vision of which was "openly articulated by unions such as the HMS (Hind Mazdoor Sabha) and HMKP (Hind Mazdoor Kisan Panchayat) and implicit in the practice of the AITUC (All India Trade Union Congress) and CITU (Centre of Indian Trade Unions)," the former two, the trade union wings of the then two socialist parties, and the latter two, those of the two "social-democratic" communist parties.[29] The railway workers could have achieved a breakthrough if the rest of the Indian working class had joined them in solidarity—sincerely, courageously, and uncompromisingly. But given the organizational and political weaknesses of the labor movement, the rest of the Indian working class did not join hands with the railway workers in a manner befitting a militancy that was the need of the hour, and hence the full potential of the strike was not realized.[30]

The organizational and political weaknesses of the labor movement stem from two structural factors: the peculiar differentiation of the Indian working class and the huge reserve army of labor. The Indian working class is differentiated on three counts, according to (a) the correspondence or not of the wage with the value of labor power,[31] (b) the caste, tribal/ethnic origins, and religion of the worker, and (c) the gender-based division of labor stemming from patriarchy. Working-class solidarity remains weak to the extent that the trade-union movement fails to struggle to secure the needs of the most exploited and most discriminated sections of the working class.

Regarding (a), based on whether or not there is a correspondence between the actual wage and the norm of a family wage, or at least a "need-based minimum wage" (the latter, formulated at the 15th Indian Labour Conference in 1956), Dev Nathan, a radical '68er, has identified four sections of the Indian working class. These are (i) workers who get more than the family wage; (ii) workers who get a wage that corresponds to the family wage; (iii) workers who get less than the family wage, but enough to meet their immediate costs of subsistence, though insufficient for the "reproduction" of labor power, that is, for what is required for sustaining a family, and have to therefore draw upon other productive resources at their command (for example, land in the village) or informal economic activity of non-working-class members of their families; and (iv) workers who are pauperized, those who get a wage which is not even sufficient to meet the immediate costs of subsistence, and do not have any other productive resource, even a tiny plot of land in the village, to fall back upon.

The miners of Chhattisgarh and Chotanagpur working as contract laborers; the bidi workers of Nipani (in Karnataka) and Nizamabad (in Telangana) working on piece rates; the power-loom weavers of Bhiwandi (in Maharashtra) and Belgaum (in Karnataka); quarry, brick-kiln, and construction workers in different parts of the country; and numerous other workers outside agriculture, many of them perennial migrants, are all part of either (iii) or (iv), which together form the bulk of the Indian working class. And, going down the wage hierarchy, the security of employment worsens, working hours get prolonged, unionization is much lower or even absent, extra-economic coercion and/or patron-client relations of dependence and obligation to employers are more prevalent, and labor laws are violated with impunity.[32]

Importantly, Dev Nathan finds little mobility between regular and casual/ contract employment, and also between low-wage and high-wage jobs. This is mainly due to caste, ethnic, religious, and gender-based discrimination, with Hindu, upper-caste men dominating the regular, high-wage jobs and a preponderance of Dalits, Muslims, and adivasis in the casual/ contract, low-wage, and dirty/heavy/onerous jobs. Most of the manual sewerage workers, for instance, are Dalits. They go unprotected into dark holes of filth and rotting garbage, clearing blockages mostly with their bare hands. Women workers are predominantly in low-wage jobs, as casual and contract workers, and in subsistence production, which makes it possible to keep the wage below the value of labor power for male workers in (iii) and (iv). In other words, where one finds oneself in the hierarchy of labor powers is considerably determined by the extent of caste, ethnic, religious, and gender discrimination one faces, and this is reinforced by one's access to the required education and training, which is also significantly determined by the degree of social discrimination one encounters. Nevertheless, Dev Nathan also remarks that it was from among the educated and trained workers—the ones who had regular, high-wage jobs—that the revolutionary cadres of working class origin came into the Naxalite movement.

"SHORT-LIVED DALLI–RAJHARA SPRING"

Organizing the unorganized sections of the working class has been one of the most difficult and demanding duties radicals have had to confront. Shankar Guha Niyogi was the organizing secretary of the Chhattisgarh Mines Shramik Sangh (CMSS) of the Dalli–Rajhara miners. Discriminated against, these contract workers were confined to a labor camp, separated from the main township administered by the public-sector Bhilai Steel Plant. Ruled by a contractor "mafia," many of the contract workers were tribal persons who had to struggle even to uphold their very dignity as human beings. What remained etched in their collective memory was the fact that they had been fired upon and twelve of their comrades died in that police firing, this on 3 June 1977, barely three months after the Emergency was lifted, signifying that for the damned of the Indian earth, Emergency or no Emergency, fierce repression of their struggles was going to continue to be the norm. They had given their labor and their working lives to the well-being of the Bhilai Steel Plant, but unlike the regular workforce, they were deemed expendable. They had no entitlements.[33]

Even as there is no evidence to vouch for the Naxalite part of it, the tale goes that Niyogi, a skilled coke-oven operator in Bhilai Steel Plant, in the 1960s was attracted to revolutionary politics amidst the Spring Thunder of 1967, went on to join the CPI(ML) and was driven underground, but eventually left the party, coming to Dhanitela, near Dalli-Rajhara, to work and organize openly in the quartzite mines over there, where he met and married a tribal co-worker, Aso. He was arrested and jailed under MISA during the Emergency, and upon his release, the miners of Dalli-Rajhara solicited his support, and it was here that the CMSS was formed in 1977.

There followed a series of struggles, these in the face of the "wrath of the powerful mining and labour contractors,"[34] and the intransigence of the management of the Bhilai Steel Plant. The demands ranged from enhancing the wage rate of the contract laborers to getting the newly formed labor cooperatives to replace the labor contractors, and even abolishing the contract labor system in what was perennial work. Besides, there was the union's innovative opposition to the management's plan to mechanize the mine and retrench most of the workers. The CMSS presented a feasible alternative in the form of a blueprint for semi-mechanization without any retrenchment.

Further, what was distinctive about the CMSS was the involvement of women workers in the struggles, with women office-bearers, rare in Indian trade unions. The CMSS went on to form its own political front, the Chhattisgarh Mukti Morcha (CMM), in 1982, which extended the struggles beyond issues of the workplace, with the Mahila Mukti Morcha (women's liberation front) a significant part of it. The participation of women workers helped rein in the scourge of sexual exploitation by the contractors, as well as the alcoholism of male workers, which had led to the proliferation of a "lumpen-degenerate culture in the streets and wife-beating and destitution in the homes."[35] The CMSS built a "Shahid Hospital," which doctors like Binayak Sen, Ashish Kundu, and Saibal Jana helped get off the ground. It established eleven schools, for the Bhilai Steel Plant didn't care to run any schools in the camp area, and it reportedly also undertook an adult educational program. Its abiding slogan was *Sangharsh aur Nirman—Sangharsh ke liye nirman, nirman ke liye sangharsh* ("Build a future for the struggle, struggle to build a future").[36]

Some CMM-affiliated unions became a force to reckon with in the Bhilai-Durg-Rajnandgaon and adjoining industrial areas where a new generation of industrialists, aggressive parvenus, had rapidly come by huge fortunes, for instance, in the Simplex group of companies. Niyogi was a marked man; on 28 September 1991, he was assassinated by unidentified assailants who pumped six bullets at point-blank range into his body while he was asleep at home. His funeral was attended by over 50,000 people, giving him a hero's farewell and vowing to carry on the struggle for a better world.

Complicity of some of the parvenu industrialists in the assassination and involvement of the district administration in the cover-up were widely believed but could not be established in the higher courts. Niyogi had spent more than a year in jail under the preventive detention provisions of MISA, which was repealed in 1977, only to reappear again in the form of the National Security Act, 1980, and he was also detained under the preventive detention provisions of this law. He never faced trial though, nor was he ever convicted of any offense; his real "crime" "was political and in an extended sense philosophical." Remembered widely in radical left circles, he continues to exist as "'the froth on the waves' of people's struggles,"[37] that which remains of each wave when it reaches the shore.

VAST REINFORCEMENT OF POTENTIAL WORKERS

The struggles must go on, though, for the churn to endure. The challenges for radical labor organizers are immense, as we have seen, more so because capital exploits the employed workforce with a vast reinforcement of potential workers at its disposal, what Marx called the reserve army of labor or the relative surplus population. In India this is the enormous pool of the unemployed and the underemployed, along with the petty commodity producers and service providers among the self-employed.

The reserve army of labor presents capital with a pool of labor available for hire; equally, it also forces "discipline" and "efficiency" on those who are already employed. The threat of unemployment and underemployment hangs like the sword of Damocles over the heads of all those who work for a wage under capitalism, and this is the real source of capitalist efficiency, the real means of increasing the rate of exploitation of the active army of labor. As Marx put it in chapter 25, "The General Law of Capitalist Accumulation," in *Capital*, Volume 1:

> The overwork of the employed part of the working class swells the ranks of the reserve, whilst conversely the greater pressure that the latter by its competition exerts on the former, forces these to submit to overwork and to subjugation under the dictates of capital. . . .
>
> . . . The industrial reserve army, during the periods of stagnation

and average prosperity, weighs down the active labour-army; during the periods of over-production and paroxysm, it holds its pretensions in check. *Relative surplus population is therefore the pivot upon which the law of demand and supply of labour works* [my emphasis]. It confines the field of action of this law within the limits absolutely convenient to the activity of exploitation and to the domination of capital.

Marx categorized the reserve army in normal times into three components—the floating, the latent, and the stagnant—and added on those engaged in illegal activity, more generally, the lumpenproletariat. Leaving aside the lumpenproletariat, for which we do not have reliable estimates, let us estimate the size of each of these components of the reserve army of labor in the Indian context in 1973.

The floating component is composed of workers who are chronically unemployed. But then, with no social security, many of these persons will not be able to survive if they remained unemployed. They desperately do what they can to earn a living, so the actual number of such chronically unemployed persons has been much lower, 1.61 percent of the "usual status" *labor force* of 240.1 million persons in March 1973, in absolute numbers, 3.9 million persons.[38]

The latent component of the reserve army of labor in the Indian context includes those who work for subsistence on own-account (as petty commodity producers/service providers) in the workforce, including in agriculture itself, as well as the other members of their families who chip in as unpaid workers, the proportion of which goes up in times of economic distress. In March 1973, the proportion of the self-employed in the usual status labor force was 61.4 percent of the usual status *workforce* of 236.2 million persons, in absolute numbers, 145.1 million persons. Roughly 50 percent of this number were petty commodity producers/service providers, 72.5 million persons,[39] constituting the latent component of the reserve army of labor in March 1973.

The stagnant component of the reserve army of labor is composed of those regular and casual workers who only manage to find extremely irregular employment (at best they are intermittent workers). In the Indian context, a significant proportion of casual wage laborers, including agricultural laborers, would be in that category. In 1972–73, 59 percent of the 50.24 million casual workers in rural areas and 61.6 percent of the 4.85 million casual workers in urban areas were intermittently unemployed and either sought or were available for work, in all, 32.6 million persons. Besides these casual wage workers, 4.2 million regular wage/salary workers, farm and non-farm, despite being designated as "regular"—that is, received their wages/salaries on a weekly or monthly basis—sought work or were available for work. The sum of these two categories of wage workers, 32.6 million persons plus 4.2 million persons, 36.8 million persons, constituted the stagnant component of the reserve army of labor in March 1973.

With a 3.9 million "floating" reserve, a 72.5 million "latent" reserve, and a 36.8 million "stagnant" reserve, the size of India's reserve army of labor in March 1973 was 113.2 million persons.[40] The active army of wage/salary-based labor in the same year was 54.4 million persons, the sum of *employed* casual wage and regular wage/salary earning "usual status" workers who were not seeking nor available for work. Thus *the size of the reserve army of labor was 2.1 times that of the active army of wage/salary-based labor,* and the former constituted the "pivot upon which the law of demand and supply of labour work[ed]," serving to restrain the rise of real wages. Inclusion of the petty commodity producers/service providers as part of the reserve army of labor is necessary because they are subjected to appropriation (by mercantile, credit and semi-feudal capital) of the profit, interest, and rent (in the case of tenancy in agriculture) respectively in the value added by their economic activity, and are left to extract their own "wages," which, invariably, turn out to be a pittance. Moreover, they suffer considerable underemployment and are therefore available for employment as wage laborers, though many of them may have given up seeking such work.

Now on the assumption that each person in the reserve army supports one dependent, then the size of the reserve army and its dependents would have been 226.4 million persons, 39.4 percent of the country's population in March 1973. By adding to this absolute number the number of "usual status" employed casual wage workers who were neither seeking nor available for work and their dependents (2 x 22.5 = 45.0 million persons, again assuming one dependent per casual wage-worker), the total becomes 271.2 million persons, or *47.2 percent of the population.* In essence, no sharp divide between the casual wage worker and the petty commodity producer is posited. The only major difference is that a significant part of the business risk is borne by the latter.

Looked at in the light of a Planning Commission estimate of the head-count ratio of poverty for 1972–73 of 51.5 percent of the population,[41] this suggests that, in 1973, those who were robbed of access to a minimum nutritional diet in terms of calorie intake extended far beyond the reserve army of labor and its dependents, and even beyond the range of the employed casual wage workers not intermittently unemployed and their dependents.

Overall, with a labor market pivoted upon a reserve army of labor 2.1 times the active wage/salary-earning army of labor, the sharp class

polarization that one encountered—islands of wealth, luxury, and civilization in a vast sea of poverty, misery, and degradation—was a ramification
only to be expected. There were a relatively small number of owners/con-
trollers of Indian big businesses and multinational corporate affiliates,
beneficiaries of the skewed distribution of surplus value, at the apex of a
steep social-class hierarchy, at the bottom of which were the massive reserve
army of labor and the remaining casual wage workers. In between, at different distances from the apex and the base of the social-class pyramid, were the
political entrepreneurs, the semi-capitalist landowners, the SME capitalists,
the merchant and moneylending classes, the administrative, professional,
scientific & technological sections of the middle class, the labor contractors/
jobbers who recruit and manage gangs of unregistered wage workers, and
the regular wage workers.

One aspect of India's underdevelopment has been its backwardness—a
low level of development of the forces of production (the material means
of production and labor-power) in significant parts of the economy, with
these spheres dominated by mercantile, credit, and "semi-feudal" capital.
Indeed, there has been a political and commercial alliance between the
"semi-feudal" landowning classes and mercantile-cum-credit capital that
has preserved the status and prerogatives of both. This, and the preserva-
tion of the large mass of oppressed peasants and other petty commodity
producers/service providers, has been at the core of India's underdeveloped
capitalism. Importantly, this state of affairs has been concomitant with backward capitalist political, ideological, and cultural traits.

The huge reserve army of labor not only circumscribes the wage and
other demands of the regular and casual wage workers, but also moderates
the producer prices of the petty commodity producers/service providers in
the overcrowded and intensely competitive supply-side of the markets in
which the latter find themselves. Thus, without mincing words, it is possible
to surmise that here was an underdeveloped capitalist system that enabled
labor exploitation of criminal proportions, utterly denying the rights of
hundreds of millions of human beings to even a bare subsistence.

SCOUNDRELS IN PATRIOTIC GARB

But, even while reflecting on the Indian system's principal economic "crime,"
there is a need to get back to the dreadful political crimes being committed,
when MISA and DIR gave the government extraordinary powers to deal
with not merely external threats but also what it perceived to be internal
intimidation affecting its stability, just like the government in colonial India
did. The Defence of India Act of 1971 was derived from its namesake of

1915, which, incidentally, came from its namesake of 1858 in the wake of the Great Rebellion of 1857–58. The provisions of the 1915 Act were extended in the widely detested Rowlatt Acts of 1919, and then again in 1939, and in 1962, in the wake of India's China war. The Defence of India Act of 1971 came into force when India openly went to war with Pakistan on December 3, 1971.

Covertly, the war broke out soon after the Pakistani Army cracked down on the Bengali nationalist movement in East Pakistan on the night of 25/26 March 1971—not merely on the Awami League led by Mujibur Rahman, the pro-Moscow National Awami Party led by Muzaffar Ahmad, and the pro-Moscow "communists," but also, and significantly, on the so-called pro-China National Awami Party led by Maulana Bhashani (the "Red Maulana") and the revolutionary left that had emerged within and without the latter. Indeed, at least for a while, it was the revolutionary left that went on to make significant gains in the rural areas politically, that is, when the Awami League, soon after the Pakistani Army crackdown, fled to safety in India alongside the massive stream of refugees. At that point, the revolutionary left took the lead, making it very hard for the Pakistani Army to control the 64,000 odd villages of East Bengal.[42]

Could the revolutionary left in East Bengal have turned the Bengali nationalist struggle into a People's War? Most unlikely, unless one chooses to persist with one's revolutionary illusions, for the Naxalite movement in West Bengal, in the face of brutal state repression, even if it were to have imagined a united communist Bengal, could not have begun the practice of such politics. Moreover, in East Bengal, it was not the Red Maulana's Awami National Party but Mujibur Rahman's Awami League that had the backing of the Bengali industrial and mercantile capitalists, kulaks, bureaucrats, the Bengali elite in the Pakistani Army, paramilitary and police who had split from their respective units, and opportunist sections of the intelligentsia. The Awami League also had close relations with the Indian establishment, which very quickly got into the act of intervention, followed by outright invasion aimed at turning East Bengal into an Indian protectorate. The Indian Army's and the Mukti Bahini's victory in East Bengal came on December 16, 1971.

Could Washington have restrained New Delhi from Indian Army intervention in East Pakistan? Article IX of the Treaty of Peace, Friendship and Cooperation of August 1971 that India entered into with the Soviet Union provided an assurance that the latter would back India in the event of external threat or actual breach of Indian security. And, as events were to unfold, the policy of *détente* between the United States and the Soviet Union in 1973 squashed any lingering doubts that Washington wouldn't adjust to the new geopolitical advantage that India had gained. And, if there was any specter of a united communist Bengal in the intelligence agencies of Washington and New Delhi, this was laid to rest by an Indo-Bangladeshi counter-revolutionary alliance in late-1973 which brought the Indian Eastern Frontier Rifles to closely coordinate its operations on the Indo-Bangladesh border with that of the Rakkhi Bahini (the counterpart of India's Central Reserve Police Force) in the newly formed Bangladesh, unleashing a terror that even seemed to have surpassed that of the Pakistani military regime of Yahya Khan.[43]

"Patriotism is the last refuge of a scoundrel," so the saying goes, but in this case it seemed like the first—Prime Minister Indira Gandhi took full credit for the victory in the war with Pakistan and the "liberation" of East Bengal, which created Bangladesh. Sections of the Indian establishment, particularly the Jan Sangh leader Atal Behari Vajpayee, hailed her as Durga, the invincible goddess of Hindu mythology, and she sought to make political capital out of what the Indian Army and East Bengali nationalist fighters had accomplished, quickly calling fresh elections in thirteen Indian states, some of which the Opposition parties governed. Such expressions of aggressive nationalism should have been a warning of what was to unfold. Her Congress Party won all these states very comfortably, except in West Bengal, where her party's landslide came because of "terror, intimidation and fraud."[44]

POLITICAL BARBARISM

Organizations for the protection of civil liberties and democratic rights (CL&DR) in independent India—the Andhra Pradesh Civil Liberties Committee (APCLC) and the Organization for the Protection of Democratic Rights (OPDR), both formed in Andhra Pradesh in 1973, as also the Association for the Protection of Democratic Rights (APDR) in West Bengal, which emerged in 1972—arose alongside the Naxalite movement and in the setting of the undeclared (pre-Emergency) emergency repression unleashed by the state and its hired hoodlums. The APCLC and OPDR came in the wake of efforts by radical intellectuals, '68ers, to protect the rights of the poor peasants, landless laborers, and their Naxalite organizers in the face of the brutal state repression of the movement in Srikakulam and parts of Telangana that began in 1968-69, as we have seen in chapter 1.

The roots of the People's Union for Democratic Rights (PUDR) and the People's Union for Civil Liberties (PUCL) can be traced to the People's Union for Civil Liberties & Democratic Rights (PUCL&DR), which was formed in 1976, mainly conceived by the Gandhian leader Jayaprakash Narayan and a retired chief justice of the Bombay High Court, V. M. Tarkunde, to oppose the repression of civil liberties during the Emergency. After the lifting of the

Emergency and with the Janata Party in power, which brought some of the PUCL&DR's political associates into office as part of the new government, the PUCL&DR was rendered relatively inactive until it was revived as the PUCL when Mrs. Gandhi rode back to power in 1980.

The PUDR began in 1977 as the Delhi unit of the PUCL&DR, but after the latter was revived at the national level as the PUCL in 1980, the PUDR began functioning as an independent organization from February 1981. The APDR, APCLC, the CPDR (the Mumbai-based Committee for the Protection of Democratic Rights, also formed after the lifting of the Emergency), and PUDR, all owed their leadership and main cadre to Marxist rebels, '68ers largely sympathetic to Maoism, who viewed their legal struggle to win civil, political, social, economic, and cultural rights as a constituent part of the revolutionary process. Along with PUCL, these organizations believed that the winning of civil and political rights are an essential part of the struggle for the realization of social, economic, and cultural rights.

What was the CL&DR movement up against when it started off in the early 1970s? An example is what APDR ran into in 1972, this in its own words:[45]

[The] orgy of slaughter and brutal repression [during the] last two years all over India was unknown even in the days of British Raj. Reckless abuse of power [by the executive] in the name of maintaining law and order . . . (v)arious detention laws of the British regime . . . brought back under old and new names [for instance, DIR and MISA], thousands . . . detained under these draconian measures . . . many others . . . implicated in cases under false charges and thrown behind (bars) . . . (p)ersons released on bail . . . rearrested within the very premises of the court under newly fabricated charges[46] . . . (the) (e)xtent of arrest(s) due to political reason(s) . . . so great . . . [the] number of prisoners . . . far surpass(ing) the capacity of the jail(s) . . .[with the] worst possible food . . . frightening sanitary condition(s) . . . facilities for (medical) treatment only in name . . . incurable and infectious diseases . . . playing havoc with the lives of the hapless prisoners . . . [and] no response from the government even after repeated appeals . . .

[P]ersons . . . detained due to political reasons . . . far from being recognized as political prisoners . . . refused even the minimum facilities . . . assured for all categories of political prisoners by the jail code . . . rights to have a weekly interview . . . not being allowed . . . [The authorities] (f)ollowing in the footsteps of the former British rulers, . . . deported [prisoners] to . . . far-off places from West Bengal . . . their relatives . . . getting no information about their wards . . . [B]arbarous torture [was] inflicted upon prisoners under the plea of extorting confession during their detention in police custody . . . [A] shameful record . . . of indiscriminate killings . . . slaughter . . . continuing outside [reference is made to mass killing outside the jails in] Barasat, Diamond Harbour, Burdwan, Kalna, Baranagore, Howrah, Bantra, Bhawani Dutta Lane . . . [A]lso . . . unarmed helpless prisoners in their hundreds . . . [were] . . . beaten or shot to death . . . under different pretexts in jails and police custody . . . [reference is made to mass killings in jails such as inside the] DumDum, Alipore, Berhampore, Midnapore, Bahkipur (Patna), Hazaribag, Gaya, Bhagalpur [prisons].

The executive organ[s] of the state . . . in complete defiance of all constitutional provisions, on their own . . . implement[ed] sentences of death, which can be decided upon by the judiciary only . . . [with the) judicial authority . . . surprisingly silent about [such] matters. [If a revolutionary, in the course of] translating his [her] ideal into reality . . . oversteps the law . . . [g]overnment . . . [has] the right to take legal action against him [her] . . . but in doing so, government too, by the same logic, cannot overstep the . . . limits of law.

The brutalization of the repressive apparatus of the state and the criminalization of politics and the adoption of Reichstag fire tactics to eliminate the left in West Bengal were evident much before the formal declaration of Emergency, whose immediate provocation, among other matters, was an Allahabad High Court judgment that declared Mrs. Gandhi's election to Parliament in 1971 null and void because of certain electoral malpractices in her campaign. As mentioned, practically all the fundamental rights enshrined in the Constitution were suspended, including habeas corpus, with an "operational moratorium on the autonomy of the country's democratic institutions." Preventive detention, which was hitherto liberally used against the radical left, was now applied to imprison all of Mrs. Gandhi's political opponents, indeed, even some of her prominent intellectual critics.[47] There were now no judicial curbs on executive power and, de facto, the status of Parliament was reduced to that of a rubber stamp.

What really distinguished the Emergency from the period immediately preceding it was that during the Emergency, Indira Gandhi and the regime she headed broke the establishment "rule" under which it was permissible to violate the CL&DR, including the fundamental rights, of the Naxalites and the wretched of the Indian earth whom they had organized, but not those of the politicians and intellectuals of the establishment. If there were some 40,000 political prisoners in jail or in police custody in 1973, come the

Emergency, that number touched 140,000, what with the ban now extending to twenty-six parties, beyond the usual Marxist-Leninist ones. The Shah
Commission's findings on the "excesses" committed during the Emergency
and the Bhargava Commission set up to investigate "encounter" deaths in
Andhra Pradesh—seventy-seven of which had been reported to have taken
place—exposed the rot that had set in, but those indicted or accused of
criminal conduct went on to make successful careers. Indeed, beyond the
investigations, the then chief minister of Andhra Pradesh, had, on more
than one occasion, claimed that he had "wiped out" the Naxalites.

"Police encounter"—a term used by the Indian police, paramilitary, military, and other security forces to explain the death of an individual whom
they have cold-bloodedly killed—is, in reality, a planned extra-judicial killing not authorized by the law or by a court of law, in most cases, staged
by planting weapons alongside the dead body to indicate the reason why
the person was killed. A first information report is lodged against the dead
person reiterating the police version of events. Truly, independent India
did not make a break from its colonial past. Just as the British colonialists
had put in place a repressive legal structure to deal with the militant section of the nationalist struggle for independence and called it "terrorist,"
maintaining all kinds of repressive sections on the statute book to repress it,
the post-Independence Indian state continued in the same vein as far as the
Naxalite movement was concerned, and also with respect to the nationalist
movements in Kashmir and the northeast.

While the Bhargava Commission was prevented from completing its
assigned task, one recalls with horror the encounter killings in Andhra
Pradesh, a few of which were investigated in detail by a committee (set up by
Jayaprakash Narayan, as president of the Citizens for Democracy) headed by
V. M. Tarkunde, and published as a report entitled *Encounters Are Murders*,
due mainly to the painstaking work done by the eminent human rights
lawyer and activist, K. G. Kannabiran, as member-secretary, and a group
of committed civil liberties activists. But the accused, allegedly responsible
for the killing of young Naxalites/Maoists in cold blood, claiming falsely
that the latter were killed in encounters (that had never taken place), were
never tried and punished for murder. The principle of ministerial and collective responsibility of the cabinet was never respected. Consequently, the
old adage that "impunity breeds contempt for the law" began to apply; the
wielders of repressive political power had nothing but scorn for the legal
code. What resulted was an ambience of "cultivated ignorance" in the sphere
of "governance" that brushed off extra-judicial killings as mere aberrations.

Kannabiran hits the nail on the head when he pins all this down to
failure to restructure the old institutions of the state in terms of the new

Constitution of independent India. The colonial value system continued
to prevail "despite an avowedly democratic Constitution" put in place on
January 26, 1950. The establishment view was that crime could not be investigated nor security preserved if the law were followed; indeed, crime could
only be investigated and security safeguarded by breaking or circumventing
the law! Kannabiran cites case law to show that the Supreme Court drew
support and inspiration from what a colonial court had decreed in a case
wherein the accused was a revolutionary of the Anushilan Samiti, a political
outfit that advocated revolutionary violence as a means for ending British
colonial rule in India. This was to the effect that "illegality [i.e. torture] in
procuring evidence does not vitiate the trial," thus persisting with colonial
jurisprudence.[48]

Indeed, in true colonial form, the "conspiracy" provisions of the Indian
Penal Code, mainly Sections 121 and 121A, promulgated by the colonial
state in Act 45 of 1860, were used to strangle the CPI(ML) by holding the
leaders of the Naxalite movement on a tight leash, in the Parvathipuram
Conspiracy Case related to the Srikakulam armed struggle.[49] Many of the
accused were killed in so-called encounters after the charge-sheet had been
filed. Such viciousness reminds one of the first Lahore Conspiracy Case,
initiated in 1915, under the Defence of India Act, against members of the
Ghadar Party, a most merciless lawsuit by the colonial state, in which out
of those of the "conspirators" tried in a special tribunal convened in Lahore
(such tribunals were also convened in Benares, Mandalay and Singapore),
forty-six were executed and 194 given life sentences.[50] Then there was
the Cawnpore (now spelt Kanpur) Bolshevik Conspiracy Case of 1924 in
which communist leaders M. N. Roy, Muzaffar Ahmed, Shaukat Usmani,
Singaravelu Chettiar, S. A. Dange, Nalini Gupta, and others were charged
with conspiring to "deprive the King Emperor of his sovereignty of British
India . . . by a violent revolution," this just a year before the formal launch
of the hitherto émigré CPI in India in 1925. Also, following the Sixth
Congress of the Communist International in July-August 1928 and publication of its "Theses on the Revolutionary Movement in the Colonies and
Semi-Colonies"[51] in December of that year, the Meerut Conspiracy Case was
initiated in March 1929. What brought on this case was colonial fear of the
spread of communist ideas in India.

In a truly colonial manner, so was the Secunderabad Conspiracy Case,
filed in August 1974, in which writers and poets of the Revolutionary
Writers Association (RWA; Viplava Rachayitala Sangham in Telugu, known
as Virasam)—T. Madhusudan Rao, K. V. Ramana Reddy, Varavara Rao,
Cherabanda Raju, M. T. Khan, and M. V. Ranganatham—were charged,
alongside Maoist revolutionaries K. G. Sathyamurthy and Kondapalli

Seetharamiah, among others. Here were writers and poets accused of sedition and "waging war against the state," the sedition charges under 124A of the Indian Penal Code, inserted by Act 27 of 1870. The spectacular growth of RWA after its formation in 1970 into a literary-political movement had obviously unnerved the Andhra Pradesh government, for the trial went on for fourteen and a half years, and with some of the alleged offenses deemed non-bailable, one of India's finest radical-left poets, Cherabanda Raju, died in jail, his contemporary, Varavara Rao suffering several years of incarceration.[52] The "continuation of British Indian traditions was responsible for the characteristically very colonial response" of the state in independent India in not only subjecting radical politics to conspiracy charges, but also in the Supreme Court's approach to the Emergency and MISA.[53]

UNABATED COLONIAL POLICY

Even the successors of the elite nationalist leadership of the anti-colonial movement were least concerned about dismantling and replacing certain colonial political structures and institutions. Moreover, India's defeat in its China war of 1962 had precipitated a huge crisis of confidence. Indian "patriots" of all hues felt deeply humiliated. The Nehru government had been aiding Tibetan separatism, claiming Aksai Chin, and demanding complete adherence to the McMahon Line. New Delhi was bent upon sticking to its former colonial master's policy with regard to the boundaries dispute with Beijing.

In 1958, it not only refused to negotiate a settlement of the border dispute, but engaged in military provocations, ultimately leaving the Chinese People's Liberation Army (PLA) no other option. In 1962, the PLA, after defeating the Indian Army in "India's China War," and with India still refusing to negotiate, unilaterally declared a cease-fire and withdrew to 20 km north of the McMahon Line (even though China then considered that line illegal), and in Ladakh too, to where they were stationed before the start of hostilities. As Neville Maxwell put it:[54]

> The Chinese withdrawal to their original lines after a victory in the field was the first time in recorded history that a great power has not exploited military success by demanding more.

This really exposed the myth of Chinese aggression; in Maxwell's view, all China wanted (*and* wants) was a negotiated settlement that would guarantee stability at its borders. But Nehru just stuck to the old colonial claims, that Aksai Chin was part of the Ladakh region of India for centuries, and so on. In the face of defeat, however, his hegemonic position in the Indian establishment suffered a jolt; in the non-aligned movement too, there was a loss of face. Nehru passed away on May 27, 1964, and the man who succeeded him as prime minister, Lal Bahadur Shastri, died of a heart attack less than two years after he took office. In the contest for the office of the prime minister that followed, with the backing of the Congress President K. Kamaraj, Mrs. Gandhi took office on January 24, 1966.

Soon thereafter, on March 1, 1966, the Mizo National Front (MNF) in India's Northeast, formed in October 1961 under the leadership of Laldenga, rose in revolt and made a declaration of independence. The MNF had been seeking the integration of the Mizo people and the liberation of their homeland, the then Mizo Hills district of Assam, from India. The Indian government retaliated with vicious air raids. On March 2, the government of India invoked the Assam Disturbed Areas Act, 1955, and the Armed Forces (Special Powers) Act, 1958, designating the Mizo Hills as a "Disturbed Area." On March 4, Indian Air Force (IAF) fighter jets strafed Aizawl, the main town, using machine guns, following this up the next day with an extensive airstrike that went on for five hours. As a Mizo Hills MLA in the Assam Legislative Assembly was to remark in the House: "The use of air force for taking Aizawl was excessive because you cannot pinpoint from the air who is loyal and who is not loyal, who is an MNF and who is somebody pledging allegiance to the Mizo Union, the ruling party in the Mizo district."[55] But the government of India even went to the extent of denying that the aerial bombing of Aizawl on March 4 and 5, 1966, had taken place, let alone apologizing to the Mizo people for this inhuman act. This was the first time that the government of India resorted to air strikes on its own civilian population. Mrs. Gandhi could not have made a more callous beginning as prime minister.

With the "colonial" deeply embedded in the so-called post-colonial, one should refrain from holding Mrs. Gandhi as prime minister individually responsible for such inhumanity. Indeed, in May 1975, again when Mrs. Gandhi was the prime minister, the Indian state "annexed" the Himalayan Kingdom of Sikkim, which was a British dependency and had become a protectorate under India in 1950. The official claim has been that this was a "voluntary" merger, but in all likelihood it was the result of New Delhi taking opportunistic advantage of a "mobilization" of the majority community of Sikkimese of Nepalese origin under a "feudal" Sikkimese leader of Lepcha origin who was implacably opposed to the Chogyal (Sikkim's traditional ruler).[56] All her pomposity and bluster notwithstanding, Mrs. Gandhi was really a captive of the colonial deep in the marrow of the "post-colonial" regime she was heading.

GREEN REVOLUTION—BYPASSING LAND REFORM

In the economy, the balance of payments was particularly strained with increasing food imports adding to the hard currency strain from the huge military hardware imports that were already underway over the previous couple of years. The international trade account was already stressed by the huge imports of plant and equipment and spares thereof that the second and third five-year plans had entailed. Under "advice" from the World Bank and the International Monetary Fund (IMF), the rupee underwent a huge devaluation in 1966, further exacerbating inflationary and industrial recessionary tendencies.

The land reform was expected to lead to significant growth of agricultural output, but it was now being realized in establishment circles that, beyond a point, such reform was not politically feasible in India. The landlords, especially the large ones, were, after all, an important constituent of the political establishment. The agrarian class structure, even after the land reform of the 1950s and 60s, was still outmoded, a serious impediment to the modernization of agriculture and to rapid rural development. Nevertheless, with the abolition of the intermediary tenures of the Zamindari era—what historians have called "subinfeudation"[57]—this on payment of compensation, about 20 million erstwhile tenants became landowners. However, most of them were not genuine cultivators tilling the land. They lived off the labor of the actual tillers, either their tenants-at-will or their hired laborers. Indeed, many such tenants-at-will, those who came from the lower castes, may have gotten evicted. Vast areas of wasteland were vested in the state. However, the large "home farms," the workable core of the estates of the Zamindars, cultivated by tenants-at-will, remained intact, with no measures even to limit their sizes. As Elizabeth Whitcombe puts it, what was left with the Zamindars was "a tenth of the Zamindari, but [with] ten times more income" after the adoption of green-revolution techniques, and with "their brothers and sons in the civil service and industry, the army and the police sending regular remittances to swell the family accounts in pre-Mutiny fashion. . . ."[58]

As regards the reform of tenancy, despite progressive guidelines laid down in the five-year plans, and some states enacting laws laying down the maximum permissible rate of rent, security of tenure, and so on, rents continued to remain at "semi-feudal" levels, insecurity of tenure persisted, and, in many cases, tenants were evicted on the plea of "personal cultivation" by the landowners. Moreover, tenancies were "pushed underground and converted into work contracts. . . . (M)ost of the leases, particularly crop-sharing arrangements, [were] oral and informal. . . . (T)he objective of ensuring fair rent and security of tenure . . . [remained] unattained in large parts of the country. [Indeed,] (h)ighly exploitative tenancy in the form of crop-sharing still . . . [prevailed] in large parts of the country.'" [59]

Land ceiling laws were enacted by the states by 1961, but "(a)ll the laws provided for a large number of exemptions. . . . (A)ll prudent landowners took steps in good time to distribute the surplus land among their relatives, friends and dependents, and in some cases they arranged paper transactions to show distribution among fictitious persons. . . . Only about one million hectares of land could be declared surplus . . . [which worked] out to be less than one percent of the total arable land in the country. . . . [Consolidation of fragmented holdings] often helped the landowner in getting rid of his tenants."

. . . "Thus the overall assessment [was] . . . that programmes of land reform adopted since Independence had failed to bring about the required changes in the agrarian structure." [60] Moreover, the close interrelation between the agrarian class structure and the Hindu caste hierarchy remained intact, albeit, with some positional changes. The ranks of landowners, formerly invariably upper-caste, were now composed of some of the former tenants, middle and backward castes. The cultivators were from the ranks of the middle and backward castes, while the landless laborers were from the lowest castes, mostly Dalits. All the tall talk of "land to the tiller" was hogwash. [61] If really meant, it would have connoted giving ownership rights to the poor peasants (tenants at the subsistence level) and landless laborers, and not permitting those who did not till the land with their own personal labor to own it. This would have then resulted in the transfer of ownership of land from the upper-caste landowners, who are averse to manual labor, to the real tillers of the soil. [62]

There was thus no basis to assume that a genuine land reform could be carried out without class struggle and the winning of that struggle by the exploited and the oppressed. [63] Overall, the post-1956 official land reforms led merely to a partial amalgamation of the old rural landowning classes-castes into a new, broader stratum of rich landowners, those not setting their hands to the plough. This included an upper section of the former tenants, all of whom, despite the various markets, were yet to rid themselves of various retrograde elements of semi-feudal culture and behavior. Yet the establishment, in the design of rural policy, kept up the pretense of an undifferentiated "village community"; it claimed to want land reforms, but without the class struggle that would inevitably accompany such a program, if it were a real one. For the peasants who took Gandhi's articulated vision of a Ram Rajya (the mythical just rule of the Hindu god, Ram) in independent India seriously, their dreams were prematurely shattered.

The story of Indra Lohar was brought to public attention in 1973 by Ashok Mitra, in his column "Calcutta Diary," in the *Economic & Political*

Weekly. Lohar, a petty sharecropper under oral lease, who despite the then more recent amendments of the West Bengal Land Reforms Act to plug loopholes, was dispossessed of the small piece of land he tilled and found to his horror a chronic denial of justice by the administration, the police, and the courts. Mitra's prose sketches a profoundly depressing portrait of deliberate and callous discrimination against the poor sharecropper, and the fact that this detrimental outcome was the almost inevitable result of the disparity in political power and economic resources between the landlord and his share-cropper tenant, made worse by the absence of a "living, pulsating organised movement of the peasantry [which] could have made a difference."[64]

"Spring Thunder," Phase I, had been crushed by then; nevertheless, it had unnerved not merely the agrarian ruling class of large landowners, but also Indian big business, the multinationals, and the entire political establishment. A technical fix was already underway, not merely in India, to contain "Communist revolution" wherever it was brewing or might ferment. The Malayan communist insurgency of 1948–60, the Huk Rebellion in the Philippines, originally against the Japanese occupation, but which continued against the Filipino government during 1946–54, and the anti-French war of resistance in Indochina during 1946–54, in all of which peasants constituted the main guerrilla base, ultimately led to the weaving of Green Revolution into the fabric of American foreign policy.[65]

As far as India was concerned, the Telangana peasant uprising of 1946–51 had unsettled the establishment. Poverty estimates (headcount ratios) from 1951 onward, based on consumption data of the National Sample Survey Rounds, didn't seem to show any time trend, but the numbers were very high in some years. For the period July 1954–March 1955, 64 percent and 46 percent of the rural and urban populations, respectively, were below the poverty line. In July 1966–June 1967 and July 1967–June 1968, likewise, the headcount ratios of poverty were 64 percent and 52 percent-53 percent of the rural and urban populations, respectively.[66]

In 1960, the Ford Foundation got the Indian government to initiate an Intensive Agricultural Districts Programme (IADP), an initial pilot run of Green Revolution techniques. In the meantime, it was food aid under Public Law 480 that was in place, which "bought time for more long-term solutions to be found to the problems of hunger and social unrest in the Third World,"[67] including India. The International Rice Research Institute (IRRI) was founded with American aid in 1962 in the Philippines to focus on developing high-yielding varieties of rice, Asia's major food crop. The CIMMYT (in English, the International Maize and Wheat Improvement Centre), though formally founded in 1966 with American aid, was already existed in the form of an American-aided program that began in 1943, and which the wheat specialist Norman Borlaug joined the following year, going on to be awarded the 1970 Nobel *Peace* Prize, raising eyebrows, for his was *not* the usual chemistry prize that such work in biochemistry might have merited.[68]

It was the new seeds from CIMMYT and IRRI alongside American aid for IADP that was the launch pad for the Green Revolution in India. Moreover, from 1966, U.S. deliveries of food under PL480 were subject to conditions. Emphasis had to be placed on the Green Revolution and population control, and the pecuniary interests of U.S. multinational corporations, especially in fertilizers and pesticides. The successive droughts of the mid-1960s had led to severe food shortages and the Indian government was enthusiastic and obliging. By 1969–70, around 37 percent and 12 percent of the total wheat and rice acreages respectively comprised high-yielding varieties.[69]

Political expediency, however, temporarily shelved the rightward shift that Washington wanted. Following the poor performance of the Congress Party in the general and state elections of 1967, during the subsequent sharp factional squabbles within the party, and with the party split in 1969, Indira Gandhi found it politically advantageous to take a leftward turn. Her government began to claim application of the principles underlying Articles 39(b) and (c) of the Constitution in framing certain laws,[70] this with political rhetoric that mouthed Nehruvian expressions such as "socialistic pattern of society" and her own coining of "*garibi hatao*" (remove poverty). Maneuvering to her own advantage, she spearheaded a motion to bring in the Companies (Acquisition and Transfer of Undertakings) Ordinance, 1969, and nationalize the fourteen largest commercial banks with effect from the midnight of 19 July 1969, soon introducing a bill to that effect, placed in and passed by Parliament. Her party, the so-called Congress (Requisition), then spearheaded the passing of the Monopolies and Restrictive Trade Practices bill in Parliament in December 1969 (just a month after the split in the Congress Party), the Indian Patents Act in 1970, the 26th Constitutional Amendment of 1971 to abolish the Privy Purses of the erstwhile royal families of the former princely states, and the Foreign Exchange Regulation Act in 1973.

With control over bank credit passing into the hands of the public sector, the Green Revolution could now be adequately financed without a hitch. After all, the supply of subsidized high-yielding seed, fertilizer, pesticide, irrigation water, and agricultural machinery, including tube-wells and pump-sets, needed liberal bank financing, and to reduce the bank-default and commercial-farming risks, agricultural pricing policy had to ensure that the government's procurement prices were well above ruling market prices. Indeed, the procurement price now acted as a floor price in the speculative trade. The heydays of the landlords, rich peasants/capitalist farmers, both of the kulak variety, and agribusiness traders had truly arrived. The output of food grains more than doubled over the next decade and a half, from 1970 onward.

With the growth of public sector industry and infrastructure sustained by drawing on the proceeds of indirect taxation and deficit financing, and the private sector in industry and agriculture liberally funded by the public-sector banks and other financial institutions, it was the terms of trade between agriculture and industry that remained the bone of contention between the landlords/rich peasants/capitalist farmers on the one hand and Indian big business and the MNCs on the other. It was this relative price that crucially affected the economic positions of these ruling classes in Indian society, as well as the process of accumulation and economic growth. A shift in the terms of trade in favor of agriculture in the initial years of the Green Revolution as a result of government intervention forced both the urban working class and the poor peasants and landless laborers to allocate a large proportion of their money earnings to food commodities, which led to a progressive shrinkage in their demand for industrial products, particularly mass consumption goods, thereby adversely affecting the pecuniary interests of Indian big business and the MNCs.[71]

This contradiction notwithstanding, the Green Revolution strategy, after an initial period of intra-ruling-class bickering over this relative price, seems to have cemented their political coalition with a fair degree of stability and durability, for the powers-that-be found a way for the landlords/rich peasants/capitalist farmers to get their high prices and subsidized industrial inputs even as Indian big business and the MNCs got their low-cost credit finance, duty drawbacks, and subsidized agricultural inputs. The whole program of industrial development was crucially predicated upon significant improvements in agricultural output per acre that would, other things equal, dampen food inflation and thereby check the rise of the industrial wage rate. But the pecuniary interests of those who were in the saddle in agriculture, the rural landed classes and the big traders of agricultural commodities, also had to be accommodated, for they were the main organizers of the rural vote banks and financiers of establishment politics in the countryside.

With the Naxalite movement crushed and the Green Revolution off the ground, the "crisis in the affairs of the ruling order" had been successfully warded off, at least for the present. Indeed, from the mid-1970s to the end of the 1980s, the real agricultural wage rate rose significantly, accompanied by significant increases in government expenditure on rural development. Together, this led to a decline in the incidence of absolute poverty in the rural areas over the same period,[72] although the absolute numbers of the poor went on increasing, and malnutrition and ill health remained endemic. The Green Revolution thus didn't turn Red, but the peasant question

nevertheless became even more germane, for with incomplete proletarianization, the numbers of the poor peasants and other petty commodity
producers/service providers swelled.

I am reminded of the way one of my best teachers, the late Professor
Nirmal Kumar Chandra, introduced the peasant question and there's no
better way I know of to pose that concern. "How can the mass of peasantry
be drawn into a revolutionary movement spearheaded by the socialists,
representing above all the proletariat?" And he goes on: "The difficulty, at
bottom, stems from the fact . . . that the peasant possesses 'two souls,' one
of the proprietor, and the other of a worker."[73] What immediately came to
mind when I read this was another difficulty, this in the Indian context. Here
this combination of the proprietor and the worker—the Indian peasant—is
imbued with *caste* consciousness, which drives him/her to strive to give up
the use of family labor in tilling the soil and in other manual tasks.

How then will the Indian peasant, especially the poor and middle one,
develop solidarity with the landless laborer, who, moreover, is most probably a Dalit? As I have hinted at earlier, in the Indian case, the institution of
caste impedes class solidarity and class consciousness, and as far as the rich
peasant goes, it induces him to behave like the landlord. The Naxalites are
yet to resolve such matters in their political practice even as they continue
to learn from their actions. The movement cannot be written off though,
however much the establishment might wish that one day it will, this in the
face of concerted state repression over the last five decades. Public memory
of the aborted/defeated peasant/plebeian struggles of the colonial and post-
colonial periods, and contemporary conditions on the ground, seem to
compel present-day peasants and proletarians to plod on.

LONG TRADITION OF PEASANT INSURGENCY

The historian Ranajit Guha, in his 1983 classic, *Elementary Aspects of
Peasant Insurgency in Colonial India*, has done much to understand the
rebel political consciousness of the peasant insurgents in India during the
period 1783–1900. As Guha puts it: "One of the direct consequences" of
the British colonialist creation of "a highly centralised state . . . that brought
into focus the refractory moments of semi-feudalism in the countryside in
a manner unprecedented in Indian history" was "the fusion of the landlord's
and the moneylender's authority with that of the sarkar" (the government),
and this is "what provided insurgency with the objective conditions of its
development and transmission."[74] So also was Kathleen Gough's historical
perspective on peasant resistance and struggles in colonial and post-colonial
India. In a 1974 essay on Indian peasant uprisings, she wrote:[75]

Indian peasants have a long tradition of armed uprisings, reaching back at least to the initial British conquest and the last decades of Mughal government. For more than 200 years peasants in all the major regions have risen repeatedly against landlords, revenue agents and other bureaucrats, moneylenders, police and military forces. During this period there have been at least 77 revolts, the smallest of which probably engaged several thousand peasants in active support or in combat. About 30 of these revolts must have affected tens of thousands of peasants, and about 12, several hundreds of thousands. The uprisings were responses to deprivation of unusually severe character, always economic, and often also involving physical brutality or ethnic persecution.

. . . [T]he fact that at least 34 of those I considered were solely or partly by Hindus, causes me to doubt that the caste system has seriously impeded peasant rebellion in times of trouble.

. . .

. . . The revolts . . . amply illustrated the remarkable organising abilities of the peasantry, their potential discipline and solidarity, their determined militancy in opposing imperialism and exploitative class relations, their inventiveness and potential military prowess and *their aspirations for a more democratic and egalitarian society* [my emphasis].

The peasantry had been affected adversely in multiple ways (listed below)[76] during colonial rule, and thus the armed struggles involving peasant partisans against those who exacted their surpluses were warranted. These included:

(i)   Ruinous taxation during the early decades of East India Company rule before and after the Permanent Settlement of Bengal, Bihar, and Orissa in 1793; the revenue used to maintain and expand the colonial system and pay for the imports of commodities for Britain, mainly Indian textiles that were earlier paid for in bullion.[77]

(ii) The land settlements created "bourgeois" private property in land. However, the landlords were deemed to be the owners of the land only if they paid the heavy incidence of tax on the assessed rent collected,[78] of course, with their tenants' "rights" highly circumscribed. Later, the British colonialists gave up much of the potential revenue from the land tax, settling for a much lower incidence of that tax than the Mughals had exacted, thus to secure the landlords' support for their rule. Tenancy reform laws[79] eventually came into force in the face of peasant struggles. The peasants' surplus was, however, by now appropriated by other "agents" besides the landlords—moneylenders, non-cultivating intermediary tenants, merchants, and lawyers.

(iii) There were encroachments on tribal hilly and forested territories and tribal oppression by planters, British and Indian, the colonial government, and landlords, merchants, and moneylenders from the plains.

(iv) The process of *de-*(proto)industrialization in the nineteenth century drove craftspersons deprived of their traditional livelihoods back upon the land as tenants or landless laborers or into the lumpenproletariat.

(v) Peasants got increasingly drawn into the cash nexus with merchants, moneylenders, landlords, and revenue officials, more so with the turn to the cultivation of indigo, opium, cotton, oilseeds, jute, pepper, and other exportable crops in the plains, and tea, coffee, cinnamon, and later, rubber plantations in the highlands. The railways connected the port cities with the hinterland and thus brought British manufactured goods, cloth, for instance, within reach of even the peasant whose produce, as raw material, was exploited by British industry.

(vi) Speculation and investment in land by merchants, moneylenders, landlords, bureaucrats, and rich peasants/farmers, the increasing commercialization of agriculture, and the growth of absentee landlordism led to an impairment of patron-client relations between landlords and tenants/landless laborers.

(vii) The famines of the colonial period were its most brutal feature, beginning with the Bengal famine of 1770 and culminating again with the Bengal famine of 1943 (the latter reawakened collective memory of the former devastation), in between twelve serious famines before the Great Rebellion of 1857, and yet more devastating ones thereafter, the most severe in 1896-97. Using B. M. Bhatia's figures,[80] Gough has estimated 20.7 million famine deaths in India between 1866 and 1943.

(vii) From the 1920s onward, with a growing population in the midst of stagnant per-capita net material product, and with modern industry incapable of absorbing even a fraction of the growing reserve army of labor, rural misery unfolded on an unprecedented scale. Such extreme distress was also a consequence of extreme fragmentation of landholdings,[81] intense competition for sharecropping and other tenancies leading to rack-renting, chronic rural indebtedness, and greater prevalence of debt bondage. What was being witnessed over the longterm was a reduction in the proportion of rich and middle peasant households with a corresponding increase in the proportion of poor and landless peasant households.

Rightly, Gough includes the Great Rebellion of 1857 among the seventy-seven peasant revolts, for as Eric Stokes, in his posthumously (1986) published *The Peasant Armed: The Indian Rebellion of 1857*, argues: the sepoys were "peasants in uniform" and the revolt was that of a "peasant army breaking loose from its foreign master," challenging British colonialism. However, it cannot be said that the assortment of people who rebelled in 1857 also supported the peasant revolts. Nevertheless, despite the disgruntled talukdars (landlords)—who had been marginalized and squeezed out by the British colonialists—assuming local leadership of the rebellion in their areas of influence, for instance, in Awadh, peasants often did take the initiative, as Rudrangshu Mukherjee, in his *Spectre of Violence: The 1857 Kanpur Massacres* (2007), argues.[82]

The rebel peasants were conscious, anti-colonial political actors, and yet, leaders of the British Indian Association, and later, those of the Indian National Congress, condemned the revolt. Jawaharlal Nehru referred to the "feudal character" of the revolt, as did the British communist Rajni Palme Dutt, who called the revolt "the last attempt of the decaying feudal forces, of the former rulers of the country, to turn back the tide of foreign domination," even as Karl Marx and Friedrich Engels, living witnesses to those times, had respectively characterized it as "a national revolt" and a "great rebellion."[83]

Another great peasant rebellion of the colonial period, the last one, which was being waged even as the elite nationalist leadership of the Congress Party and the Muslim League were negotiating the terms of the "transfer of power," was the 1946–51 armed struggle of the peasantry in Telangana under communist leadership. As the eminent historian Ranajit Guha characterizes this armed peasant struggle:[84]

Starting off as a movement against eviction and extortion it assumed, by 1946, under communist leadership, the size and character of a peasant war aimed at the destruction of the princely state of Hyderabad ruled by the Nizam, the largest and most powerful of all the many feudal principalities lovingly fostered by the raj. The struggle, limited at first to 150 villages, had already involved ten times as many by the summer of 1947 when India became independent. A number of liberated zones complete with people's courts and people's militia had already emerged out of the guerrilla war by 1948 when the new regime headed by Nehru and Patel (Vallabhbhai Patel, India's first home minister) sent in its army with the twin objectives of annexing the Nizam's territories *and* liquidating the peasant rebels [my emphasis]. The outcome of this "police action" was the rewarding of the Nizam with a vast pecuniary compensation for the loss of his dynastic kingdom and with elevation to the status of a titular head of state (Rajpramukh) in the new republic when its constitution was inaugurated in 1950. Neither the oppressive officials who had acted as the instruments of the Nizam's despotism nor the landlords and moneylenders who constituted its social base, came to any harm. On the contrary, a feudal restoration was actively promoted by the Indian army and in its wake the armed constabulary wherever they established themselves in any of the liberated zones. Encouraged and supported by them the landlords and moneylenders flocked back to the villages from which they had fled for their lives and seized again the lands, grain and other property which the peasants had expropriated. The sons of the soil who had fought for the end of feudal rule and for democracy in Hyderabad, who had effectively undermined the Nizam's authority long before the Congress party leaders were to recognize in him a potential threat to the Indian republic, had their efforts rewarded by a reign of terror imposed on five Telangana districts where the revolt had made the most headway.

It is also necessary to mention the Tebhaga movement in Bengal—initiated in 1946 and led by the Kisan Sabha, the peasant front of the CPI—which demanded that the sharecropper, the *bargadar*, has the right to two-thirds of the produce, leaving only one-third of it for the landlord, the *jotedar*. The "Great Rebellion" of 1857, Telangana, 1946–48, and Tebhaga, as well as the many other peasant revolts of the colonial period that Kathleen Gough lists, might then be seen as precursors of "Spring Thunder," Phase One, and its following phases. Spring Thunder, like the many peasant struggles of the past, at its core, is a battle for democracy. The Indian republic is a rotten liberal political democracy, and the roots of this decay can be traced back to the time of its birth and to the colonial period.

ABORTED DEMOCRATIC REVOLUTION

By the mid-1940s, people's democracies seemed a distinct possibility in the countries where socialist or national liberation struggles were being waged, especially in mainland China, where the forces of the Communist Party of China played a stellar role in the anti-Japanese resistance in the period 1937–45, thereby shifting nationalist opinion progressively in its favor. But also in the national liberation struggles in Vietnam and Indonesia. Moreover, from 1918 onward, British imperialism seemed to be in relative decline, economically, politically, and militarily, and by the end of the Second World War, the United States had emerged as the foremost imperialist power.

India, despite the ideological and political weakness of the CPI and the near absence of revolutionary leadership within it, could also have taken the militant people's democratic path to liberation. As Ranajit Guha argues, British imperialism, which then had the world's largest colonial empire,

> recognized the writing on the wall in the Quit India movement, in the militant nationalist (though wrong-headed) response to [Subhas Chandra] Bose's Indian National Army [he took help from Nazi Germany and Imperial Japan during World War II to try to rid India of British Rule], in the massive strikes of workers, students and poor middle-class employees in the cities, in the emergence of a democratic peasant movement under communist leadership, and most ominously perhaps in *the mutiny of the Indian ratings of the Royal Indian Navy* [RIN] *and spreading disaffection among the Indian ranks in the army and police forces* [my emphasis]. Faced thus with the prospect of an armed anti-imperialist upsurge the British government decided to defuse the charge by decolonizing which, in the Indian context, was nothing but a pre-emptive strike against what could have exploded as a full-scale liberation war the size of the vast subcontinent. Hence decolonization was achieved, appropriately enough, not by the destruction of the old colonial state and seizure of power by the people, but by *a "transfer of power" from the British to the Indian elite representing big landlord and big business interests which had many links with imperialism and shared with it a common fear of revolutionary developments in the country* [my emphasis]. Consequently, the post-colonial state, the product of a legal transaction between the dominant elite groups of Britain and India, found it easy to continue, even as a sovereign republic, much of what was undemocratic—and a good deal was—in the political institutions and political culture of the raj.[85]

It must be emphasized that all the post-war unrest and rebellion referred to above took place independently of the Congress Party and often in defiance of it. Indeed, even Gandhi condemned the Hindu-Muslim unity of the RIN revolt and the massive militant people's support it got; he referred to this solidarity as an "unholy" alliance/combination that, in his view, "would have delivered India to the rabble." He reportedly even went on to say, "I would not want to live up to 125 years to witness that consummation. I would rather perish in the flames."[86] One only has to recall his "repudiation of all responsibility for the "Quit India" movement, his condemnation of sabotage and underground activities associated with it, and his instruction to underground workers to surrender."[87] There seems to have been, at the time, "a certain convergence of interests of . . . Indian and British capitalists . . . reinforced in the face of the rising militancy of the Indian working class and peasantry, the unrest among the armed forces and the rise in the influence of the Left political forces in the country." Indeed, there was an "overall meeting of minds between the imperialist rulers and the Congress leaders about the growing threat from the Left."[88] As "far as the oppressed people were concerned, Congress and Muslim League were on the same side of the barricade as the raj."

Cooptation of elite nationalists was an important part of British colonialist strategy ever since the aftermath of the Great Rebellion of 1857, and these "nationalists" were willing collaborators in the face of militant struggles of peasants and tribal people that targeted both colonialism and the collective power of the *sarkar*, *sahukar*, and *zamindar*. Of course, the terms of such collaboration/cooption were always under contention. The Government of India Act of 1858, passed by the British Parliament, disbanded Company rule and brought India directly under British sovereignty. Soon to come was the Indian Councils Act of 1861, under which legislative councils with a few non-official Indian members were formed, followed by the same Acts of 1892 and 1909 extending the influence of locally elected[89] provincial councils, and then the Government of India Act of 1935. Taken together, these can be seen as part of a concerted colonialist strategy of progressively devolving power to elite nationalists in the provincial echelons of what was officially claimed to be an emerging federal structure. For the colonialists, the involvement of Indians was a must, with those deemed "politically dangerous" easily disqualified from electoral candidature, and the provincial governors were bestowed with enormous powers. They could jettison any bill that was passed by the legislature, and take over the province from an elected majority ministry on law and order grounds, for the center was strictly under imperial control. The ground was firmly laid for the rotten liberal-political democracy to come.

The vast numbers of ordinary people who had, right from the 1920s, supported/participated in the nationalist elite-led part of the movement for independence were betrayed. But they didn't realize it, for there was no revolutionary leadership, politically and ideologically mature, to guide them. The people thus "cherished illusions about the goals of the political representatives" of Indian big business, Congress, and Muslim League leaders, elite nationalists, "who were out to strike a bargain with imperialism." Indeed, "within less than a year [following 1946] a qualitative change in the situation was brought about by the skilful moves of the raj and its collaborators." And, in "less than two months and a half this vast subcontinent was partitioned, boundaries demarcated, assets divided and two new dominions brought into existence!" It can also be said that all these imperialist maneuvers were put through "because Congress and Muslim League were willing participants in it."[90]

Clearly the Indian nation in the making was not a uniform and homogenous entity—the dominant and the exploited classes in the nation had conflicting interests and needs. The nation was largely imagined and depicted by elite nationalists in an iconography that was Hindu, these nationalists representing the interests and rights of non-Muslim big business but camouflaging the same as the nation's interests and rights. In reality, what was being created was the ground for a dependent "independent" nation with sections of that big business already forging ties with U.S. monopoly capital. Elite nationalism was undermining the nation, for independence was to be brought about via a gentle decolonization, the two dominant arguments in the aftermath of the Second World War being the British colonialists' "change of heart" and the efficacy of non-violent opposition. Gandhi was adept at playing the "dual role of saint for the masses and champion for big business," as the discerning American journalist Edgar Snow is said to have pithily remarked.

Gandhi and the Congress Party's role and attitude in one of the freedom movement's most significant high points, in 1945–46, have already been touched upon. In the three other high points, mass movements against British rule, the ones initiated by the Congress Party with Gandhi in the lead, complete control over the masses was a precondition. In the first of these, the Non-Cooperation Movement (1921–22), mass rage and fervor had already been aroused earlier by the Jallianwala Bagh Massacre and Khilafat, and when violence erupted in Chauri Chaura, the movement was called off, and the masses fell in line, for they looked up to Gandhi the saint, indeed, Gandhi alone, for guidance. The Congress Party and Gandhi insisted on, in his words, "peaceful rebellion" in the Civil Disobedience Movement (1930–34 with breaks in between) too, with no-rent campaigns against the landlords, dependent allies of the colonialists, simply not permitted, for despite the stated goal of "complete independence," in reality, it was intended to be a controlled mobilization for forcing constitutional concessions. Incidences of violence, including those in Chittagong,[91] Peshawar, and Sholapur, did not however lead to its suspension, for, in the courting of arrest, the Congress leaders were out of the way of the masses. But unlike the Hindu-Muslim unity of the Khilafat and Non-Cooperation years of 1919–21, Muslim participation in the Civil Disobedience Movement was low, this because of inter-religious communal strife in the 1920s.

Mass anger and disgust against British rule was at a peak in 1942, and so the "Quit India" movement was violent right from the beginning, more so because the Congress leadership was forced out of the way of the masses by the pre-emptive arrests, because of which the Congress organization couldn't intervene to condemn, denounce, and put an end to violent rebellion. It was only when Gandhi was released from jail in May 1944 that he began to severely condemn the underground movement and called upon the rebels to surrender. But by then the movement had gone through three phases of militancy—the first, violent protests in the cities, the second, the shift of militancy to the countryside, with underground activity, including the use of revolutionary terror, especially in the United Provinces and Bihar, and the third, the running of parallel governments in places like Satara in Maharashtra, Midnapore in Bengal, and Talchar in Orissa. Gandhi, Nehru, and the Congress Party always condemned militant actions, especially peasant, tribal, and urban bouts of violence, strikes, and, of course, revolutionary terror.

With the brutal crushing of the Quit India Movement, in the context of the Second World War and what then seemed like an imminent Japanese invasion of India, and earlier, the post-1905 armed struggles in Bengal, the Ghadar movement, the Hindustan Socialist Republican Association, the Chittagong uprising, and the RIN revolt of February 1946, independence was not to be the precursor of a democratic revolution. As the historian Indivar Kamtekar put it: "Independence" was a handing over "at one stroke" of the entire territory and state apparatus of the Raj "to the leaders of the Congress and the Muslim League" in a "single negotiated transaction." The courageous soldiers and officers of the Indian National Army were refused admission into the ranks of what became the Indian armed forces. And, no one, not even Marxist historians, bothered to ask about the fate of the 20,000 mutineers of the RIN.[92]

The elite nationalist leaders simply substituted themselves to take the place of the British colonialists in office, primarily to secure their own power and privileges and to transfer to Indian big business the unfair advantages that were a legacy of the colonial period, all within the framework of dependence on the dominant imperialist powers. U.S. imperialism had, after all, been pressuring its British counterpart to dismantle its empire and this was exactly what was to transpire. Very soon, the elite nationalist leaders were to prove their utter insensitivity to mass misery. The poor peasants in the Telangana countryside in the late 1940s, fighting for New Democracy, were humiliated, beaten, and tortured by the Indian Army, sent in by the elite nationalists to bring back the landlords and the moneylenders, and thereby restore the status quo. Driven to the wall, it was not easy for these unlettered peasants to turn into revolutionary fighters—this could never have been the first time around.

In power after independence, the elite nationalists of the Congress Party promoted a historiography of a heroic past, largely the part of the independence struggle they had led, and even historians calling themselves Marxists joined the bandwagon. The state embarked on a multiplication of its offices, privileges and pelf—"development administration" was the new kid in town and on the block—with the elite nationalist patrons directing the process from the top downward. During a crisis of legitimacy, however, adept maneuvering in a parliamentary democracy based on universal adult franchise didn't come easy, as was evident in the two years preceding the Emergency.

POPULAR UPHEAVALS PRECEDING THE EMERGENCY

Despite Mrs. Gandhi's huge electoral victories in the parliamentary and state assembly elections of 1971 and 1972, these following the 1969 split in the Congress Party, two states, Gujarat and Bihar, were headed for popular flare-ups.[93] In Gujarat, the home state of Mrs. Gandhi's main political opponent, Morarji Desai, the state Congress committee opted for Desai's Congress (Organization), Congress (O) hereafter, but after the 1971 elections, Mrs. Gandhi's Congress (Requisition) increasingly attracted opportunist defectors from its rival. Feudal allegiance to Mrs. Gandhi was all that seemed to count, with each contending faction within her party claiming to be more loyal than the others. Political degeneration took hold, and, very soon, public cynicism about the *garibi hatao* (remove poverty) program ran high, even as the Congress (Requisition) rode comfortably to power in the 1972 state assembly elections in Gujarat.

In the internal scramble for power that followed, backed by the Congress "High Command" and the state's rich peasantry and wealthy agricultural commodity merchants, an astute manipulator, Chimanbhai Patel, became the state's chief minister in July 1973. Protests by engineering students over inflated hostel-mess bills in the wake of rising food prices soon turned into a popular, state-wide, anti-price rise agitation, led locally by Navnirman Yuvak Samitis (youth for reconstruction committees). In the face of police retaliation, the Navnirman agitation metamorphosed into one demanding the resignation of Patel and his ministry, and the dissolution of the state assembly. The Congress (O) and Jan Sangh, taking advantage of the volatile situation, raised the question of the electorate's "right to recall" elected representatives, and with Desai undertaking a "fast unto death," Mrs. Gandhi's government at the center had no other option but to "advise" the president to dissolve the Gujarat state assembly. In the state elections that followed, a coalition of Congress (O), Jan Sangh and other opposition parties came to power.

In Bihar, from 1967 to 1972, no party or alliance of parties was able to form a stable government. Like in Gujarat, corrupt, opportunistic defections turned the tables, more so after Congress (Requisition)'s huge electoral victory in the 1971 general elections. The 1972 state assembly elections gave Mrs. Gandhi's party a majority even though it secured a mere one-third of the vote, but with a relatively strong, combined opposition of mainly Samyukta Socialist Party and Jan Sangh MLAs (Members of the Legislative Assembly), political instability persisted. An alliance of the Samyukta Socialist Party and Jan Sangh student wings had won the Patna University student elections in 1973, with many of the socialist student leaders from the Yadav, Kurmi, and Koeri (backward) castes. In March 1974 these students launched what became the JP movement in Bihar, when they invited the elderly (72-year-old) Sarvodaya socialist, Jayaprakash Narayan (JP), to lead them. JP, a former prominent socialist politician, quickly renewed his links with his former socialist comrades and launched a political program that, he claimed, would take the state from *raj niti* (ruler-oriented policies) to *lok niti* (people-oriented policies). He got the students and youth to form Chhatra Sangharsh Samitis (student struggle committees) and Jana Sangharsh Samitis (people's struggle committees) and demanded the dismissal of the Congress state government. The political opposition, especially the socialist parties and the Jan Sangh, the latter, opportunistically, soon began to ride high on the JP bandwagon.

Indeed, in June 1974, when JP declared that the Bihar movement was for *sampoorna kranti* (total revolution), though these opposition parties didn't want any kind of revolution, their sole purpose being the overthrow of the Congress government and the installation of themselves in power, they began spreading the line, "give us the reins of government and the rest [JP's *sampoorna kranti*] will follow." Soon JP reckoned that his idea of *sampoorna kranti* had gripped the national imagination, just like Mrs. Gandhi's earlier slogan *garibi hatao* had, and he decided to launch his movement at the national level. Addressing a public rally at the Ram Lila grounds in Delhi on 25 June 1975, with the other opposition leaders on the dais, JP demanded the resignation of Mrs. Gandhi, called on the police and the army not to obey any "illegal orders of the government," and appealed to the Indian public to join a nationwide non-cooperation movement from June 29.

An apprehensive Mrs. Gandhi reacted at breakneck speed; like Jawaharlal Nehru, her threshold of tolerance and accommodation of opposition was low, set as it was by the interests of Indian big business. Around midnight

June 25–26, the president was made to sign the proclamation of *internal* Emergency,[94] and the cabinet ex post facto was made to approve of it early next morning. When the nation came to know of it, "not a dog barked," as the then Defence Minister Bansi Lal was reported to have boasted. "Even I was astonished," observed Mrs. Gandhi, ". . . there was not a murmur at all."[95] It was indeed an eye-opener that the arrests of the top leaders of all the opposition parties and of Jayaprakash Narayan didn't provoke spontaneous strikes, demonstrations, and/or uprooting of rails, as used to happen when prominent leaders of the national movement were treated like this by the colonial authorities. The ban on twenty-six parties and detention of some 140,000 political prisoners were to follow.[96]

There were expectations that the JP movement would go on even with JP incarcerated, but such expectations and hopes were belied. Where was the mettle of the regime's opponents? The Naxalite movement had by then almost been decimated by the state's brutal repression, and what remained had split into many factions. The establishment opposition claimed to be fighting for democracy, but Mrs. Gandhi didn't even need any large-scale deployment of the police, for most of her establishment opponents now chose to be mere passive adversaries. So she didn't need to create any new repressive machinery, for the run-of-the-mill bureaucrats and police officers did what they were told to do, even as decision-making was concentrated in the hands of a few loyalists, as it was before. The regime's establishment opponents, just like in British colonial times, by and large "sought a negotiated settlement with the government." Indeed, in December 1976, bigwigs of the Congress (O), the Jan Sangh, the Socialist Party, and the Bharatiya Lok Dal tacitly approved what the widely respected socialist intellectual C. G. K. Reddy called a "'pure and simple surrender document.'"[97]

At no time during the Emergency was there any real threat to Mrs. Gandhi's authoritarian regime, even though it did some horrible things, like the *nasbandi* (forced sterilization) campaigns and the "beautification" drives, in both of which Muslims were the first targets. Government medical personnel accompanied by contingents of police personnel entering a village or an urban locality invariably targeted the Muslims first in the forced vasectomies they conducted. Even Muslim youth who had barely entered adolescence were sterilized. And the "beautification" drives began in Muslim settlements, in Delhi, at Turkman Gate and the Jama Masjid area. The hypocrisy of it all reached such levels that the word *secularism* was inserted into the Preamble to the Indian Constitution by the 42nd Amendment, which was passed by Parliament in November 1976. Indeed, before this amendment, India was described in the Constitution's Preamble as a "Sovereign Democratic Republic" and after the amendment, as a "Sovereign Socialist

Secular Democratic Republic." Was there a better way to discredit secular-ism and socialism?

JP's most fatal political error was his embrace of the semi-fascist Rashtriya Swayamsevak Sangh (RSS), its political party, the Jan Sangh, and its student wing, the Akhil Bharatiya Vidyarthi Parishad. Till then, the RSS, one of whose presumed cadre had assassinated M. K. Gandhi, was a politi-cal pariah at least as far as progressive political circles were concerned, but JP even went to the extent of declaring that if the RSS was fascist, then he too was a fascist. The RSS and its various wings took full advantage of JP's endorsement, even going on to claim that it played a leading role in India's "Second Freedom Struggle" during the Emergency when the reality "was the abject attitude of RSS chief Balasaheb Deoras, in his letters to Indira Gandhi from Yeravada jail in Poona [now Pune]. Deoras promised that his organi-zation would be at the disposal of the government 'for national uplift' if the ban on the RSS were lifted and its members freed from jail."[98]

SEEING THE LONGER PROCESS

The narrative has moved across time and space, between "1857" and "1968" India in order to trace the roots of the latter and clarify the ways in which India's "modern" past and India's "1968" are connected. What has been dis-cerned includes what was new in "1968" India and what was part of a longer process, the interplay of continuity with change. The longer process is a series of rebellions for justice and well-being by ordinary people—poor and middle peasants/workers/revolutionaries. These revolts incurred the wrath of the state and were crushed by brutal repression, and laws were instituted to suppress and punish the rebels, harshly and unfairly. This was followed by reform, and laws to that effect, and political encouragement of a reform-ist strand among the nationalist elite, whose dependability was gauged by the extent to which it went in condemning the rebels/revolutionaries and expressing faith in the establishment's will to bring progressive institutional change. The colonialists devolved more and more powers to the national-ist elite they had co-opted, with the latter contending and negotiating over the extent of such prerogatives, taking advantage of the persistence of the militant struggles to enhance its own bargaining power. Such opportunis-tic politics by the elite guaranteed the failure or the falsity of the reforms, the persistence of "subaltern" rebellions and the spawning of new ones, the many Naxalbaris of Spring Thunder, Phase One, being the latest in the series up to "1968."

The longer process can thus be discerned in terms of a series of recur-ring rebellion–repression–reform sequences, with the nationalist elite collaborating with the colonial power against the militant opposition and engaging in an open-to-reason face-off with the colonial power on the question of the extent to which it must devolve power to them.[99] Over time, and two decades after independence, democratic consciousness, if some of it had indeed come into being in the awareness of the nationalist elite, was shallow, as the '68er Primila Lewis realized when she took on the absentee owners of Mehrauli's "model farms" in the 1970s. The March 4–5, 1966, IAF airstrikes on the civilian Mizo population of Aizawl revealed how low the threshold of the establishment's tolerance and accommodation really was, this atrocious act of the Indian state taking place almost a decade before the internal Emergency came into force.

For the '68ers, the Emergency was the exact opposite, the very antithesis of the dawn in the longing for which they had set out. If they now found some kind of "anchorage for the ship of heartache,"[100] it was in the many Naxalbaris where the "notion of witness" was practiced; it was in the Chipko movement that hugged the trees; it was in the Dalit Panthers who took their cue from America's Black Panthers; it was in the small, yet spirited, autonomous women's movements that were sparked off by widespread outrage over the Mathura rape case; it was in the "short-lived Dalli-Rajhara spring"; it was in the twenty-day all-India railway strike; it was in the budding civil liberties and democratic rights movement; it was in the Navnirman and JP movements; it was in the active opposition to the Emergency. Yes, even in those last two movements and in the active opposition to the Emergency, there were Sarvodaya and socialist activists, '68ers, who earned the loyalty, respect, and affection of people who came to know of their good deeds, and their aversion to the devious, scheming, and unprincipled politicians who had opportunistically hitched on to the JP bandwagon.[101]

And surely the '68ers in all the above-mentioned struggles derived some of their inspiration and courage from the public memory of the militant struggles of ordinary people in the colonial period. In the Great Rebellion of 1857; in the many other peasant resistances; in the struggles for forest rights in Kumaun and Tehri Garhwal in 1921, 1930, and 1944–48; in the planned Ghadar uprising of 1915 that was nipped in the bud; in Chauri Chaura; in the militant activities of the Chittagong branch of the Indian Republican Army and those of the Hindustan Socialist Republican Association; in the Non-Cooperation and Civil Disobedience movements; in the massive anti-imperialist upsurges of 1942 and 1946; and in the Telangana Armed Struggle.

In the course of resistance, there surely comes a time when the partisans, who were ordinary people—poor peasants and landless laborers, artisans, workers, middle-class youth—become historical persons. They seriously begin to reason, critically view the world, and assume responsibility for their actions. They are then no longer "things," alienated human beings available to be manipulated by unprincipled leaders. Their creative energies then unfold, unconstrained by the fiat of the "Old Left" parties. India's "1968" was such an historical moment, and it endured right up to the first half of the 1980s.

Most significant during the latter moment was the Bombay textile strike of 1982–83,[102] unparalleled in that it could sustain itself for a year and a half with a significant section of the 250,000 workers of sixty textile mills actively involved. This in the face of close links between the mill managements, the Congress government, and leaders of the Rashtriya Mill Mazdoor Sangh, a union that had been imposed on the workers by the Bombay Industrial Relations Act of 1946, and whom the workers had rejected. Not to mention the police, the judiciary, and mass media. For some of the leftist students and radical youth in active solidarity with the workers (and with the trade union leader Datta Samant who was urged to lead the workers), the one-and-a-half-year-long strike that began in January 1982 was one that took them to a higher level of political consciousness, a reasoned critical understanding of the defeat of the strike and the subsequent planned transformation of central Mumbai's historic industrial lands into expensive real estate in the evolution and growth of Bombay's Manhattan.

India's "1968" was a period when poor peasants and landless laborers, industrial workers, Dalits, "tribals," middle-class youth, and women had variously begun to revolt against the demons that oppressed them— "semi-feudalism," backward capitalism, patriarchy, and so on. Some of these revolts were violent, and the state's violence against them was undoubtedly on behalf of the oppressors, unleashed against the oppressed in the name of democracy and law and order. For reasons best known to them, most liberals refuse to make a distinction between the violence of the oppressors and the violence of the oppressed, this even though the latter has made important contributions to freedom and democracy in the past and in the present.

Speaking to the House of Commons in the aftermath of the RIN mutiny in 1946, and in reply to a question from Winston Churchill, the British Prime Minister Clement Attlee apparently disclosed the "real reasons for granting independence to India."[103] The ordinary soldiers of the British Indian Army were no longer loyal to Britain, and Britain could not afford to have a large British Army to hold down India. The contribution of violent resistance to bringing freedom is rarely acknowledged. What then about non-violent resistance, fasting-unto-death, for instance? According to Gandhi, himself, as interpreted by David Hardiman, this "was best used only in cases in which the two parties knew each other personally and enjoyed a mutual respect,"[104] as apparently, Gandhi enjoyed with the British colonialist administrators.

Arguably, the violent resistance of the Telangana and Tebhaga movements of the 1940s brought land reforms with a sense of urgency onto the official agenda in the 1950s and 1960s. And the Naxalite movement, in Srikakulam, for instance, forced "an amendment (popularly known as 1 of 1970) to the existing Land Transfer Regulation Act of 1959 to prohibit transfer of tribal lands."[105] Indeed, in Mrs. Gandhi's manifesto of the Emergency, of her twenty-point program, five points had a bearing on the very questions of land and livelihoods that the Naxalites had raised with great force—point 2 on implementing the ceilings on agricultural land and the distribution of surplus land; point 3 on homestead land for the landless; point 4 on abolition of bonded labor, mainly debt servitude, outlawed in the Constitution's Article 23, and then again, subsequently, in the Bonded Labour System (Abolition) Act, 1976; point 5 on liquidation of rural indebtedness and a moratorium on recovery of debt from landless laborers, small farmers and artisans; and point 6 on review of laws on minimum agricultural wages.[106]

Importantly, the CPM-led Left Front government, which came to power in the state of West Bengal in 1977, after the Emergency, launched *Operation Barga* in June 1978, and later backed it with legal reforms, to enumerate the sharecroppers and legally record their tenancy, which did a lot to prevent peasant-tenant eviction and ensure that the tenants got their "fair" share of the crop. The CPM has rightly been credited for plugging some of the key loopholes in West Bengal's agricultural tenancy law; its peasant organizations assisted many of the *bargadars* (sharecroppers) in winning their rights.[107]

One can think of the CPM here as the "moderates," but there were also the "extremists," the Naxalites, who had already played the most indispensable part, for, more than any other political force, it was this section of the left which brought the agrarian question to the center of politics in West Bengal in the late 1960s and early 1970s through the armed struggles it led. The Naxalites aroused the social conscience of the people of West Bengal against landlordism in a manner not witnessed before. It was the CPM, however, that reaped the benefit because of its pragmatism in instituting a limited but effective tenancy reform, which among other things, helped it to retain power (it was repeatedly voted into office) over the next thirty years in West Bengal. Indeed, the "moderates" broke the force of the radical opposition that came from the "extremists," but they failed to accomplish anything resembling a thorough democratization of West Bengali society over the thirty-four years that they were in power, and were dislodged by Mamata Banerjee and her Trinamool Congress party—with leftist rhetoric and militancy a significant part of her political repertoire—in the state assembly elections of 2011.

The focus so far has been on human volition, human beings in resistance turning into active agents, historical persons, their creative energies unfolding and, in turn, molding the reality of "1968" India. The '68ers were, however, defeated, and I'm certainly not going to make what I think would be an absurd claim if I were to say that in the long run history is going to be on their side. Nevertheless, "1968" didn't die; the quest for an egalitarian, democratic India goes on. Reform forced from below and technical fixes of the Green Revolution-type apart, the ruling classes and their political representatives have been the keepers of the past, and as Paul Baran forcefully wrote in 1952—and we began this chapter with his incisive remark—"The keepers of the past cannot be the builders of the future." There was a reason why I chose that sentence from Baran, for strangely, within the parliamentary left in India, there is a peculiar prejudicial view that the so-called national bourgeoisie *ought* to lead the country into its future. It's time then to track down the evolution of the contemporary class structure of the ruling classes, and in this, Paul Baran's *The Political Economy of Growth* (1957) is indispensable as the starting point. Having so far given primacy to human actions driven by collective resolve, it's time now to turn to the bare economic facts, structural economic change, unequal development (the tendency of the system to produce poverty as well as wealth), and the evolution of the Indian big business–state–multinational bloc.

3

Unequal Development and Evolution of the Ruling Bloc

My voice is a crime,
My thoughts anarchy,
Because
I do not sing to their tunes,
I do not carry them on my shoulders.

—CHERABANDA RAJU[1]

Unequal development is a process in which there is a tendency of the socioeconomic system to generate poverty as well as wealth, misery as well as luxury, degradation as well as civilization, islands of the latter in a vast sea of the former, more succinctly, underdevelopment all around with small pockets of development. It is necessary to try to grasp this process as it has been unfolding in India over the long term, to understand its working and where it is taking India.

A large proportion of the workforce has been earning a livelihood through petty commodity production of goods and/or services. The process of "proletarianization," wherein wage labor increasingly becomes the principal form of employment, has been limping. The persistence of huge differences between the returns to labor in India and the same in the developed capitalist world, much more than the corresponding differences between their respective labor productivities, has been a distinctive feature. And a reserve army of labor whose size is greater than that of the active army of wage labor has also been a telltale sign of economic backwardness. The huge reserve army of labor—its size 2.1 times that of the active army of wage/salary-based labor in March 1973—just doesn't get drained, a phenomenon that is at the heart of India's unequal development.

The evolution of the Indian economic system over the long term, a process of unequal development, spans a vast canvas in space and time covering both the colonial (1757–1947) and post-independence (1947 onward) periods taken together. It has led to the consolidation of an Indian big business–state–multinational bloc that has been directing the process of development of India's underdeveloped capitalism since the late 1950s.

In the course of colonization, India made a transition from what was then a petty-commodity, tribute-paying social formation in decline in the first half of the eighteenth century to an underdeveloped capitalist one by the second half of the nineteenth century. A bloc of the colonial Indian state, British managing agency capital, Indian big merchant-cum-financial capital, and the big landowners took hold to steer the development of underdeveloped capitalism. Over time, Indian big merchant-cum-financial capital took on industrial assets, and the British managing agency houses were eventually overshadowed by the rise of the subsidiaries and affiliates of the modern MNCs. At India's independence, nationalist rhetoric notwithstanding, the economic base and the political superstructure were conducive to the eventual consolidation of a big business–state–multinational bloc in the latter half of the 1950s. It is this ruling bloc that has since been driving the process of development of Indian capitalism, and the narrative traces this process up to the second decade of this century. The big landowners, largely cut down to size, many of them now akin to kulaks,[2] have continued to be a part of the ruling bloc, especially at the provincial and district levels.

PASSAGE TO COMPANY-STATE RAJ

With regard to the Mughal Empire in the seventeenth century, one can speak of a petty-commodity, tribute-paying social formation, one wherein the *zamindars* (rural intermediate land-controllers) and the ruling class combine (*jagirdars*, *mansabdars*, and the emperor) extracted the "tribute" (a massive state extraction of surplus that was commoditized) from the peasantry in village communities. This extraction of tribute, made possible by the political and military power of the ruling classes, left the poorer peasants and landless laborers (the rural toilers) with a bare minimum necessary for survival.[3] The state owned the principal means of production, cultivable land, and the toilers had virtually no political rights.

Mercantile and financial wealth, especially the section of it that had benefitted from the large inflows of precious metals that came from the export trade, was also beholden to the ruling aristocracy, for the towns and their commerce were dependent on state-enforced agrarian exploitation. There were thriving urban manufactories (*karkhanas*) producing luxury consumption goods for the nobility and run by it, and a putting-out system of household craft production of commodities organized by merchant capital, which also fed the expanding export trade. Indeed, the wealthiest of the merchants had their own merchant shipping, but it was handicapped because there was no corresponding naval power to back it, and it had to rely, initially, on the Portuguese, and then on the Dutch and the British navies for "passes" to remain in the business. The seventeenth century was a period of vast growth in worldwide trade, a commercial revolution of sorts, and Indian mercantile and banking capital was an integral part of it. The system of credit and banking that supported the long-distance, including international, trade organized by merchant capital was quite sophisticated. An order of payment could become commercial paper, discounted by indigenous bankers.

However, with the onset of a crisis of the petty-commodity, tribute-paying social formation, the Mughal central authority suffered terminal decline, and regional political formations became relatively stronger by the 1740s, especially in Bengal, Awadh, and the Deccan, after the 1739 ransacking of Delhi by Nadir Shah from Iran. The regional formations were, however, undermined by the East India Company,[4] Britain's merchant monopoly capitalist enterprise for its trade with the East that had been making inroads in India since 1619, when it established a "trading post" in Surat. The Company went on to wrest political power from the regional Indian rulers, beginning with its conquest of Bengal in the 1750s and 60s and completing the colonization of India with the subjugation of the Punjab and the final annexation of Awadh in the 1840s and 50s. In a world-historical context, it was the Seven Years' War (1756–1763) that opened the way for the British takeover of India and attainment of supremacy in the Indian Ocean. It must be remembered that it was commercial interests, commercial capital, that politically triumphed in the English revolution of the seventeenth century.

In this context, what is significant is the close collaboration of wealthy indigenous merchant and financial bigwigs, especially the section that undertook long-distance trade and finance, which quickly switched its loyalty to the Company. These magnates were to give substance to, in no small measure, the economic integration of the vast areas of the sub-continent, cemented later with the spread of the railways and the telegraph. With their links at various levels in the structures of power, they knew exactly when to connive with the Company and when to withdraw their support to the rulers of the regional political formations.

The role of the wealthy indigenous bankers Jagat Seth and Omichand in 1757 comes to mind, as also that of Seth Naomal Hotchand in the British conquest of Sind in 1842. And, following the death of Ranjit Singh in

1839—he had held state power in the Punjab since 1799—the East India Company, with the collusion of some wealthy Sikh financiers, annexed the Punjab in 1849. The Hindu Dogra ruler of Jammu, Gulab Singh, who aided the British in the conquest, was handed over the Kashmir Valley in 1846 for a huge sum of money and a pledge of perennial homage to the British of all his male heirs to come. Obviously, as long as loyalty as junior partners in commerce-cum-banking or local governance assured a raking-in of the *moolah* or royal privilege, and the Company-State guaranteed military security, all these wheeler-dealers were willing to tolerate racial discrimination.

This was how the East India Company, with its superior military power and having gained the loyalty of wealthy indigenous merchants and bankers, reached the pinnacle of its profession as a Company-State. It was a period when proto-manufacturing was subservient to merchant capital. Following the grant of *diwani* (the right to collect the land revenue from Bengal) and the Permanent Settlement of Bengal Revenues of 1793, the Company-State bestowed ownership of revenue-paying land to the zamindar. As long as the latter paid the stipulated amount of revenue, which was a high proportion of the assessed rent he "earned," he had the right to sell or mortgage the land and pass it on to his heirs, as well as the power to take away tenancy from peasants who failed to pay the rent and re-allot it. But failure to fulfill his revenue payment obligations resulted in confiscation and auction-sale of his land.

SWITCH FROM "OLD" TO "NEW" COLONIALISM

Enriched with the flow of land revenue into Company coffers, the import of silver, which was hitherto used to pay for India's exports, stopped; the land revenue was now used to make such payments. The very appropriation of such revenue changed the class structure of Indian urban society, unrolling a set of compradors. Part of the land revenue also financed further military expeditions in India and the East. (India actually paid for its own conquest and subjugation and for the extension of the British Empire in the East!) Of course, the Charter Act of 1813 abolished the Company's monopoly over India's foreign trade, and the triumph of industrial capitalism in England led to a swamping of the Indian domestic market with British factory-made goods and the turning of India into a primary producer for the British industrial system.[5]

"Old" colonialism gave way to "new" colonialism. From a major exporter of cotton goods, India was converted into a major importer of the same. This story is well known, but it is presented here with a focus on monopoly (oligopoly, more precisely) as one of the key elements in the evolution of India's underdeveloped capitalism, with the East India Company at the heart of it, from 1757, and even after 1813, up to 1858, and then the British agency houses and their Indian big-business imitators. That the British-controlled managing agency houses, and later, the Indian large business houses and the modern MNCs generally had their fingers in the pies of trade, finance, *and* production in their drive to gain monopolistic advantage, and that in this single-mindedness they sought and competed among themselves for state-political backing shouldn't come as a surprise to any serious student of modern Indian history.

PEASANT AND ARTISAN—DEGRADED

The colonial government nurtured the British-controlled managing agency houses, not their Indian counterparts, who became the political favorites only after independence. But the dynamism of industrial capitalist growth that emanates from linkages between the manufacture of consumer goods and those of the means of production, including capital goods, both within the same economy, was, in the colonial period, marked by its almost complete absence. The backward linkages of the growth of the textile industry in England triggered the expansion of the basic, intermediate, and capital goods industries, bringing about an integrated development of the industrial sector of the British economy. India's economic underdevelopment was, however, rooted precisely in such development. The process of industrialization in England drove the twin processes of India's *de-*(proto)industrialization (the destruction of native, competitive proto-industry from ruinous competition) and agricultural commercialization (forced cultivation of opium and indigo, but also the market-driven sowing of raw cotton, wheat, jute, oilseeds, and sugarcane), more so after the opening of the Suez Canal in 1869 and the building of India's rail network inland from the major port cities in the 1880s.

While *de-*(proto)industrialization brought about the destruction of craft and manufactory production of the putting-out type, where merchant capital advanced the raw materials and placed orders for the final goods, the commercialization of agriculture and the commodification of land brought about the "formal subsumption" of agricultural labor to capital. Recall Marx's sharp comment on the plight of the small peasant in developing capitalist France in *The Eighteenth Brumaire of Louis Bonaparte, 1848–1850*:[6]

> . . . [I]n the course of the nineteenth century the urban usurer replaced the feudal one, the mortgage replaced the feudal obligation, bourgeois capital replaced aristocratic landed property. The peasant's small holding is now only the pretext that allows the capitalist

to draw profits, interest, and rent from the soil, while leaving it to the agriculturist himself to see to it how he can extract his wages.

This does not imply a correspondence of the plight of the French and Indian peasant. It merely indicates the subordination of the peasants to capital, but of a kind wherein capital didn't directly takeover the process of cultivation, except in the plantations. Nor did capital bring in techniques that would have increased the capital-labor ratio and labor productivity by reinvestment in agriculture itself of part of the surplus it appropriated, what Marx called the real subsumption of labor to capital. If the latter had happened, the peasants would have been evicted and only some of them re-employed as agricultural wage laborers. But this didn't happen, and so the landowner continued to extract rent; the merchant continued to buy cheap and sell dear; and the moneylender/creditor continued to lend at usurious rates of interest, leaving the peasant to extract for himself his "wages," as best he could.

The processes of *de*-(proto)industrialization and agricultural commercialization—these in the face of the institution of the Permanent, the Ryotwari[7] and the Mahalwari[8] settlements—furthered the commodification of land, in turn adversely affecting the "customary" rights of poor peasants and landless laborers. The high revenue demand in the areas of Ryotwari Settlement caused acute peasant distress, which reached its limits in times of agrarian depression, forcing large-scale labor migration, part of this overseas as indentured labor. And, following the commodification of the cultivating fields, the grazing grounds were reclaimed as "wastelands" and the forests came to be recognized for their commercial value. "Transgressions" of these enclosures to graze cattle and collect fuel-wood began to be dealt with quite severely. With the spread of the railways from the middle of the nineteenth century and international expansion of the British Royal Navy, the demand for durable timber boomed, and the forest department, which was created in 1864, "enclosed" the forests and began to deal even more severely with infringements by commoners.

Nothing but contempt for and callousness toward ordinary folk, "uneducated rustics," is what one senses. In this intricate story of the impact of colonialism on various classes in India during the phase when industrial capital was dominant in Britain, it is necessary to highlight what the destruction of proto-industry did to the skilled artisans and craftspersons involved therein. There is disagreement among scholars on this score, but at least most of them agree that the proportion of the labor force in manufacturing did not rise at all over the century, despite the emergence of modern textile and jute mills in the latter half of the period.[9]

The ruination of artisans/craftspersons in competition with imported manufactured goods from England, their degradation into unskilled laborers in mines or plantations, or after being forced to fall back upon the land, as disguised-unemployed labor in agriculture, or into servile trades in the services sector should not be lost sight of. Many of the artisans/craftspersons were turned into "unproductive laborers," doing jobs that would have been absent if society had been more rationally and humanely ordered. Indeed, the historical genesis of the phenomenon of India's huge reserve army of labor—which, as we have noted, was 2.1 times the size of the active army of wage labor in March 1973—a vast pool of pauperized labor with no prospect of a better tomorrow, can be traced to the process of *de*-(proto)industrialization in the nineteenth century.

There is another tragic dénouement in the *de*-(proto)industrialization story. This is that the process of *de*-(proto)industrialization obstructed what Marx called "the really revolutionary path" to industrial capital, wherein class differentiation within artisanal/craft production gives rise to the emergence of industrial capitalists from the ranks of the artisans/craftspersons themselves. De-(proto)industrialization blocked this path even more than it did the conservative path to industrial capital wherein merchant capital takes control of and reorganizes the process of artisanal/craft production by turning all the artisans/craftspersons into wage workers. The relation of industrial capital to the sphere of production that emerges in these two distinctly dissimilar paths is radically different as far as its approach to and appreciation of those whose knowledge and skills reside in technology and the labor process. The relative attenuation of "the really revolutionary path" to the emergence of industrial capital in India is one of the root causes of contemporary technological dependence and technological underdevelopment, which I will touch upon a little later in this chapter. Indeed, in modern times, the very misconception of the artisan as a "'skilled manual worker' without 'intellectual' or 'imaginative' or 'creative' purposes"[10] says a lot about her/his degradation, besides, of course, the devaluation of such work and the persons deriving their livelihoods from it, both rooted in the ideology of the caste system.

TASTES–OPINIONS–MORALS–INTELLECT

Ideology is a process accomplished by the so-called thinker consciously indeed but with a false consciousness. The real motives impelling him remain unknown to him, otherwise it would not be an ideological process at all.
—FRIEDRICH ENGELS, "LETTER TO MEHRING," 1893[11]

With vast numbers of people unable to fulfill any of their reasonable aspirations, social unrest was in the air, as was insurgency. The Santal *hool*

(rebellion) of 1855–56 and the Great Rebellion of 1857 shook the very foundations of the Empire. In the aftermath of the latter rebellion, the Company's
powers were transferred to the Crown. From now on, all the more, the
Indian aristocracy—the landlords and the princes—the mercantile and the
financial classes, and the educated, high-caste Hindu middle classes were
to be co-opted as allies to legitimize British rule. How else can one explain
the extent of the colonial drain (transfer) to Britain amounting to 10 percent of India's gross national income each year in the early decades of the
twentieth century, but for the political subordination of these elites as junior
partners in the squeezing of more of the surplus from the "underfed, under-
clad, underhoused, and overworked masses"?[12] The British Indian Army was
reorganized, not merely to maintain the "peace" within the country, but also
for overseas colonial military expeditions financed from government revenue. And rich "cultivators," who lived off the surplus appropriated from
those who actually tilled the land as tenants-at-will, benefited from a series
of tenancy laws, the Rent Act of 1859, the Bengal Tenancy Act of 1885, its
amendment in 1928, and another in 1935.

Of course, to hold out hope in the midst of all this misery, the British colonialists had to present their ideas as the "only rational, universally valid ones,"
the "ruling ideas of the epoch."[13] Much earlier, Thomas Macaulay's oft-quoted
"Minute" on Indian education of 1835 made a beginning on this score:[14]

> We must at present do our best to form a class who may be inter-
> preters between us and the millions whom we govern—a class of
> persons Indian in blood and colour, but English in tastes, in opin-
> ions, in morals and in intellect. To that class we may leave it to refine
> the vernacular dialects of the country, to enrich those dialects with
> terms of science borrowed from the Western nomenclature, and to
> render them by degrees fit vehicles for conveying knowledge to the
> great mass of the population.

The stage was thus set for diffusion of the culture and ideology of the
colonialists, and with this unfurling, inculcation of a social psychology
based on a false presumption of superiority of the colonizer and inferiority
of the colonized. Elite groups could then be fostered as junior partners of
the colonialists in this the heyday of the Company-State when "economism"
as an ideological construct was making waves—an understanding that the
economic logic of capital must override all other considerations, even to the
extent of violating the autonomy and integrity of the political sphere.

For the Company-State and, later, the Raj, economism underlay the whole
gamut of commercial relations that ensured the "drain" of a considerable

part of the economic surplus[15] to Britain. Indeed, in the fourth quarter of the nineteenth century, the Indian government was the largest purchaser of British exports, a huge employer of British civil servants at high salaries, and a mega provider of manpower for the military might of the British Empire.[16] Moreover, the administration and military expenses of the Indian government in Britain (called "Home Charges") were paid for from Indian government revenues.

In the late nineteenth century, Britain was, however, in relative decline as a producer and exporter of manufactured goods, and it ran huge trade and current account deficits with Europe and the United States. How was it to maintain the pound sterling as the world's reserve currency and London as the world's premier financial center? The retention of much of its wealth and power now depended on protecting this turf. It had to somehow increase not only its bilateral trade surplus with India and its other colonies, but also politically impose more liabilities in the form of "invisible" charges (invisible earnings not actually earned) to thereby increase its current account surplus with them. Britain seemed to have found a way through appropriating the export surplus of India (and its other colonies) with the rest of the world by politically imposing invisible charges to match India's (and its other colonies') high *net* export earnings with the rest of the world. In effect, the colonial "drain" to Britain allowed it to cover its deficits with Europe, the United States, and other regions of white settlement, keep up its profitable capital exports to these regions, and thereby preserve the pound sterling as good as gold and maintain the hegemony of London as the world's premier financial center, at least up to 1914.[17]

How could the Indian ruling elite have consented to the "drain" of a considerable part of the economy's surplus to prop up Britain's faltering international financial position at onerous costs to the well-being of the Indian people? A part of the answer might be buried in the making of these elites, molded as "English in tastes, in opinions, in morals and in intellect." Comprador capitalists and comprador culture were fostered. The Indian mercantile-cum-financial bourgeoisie had switched its loyalty, first to the Company, and then to the Raj, and with the dispossession of many peasants in times of financial distress, it had even appropriated cultivable land. Following the Indian economy's integration in the capitalist world-system, it was this local bourgeoisie and the British managing-agency firms who now handled the wholesale trade of British manufactured goods in the domestic market and the produce of the commercial crops for the international market as middlemen/agents of colonial commerce. In the Bombay Presidency, for example, in the first half of the nineteenth century, Gujarati and Parsi merchants procured raw cotton and opium as the agents/middlemen for British firms; some of these merchants reaped windfall profits during the American Civil War (1861–65), from the export of raw cotton to Lancashire. More generally, a great many local businessmen, landlords, rich peasants, and professionals and civil servants were recipients of the appropriated surplus and owed their benefits to British rule.

BLOSSOMING OF INDIAN BIG BUSINESS

Capitalism is a global system consisting of two sub-systems, a "center" and a "periphery." Britain was part of the center where capitalism had emerged from its own internal contradictions, the accumulated merchant wealth of the commercial revolution of the seventeenth century, and overseas conquests. India became a part of the periphery where capitalism was initiated by and for Britain, imposed on India from outside, leading to Britain's "development" and India's "underdevelopment," both the result of a world-wide process of capital accumulation. The transition in India from a declining petty-commodity, "tributary" social formation in the first half of the eighteenth century to "underdeveloped capitalism" by the mid-nineteenth century involved a number of basic changes, foremost among them the institution of bourgeois private property in the means of production, which were then mainly cultivable lands, but also a bourgeois government *and* legal system. India's economy and society were adapted and manipulated to serve the imperative of the accumulation of capital in Britain. The peasant, under the threat of eviction, was now subject to economic coercion, made worse by the pauperization of artisans following *de-*(proto) industrialization.

The landowners, employing intermediaries to manage their relations with the peasants, established themselves in the cities, where, in due course, their educated sons developed urban commercial interests and other "petty-bourgeois" careers for themselves. Over time a new class of de facto landowners came into being; "superior" tenants who acquired "occupancy" rights emerged as *jotedars*, the new landowners exploiting tenants-at-will. And importantly, there was a separation of political from economic power, earlier vested in the same person at the local level. Now the landowners held economic power, while their political counterpart was vested in the colonial state.[18] A caveat would, however, be in order regarding the separation of political from economic power. While this was as per legal right, in reality, in the hinterland, the landlords continued to exercise judicial and police powers. They presided over the village *panchayat* in the settlement of disputes and they also maintained private hired armed gangs to take on rivals, threaten recalcitrant peasants, and violently suppress the rebellious ones.

Meanwhile, the comprador bourgeoisie had accumulated sufficient wealth in long-distance trade as agents of the East India Company, and later, of the British managing agency firms, and in indigenous banking as intermediaries (*shroffs*) of the British joint-stock banks. The "original" accumulation of capital of the business house of the Tatas came from the fortunes its founders had made as middlemen in the opium trade and as suppliers of the Bombay Presidency Army in Ethiopia in 1868. More generally, the Indian compradors handled the wholesale trade in British manufactured goods, procured agricultural commodities (raw cotton, jute, etc.) from the hinterland for British merchant firms, and supplied provisions to the British Indian Army in India and abroad. Besides these business activities, some of them also made fortunes from speculation on the commodities futures markets and the stock market. The original accumulation of the business wealth of the Bombay and Ahmedabad mill owners—who, sensing huge profit margins despite foreign technological and managerial dependence, ventured into modern spinning and weaving mills from the 1850s and 1860s onward—was also from a combination of businesses in long-distance trade, finance, and speculation.[19]

This was the beginning of a structural transition of the Indian economy from a position where it was essentially an importer of manufactured consumer goods and an exporter of primary commodities (mainly agricultural) to one wherein it imported capital goods to develop a modern consumer goods industry (for example, cotton cloth, sugar, matches), the exports of primary commodities paying for such imports.[20] With the relative decline of industry in Britain from the late nineteenth century onward in the wake of competition from the late industrializing nations of Germany, the United States, France, and Belgium, the rise of oligopolistic capitalism, the advent of modern multinational corporations (MNCs), and a changing international division of labor, protective tariffs for import substitution in the relatively older branches of industry came into place in the 1920s and 1930s. A substantial amount of the capacity of modern industry was until then British owned and controlled.

The war compulsion had forced the colonial power to encourage the production of iron and steel in India, but overall, industrial development was constrained by what was permitted within the framework of tariff protection. As of 1939, there was no capital goods industry worth the name and a number of manufactured goods markets were under the firm control of MNCs like Unilever, Dunlop, ICI, and General Motors. The interwar years had, after all, witnessed the entry of the subsidiaries and branches of the MNCs—ICI, Unilever, Philips, Union Carbide, Glaxo, Goodyear, Colgate Palmolive, General Motors, Ford, Standard-Vacuum, Caltex, Firestone, Dunlop, British Oxygen, Swedish Match, Metal Box, Bata, Remington

Rand, Indian Aluminium (an Alcan subsidiary), and so on. Indian big business, which had by then already consolidated its position with industrial corporations, joint-stock banks, and insurance companies, also began to forge collaborations with US MNCs, for the United States had ascended over Britain as the world's leading capitalist power. It was when Indian big merchant-cum-financial capital took control of industrial assets to become Indian big business that its relationship with foreign capital (British managing agency and multinational capital) turned ambivalent.[21] From now on, it was no longer merely in collaboration with foreign capital, but competing *and* collaborating with foreign capital.

Colonialism was, however, the most important obstacle to integrated industrial development.[22] Russia and Japan witnessed a rapid interlinked, integrated development of their railways, coal, iron and steel, and engineering industries at the very time when Bombay (now Mumbai), Calcutta, (now Kolkata), Delhi, and Madras (now Chennai) were being linked by the Indian railways. And yet, the whole Indian railway network was put together with imported locomotives, rolling stock, tracks, and signaling, and even the engineers and managers were brought in from Europe.

Economic and technological dependence in a colonial setting had thwarted the dynamism of capitalism in India, and it was Paul A. Baran's *The Political Economy of Growth*, first published in 1957,[23] that laid the foundations of a modern Marxist analysis of such attenuation, which took a long time to remedy in the post-independence period. Baran's was a path-breaking analysis of the roots of India's economic backwardness, this in the sharp contrast he drew between Japan's independent capitalist development after 1868 and India's dependent capitalist underdevelopment with native compradors as junior partners.[24] In the words of the editors of the independent socialist magazine *Monthly Review*, with respect to India, Baran showed "what happens to a country which remains under the control of imperialism and native compradors," and, in sharp contrast, with respect to Japan, "how a fiercely nationalist ruling class in an undeveloped country could devise a development strategy which kept foreign capital at arm's length, concentrated economic power in the hands of the state, and led in a significantly short time to becoming one of the leading advanced capitalist countries."[25]

Following independence in 1947, however, the Indian ruling classes got a second chance. But the Congress Party, their main political representative, squandered the opportunity. Baran wrote of the sharp contrast between that Party's precepts and practice:[26]

Setting out to promote the development of industrial capitalism, it does not dare to offend the landed interests. Seeking to mitigate the most outrageous inequalities of incomes, it refrains from interfering with the merchants and money-lenders. Looking for an improvement of the wretched position of labor, it is afraid to antagonize business. Anti-imperialist by background, it is courting favors from foreign capital. Espousing the principles of private property, it promises the nation a 'socialist pattern of society.'

Meanwhile, the heart of the international financial system had been transplanted from London to New York City; the United States was now the world's largest manufacturer and trader, and the international monetary system was tied to the dollar. Nevertheless, alongside U.S. MNCs, Japanese, German, and other West European firms also bid for business in the opportunities presented by India's import substitution-led industrial development, for which state enterprises from the Soviet Union and Eastern Europe in technical collaborations with Indian governmental enterprises were also not too far behind. The Indian state and Indian big business were in a much better bargaining position than ever before. Oligopolistic rivalry among the MNCs of the developed capitalist countries made foreign direct investment (FDI) in large third-world countries like India a strategic necessity. The governments and big businesses in some of these countries, India and Brazil among them, relative to their counterparts in most nations of the third world, were neither weak nor backward. Together, the state and big business steered the course of national politics, and, in the economy, there was an understanding that the state, more specifically the central government, would act to prevent the MNCs from expanding too much at the expense of Indian big business. The definition of too much, that is, the delicate balance of the interests of Indian big business and the MNCs—between "nationalist" economic policies and those that favor the MNCs—was left to Indian big business to define and redefine, but the MNCs proved to be much more flexible than what was normally expected of them.

A study of India's large business houses (LBHs) in the private corporate sector (PCS) and the Indian economy for the period 1931–75 by Nirmal Chandra[27] found an increasing share of the assets of the LBHs as a proportion of the total assets of the private corporate sector, of which they were an integral part. Mercifully, their share in the total reproducible tangible wealth of the country betrayed a negative trend over the same period, even as the share of the PCS or the organized private sector in net domestic product manifested a positive drift. Typically, a large business house/group was composed of a set of interconnected companies and was of a minimum size in terms of total assets. Management control over all the interconnected companies of the group was established through inter-corporate direct investment and interlocking company directorships, and the group as a whole acted as a large conglomerate firm. The companies in the group were financed by the public-sector banks and financial institutions and funds mobilized through the stock markets from passive shareholders. The large business house/group could thus be controlled by its promoters as long as they acted as a single cohesive authority. In effect, a small set of wealthy promoters could secure management control over a massive asset base without commensurate ownership of it.

India had never been through a phase of competitive capitalism; the Indian PCS firms, with an eye to quick profits and control of the labor process, found the adoption of contemporary Western technology licensed from the MNCs much too attractive. The companies of each large business house retained or expanded their market power

> not so much through superior efficiency, but by controlling the supply of raw materials and intermediates, by nurturing intimate links with the state machinery at various levels, by resorting to restrictive selling practices designed to shut out smaller firms, and by gaining access to cheap institutional finance, which are effectively denied to the vast majority of small capitalists.[28]

Apart from the large multinational corporate subsidiaries that were a part of monopoly capital, most of the companies that were grouped in one or the other LBH were controlled by Indian big business groups—the Tatas, the Birlas, the Mafatlals, Thapar, Sriram, Bangur, J. K. Singhania, etc.[29] Over time some more business groups, like Reliance, Escorts, Godrej, Gujarat Ambuja, O. P. Jindal, etc., joined the ranks of the LBHs. Even as most of these big business groups have been technologically dependent on the MNCs, and could not have derived quick profits without access to contemporary Western technology, they have resented the entry and consolidation of MNCs in the form of branches or wholly-owned subsidiaries, preferring instead that the MNCs collaborate with them either in joint ventures or simply by repeatedly transferring the most recent vintage of the technology to them.

INTEGRATED INDUSTRIAL DEVELOPMENT—AMBIVALENT INTENT

The government could, however, be quite flexible in the application of its industrial policy. Although the industrial policy of 1948 assigned the state the responsibility of developing the oil industry, the government instead invited Burmah Shell, Standard Vacuum (Esso), and Caltex to set up oil refineries in India. These MNCs, profit-oriented, vertically-integrated capitalist enterprises, with international operations from the stage of exploration and extraction of crude oil to the marketing of petroleum products, extracted very lucrative terms for the proposed refineries, reaping for themselves the benefits of movements in the price of crude oil and reductions in transportation costs.

Indian big business, aware of such multinational business conduct, had, in their so-called Bombay Plan of 1944,[30] envisaged a great deal of infrastructure and industries, the development of which was to be the responsibility of the public sector. These were industries in which capital outlays were huge, gestation periods long, and profitability low in the short and medium term, and in which the Indian private sector was not willing to undertake such investment because the expected net private gain was not deemed sufficient. Indeed, this was what Indian development planning of the post-independence period went by; public investment in public enterprises in infrastructure and certain designated industries served to boost private investment. Nevertheless, the implicit policy of "live and let live" was not abandoned. Nehru made a significant statement in favor of the role of MNCs in India's industrial development in the Constituent Assembly in April 1949 and from then on until the late 1960s government officials seemed to treat MNCs on par with Indian big business.

More generally, there was never any anti-private enterprise strategy, even in the nationalization of air transport in 1953, the Imperial Bank in 1955, and life insurance in 1956, for these nationalizations were, in the circumstances, just what Indian big business needed.[31] Indeed, J. R. D. Tata, a pioneer of civilian air transport in India, was appointed the chairman of the new public sector Air India; the private sector simply didn't have the investable resources to expand air transport services throughout India and on the major international routes. The Imperial Bank became the State Bank of India in 1955 when India's central bank, the Reserve Bank of India, bought 60 percent of its paid-up equity capital, this because the huge expansion of domestic credit and the change in its structure that were necessary for rapid capitalist development was beyond the wherewithal of the then big five private-sector banks—the Central Bank of India, Punjab National Bank, Bank of India, Bank of Baroda, and United Commercial Bank. The nationalization of life insurance contributed immensely to the supply of long-term credit for private investment; besides, the industry had to be "cleaned up" after the public disgrace it had suffered in the wake of scandalous corruption that had tarred its image.

As far as industrial finance was concerned, the public sector played a major role in extending long-term credit to the PCS through the setting up of public financial institutions. These, together with public-sector investment institutions like the Life Insurance Corporation and the Unit Trust of India, also went on to subscribe to significant amounts of the equity share capital in Indian PCS companies as *passive* shareholders. Among the major public-sector financial institutions that aided the Indian PCS companies in this manner were the Industrial Finance Corporation of India (set up in 1948), the National Industrial Development Corporation (started in 1954; it financed the much needed modernization of cotton textile and jute mill companies), the Industrial Credit and Investment Corporation of India (floated in 1955), and the Industrial Development Bank of India (began functioning in 1964).[32]

Public-sector financing of the PCS notwithstanding, there followed another wave of nationalizations from the late 1960s to the mid-1970s, that of

- a number of Indian private-sector banks in 1969, including the big five, which, after government takeover, among other things, helped meet the requirements of agricultural credit for the success of the Green Revolution (chapter 2);
- the Indian Iron and Steel Company (IISCO) of the Martin Burn group that was desperately in need of technological modernization but bereft of surpluses that had been siphoned off over the years through managerial remuneration, sole selling agency, and purchase contracts;
- a number of textile and engineering firms, and a few British-controlled managing agency houses, all on the brink of insolvency;
- companies mining both coking and non-coking coal that had resorted to reckless, irrational, quick-profit seeking practices which had made sections of the resource in the ground irrecoverable at a subsequent date and also had increased the risk of mine fires;[33] and
- the multinational petroleum companies, Esso, Caltex, and Burmah Shell, inspired by the example of the Middle East oil producers, which had then undermined the Western petroleum MNCs in that region of the world.[34]

The initial priority for public investment was the development of infrastructure (electricity, major irrigation, railways, etc.), although its outputs were systematically underpriced, directly subsidizing the private sector and thereby boosting its profitability. But in the Second (1956–61) and Third (1961–66) five-year plans, steel, cement, fertilizer, metallurgical equipment, organic chemicals, heavy electrical equipment, earth-moving equipment, heavy plates and vessels, aluminum, and railway equipment manufacturing companies, and an oil exploration and extraction commission and an oil refinery company were set up in the public sector. The public sector, itself, was the major customer of the products of these companies, but so also was the private sector, and it too was a supplier of some of these products, and so pricing became a major bone of contention.

Nevertheless, the period 1951–65, like the one during the 1920s and 1930s, witnessed a notable expansion of industrial output, mainly because of tariff protection and import substitution. However, the 1951–65 period, and especially 1956–65, unlike that of the 1920s and 1930s, was one wherein the economy began producing the means of production, including capital goods, not only for its consumer goods industry, but also for its intermediate and capital goods industry. Indeed, between 1960–61 and 1965–66, around 29.9 percent and 25.6 percent, together 55.5 percent of the growth of net value added in the registered manufacturing sector was contributed by basic intermediate goods (steel, cement, fertilizer, etc.) and capital goods, while consumer goods, including consumer durables (4.8 percent), contributed only 31 percent. Such figures for the 1980s and 1990s, however, show a sharply diminished contribution of capital and basic intermediate goods to the growth of registered net manufacturing value added.[35] This was because the process of laying the structural foundations of internally integrated industrial development—development of a fully-integrated production structure within the domestic economy composed of manufacture of consumer goods, the means of production (including the capital goods) of consumer goods, and the means of production (including the capital goods) of the producer goods industry[36]—was cut short after the mid-1960s, and was only half-heartedly pursued thereafter until the end of the Fifth Five-Year Plan (1974–79). The manufacturing sector thus could not attain the central role that the main architect of the Second Five-Year Plan (1956–61), Professor P. C. Mahalanobis, envisaged for it.

It is a matter of conjecture, given the class structure of the ruling classes, whether the Mahalanobis strategy would have been allowed to run its course. Much of the mobilization of tax revenue was from indirect taxes such as excise duties rather than direct taxes. And, in registered manufacturing, there was a sharp increase in the capital–labor ratio, a significant decline in the share of labor in net value added, and sluggishness in the expansion of employment. Besides, a widening gap between the value of output in registered manufacturing and the aggregate purchasing power of its employees compelled the managements to rely increasingly on the primary, unorganized-secondary, and tertiary sectors, along with exports, to sell what was being produced.[37] Much earlier, the Congress Party engineered a split in the All India Trade Union Congress in 1945 in order to defuse worker militancy, and formed the Indian National Trade Union Congress in

1947. Governments at the center and in the states that the Congress Party led patronized the latter, thus dividing and thereby weakening the working class[38] and adversely affecting the growth of its purchasing power. Moreover, these governments also had a virtual monopoly over public resources that were available for such private patronage.

A mention should also be made of the external assistance that the government of India was able to mobilize because of its foreign policy stance and the advantage it derived from East-West rivalry. The Bandung Conference of Asian and African countries in 1955 and the subsequent flowering of the non-aligned movement paved the way for the hegemony of the ideology of independent, national-bourgeois development in a couple of third world countries, prominent among them India, Egypt, and Indonesia, because of the respective stellar roles played by Nehru, Nasser, and Sukarno. Moreover, the United States, UK, West Germany, and Japan seemed bent on ensuring the success of "democratic planning" in India over "authoritarian planning" in China.

To this effect, an Aid India Consortium was constituted in 1958 by the United States, Britain, West Germany, Canada, and the World Bank to finance India's "democratically planned" projects, but surely the Mahalanobis strategy must have been some cause for embarrassment, for the economics of it had a close resemblance to a model developed by the Soviet economist G. A. Feldman in 1928. External support for the Mahalanobis strategy nevertheless came from the Soviet Union together with Czechoslovakia and Poland when they offered technical assistance and soft loans to India for industrial projects related precisely to its public sector-led heavy-industrial development program. However, in the wake of a foreign exchange crisis in 1957, it was the U.S. government that came forward with considerable "aid"—euphemistically called "development assistance"—not only in absolute terms but also relative to the size of India's Second Five-Year Plan, and the government began to encourage even more FDI in the form of equity capital in joint ventures.

Gross fixed capital formation in the public sector faltered from 1966–67 to the mid-1970s, recovering in 1976–77, although by then the structure and character of such investment had changed, more of it going into coal (which was nationalized in the early 1970s) and electricity, and the services sector. Indeed, the post-1966 industrial "stagnation" up to 1974–75 as compared to industrial growth in the period 1951–65 has been attributed, among other things, to this slackening of public investment, for it dragged down total investment (both as a proportion of GDP) with it.[39] Private corporate investment (as a proportion of GDP) diminished sharply in 1965-66 and did not recover in the 1970s. The deceleration of industrial growth was, however,

mainly in capital and basic intermediate goods industries, partly a consequence of diminishing import-substitution opportunities,[40] but mainly due
to slackening demand in the face of faltering public investment in infrastructure, for example, in the railways.

A closer look at inter-public enterprise transactions makes it clear that
the slackening in public-sector investment affected the order-book positions
of the public enterprises the most. In addition, over the years, many decisions to import technology and capital goods when these could be supplied
by public enterprises marred the process of learning-by-doing. There were
cases when either marginal-cost pricing in conditions of industrial recession,
non-price stipulations, project-related tied aid, insistence on international
competitive bidding, or plain favoring of multinational corporate rivals
effectively checkmated the chances of public enterprises bagging orders for
capital goods. Large investment projects in the public sector were not evalu-
ated from the point of view of the possibility of the entire public enterprise
system supplying the demand for capital goods and engineering services
that such investment generated. Even as the public purpose of public enterprise was constantly being evoked, the private interest usually prevailed.[41]

The government stake in the equity capital of the union public-sector
companies is held by the president of India, and on his or her behalf, the
union government appoints the chairman, the managing director, and the
other members of the boards of directors. Besides, the government insisted
on a host of approvals—of investment proposals and pricing, for example,
and even in the awards of contracts to companies and commissions to agents.
Ultimately it was the priorities of the top political authority that determined
the objectives with which the public enterprises were run.

Economic self-reliance was ostensibly one of these aims, but the public
enterprises were not able to do much to help the country overcome technological dependence and technological underdevelopment.[42] In earlier
research by this author, it was found that the Indian integrated steel industry
systematically relied almost wholly on the adoption of innovations generated in the developed capitalist or the centrally planned economies. The
imported technology was not significantly absorbed, adapted, and modified, nor was there generation of a significant set of incremental innovations
or autonomous development of imported technology. There seemed to be a
structural propensity to systematically rely on imports of technology with
little significant adaptation and modification and hardly any autonomous
innovations. These facts led to the conclusion that despite the public sector's stated objective of technological self-reliance, it continued to be rooted
in a state of technological dependence as far as iron and steel technology
was concerned. A certain weakness and lack of development of local R&D,

design and engineering, capital goods design and manufacturing, and equally important, their lack of integration with the steel plants in the process of technological development, apart from tenuous linkages among and between the various organizations in the social division of technological labor, was also discernible. This situation seemed to persist over a considerable period, which prompted the conclusion that the integrated steel industry was weighed down in a state of technological underdevelopment.[43]

In contrast, Japan imported iron and steel technology without falling into a state of technological dependence. It actively adapted, modified, and further developed the iron and steel technology it imported. Indeed, the import of iron and steel technology in Japan supported local technological development rather than substituting for it. In sharp contrast to their Indian counterparts, Japanese enterprises in the steel industry seemed to have invested considerable complementary resources in the absorption and subsequent development of iron and steel technology. A precondition for overcoming technological underdevelopment was the creation of sufficient demand for the potential outputs of local ferrous metallurgical R&D, design and engineering, and capital goods manufacture. The logic of India's industrial development strategy, rather than nurturing infant technology, seems to have allowed the leakage of this demand through continuous and systematic technology imports. Drawing on other research on technology transfer and development, one finds that technological dependence and technological underdevelopment continued to prevail in other industries too in which the public sector had taken a leading role.[44] The repeated technological alliances that India's public enterprises struck with MNCs seem to have only perpetuated their technological dependence on these corporations, and in this respect they proved to be no different from their counterparts in the private sector.[45]

To what extent, then, did the public enterprises and the Indian private corporate enterprises together act as a counterweight to counterbalance the leverage of the MNCs in India? The 1944 Bombay Plan was against excessive state ownership in counterbalancing the influence of the MNCs. Moreover, the public enterprises, even as they made headway in the second and third five-year plans, failed to generate the required profit income whose retained earnings after dividend payouts would have otherwise significantly financed their capital formation, this mainly because of the pricing policies they were obliged to follow in order to benefit the private sector. Anyway, lack of technological capability, a hard foreign exchange constraint after 1956, and the availability of World Bank and other Western "aid" with strings opened the pathways for FDI in a number of industries, even as the offer and acceptance of Soviet and East European loans and technology transfer improved India's bargaining position.

KEEPING THE MNCS AT BAY—DUBIOUS RESOLVE

India's hard currency reserves ran out again in the wake of food shortages in the mid-1960s, necessitating huge imports of grain, and Western governments again came to the rescue, as usual with strings attached. The fertilizer industry was opened to the private sector, including the MNCs. But then came Mrs. Gandhi's sharp populist, left-nationalist turn (chapter 2). The 1967 general and state assembly elections witnessed a significant erosion of the Congress Party's electoral support base, and then the 1969 split in the Congress Party forced Mrs. Gandhi's Congress (Requisition) to undertake a strident left-nationalist turn.

In this context, the Monopolies and Restrictive Trade Practices (MRTP) Act of 1969, the Indian Patents Act (IPA) of 1970, and the Foreign Exchange Regulation Act (FERA) of 1973 need mention. The MRTP Commission obstructed the expansion plans of large companies, including MNCs. The IPA stimulated the emergence and growth of Indian companies in agrochemicals and pharmaceuticals, competing successfully with the MNCs, for there were now no product patents in these lines, only process patents with a validity period of five years from the grant of patent or seven years from the filing of complete specifications, whichever was shorter. And FERA obliged foreign branches of the MNCs to convert themselves into companies under Indian company law, and all such companies were required to dilute their shareholding to 40 percent or below if they were not in "priority industries" or didn't meet the required export and/or high-tech stipulations. Refusal to do so meant winding up, and as we know, IBM and Coca-Cola opted out.[46]

The government, however, didn't systematically favor Indian companies, including public-sector companies, over MNCs, as for example, in the fertilizer industry,[47] or in Bharat Heavy Electricals Ltd's collaboration with Siemens.[48] And again, in the wake of a balance-of-payments crisis in 1980 and IMF loan preconditions, FDI policy moved in favor of MNCs, for instance, in the Suzuki-Maruti joint venture in automobiles, but curiously, the industry was shielded from the entry of other MNCs for a decade. As a correspondent put it, Maruti was simply the auspicious Hindu prefix for the Japanese Suzuki. In the mid-1980s, a consortium of machine tools manufacturers led by the public enterprise Hindustan Machine Tools (HMT) made offers for the supply of machinery to be used by Maruti for the manufacture of auto components for the Suzuki engine, and again for the supply of machinery for the manufacture of auto components for the transmission, but in both instances the offer was rejected in favor of imports from Japan.[49]

However, MNC influence in the PCS of the Indian economy diminished in the aftermath of FERA–MNC (including minority MNC affiliate) share in dividends and sales of the PCS fell from an average of 57.6 percent and 36.5 percent respectively in 1970/71–72/73 to 47.0 percent and 28.0 percent respectively in 1979/80–80/81—only to rise again to 63.6 percent and 37.5 percent in 1982/83–84/85 in the aftermath of IMF "conditionalities."[50] This does not imply that the MNCs and their joint ventures with Indian big businesses had a field day. In light commercial vehicles, for instance, TELCO's (now, Tata Motors) indigenously developed models (206, 407 and 608) did commercially better than the high-import-content Indo-Japanese joint-venture vehicles of Allwyn-Nissan, DCM-Toyota, Swaraj-Mazda and Eicher-Mitsubishi.[51]

Not for nothing did the 1980s witness a significant decline in the contribution of capital and basic intermediate goods to the growth of value added in the registered manufacturing sector, 13.3 percent and 18.9 percent respectively, compared to 25.6 percent and 29.9 percent in 1960/61–1965/66. The contribution of consumer durables was, however, 15.6 percent compared to the earlier 4.8 percent, prompting some of us to prematurely conclude that an elite consumer durables-led industrial growth pattern had taken shape, based on the booming demand for Maruti-Suzuki cars and consumer electronics, geared by the Fourth Pay Commission's incomes-policy bonanza for the bloated government bureaucracy in public administration.[52] Certainly, there was a sharp increase in the government's current expenditure, including that on subsidies, but public investment in the electricity and transport sectors also contributed to giving a fillip to private corporate investment.

Indeed, the 1980s witnessed the movement of the Indian economy on to a higher growth path, but this was because the tertiary sector assumed an even more important role in the growth process. From around 1980, the services sector began to make a greater contribution to the growth of GDP than the industrial sector, and at least as far as the 1980s go, it was the public sector, and especially the part of it in the tertiary sector, that led the growth process, not the private organized sector. Come the capitalist triumphalism of "1989," however, and the tables began to dramatically turn in favor of the organized private sector, especially its corporate component, in the 1990s and beyond. In December 1989, the World Bank released a report, *India: An Industrializing Economy in Transition*, that was contrary to the Planning Commission's draft "Approach Paper to the Eighth Five-Year Plan," but the Bank's, not the Planning Commission's, word went on to lay the basis of India's "New Industrial Policy" of July 1991.

Looking back at the period 1951–89, it can be argued that it was the implementation of the Mahalanobis strategy, which gave priority to production of the means of production (including capital goods) of the producer goods sector, which brought the economic contradictions between the

MNCs and the Indian state to a head. Western foreign "aid" and collaborations of Indian public and private enterprises with the MNCs sought to ensure not only dependence on imports of the means of production for India's producer goods industry but also over-reliance on imports of the means of production for India's consumer goods industries. If India were to have persisted in implementing the Mahalanobis strategy, not only would it have significantly reduced imports of the means of production for its producer goods industry, but, given its low-wage advantage, it would have emerged internationally competitive in some of these means of production, including capital goods to manufacture producer goods, and would have exported these goods and thereby diversified its export basket toward high-tech items in competition with the MNCs worldwide. India's production structure would have then turned auto-centric. The MNCs didn't want this to happen, and there were large sections of Indian big business whose accumulation of wealth was based on their junior partnership with the MNCs that also didn't want this to happen. Perennial dependence on contemporary Western technology (rather than concerted investment in one's own R&D with the attendant risks) was much too attractive for Indian big business on the lookout for quick profits.

The state, which in agreement with Indian big business—congruity between the Second/Third Five-Year Plan and the Bombay Plan—had earlier confined its investment to both high-tech industry *and* infrastructure, decided later to restrict its investment only to the latter, this to the satisfaction of both Indian big business and the MNCs. The public enterprise Indian Telephone Industries (ITI), a major manufacturer of telecommunications equipment, for example, was starved of investment for modernization and technological up-gradation just when it had to compete with imports of such hardware from Alcatel, Ericsson and Motorola, and when the induction of wireless telephony was leading to unprecedented growth in the market for telecommunication services.[53]

HEYDAY OF MNCS AND INDIAN BIG BUSINESS

As events unfolded, another balance-of-payments crisis in the wake of the Gulf War in 1990 and IMF stabilization and World Bank structural adjustment loan preconditions brought about further FDI and import policy liberalization from the 1990s onward. And, the Uruguay Round of the General Agreement on Trade and Tariffs (GATT) agreements, especially the Trade-Related Intellectual Property Rights (TRIPS) and the Trade-Related Investment Measures (TRIMS) agreements, eventually obliged the Indian government to institute a strong patents law and prohibit the imposition of domestic content and export requirements as entry preconditions for FDI. The spirit of "1989" was in the air, following the collapse of the Berlin Wall that unleashed a huge wave of capitalist triumphalism from which India could hardly remain immune. The stage was set for India's own "1989," providing the setting for weakly regulated entry and expansion of MNCs in India. Today, the MNCs and Indian firms can import final goods (after paying a relatively low import tariff) or produce them in India. If they choose domestic production, in a relatively free international trading regime, they can manufacture the final good with the use of imported materials, components, and capital goods or by buying local.[54] The final good so produced can be exported or sold in the domestic market, and the profits, as far as the MNCs are concerned, can be repatriated or reinvested in India. Indeed, for the MNCs, disinvestment of capital and its repatriation overseas is now a relatively easy option.

Looking at the post-independence period of so-called national-bourgeois development, which came to a close with the inauguration of India's "1989" in July 1991, it seems clear that the foundations for dependent economic development were laid with the cementing of what eventually became a ruling bloc of Indian big business, the Indian state, and the multinationals in the aftermath of the foreign exchange crisis of 1957. It was then that the Indian state, with the consent of Indian big business, de facto adopted a liberal policy with respect to the MNCs, which needed domestic market access in the wake of India's adoption of an import substitution industrial policy. This phase of public policy toward MNCs lasted until 1970, when the MRTP Act became operational, followed by the Indian Patents Act of 1970, which came into operation in 1972, and FERA, which began to be applied in 1974. The MNCs, however, proved to be remarkably flexible. They met the FERA stipulations to reduce their equity stakes to 40 percent or below by inducing more paid-up equity capital from the Indian capital market, making sure that the remaining Indian-owned 60 percent was widely dispersed. Indeed, MNC affiliates having a foreign equity capital share as low as 10 percent to 25 percent could ensure management control through incorporation of a stipulation to that effect in the articles of association of those companies. Once they came out of the FERA orbit, the MNCs could expand their operations with the same freedom allowed to Indian big business, for they were now entitled to be treated on par with Indian big business, subject to the same set of policies.[55]

This only goes to demonstrate the propensity of the MNCs to share the surplus they controlled with Indian investors as long as they could thereby expand their operations to increase the size of that surplus. The bloc of Indian big business, the Indian state, and the MNCs thus weathered the "nationalist" phase of the 1970s quite well, mainly due to the immense flexibility displayed by the MNCs, for they knew that unlike Indian big business, they have vast alternative business opportunities elsewhere in the world, whereas for Indian big business, India remains its main realm of operation. The MNCs, or for that matter, the Indian state and Indian big business, are no doubt powerful; they make their own history, but they cannot do so as they choose. Their Indian subsidiaries have shaped the Indian economy but have also been shaped by it, so they also have to adapt to Indian economic policy and indeed they do, quite flexibly, as we have seen.

But once again the tables turned, from July 1991 onward, this time in favor of the MNCs. Even before FERA was repealed, MNCs that had earlier been induced to opt for minority affiliates began to acquire majority equity stakes, turning such affiliates into subsidiaries. Indeed, the 1991 New Industrial Policy brought about a drastic reduction in the number of industries reserved for the public sector, and there was a further pruning of the list when big business began to call the policy shots. Besides, multinational subsidiaries were, in effect, no longer bound by the stipulations that had confined them to "priority industries" or the ones that had imposed export and high-tech obligations on them. Moreover, the protection provided for the small-scale sector was reduced, and industrial licensing by and large dismantled, even for "items of elitist consumption" (cars, entertainment electronics and "white goods"), what the MNCs particularly have a competitive advantage in, with their brand names now freely permitted to be used as a competitive weapon. The monopolies part of the MRTP Act was virtually repealed. Mergers, amalgamations, takeovers, including hostile ones, soon seemed to be the name of the game.[56]

The MNCs began ousting their Indian partners in their joint ventures. For example, Indian Shaving Products, a joint venture of Gillette with the Poddars, became Gillette India, which then went on to acquire its major Indian competitors, two companies, Wilkinson and Harbans Lal Malhotra & Sons, to overwhelmingly dominate the shaving products market. And, TVS Whirlpool, after Whirlpool acquired Kelvinator India and bought TVS' shares from Sundaram, became Whirlpool of India Ltd. But the Munjals of the motorcycle manufacturer Hero Honda resisted, even though they were technologically dependent on Honda; eventually they parted ways with Honda, with the latter selling its stake to Hero and focusing on its own subsidiary, Honda Motorcycle and Scooter India. Several MNC affiliates with minority equity share stakes made themselves subsidiaries—so Indian Photographic became Kodak India; Carrier Aircon became Carrier India; and Indian Oxygen became BOC India. But the Indian management of ITC Ltd resisted; BAT Industries (BAT Plc.), which owned 31.5 percent of the paid-up equity capital of ITC couldn't increase its stake to 51 percent. Soon a Bombay Club of some of the patriarchs of Indian big business got nervous and began demanding ways and means to acquire full control over the companies that in the past they had managed with mere minority stakes. In turn, the MNCs that had technical collaborations with Indian companies began to demand equity stakes in those entities. BPL's technical collaboration with Sanyo would eventually metamorphose into a Sanyo–BPL joint venture, and Toshiba India would eventually emerge from what was then a mere technical collaboration with Videocon.

Indeed, some consumer goods markets, dominated by Indian firms, overnight turned into MNC bastions. The Indian soft drinks market, which Indian firms had taken over after Coca-Cola, refusing to comply with the provisions of FERA, exited in 1977, was "recaptured" by the likes of PepsiCo and Coca Cola within a span of five years in the first half of the 1990s. In general, MNCs made huge inroads mainly in a whole range of elite consumer goods, entertainment electronics included, computer and telecommunications hardware, and automobiles.[57]

But the Indian auto-components manufacturers, which had eventually become internationally competitive because of the government's insistence in the 1980s that the auto-MNC joint ventures increasingly buy local, not only profited from supplying parts to the auto assembly plants in India, but also made hay by entering into strategic alliances with the auto MNCs. Sundaram Fasteners forged a strategic alliance with GM, Bharat Forge with Mercedes-Benz, and so on, for the supply of key components to the latter's assembly hubs overseas. India, however, still remains poorly rated as an export platform compared to China, Mexico, Malaysia, Thailand, and Indonesia, the Indian auto-component manufacturers' strategic alliances with the auto MNCs notwithstanding. But it was the industrialists who had benefitted from such strategic alliances with MNCs that were the ones who were in the forefront in the Confederation of Indian Industry's bid to preserve the Indian big business–state–multinational bloc.

As far as outsourcing is concerned, besides the strategic alliances of India's major automotive-parts manufacturers with the automotive MNCs, the other outsourcing big business that emerged was in Information Technology (IT) and IT-Enabled Services (ITeS). Indian IT entrepreneurs famously made India the "back office of the world" by adopting a business model based on labor-cost arbitraging, pioneered by TCS, Infosys, Wipro, and HCL Technologies. The media hype surrounding these business stars reached a new high when, not long ago, the *New York Times*'s celebrated columnist Thomas Friedman predicted that India's IT sector will "flatten" the world, meaning, in fact, that the country's young, educated "Zippies" are able to undertake a whole spectrum of Western white-collar jobs at a fraction of the cost.

It did not, however, take many years for the large western software services MNCs like IBM, Capgemini, Accenture, and EDS to move in and emulate the labor-cost arbitraging business model pioneered by the Indian IT/ITeS majors. The so-called "captives," foreign subsidiaries that provide ITeS for their parent firms, for example, British Airways setting up its own call centers, or Nokia establishing its own software development center in India, were not far behind. The government, as regards what to do to promote the IT–ITeS business, simply decided to cede the policy ground to the National Association of Software and Service Companies, popularly known by its abbreviation, NASSCOM. So far at least, the Indian entrepreneurial aspiration in this field is merely to be the "back-office of the world,"[58] another instance of successful steering of dependent development by the Indian big business–state–multinational bloc.

Overall, since the early 1990s, both multinational and Indian big business companies have gained enormously relative to Indian state enterprises. FDI inflows have increased quite significantly, from an average of 1 percent of India's gross fixed capital formation in 1991–95 to 3.3 percent in 2000–05, and to 6.3 percent in 2006-12. But the bulk, 55.9 percent of the FDI equity inflows in 2000–12, have been in the tertiary sector compared to 30.3 percent in manufacturing, almost half of which was through acquisitions of incumbent companies, the most prominent ones in pharmaceuticals and cement.[59] There is some evidence that private equity (PE) and venture capital (VC) inflows may have contributed significantly to the large increase in FDI inflows from 2006 onward. As is well known, PE and VC investors have a much shorter investment horizon than conventional MNCs; indeed, they invest with an intention to exit with the booking of short-to-medium-term capital gains. Moreover, round-tripping (RT) by Indian companies/investment funds—the channeling of local funds to tax havens like Mauritius and Singapore only to return as foreign investment—must also be reckoned with. Such "FDI," namely, foreign financial investments, not reckoned as foreign portfolio investment, from PE and VC funds, and due to RT, has been estimated to be significant in construction and real estate, telecommunications, and IT/ITeS, among others, and has come in mainly from tax havens like Mauritius and Singapore. Indeed, some of these overseas PE and VC funds have been promoted by Indian big businesses themselves.[60]

A significant part of the overall FDI has been associated with cross-border acquisitions. Most of the mergers and acquisitions following India's "1989," whether in manufacturing or services, seem to have been "horizontal" in nature, leading to a tendency of increasing product-market concentration, and in many a case, the equity capital stakes of the Indian large business houses in joint venture companies with MNCs have been bought off by the latter. There are, of course, instances where the Indian large business house has bought the equity capital stake of the MNC, but these are fewer in number. In the case of the Hero group buying Honda's stake in Hero-Honda, most analysts have not expected such acquisition to have a product-market concentration enhancing effect because the Indian partner has lost access to the MNC's technology, which was the major source of competitive advantage of the joint venture.

More generally, the picture since the 1990s is one of a few companies of the large business houses and the MNCs coming to dominate important "product" markets in goods and services. The MNCs seem to be dominant in the markets for cars, refrigerators, a whole range of elite food products (certainly in soft drinks), and shaving products, but Indian big business companies are also significant players alongside the MNCs in other markets, for instance, in soaps and detergents, pharmaceuticals, paints, tea and coffee, ice cream, footwear, electrical machinery, TVs, air conditioners, washing machines, lubricants, and so on. And, indeed, MNCs seem to have largely left the dominance of certain other product markets to Indian big business companies, for instance, practically the whole range of petrochemical products (where the Reliance group rules the roost), heavy and light commercial vehicles, and aluminum products (where the A. V. Birla group calls the shots).[61]

In banking, in both deposits and credit, the public sector and Indian private banks together dominated the market, the multinational banks remaining secondary due to regulations that have hindered their expansion. In insurance, the MNCs have been allowed only in joint ventures with Indian promoters. In cellular mobile telecommunications services, the dominant four "players" are Airtel, Reliance Jio Infocomm, Vodafone and Idea Cellular, the first, second, and fourth being companies of the Bharti, Reliance, and A V Birla large business houses, and the third, one of the leading MNCs in that business. (More recently, Vodafone and Idea have announced a merger to take on the aggressive new entrant, Reliance Jio.) In petrochemicals, after the Reliance group acquired the public-sector petrochemical giant IPCL, and with its takeover of the polyester divisions of other private corporate sector companies, it came to enjoy overwhelming market power in a number of petrochemical derivative products, for instance, in linear alkyl benzene, ethylene glycol, polyester staple fiber, polyester filament yarn, and poly vinyl chloride. So, too, the dominance of the A. V. Birla group in some aluminum products, albeit to a lesser extent, after its takeover of the Canadian multinational Alcan's subsidiary, Indalco. Competition policy has been given the go-by in mergers and acquisitions that have significantly enhanced market power. However, the virtual market for corporate control that the MNCs wanted—which seemed to be in operation from 1993 for a few years, and which rendered the companies of the Indian large business houses vulnerable to hostile takeovers by the MNCs—shriveled after heavy lobbying against it by Indian big business.[62]

But, in the course of India's "1989," with the political swing to the right and consequent relative shift of economic activity from public sector companies to the private corporate sector,[63] the balance of power in government-big business relations seems to have shifted decisively in favor of big business. Overall, at the risk of some exaggeration one can possibly conjecture that a few Indian large business houses—the Tata, A. V. Birla, and Reliance groups among them—and MNCs have come to dominate not only in important product markets but also in their influence over government decisions related to incentives for investment.

Interestingly, however, although Indian big business and the MNCs have stolen a march over public enterprises in the wake of India's "1989," there has been some reluctance on the part of successive governments to go the whole hog on privatization. Early on, Maruti Udyog, in which the Japanese MNC Suzuki had a minority stake, was privatized by selling the government stake to Suzuki. Then, during 1998–2004, a more rightwing BJP-led government did privatize a dozen public enterprises, among them, some major ones, like IPCL, the petrochemicals giant, which was sold to the Reliance group; VSNL, the long-distance telecom services major, which was taken over by the Tatas; and Bharat Aluminium and Hindustan Zinc, over which the multinational Vedanta Resources group took management control. But besides these, there has been little else of any significance on the privatization front. The petroleum public enterprises are not allowed to avail themselves of the advantage of international price parity as their private counterparts do, and the main public sector power utilities sell electricity at prices much lower than their private competitors.[64] Overall, although the state gave up its near monopoly of a number of lines of business, for instance, in telecommunications, petroleum, electricity generation and distribution, air transport, and so on, India's "1989" didn't witness the executive of the Indian state relinquishing control over all its major public enterprises.

THE LONG VIEW

What then of the evolution of the structure of the ruling classes and the process of unequal development over the long term? Interestingly, in 1956 Paul Baran, reflecting on the long-term effects of imported manufactured commodities invading the markets of indigenous craftspersons and artisans, the rise of wealthy domestic merchant capitalists as junior partners of foreign enterprises, and what he called the regime of "industrial infanticide" that had checkmated the blossoming of competitive industrial capitalism, viewed the subsequent emergence of "native industrial monopolists" . . . "interlocked and interwoven with domestic merchant capital and with foreign enterprise" as ultimately leading the way to stagnation.[65]

Indeed, development planning by India's Planning Commission didn't alter the situation much. The long-term trend of stagnation in terms of per capita net material product (per capita real value added in the primary and secondary sectors) from 1900 continued to prevail when the time series of such data was extended up to 1975.[66] But, of course, the combination of the green revolution strategy in agriculture and the Mahalanobis strategy in industry, however flawed in its implementation, did eventually help overcome the stagnation in per capita net material product. "Qualitative" stagnation—as much as 70 percent of the total labor force remained in agriculture and livestock in 1971, the same as it was in 1901—however, still prevailed. In fact, in 1971, "non-household manufacturing" employed just 6.7 percent of the workforce.

Nevertheless, Indian big business, manifesting shrewd political and business sense, allied with the Indian state and ambivalently competed and collaborated with the MNCs to concertedly improve its relative position in India vis-à-vis the MNCs. Indeed, as part of their competitive and collaborative strategies, some of the companies of India's large business houses have even developed the capacity to acquire companies in the developed capitalist countries. In April 2007, Tata Steel Ltd acquired 100 percent of the equity capital of Corus Group Plc (UK) for $12.695 billion, taking management control of the latter. Another Tata group company, Tata Motors, acquired the South Korean truck manufacturer Daewoo Commercial Vehicles Company in 2004 and the British premium car manufacturer Jaguar Land Rover in 2008. Or take another Indian big business bloc, the Aditya Birla group; in May 2007, its Hindalco Industries Ltd acquired 100 percent of the equity capital of Novelis Inc (U.S.) for $5.766 billion, placing itself in the saddle of the latter. One should not, however, underestimate the economic and political power of the MNCs. They are not external to the Indian social formation. Besides advancing their interests through their own presence, organizations and resources, their home states negotiate and mediate on their behalf with the Indian state, and the World Bank, the IMF, and the WTO as organizations also work to advance their interests.

The problem of India's long-term "qualitative" stagnation nevertheless remains. Right from the latter half of the nineteenth century in the colonial period, India has always had an overdeveloped state and a bloated tertiary sector. Harbors, ports, railways, roads, canals, and the telegraph were public-sector infrastructure that was essential for the smooth functioning of the foreign export- and import-oriented businesses and those of their junior partners, the domestic merchant capitalists. This infrastructure was also indispensable for the British Indian Army, police, and paramilitary, and for the public administration of the subcontinent. The colonial state was overdeveloped, as Hamza Alavi argued,[67] in relation to the economic base in terms of its powers of control and regulation, and the bureaucracy, the military, and the polity in independent India had a vested interest in continuity rather than change on this score. The educated salaried middle classes—Macaulay's "class of persons Indian in blood and colour, but English in tastes, in opinions, in morals and in intellect"—entrenched themselves in the upper echelons of the bureaucracy and the military, and even the polity,[68] and later, as managers in the public and private corporate enterprises, including the multinational subsidiaries.

Yet, the expansion of tertiary sector activity in the public and private sectors was not accompanied by an increase in per capita net material product, at least up to 1975. And the services sector has grown faster than the rest of the economy since 1980, and in the period after 1995 such growth has been led more by the private organized sector rather than the government, eventually leading to the private organized sector's share in services sector GDP approaching and eventually surpassing the public sector's share in services sector GDP.[69] Overall, over the longterm, 1901–2011, India has made the switch from an economy dominated by the primary sector to one in which the tertiary sector is preeminent. Fundamentally, the more rapid increase in the share of the tertiary sector in GDP after 1980, and this led by the private organized sector after 1995, reflects the adjustment of India's capitalist system to an arrangement wherein labor productivity consistently rises faster than the wage rate in the primary and secondary sectors. This bloated services sector is a systemic necessity, essential for the realization of the surplus generated in the primary and secondary sectors. Moreover, "backwardness" (lack of development of the productive forces) and huge merchant margins derived from buying cheap from the mass of small producers makes for low wages in the advanced part of the economy, even though productivity is high.

In a fundamental sense, India's capitalist development strategy over the longterm has really been one of non-industrialization rather than industrialization in that no vast industrial working class (relative to the size of the labor force) has been created. The de-(proto)industrialization of the nineteenth century, which ruined the traditional craftspersons/artisans with little, if any, re-absorption in modern industry, continues, replenishing the huge reserve army of labor. More generally, vast numbers of people have been left out of the development that was supposed to accompany the growth of modern industry. The capitalist development that was steered by the big business–state–multinational bloc didn't lead to a distribution of income that would have made it possible for the Indian people to have sufficient food to eat, clothes to wear, houses to reside in, and medicines to take when disease and illness strike. Let alone enabling them to overcome gross misery and have some degree of security and control over their own lives, it led to widespread undernourishment in infancy itself. In fact, such capitalist development merely made way for a prosperous upper-middle class and defended the privileges that came from ownership of the means of production, including land, and other assets.

LABOR STILL MASSIVELY IN RESERVE

To reprise, data on mass poverty and the huge reserve army of labor relative to the active army of wage labor for 1973 indicated that the headcount ratio of poverty was 51.5 percent of the population and the reserve army of labor was 2.1 times the fully active army of wage labor. What has happened since then, say by 2011–12? As we have seen, Marx categorized the reserve army in normal times into three components—the floating, the latent and the stagnant, and added on those engaged in illegal activity, more generally, the lumpenproletariat, which will have to be kept out of this estimate because of lack of reliable figures. The floating reserve army of labor was 5.6 percent of the "current daily status" labor force of 440.4 million persons in 2011–12, in absolute numbers, 24.7 million persons.[70]

What then of the latent reserve army of labor? In 2011–12, a "normal" year, the proportion of the self-employed has been around 51.9 percent of the workforce as estimated on a "usual principal plus subsidiary status" basis, which was 245.3 million persons. Roughly 70 percent of this number were petty commodity producers/service providers in 2011–12; so the size of the latent reserve army of labor was 171.7 million persons in that year.[71]

What is the estimated size of the stagnant component of the reserve army of labor? According to India Census 2011, the proportion of "marginal workers" in the census workforce, those who found employment for only less than three months in a year, was 18.6 percent of that workforce. Assuming the proportion of marginal workers among all wage laborers and salaried employees to be the census figure of marginal workers in the workforce, 18.6 percent, in 2011–12, and the proportion of "marginal workers" among casual wage laborers to be six times the proportion of the same among regular salaried employee/wage laborers, we roughly get the proportions of "marginal workers" among the casual wage laborers to be 30 percent and among the regular salaried employees/wage laborers to be 5 percent. The stagnant component of the reserve army of labor comprises those wage laborers and salaried empoyees who find only extremely irregular employment (at best they are intermittent workers), and the "marginal" wage laborers/salaried employees seem to fall in that category. The size of the stagnant component of the reserve army is therefore the sum of 30 percent of the 138.6 million casual wage laborers and 5 percent of the 88.8 million regular salaried employees/wage laborers—46 million persons.

With a 24.7 million "floating" reserve, a 171.7 million "latent" reserve, and a 46 million "stagnant" reserve, the total size of India's reserve army of labor in 2011–12 was *242.4 million persons*. The fully active army of labor in the same year was the sum of 70 percent of the 138.6 million casual wage laborers and 95 percent of the 88.8 million regular salaried employees/wage laborers—181.4 million persons. Thus the size of the reserve army of labor in 2011–12 was 1.3 times that of the active army of labor, a formidable force that restrained the rise of real wages.[72]

Assuming that each person in the reserve army supports one dependent, then the size of the reserve army and its dependents would be 484.8 million persons (40.1 percent of the country's population). To this absolute number if the number of non-"marginal" casual wage workers and their dependents (2 x 0.7 x 138.6 = 194 million persons, assuming one dependent per casual wage worker), is added, the figure rises to 678.8 million persons, or 56.1 percent of the population.

Now, in multidimensional terms, that is, taking account of deprivations at the household level as indicated by child mortality, nutrition, years of schooling, child enrollment, and living standards as evident from the cooking fuel used, access to safe drinking water, electricity, toilets, type of flooring, and assets owned, and deeming a person poor if she/he is deprived in at least 30 percent of the weighted indicators, in 2005, the UNDP and Oxford University estimated that 55.4 percent of India's population was poor.[73] Assuming that this multidimensional poverty estimate holds for 2011–12 too, then it is likely that the reserve army of labor and their dependents and the non-"marginal" casual wage laborers and their dependents constitute the "multidimensionally poor." And yet, instead of improving and extending public provision, both Congress and BJP, which have been alternating in power at the center, have promoted the privatization of education and medicare, and the private provision of water, electricity, housing, and transport.

Thus, just like in 1973, there is a sharp class polarization in India today—islands of wealth, luxury and civilization in a vast sea of poverty, misery and degradation. There are a relatively small number of owner-controllers of the oligopolies, beneficiaries of the skewed distribution of the surplus, at the apex of a steep social-class hierarchy, at the bottom of which is the massive reserve army of labor and the remaining casual wage workers. The ratio of the income of a billionaire to that of a casual laborer is of the order of 10^6! In between, at different distances from the apex and the base of the social-class pyramid, are semi-capitalist landowners, SME capitalists, the merchant and moneylending classes, the administrative, professional, scientific and technological sections of the middle class, the labor contractors/jobbers who recruit and manage gangs of unregistered casual wage workers, and the regular wage workers.

The huge reserve army of labor in an underdeveloped capitalist country like India doesn't merely circumscribe the wage and other demands of the "usual principal status" employed regular and casual wage workers, but also moderates the producer prices of the petty commodity producers in the overcrowded and intensely competitive supply side of the markets that the latter find themselves in.

UNEQUAL DEVELOPMENT—PRINCIPAL CHARACTERISTICS

What then have been the principal characteristics of unequal development in India?

One is that, to a considerable extent, labor in Indian agriculture has not been dispossessed of the principal means of production, land, and has not been free of caste obligations to powerful landowners. Indeed, in the countryside, aspects of caste relations are a part of the relations of production. Also, labor in agriculture has not been free of extra-economic compulsion (for example, threat of violence from the landlord's or the kulak's hired hoodlums) in the extraction of the agricultural surplus; indeed, it has been subjected to both economic and extra-economic forms of compulsion in the process of surplus extraction.

Two is that the zamindars didn't have full rights of ownership. Just as the possession of land by the peasant is contingent on his payment of rent to the landlord, so also the ownership of land by the landowner was contingent upon the payment of land revenue—of a high order in the initial decades after the Permanent Settlement of 1793. Moreover, the rents paid by the peasants (the actual cultivators) were much higher than the typical incidence of what would have been *capitalist* ground rent, the latter, 10 percent to 20 percent of net output. Indeed, the incidence of ground rent was, not long ago, as high as the typical minimum rate of *feudal* ground rent, 50 percent of the *gross* output. The high rate of rent was, importantly, also because of "subinfeudation" (chapter 2). Both market forces *and* custom, and the extra-economic power of the landowners together seemed to determine the levels of the rent as a proportion of net output. Paraphrasing Paul Baran, one might say that the "obscurantism and arbitrary violence" inherited from the tributary social formation of the past has been combined with the "rationality and sharply calculating rapacity of . . . [the] capitalist present."[74]

Three, there has been mostly a formal subsumption of agricultural labor to capital; the extent of real subsumption of labor to capital, where capital directly takes over the process of cultivation, hires wage labor, reinvests the surplus and adopts new production techniques has been very limited.[75] Further, generalized commodity production has not prevailed; the system of "production of commodities by means of commodities" with labor power as a commodity has not been the rule. And there has not been any continuous drive toward technological progress in the agricultural sector, which has been the main source of livelihood in the Indian economy, where *kisans* (peasants) and *mazdoors* (landless laborers) have toiled for the *maliks* (the landowners) and all they have got in return has been a pittance.[76]

Four, over time, operational holdings of land have split, this in keeping with the cycle of the family (demographic differentiation), resulting in cultivation of very small, almost unviable, plots of land. Besides, in recent times, a host of neoliberal policy measures have adversely affected the economics of cultivation, with farm risk enhanced by capital's, including multinational capital's control over the new hybrid seeds. The insensitivity of the ruling elite to peasant indebtedness has only made matters worse, leading to thousands of suicides.[77]

Five, in the countryside there has been a *de facto* fusion of political and economic power; the landlord or the kulak has been adjudicating (in backward areas) disputes at the local level and has his own hired armed hoodlums to enforce his writ. Peasant uprisings, even though they have not been endemic and pervasive, have inevitably been violent. Peasant, including tribal peasant, unrest and even insurgencies didn't cease after 1858. Unlike the elite nationalists, the tribal people and poor peasants took on the sarkar (the colonial state) *and* its local collaborators, the sahukars (moneylenders), merchants, and contractors in the tribal areas. And, such violent peasant struggles still go on in contemporary India.

Six, the proportion of the workforce engaged in manufacturing and the secondary sector in general didn't show a rising trend over the long-term, 1901–71. As per the census figures, the industrial workforce remained stagnant over the period 1901–71, roughly between 9 percent and 11 percent with no rising trend. Agriculture, in turn, employed the bulk of the workforce in the period 1901–71—67.5 percent to 70.4 percent of the workforce with no declining trend.[78] In other words, most of the working population was engaged in producing food and other primary commodities, and still does so, albeit, to a lesser extent. Development, identified with industrialization and the accompanying technological progress, has not yet brought about the required increase in output and consumption per head so that a small proportion of the workforce would be able to meet society's food and other primary needs, and the remaining large proportion of the workforce would be available for industry and other gainful economic activities. Indeed, the internal class structures that have been impeding such development have not been dislodged.

Seven is the phenomenon of economic dependence. India, as we have seen, was once a colony, a non-sovereign country belonging to and under the direct rule of a single imperialist country. In contrast, China was once a semi-colony, *formally* sovereign, but, in *reality*, politically, economically, diplomatically, and militarily dependent on *more than one* of the imperialist powers. A neo-colony is distinctively different. While it is also formally sovereign, in reality, it is politically, economically, diplomatically, and militarily dependent on a *single* imperialist power. India is neither a semi-colony nor a neo-colony. India is a sovereign country, but it is politically, economically, diplomatically, and militarily dependent, mainly on the world's major imperialist power, the United States. The main characteristics of India's economic dependence are:[79]

- Significant penetration of MNCs in the advanced "islands" of its economy;
- Continuous and systematic reliance on the import of technology (i.e., technological dependence) in those "islands," which does not raise labor productivity in the rest of the economy;
- Export specialization in primary and labor-intensive manufactured goods, and, more recently, in ITeS;
- An elite consumption pattern that emulates those of the developed capitalist countries, which has a considerable impact on the kind of industries that are set up;
- Unequal exchange in international trade with the developed capitalist countries because the difference in the respective wage rates far exceeds the gap in the corresponding labor productivities.

The stress on national economic strength or the lack of it comes from an economic nationalist belief that, in the international arena, national economic power is a major determinant of political power. A colonial, semi-colonial, neo-colonial, or sovereign-dependent country can be contrasted in terms of the degree to which each is subordinate to imperialism—a colonial country, the most, a sovereign-dependent country, the least. But whether colonial, semi-colonial, neo-colonial or sovereign-dependent, an underdeveloped country's economic structure and the class structure of its ruling classes are shaped to a considerable degree by the extent and the nature of that subordination. Imperialism here must be understood as a process by which a developed capitalist country's corporations and state "team up to expand their activities, their interests, and their power beyond their borders."[80]

Eight, one can trace the roots of the contemporary big business–state–multinational bloc to the deals of the East India Company with the Jagat Seths, Omichands, Hotchands, and Gulab Singhs, Indian merchant-cum-financial magnates, regional political autocrats, and the big landowners. Over the course of the first half of the nineteenth century and with the British Crown taking over the colonial state in 1858, the metropolitan-local ruling class partnership metamorphosed into a bloc of the colonial state with British managing-agency-house capital and Indian merchant-cum-financial big business, and the big landowners. But, in the 1930s and 40s, the British managing agency houses had to give way to the modern MNCs. Subsequently, come Indian independence, and with the foreign exchange crisis of 1957, the Indian big business–state–multinational bloc emerged to pilot the course of unequal development, with the big landowners largely cut down to size, but still part of the ruling bloc at the provincial and district levels alongside the kulaks. The process of unequal development eventually took India from peripheral underdevelopment to semi-peripheral underdevelopment, evident in the greatly enhanced power of the Indian state and the burgeoning wealth of Indian big business.

Nine, it is not capitalism per se that transforms a non-capitalist region but significant entry of big business that brings this about, for big business comes with all the necessary political support to accomplish the mission. One can think about this in the light of the inroads of the East India Company from 1757 onward; later, the British managing agency firms; and still later, Indian big business and the multinationals.

Ten, the Indian underdeveloped capitalist social formation, the result of prolonged evolution in a colonial setting with the superstructure conditioning and circumscribing the development of the economic base, has an overdeveloped state and a bloated tertiary sector. Unlike in developed capitalist social formations, the economy in underdeveloped capitalism is not much of an autonomous sub-system.

Eleven is the monstrous class polarization, epitomized by the emergence of dollar billionaires in the small islands of wealth, luxury, and civilization amidst the vast sea of poverty, misery, and degradation, wherein a huge, non-depleting reserve army of labor and its dependents signifies the irrelevance to which the ruling classes and their political representatives relegate a majority of the Indian population.

Twelve is the parasitical reliance of Indian big business on the state for its self-expansion, indeed, historically, the state fostered Indian big business more than the other way around,[81] and so the controllers of the state's assets have been part and parcel of the ruling classes. Politics dominates economics, and unlike in the developed capitalist countries, the economic structure is *not* largely an autonomous sub-system in the social formation.

EXPLOITATION–STATE OPPRESSION–RESISTANCE

Theory is necessarily abstract, while history and the present as history are necessarily concrete, but theory, even though in this narrative it has been deliberately kept to bare essentials, is essential to a deeper understanding of history and the present as history. As will be evident by now, I am a libertarian socialist; my worldview stems from Marxism and the civil-liberties legacy of liberalism. Paul Baran's and Samir Amin's Marxist theoretical perspective and analytical framework that I have drawn upon emphasizes class contradictions, exploitation, and class polarization, ceaseless accumulation of wealth by the ruling classes, the state as a major instrument of class oppression, and the resistance of the victims. All these elements have been a primary part of my narrative. It's time then to turn once more to Maoist resistance, for the struggling and fighting poor peasants and tribal forest dwellers led by the Maoists are the true legatees of their counterparts in the colonial period.

As has been stated, Rosa Luxemburg defined imperialism as "the political expression of the accumulation of capital in its competitive struggle for what remains still open for the non-capitalist environment"[82] within a capitalist country's own borders and beyond, through militarism and war. In this respect, there seems to be a continuity in the development of underdeveloped capitalism in independent India vis-à-vis the colonial period, evident in the penetration of the Indian state, Indian big business and the MNCs into the tribal areas of central and eastern India, and the Indian state's engagement in a "war against its own people" as part of the land and mineral grabs.

Of course, in the tribal areas of central and eastern India, where there is Maoist resistance, the process of capitalist development has turned increasingly more violent and catastrophic, what with the escalation of militarism and war by the Indian state leading to an inevitable cultural and economic ruin of the tribal communities. As Luxemburg wrote, albeit with respect to what colonial capitalism did in the non-capitalist parts of the world, and her passionate account, in parts, might well apply to what is presently happening in the undeclared civil war that the Indian state has unleashed against its own people in central and eastern India:[83]

> . . .primitive conditions allow of a greater drive and of far more ruthless measures than could be tolerated under purely capitalist social conditions. . . .
>
> The unbridled greed, the acquisitive instinct of accumulation . . . is incapable of seeing far enough to recognise the value of . . . an older civilisation. . . .
>
> Force, fraud, oppression, looting are openly displayed without any attempt at concealment, and it requires an effort to discover within this tangle of political violence and contests for power the stern laws of the economic process.

With a grasp of India's "1968" as history and an understanding of the process of unequal development that has consolidated the Indian big business–state–multinational ruling bloc, let's then take the story of Maoist resistance ahead.

4

Naxalite! "Spring Thunder," Phase II

[A people's] war can be waged only by mobilizing the masses and relying on them.
—MAO ZEDONG IN 1934[1]

Successfully mobilizing and relying upon the people was the foremost challenge that occupied the Naxalite revolutionaries in phase II of the movement. The narrative thus returns to writing about "ordinary people in extraordinary circumstances." Despite defeat, a section of the revolutionaries re-emerged, gathering strength once again and augmenting its forces. One would have expected these people, in the face of the lawless brutal power of the Indian state, to give up the fight, but they didn't. Militant politics, in search of a solution to the problems that plagued the oppressed in rural India from colonial times, made a new beginning in the post-Emergency period. As the radical Telugu poet Varavara Rao put it:[2]

> How long
> Can prison walls
> And iron bars
> Cage the free spirit?

Against the background of the discussions on "'1968' India as History" and "Unequal Development and the Evolution of the Ruling Bloc," it will now be easier to examine the events that unfolded without losing track of the processes of which they were a part. Further, it will be evident that the forms of the struggles of the oppressed, led by the Maoists, have, among

Map 2: Political Geography: "Spring Thunder," Phase II (1978–2003)

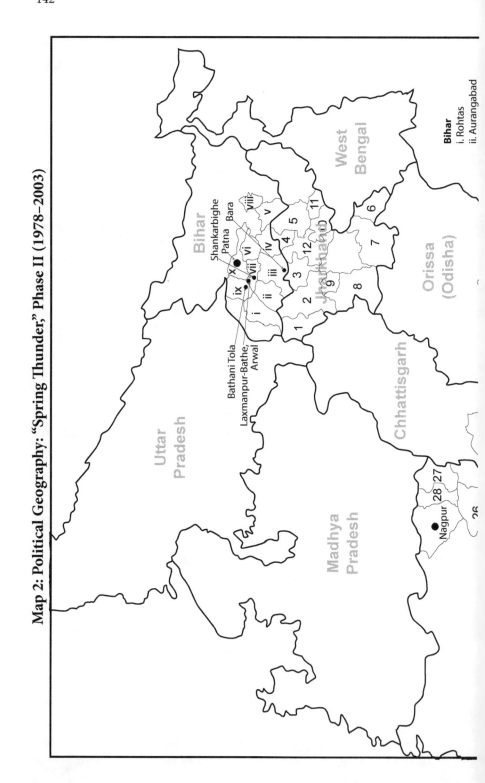

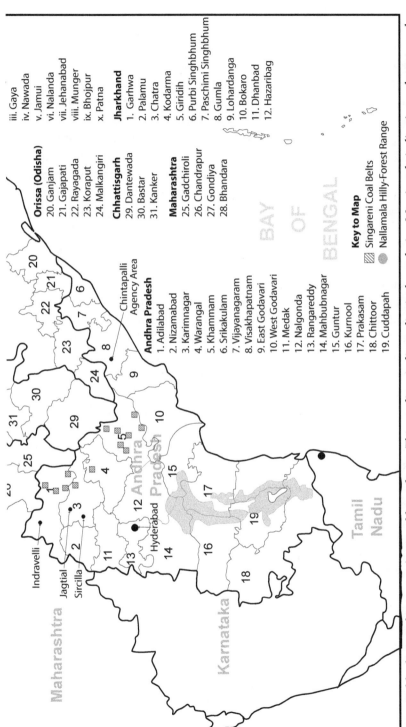

Note: Bolder lines indicate state/national boundaries. Thinner lines indicate district boundaries. Map is only indicative and not to scale.

Source: Map adapted from www.d-maps.com using information in Census of India.

other factors, also been determined by the brutally repressive acts of those who govern on behalf of the ruling classes. Over years of association with the civil liberties and democratic rights' movement, I have come to learn that, invariably, chief ministers and home ministers assure the top police officers, off the record, of carte blanche for their lawless actions to "contain" the Naxalite/Maoist "problem." Nevertheless, and willing to face the dire consequences of their radical politics, Kondapalli Seetharamaiah (KS), one of the Naxalite movement's more accomplished strategists and organizers, and his close comrades in the then province of Andhra Pradesh began to practice the fresh tactical line they had formulated, and the first seeds of what they sowed began to sprout in the peasant movement in Karimnagar and Adilabad districts of North Telangana soon after the Emergency was lifted. (The accompanying India map will be of help right through this chapter.)

The young men and women involved had all read three short pieces penned by Mao Zedong: "Serve the People," "In Memory of Norman Bethune," and "The Foolish Old Man Who Removed the Mountains." From the latter, "Be resolute, fear no sacrifice, and surmount every difficulty to win victory" conveys the notion that courage and determination in the face of adverse circumstances are the most essential attributes of a revolutionary. From "Serve the People," there's this guidance: "If, in the interests of the people, we persist in doing what is right and correct what is wrong, our ranks will surely thrive." And, from "In Memory of Norman Bethune,"[3] there's this ideal: "A man's [woman's] ability may be great or small, but if he [she] has this spirit [Bethune's "selflessness"], he [she] is already noble-minded and pure, a man [woman] of moral integrity and above vulgar interests, a man [woman] who is of value to the people."

"DISTURBED AREAS"

For a significant number of those guided by Mao's thought among the 40,000 in jail or in police custody in 1973, despite the adversity, those feelings of optimism and resolve, the stuff of revolutionary romanticism, had not been snuffed out. With a new lease on life following the release of political prisoners in the brief interregnum after the Emergency, the revolutionaries in the making were back to the countryside. And there were those who had come on board in 1973 and 1974, and during the Emergency that followed. Sircilla and Jagtial taluks in Karimnagar district of North Telangana were among the new flash points soon after the Emergency. Incidentally, the present general secretary of the CPI(Maoist), as the party is known today, Mupalla Laxman Rao (alias Ganapathy), hails from Karimnagar and it was he who led the Jagtial struggle in Karimnagar district. A teacher and a soft-spoken writer, Ganapathy got politicized in 1974, and later became Karimnagar district secretary of the CPI(ML)(People's War), then, Andhra Pradesh Party Secretary, and, by 1989, was elected as the general secretary of the party.[4]

The Andhra Pradesh Suppression of Disturbances Act, passed in 1948 to suppress the then raging Telangana peasant insurgency, was applied in October 1978 to declare the Sircilla and Jagtial taluks "disturbed," this because there was organized peasant resistance against the landlords and kulaks, militant opposition against eviction, and insistence on implementation of the legally prescribed minimum wage. Police got the power to "shoot at sight," indeed, with a carte blanche to highhandedly do so, for any intended legal action by the victims now required previous government sanction! Frankly, the areas were declared "disturbed" because there was peasant resistance to their exploitation by the landlords and the kulaks, and all the government wanted was to suppress that resistance so that the landlords and the kulaks could go on "peacefully" exploiting the peasants. It didn't matter that, in the process, the rights of the peasants to life, to legal remedy, and to freedom from exploitation were taken away.[5]

The peasant struggle, however, spread elsewhere in north Telangana, and the Maoist mass organizations—the Revolutionary Writers' Association, Virasam in its Telugu short-form, the Jana Natya Mandali (JNM), the Radical Students' Union (RSU), and the Radical Youth League (RYL)—nurtured in the first half of the 1970s now came to fruition. In the midst of this renewal of the Naxalite movement in Andhra Pradesh, the CPI(ML)(People's War)—CPI(ML)(PW)—was formed on April 22, 1980, with the medium-term aim of building "guerrilla zones" in the countryside of North Telangana and Dandakaranya (the forest area situated in the border and adjoining tribal districts of the states/regions of Andhra Pradesh, the Chhattisgarh part of Madhya Pradesh, and Maharashtra and Orissa) by the early 1990s.[6] Guerrilla zones are tracts where the agrarian revolutionary movement is strong, but where the Party and its mass organizations are in power only as long as the guerrillas have the upper hand over the state's forces; power reverts to the Indian state when the guerrillas are forced to retreat.

WORKER–PEASANT ALLIANCE

With the organized peasant struggle bringing increasing numbers of poor peasants and landless laborers into the Naxalite fold, a Rythu Coolie Sangham (RCS, translated as peasants and laborers association) was formed in 1980–81. And workers in the Singareni coal fields in North Telangana were organized in the Singareni Karmika Samakhya (SIKASA, translated as the Singareni collieries workers' federation) in 1980–81. Underground organizing of the coalminers had of course begun in 1975 itself by radical students and other youth (then known as "the radicals"), and continued in the period leading to the formation of the union.

SIKASA was particularly important in building the proletarian base of the Party in North Telangana and establishing a worker–peasant alliance, both essential for any party claiming to follow Lenin and Mao. The Singareni coalfields and the adjoining industrial belt spread across Adilabad and Karimnagar districts—the former, where the peasant movement in Telangana got a new lease of life, the latter, where the tribal people were organized to win their rights to the forests. The Singareni workers, or at least a significant proportion, had their roots in the villages of these two districts, so they could not have remained unmoved by the "land to the tiller" and "full rights to the forests" struggles waged by the Naxalites over there.

We mention SIKASA because it was here in Singareni, more than in any other place in this vast country—except in the industrial belt of Bhilai, where the Shankar Guha Niyogi-led Chhattisgarh Mukti Morcha did the same— that the workers began to respond to cases of abuse and tyranny no matter which section of the wretched of the Indian earth was the victim. SIKASA took up a range of issues, including those concerning "bread," against slum (shanty) demolition (safeguarding the hearth), and the organization of the labor process in the mines. And the rape and murder of Rajeshwari, a maid who worked in the house of a personnel manager, by his son—who hung her dead body in the car shed to hoodwink the people into believing that it was a suicide—aroused the wrath of the union and its members as if she were their own. In a way, she was their own, for she and her husband, part of the millions of "footloose" laborers, had come all the way from the Rayalaseema region in search of a livelihood, though the only jobs they managed to get were that of servants in the personnel manager's house.

State repression of the mass organizations of the CPI(ML)(PW) intensified soon after the Party's formation in April 1980. Police firing on April 20, 1981, at Indravelli in Adilabad district killed many tribal people. The organized tribal people were attacked when they gathered to attend a district-level conference of the Girijana RCS (tribal peasant and agricultural labor union), affiliated to the CPI(ML)(PW). At the root of the conflict was the Girijana RCS' organization of the struggle for rights to the forest and against moneylenders. Indeed, by 1983 the authorities sought to stifle the voice of all the mass organizations of the CPI(ML)(PW), and the May 1985 disruption of a state-level conference of the RCS seemed to have driven the message home that no open, legal political work of the CPI(ML)(PW) was going to be permitted. The mass organizations were, in effect, being driven underground. But the movement had by then expanded to encompass parts of Dandakaranya, the forest areas in the border and adjoining tribal districts of the states of Andhra Pradesh, Madhya Pradesh, Maharashtra and Orissa.

ACROSS THE GODAVARI

Party accounts date the beginning of the struggle in Dandakaranya to 1980 when teams of revolutionaries in Karimnagar and Adilabad crossed the Godavari River and entered the then Gadchiroli sub-division of Chandrapur district (and later, Bhandara district) of the province of Maharashtra to the north.[7] Indeed, one of the first martyrs was eighteen-year-old Peddi Shankar, the son of a coalmine worker from across the border, allegedly killed by the Maharashtra police. Shankar was part of the first team of revolutionaries who had crossed over into Maharashtra.

Another team went to Bastar district (the movement was later to extend into Rajnandgaon and Balaghat districts), then part of the province of Madhya Pradesh. Soon thereafter, in 1981, the Dandakaranya Adivasi Kisan Mazdoor Sanghatan (DAKMS, Dandakaranya tribal peasants and workers' organization) began organizing the poor among the tribal people (the Gonds) against the oppressive forest, revenue, and police department officials, and the contractors, traders, and moneylenders. The DAKMS took up the question of *pattas* (instrument of ownership right) on forest land brought under cultivation, as also the winning of rights on cultivable land in forest villages through bitter struggles against the forest department. The DAKMS also exercised control over the collection and sale of minor forest produce (for instance, the tendu patta) in favor of adivasi women who plucked the tendu leaves, ensuring them a "fair" rate per bundle of leaves collected. So, also, the wage rates for cutting bamboo which is the principal raw material of the paper mills run by companies controlled by the Birlas, the Thapars, and the Bangurs. All this activity generated opposition from the landed proprietors, the traders, the contractors, and corrupt forest and revenue department officials.

The DAKMS's *sanghams* (unit of the Maoist mass organization at the village level), nevertheless, eventually displaced the village mukhias and other traditional village headmen, leading the decision-making process on local issues and even settling disputes. It must be mentioned that this was far more difficult than taking on the forest department and the police, for it entailed gaining the affection of the tribes, mainly the Koyas and the Madias. The Maoists who had come from North Telangana gradually learned the Gondi language and later even began to compose and perform songs and plays in the local idiom to express their political feelings. The DAKMS flag, though red with hammer and sickle, also carries a drawn bow and arrow.

AGAINST PATRIARCHY

The Dandakaranya Krantikari Adivasi Mahila Sangh (DKAMS)—which Arundhati Roy refers to in her celebrated essay, "Walking with the Comrades,"[8] as what may very well be India's largest women's organization—was also started in 1981. Over the years, it has not only come to grips with gender oppression, but also has linked it with class exploitation and the oppression of adivasis (that is, on the basis of their ethnic identity). As regards the latter, namely, with respect to adivasi culture, unlike those who practice identity politics, the Maoists do not think that "the traditional" is *not* oppressive; indeed, they have been trying to persuade the adivasi community to do away with certain sexist practices.[9] Moreover, as a result of various anti-patriarchal campaigns in the guerrilla zones, men are now increasingly participating in household tasks, including child care and socialization.[10] One of the visible changes on the ground has been the significant participation of tribal women in the People's Guerrilla Army (PGA), which was formed in 2000, with women leading some of the armed squads, platoons and companies.

The Viplava Mahila Sangham (VMS), the CPI(ML)(PW)'s mass women's organization in Andhra Pradesh, came into its own during the anti-arrack agitation in the 1990s, directed against the sale of and addiction to a local alcoholic beverage made from a palm extract or brewed from jaggery. VMS worked closely with RCS, and in the Singareni collieries areas, where alcoholism was a scourge, with SIKASA. The joint work with RCS led to women gaining titles to cultivable land seized and distributed by RCS. Indeed, in 1995, at a "Special Conference" of the CPI(ML)(PW), the Party included women's liberation as part of the objectives of the "New Democratic Revolution" it was fighting for, and so patriarchy had to be fought within the Party too. Empirical studies of women who were activists in the Naxalite movement in the late 1960s and early 1970s suggest that they were confined to supporting roles and that their middle-class male comrades displayed much of the same patriarchal morality that is prevalent outside the movement.[11] Clearly, the Maoist movement needed a feminist perspective.

The struggle has been an internal one, against oneself, with the deeply personal—man-woman relationships, sex, conjugal rights, marriage, family, children—becoming the political. The more women assume leadership roles within the Party, the mass organizations, and the guerrilla army, the better. The internal struggle against patriarchy has been a difficult one. An undated internal rectification paper of the party titled "Fight against Patriarchal Thinking within the Party and Promote Proletarian Culture" is brutally honest. For instance, "our thinking . . . embraces and sometimes champions values, traditions and habits of the old exploitative society and these are reflected to some extent in the revolutionary party too." Further, "looking down upon women, treating them as weaklings and as objects that fulfill the sexual desires of men, abusing and beating wives, making them feel inferior, regarding them as personal property, suspecting wives when they move closely with other men," all these feudal-patriarchal forms of thought and behavior "are prevalent to some extent among the male members of the party."[12] Clearly, the fight against patriarchy, within the Maoist movement and in Indian society, is going to be a long and hard one; the cultural, social, political, and economic practices that discriminate against women would likely persist even after the revolution.

All the more, within the movement, the need for women to form half the struggle—"half the party, half the military formations, half of the students', peasants' and workers' organizations and half of the alternate people's power structures"—is increasingly being felt by women in leadership positions in the Maoist parties in India, Nepal, and the Philippines.[13] After all, didn't Mao once, famously and evocatively, say, "Women hold up half the sky"?

"GO TO THE PEOPLE"

There are many aspects of the mass-struggle phase of the Naxalite/Maoist movement (1978–85)[14] that seem to have been forgotten and need to be brought to the fore. Compared to the establishment left, Naxalites/Maoists have been particularly sensitive to the caste question. The 1970s was a period when, among the so-called lower castes and Dalits in Telangana, it was mostly the first time that young men and women were making their way into higher education, and it was a part of this section of youth that joined the RSU and the RYL. Their grandparents or great grandparents had been one or the other of the following: carpenters (*vadla*), blacksmiths (*kammari*), toddy tappers (*goudas*), barbers (*mangalis*), dhobis (*chakalis*), potters (*kummaris*), landless laborers of the *Madiga* and *Mala jatis* among the Dalits, known as *vetti madigalu* and *vetti malollu*, and poor peasants.

The CPI(ML)(PW) and its mass organizations made a conscious attempt to draw these people into the movement. In the "Go to the Villages" campaigns, in which the RSU, RYL and the JNM coordinated with the rural mass organization (the RCS in the making, and later as a full-fledged organization) to win over the rural poor, it was the lower caste and Dalit students that were prominent as activists, and later on, many of these student-youth activists assumed local leadership positions within the mass organizations and the Party.[15]

As far as the struggle went, it was tactics such as social boycott and public hearings (the latter also a feature of the CPI's forms of struggle in Telangana in the 1940s) that were the principal non-violent means. Refusal to perform certain tasks in the social division of labor could paralyze the rural gentry, and public hearings highlighted the different forms of oppression and exploitation, including usury, evictions, forced labor, usurpation of common property resources, and payment of pitiably low wages, as well as atrocities. The rural gentry organized private militias to break the network the RCS had established with the RSU, RYL and JNM, and, indeed, to wipe out the RCS itself, and when they couldn't accomplish the task on their own, the repressive apparatus of the state was brought in and the Suppression of Disturbances Act of 1948 was applied to designate the zones of activism as "disturbed areas."[16]

The movements in North Telangana and parts of Dandakaranya witnessed intense police repression, including combing of the paramilitary forces to eliminate the armed squads of the Party, "encounter" (extrajudicial) killings, Pinochet-style cases of "missing," demolition of martyrs memorials, and so on. Even DKAMS was not spared. The mass organizations could henceforth no longer function in an open, legal manner; they were driven underground. But they organized very successful *bandhs* (complete shutdowns) in the adjoining towns and, even, state-wide against the extrajudicial killings, against police repression of open, legal political activity. The police, in turn, came down with a heavy hand on such forms of protest.

In one such case, a young radical was apprehended in Kamareddy town in Nizamabad district on May 15, 1985, by the police when he was going around asking shopkeepers to pull down their shutters to protest "encounter" killings. The police took the radical youth to a busy crossroads, and there, in the public view, beat him to a pulp with their rifle butts the way people who are afraid of a poisonous snake crush it to death with weapons readily at their command. Later, a butcher who had witnessed this lynching, deposed before the sub-divisional magistrate at Kamareddy describing what he saw, prompting the radical Telugu poet Varavara Rao, then a political prisoner, to pen the following lines that in extraordinarily sensitive verse expresses the anger and revulsion of the witness:[17]

> I am a vendor of flesh
> If you want to call me a butcher
> Then that is as you wish
> I kill animals every day
> I cut their flesh and sell it.
> Blood to me is a familiar sight

But
It was on that day I saw with my own eyes
The real meaning of being a butcher

. . .

I too take lives
But never with hatred
I do sell flesh
But I have never sold myself

. . .

To me who kills goats every day
The meaning of the cruelty that
Combines and conspires to take a life
Was revealed that day.

UNLEASHING STATE TERROR

The burning of forty-six Kondh tribal hamlets consisting of 638 homesteads by the police in the Chintapalli Agency area of Visakhapatnam district of Andhra Pradesh in early May 1987 was ghastly and horrendous. The reason? Because this tribal community was harboring—giving food and shelter to— Naxalites. The Indian People's Human Rights Commission set up a tribunal to investigate and adjudicate this macabre case of gross violation of the right to life itself by the state, this when the existing legal machinery had proved to be most inadequate in providing any kind of redress against such atrocities committed by the state. What else could civil liberties' activists do to combat the state's growing lawlessness? The police warned the tribals—"if you go to the inquiry [organized by those 'civil liberties bastards', that's what the police called the Andhra Pradesh Civil Liberties Committee (APCLC) activists, of course, behind their backs] we will break your limbs and burn your houses once again."[18]

The political establishment had given the police complete freedom to do what it thought fit to terrorize the mass support base of the Naxalites. First, the police burned the Kondh tribals' houses for their act of giving food and shelter to the Naxalites, and then they assaulted them for telling the "civil liberties bastards" about it. The police organized a mob that fell upon the place where the tribunal was conducting its first hearing, on December 11, 1987, and assaulted the deponents. But what needs to be understood is why, despite the dire warning, the Kondhs still came for the inquiry. It was because these judges and civil liberties persons had taken so much trouble, come all the way to give these wretched folks a chance to express what they had suffered. The civil liberties' activist K. Balagopal sensitively expressed what one tribal youth who was deposed before the tribunal felt: "For the first time he had been told there was . . . no sin in his existence, for the first time he had not been scolded, not been abused, for the first time the wretched guilt of an unlawful life had been lifted from his shoulders."[19] The tribunal's judgment acted as a voice of the public conscience against the state's growing lawlessness.

There were definite limits, nevertheless, to which a civil liberties' organization could curb the state's growing criminality. The Maoist movement was forced to resort to the kidnapping of state officials or prominent mainstream politicians as a means of getting their comrades released from jail or produced in court, or just to extract the facts about their whereabouts in the "missing" cases. On December 27, 1987, an armed squad of the CPI(ML) (PW) abducted seven Indian Administrative Service (IAS) officers, including the widely-respected S. R. Sankaran, when they had gone into the interior in Gurthedu in East Godavari district to discuss the tribal welfare programs with the intended beneficiaries themselves. The armed squad, *dalam* as it is locally called, promised to set the IAS officers free in return for the release of eight of their comrades from Rajhamundry jail, and successfully got the state to do its bidding without causing any harm to the government officials. Officers like S. R. Sankaran were truly committed to tribal welfare, and so it seemed odd that the dalam had picked on them. In fact, KS seemed to have made it a point later to emphasize that the dalam would never have harmed those officers: "Do you really think that we would have killed the IAS hostages if our prisoners were not released? No, we would have never done it."[20]

Gurthedu merely reflected the helplessness of the Maoists in the face of the lawlessness of the repressive apparatus of the state and the failure of the judiciary to provide any redress. The police, too, seemed to have viewed it as such and took the cue to further step up its criminal ways of suppressing the Naxalite movement. The unlawful activity of the police thus got compounded, the enactment of the Terrorist and Disruptive Activities (Prevention) Act (TADA) in 1985 only emboldening them to engage in such acts with impunity. The numbers of encounter killings and deaths in police lock-ups of Naxalites went up significantly, and the cases of forced disappearance (Latin American-style "missing")—of Velupula Venkateshwara, Gopaganni Ilaiah, and Ravinder—widely reported, were simply ignored, even as the APCLC demanded that the missing be produced in the courts. Indeed, a commando force, the Greyhounds, was created in 1989 to strengthen the state's repressive apparatus against the Naxalites, giving rise to apprehensions of an impending major crackdown. However, elections and electoral promises by the main opposition party to relax state repression and restore democratic rights if it came to power led to a change of government from the Telugu Desam to the Congress Party.

In late 1989–early 1990, the new Congress government agreed to release political prisoners and allow the mass organizations to conduct open, legal political work. Massive demonstrations and rallies and huge public meetings organized by the mass organizations followed. When the question of peace talks came up, the Party demanded the civil liberties and political rights that a regime claiming to be a liberal-political democracy should have had no problem in granting, including the disbanding of the notorious Greyhounds, the commando force raised by the Andhra Pradesh Police to eliminate the Maoists. But the state didn't relent.

In the ten years since the foundation of the CPI(ML)(PW), there had been an unprecedented expansion of the Party's mass base. A two-day RCS state-level conference in Warangal in May 1990 attracted about 1.2 million peasants at the public meeting organized on the second day, and the government was afraid to agree to peace talks lest the grant of democratic rights were to lead to a further consolidation and expansion of the movement. Thousands of acres of government land usurped by the landlords had already been seized and distributed among the poor peasants in North Telangana. Indeed, the process of occupation and distribution of landlords' *patta* lands under the leadership of the RCS began in May 1990, and, in some cases, collective cultivation of such plots of land was also initiated. The RCS began running praja panchayats, with the Sanghams adjudicating in disputes at the village level (this was the landlords' prerogative earlier). Moreover, SIKASA came into its own in advancing the worker-peasant alliance.

The movement was touching the lives of the common people in North Telangana in various ways—in the occupation of forest land, the increase in wages of the tendu-leaf pickers, diminution in the incidence of atrocities perpetrated by the landlords, and so on. The Naxalites organized the rural poor to grab and occupy the surplus and *benami* lands of the landlords and, in many cases, got lawyers and revenue officials to register the occupied lands. And they set up "people's courts" that handed out "plebeian justice," this despite all the mistakes and the excesses that could be held against the plebeian judges presiding over these people's judicatures. Listen to the civil-rights activist K. Balagopal who, while acknowledging the excesses, has this to say about the people's courts: "There have been a large number of cases where disputes have been resolved and justice rendered in a fair and humane way."[21]

The state was planning to launch another round of severe repression of the Maoist movement—encounter killings, "missing," and the like—and anticipating this perhaps the Party had no other choice but to tilt the balance between mass movement and armed struggle heavily in favor of the latter. There seemed to be no other way of defending the gains made over the decade just gone by. Select areas of the countryside of North Telangana and Dandakaranya, in the Party's view, had to be turned into guerrilla zones.

These generalized observations about the movement are drawn mainly from its practice in Karimnagar and Adilabad districts where it all began, Warangal, where KS began organizing the students from 1966, giving the movement a prominent part of its present leadership and cadre, as also Khammam. In Adilabad and Khammam, the winning of forest rights came to the fore. And in the Singareni collieries and industrial belt, SIKASA, in its heyday, had a membership of over 100,000 workers. The movement had also spread to the forest areas of East Godavari and Vishakhapatnam districts of Andhra Pradesh, and to Malkangiri and Koraput in the province of Orissa. In Andhra Pradesh, apart from the movement's strongholds in North Telangana, it had also made inroads into Nalgonda, Mahbubnagar, Medak, and Rangareddy districts in South Telangana, and in the Nallamala hilly-forest range (a section of the Eastern Ghats) of Mahbubnagar, Guntur, Prakasam, Kurnool, and Cuddapah districts.

CASTE DEFINES THE CULTURE OF EXPLOITATION

The other major state where the Naxalite/Maoist movement made significant inroads was Bihar, where three parties led the way—the CPI(ML) (Liberation), the CPI(ML)(Party Unity) [CPI(ML)(PU)], and the Maoist Communist Centre (MCC), all of which had learned from the failures of the period 1967–75 and launched their respective mass organizations, hoping to gain a mass following.

The movement led by the MCC and its mass organization, the Krantikari Kisan Sangh (revolutionary peasant association), first took off mainly in parts of the countryside in Gaya and Aurangabad—both then very large districts—in what was then part of central Bihar, and in Hazaribagh and Giridih in the then southern part of the province (now part of the province of Jharkhand), and from there it spread to other districts. The struggles led by the CPI(ML)(PU) got off the ground in the districts of Gaya, especially in the Jehanabad sub-division of that district in central Bihar, and Palamu in the south (now one of the strongholds of the movement in the province of Jharkhand), and from there, they spread to other districts. It was in Palamu in June 1984 that the CPI(ML)(PU) lost one of its most able leaders, Krishna Singh—he came from a poor peasant family and made his livelihood as a transport worker—General Secretary of the Mazdoor Kisan Sangram Samiti (worker–peasant struggle association), the Party's mass organization, killed by an armed gang organized by Rajput landlords when the movement was in its initial stage.[22]

The CPI(ML)(Liberation) had its roots in the heroic Bhojpur struggles of the first half of the 1970s, led by Subroto Datta (Jwahar). The formation of the Bihar Pradesh Kisan Sabha (BPKS) in February 1981 marked the start of the period of mass struggles it led. The following year witnessed the formation of the Indian People's Front (IPF), this when the Party was underground, but which created an avenue for party members to gradually come above-ground to engage in open political activity. The IPF also engaged in electoral politics, one of its leaders, Rameshwar Prasad, winning the Arrah Lok Sabha seat in the 1989 parliamentary elections. In the 1990 Bihar Legislative Assembly elections the IPF won seven seats, but in 1991–92 four of its Members of the Legislative Assembly defected to the Janata Dal, then leading the government with Lalu Prasad Yadav as chief minister. This was at the height of the political polarization around the issue of reservations for Other Backward Classes in the wake of the implementation of the Mandal Commission's Report. Then in 1994, the IPF was dissolved and the CPI(ML)(Liberation) came above-ground as a recognized political party of the left, similar to the CPM, which marked the beginning of the end of the Party's Naxalite character as it finally managed to "break out of the old theoretical-strategic model of the Naxalite movement."[23] The CPI(ML)(Liberation) has since been trying to put together an effective left confederation with the mainstream CPI and CPM, but with not much success so far.

As regards the CPI(ML)(PU), it was in the Jehanabad sub-division of Gaya district that the Party launched its mass organization, the Mazdoor Kisan Sangram Samiti (MKSS), becoming a force to reckon with, this despite the political and economic clout of the mainly Kurmi (backward caste) rich peasants, and (new) landlords, and the support the latter got from the state's administrative and police wings. The Arwal Massacre in April 1986 perhaps reflected the state's growing nervousness in the face of the rapid growth of the MKSS along class lines, with landless Dalit militants at the forefront. In the Arwal block of Jehanabad sub-division of Gaya district, a dispute was raging over a tiny piece of government land that was appropriated by a landlord but on which nine landless households had set up their homesteads. The landlord had evicted them and constructed a wall around the land. The poor households got organized under the banner of MKSS, which, on April 19, 1986, led a *morcha* (rally) that demolished the wall and then proceeded for a public meeting in the compound of a nearby Gandhi library. But the gathering was fired upon in a "'highly indiscriminate, unnecessary and unjustified'" manner, killing twenty-one persons. A local leader of the MKSS was taken into police custody and killed. But didn't the poor "'have a legitimate compulsion to occupy some land for housing themselves'"?[24] The political establishment and the police couldn't have cared less.

The three main immediate objectives of the Naxalite movement in Bihar in the 1977-2003 period, indeed, the movement's achievements, were the seizure of illegally occupied land and its distribution among landless laborers and poor peasants, the assertion of "izzat" (human dignity) of the Dalits and the most backward castes, and the winning of higher wages.[25] In the aftermath of Zamindari abolition, unsurprisingly, with adequate compensation, intermediaries of the Zamindars and occupancy tenants, upper-caste persons and some upper-backward caste ones too, benefited from the acquisition of land ownership, apart from their illegal encroachment on land. The landless, if they were allotted any land by the government, were unable to take possession of it. There was a huge underreporting of tenancy (*bataidari*, sharecropping); perhaps, in the 1980s, 35 percent of the cultivable land was under some form of tenancy, even though there had been a shift from bataidari (tenancy) to wage labor.

A person's identity was, however, invariably primarily conceived in terms of caste. Besides the utter economic deprivation of the landless laborers, importantly, they also suffered humiliation at the hands of the dominant castes. The Rajput- and Bhumihar-caste landlords generally have an aggressive mentality, with a callous and intimidating attitude toward the landless laborers, and particularly with no concern for the dignity of women. As Professor Anand Chakravarti succinctly put it, albeit with respect to North Bihar, but valid in central Bihar too: "Caste defined the culture of exploitation."[26] Landless Dalit laborers have, apart from a proletarian consciousness, Dalit awareness, stemming from the reality of their being considered "Untouchables," their "izzat" (sense of human dignity) being violated all the time.

The struggle for "izzat," including the fight against sexual abuse of Dalit women, has been a protracted one. Many landless Dalit laborers, being Naxalites themselves, had been able to organize armed defense of the Dalit *tolas* (hamlets) of their villages in the form of local militia with country-made weapons. But the typical Naxalite armed squad had to cover several villages as part of its assigned jurisdiction, in the process leaving many Dalit tolas vulnerable to attack. The upper-caste landlords, given their links in the bureaucracy, the police, the political establishment and the judiciary, had openly organized "senas" (armies, but in reality, armed gangs) that committed atrocities against the Dalits once the latter stood up. These atrocities provoked Naxalite retaliation, in some instances almost matching the cruelty and brutality of the senas.

Worthy of note was the Bara Massacre of February 12, 1992, in the district of Gaya, by an armed group of the MCC, which came in search of Ramadhar Singh (alias "Diamond"), the supreme commander of a sena of

Bhumihar landlords called the Savarna Liberation Front. Not finding their target, the MCC armed group singled out thirty-seven men (note: male adults only) of the Bhumihar caste, supporters of the Savarna Liberation Front, and hacked them to death in a most gruesome manner, this in retribution for the Mein-Barasimha Massacre of December 1991 in which men of the Sarvarna Liberation Front killed ten Dalits who were supporters of the MCC. So intense was the resentment of the Dalits that a prime accused in the Bara Massacre, Bihari Manjhi, an MCC activist, reportedly told a journalist: ". . . the character certificate of Bara's men folk should be obtained from the Harijan women of the area."[27] Dalit Naxalites feel the same sense of outrage, the same sense of indignation as ordinary Dalits feel. The need to take revenge for the atrocities committed on Dalits is all-consuming; they share the same set of standards that ordinary Dalits have of what is just retribution in the face of such barbarities, and the MCC seemed to go along with them in such situations.

Nevertheless, the Bhumihars in Bihar are certainly not all "casteist" landlords. In the villages, there are Bhumihar landlords, but there are also Bhumihars who are small landowners. Of course, they consider it below their dignity to labor in the fields, especially ploughing the land, and as a result of their caste loyalty, they are politically on the same side as the big landowners of their caste. In urban areas, Bhumihars can be professionals, teachers, bureaucrats, judges, factory workers, coal miners, and even loading mazdoors. In other words, the caste–class correlation is not a simple one; the MCC should have been trying to win over the poorer sections of the upper castes. Instead, its action only strengthened the caste divide. A sharp division between the poorer sections of the upper castes and the Dalits makes the goal of "land to the tiller" and legitimate decentralized political power to the revolutionary committees of the poor peasants and landless laborers—part of the Party's agrarian program—non-viable.

Caste divides the exploited all along its ranks. Why only the upper castes, even the upper-backward castes like the Kurmis, the small landowners among them, whom the CPI(ML)(PU)'s MKSS had brought into its fold, harbored the usual prejudices about the Dalits, and this adversely affected the internal harmony that has been so essential to effective organizational functioning. The Dalits in the MKSS, identified mainly as Musahars and Dusadhs, resented the influence the Kurmis began to wield in the MKSS.[28] They, however, wanted the armed squads of the CPI(ML)(PU), of which they too were a part, to continue to defend the Dalit tolas from the landlord senas. The latter, at that time in the 1980s and the early 1990s, were the Bhoomi Sena (of the Kurmi landlords), the Lorik Sena (of the Yadav landlords), the Brahmarshi Sena (of the Bhumihar landlords), the Sunlight

Sena (of the Rajput landlords), and the Savarna Liberation Front (of the Bhumihar landlords).

Many massacres were carried out by the senas, examples of which include the Bathani Tola, Laxmanpur-Bathe, and Shankarbigha massacres. On July 11, 1996, at about 1 p.m., 150 armed men of the Ranvir Sena (formed in 1994 by affluent landlords of the upper castes) entered Bathani Tola (in Bhojpur district) and killed twenty persons, Dalits and Muslims, eleven of them women and nine children, including an infant. Fourteen years later, a Sessions Court in Arrah convicted twenty-three Ranvir Sena men, but on April 26, 2012, the Patna High Court acquitted all the accused, citing "unreliable" evidence, and almost mocking the witnesses.[29]

On December 1, 1997, in the dead of night, around 100 armed goons of the Ranvir Sena entered Laxmanpur-Bathe (in the Arwal block) after crossing the River Sone and attacked and killed fifty-eight Dalits—twenty-seven women among the dead, eight of whom were pregnant, sixteen children, the youngest, a one-year-old—eliminating or seriously injuring almost all the residents of the Dalit tola. Many years later, on October 9, 2013, the Patna High Court acquitted all the twenty-six accused in a reversal of the decision of the lower court, this on the grounds that the witnesses were "unreliable."

Again, on January 25, 1999, in the dead of night, Ranvir Sena men killed twenty-three persons in Shankarbigha (Jehanabad district), all of them from landless labor households, most of them Dalits, five women, seven children, including an infant. On January 14, 2015, a Trial Court in Jehanabad acquitted all the twenty-four accused members of the Ranvir Sena. It may be noted that the Ranvir Sena had proudly claimed to have carried out the massacre, and all the forty-nine witnesses, out of fear, had turned hostile, declaring that they were unable to identify the accused.[30]

That these massacres took place in the context of one or the other radical-left party—the MCC, the CPI(ML)(PU), which merged with the CPI(ML)(PW) in August 1998, or the CPI(ML)(Liberation)—organizing and leading the Dalits in their struggle for "izzat" must be kept in mind, besides the fact that the Ranvir Sena had friends in high places. The bias of the police in investigating these massacres, in the inadequate evidence it made available in the prosecution of the cases, is also evident. But, more important, a commission appointed in the wake of the Laxmanpur-Bathe Massacre, headed by retired Justice Amir Das, was disbanded by the Nitish Kumar government in 2006 when word came that it was going to name certain politicians who patronized the Ranvir Sena, some of whom were Kumar's allies in the state government, particularly, the then Deputy Chief Minister Sushil Kumar Modi of the Bharatiya Janata Party, and a senior leader of that party, Murli

Manohar Joshi. Moreover, a sting operation carried out by investigative journalists of the website *Cobrapost* has unearthed evidence to suggest that the Ranvir Sena was able to procure sophisticated (albeit rejected) weapons of the Indian Army; it could swing this deal because of a recommendation made to the Indian Army by the then Prime Minister of India, Chandra Shekhar, sometime during November 1990–June 1991.[31]

The powerful upper-caste landlords of Bihar thus had not only the police and the courts on their side, but also sections of the political establishment, including a prime minister, whom the Indian Army listened to and made available sophisticated, albeit rejected, weapons that it knew were going to be used against the Naxalites and their Dalit supporters. Moreover, the shift in the power structure of the state at the provincial level from the upper castes to the upper-backward castes seems to have not been of any benefit to the Dalits.

Despite the concrete tactical advances that the Maoist/Naxalite movement has made in addressing the caste–class reality of oppression and exploitation, atrocities against the Dalits have been ongoing. The younger, politically more conscious generation of Dalits has rejected their community's social and political subordination to the upper- and upper-backward caste landowners and has even refused to be submissive to the leaders of the political parties controlled by them. The upper- and upper-backward caste landowners cannot countenance such anti-caste, democratic assertion on the part of the Dalits, and they have, from time to time, organized gruesome assaults on Dalits to reassert their class–caste domination.

Besides the caste-Hindu landowners' attacks on Dalit landless laborers in Bihar, the Karamchedu and Chundur killings of Dalits in Andhra Pradesh— the former, on July 17, 1985 (organized) by Kamma caste landowners in the village of Karamchedu in Prakasam district, and the latter, on August 6, 1991 (organized) by Reddy caste landowners in the village of Chundur in Guntur district—are both reflective of the fact that the various caste-Hindu landowners cannot countenance any independent political assertion by the Dalits of their basic democratic aspirations.[32] A section of the younger generation of Dalits has been taking pride in its newfound political identity derived from the memory of B. R. Ambedkar, one of the principal architects of the Indian Constitution. Alternatively, another section of this generation of Dalits has been uncompromisingly struggling to win its democratic rights after having joined the Naxalite mass organizations. The caste-Hindu landowners have found such independent forms of democratic assertion on the part of the Dalits impossible to stomach and have periodically subjected the Dalits to an unprecedented degree of brutal violence as vengeance against those propagating the goal of "annihilation of caste."

But precisely at this time when the revolutionary forces needed most to jointly confront the aggressive onslaughts of the caste-Hindu landowners on the Dalit landless laborers, the 1990s witnessed internecine clashes between the revolutionary forces, both in Bihar and in Andhra Pradesh. In Bihar, incidents of such internecine hostilities multiplied, between the MCC and the CPI(ML)(Liberation), and later in the decade and in the early 2000s, also between the CPI(ML)(PW) and MCC, mainly due to each of these party's insistence on carving out exclusive zones of influence in districts where all three or at least two of them were active. Similar clashes over territory had taken place in pockets of Andhra Pradesh between CPI(ML)(PW) and CPI(ML)(Janashakti), the latter, then led by one of the late Chandra Pulla Reddy's followers. Such internecine clashes, in some cases even resulting in loss of lives on both sides, suggest an intolerance unbecoming to parties struggling to bring about a "New Democratic" India, and constitute a "black chapter" in the history of the Maoist/Naxalite movement in India, as MCC and CPI(ML)(PW) have suggested later in a reflective moment of self-criticism. That the Naxalites were engaging in such fratricidal politics must have made the counterinsurgency ecstatic!

FULL-SCALE COUNTERINSURGENCY

In the early 1990s, with the spread and deepening of the movement in Bihar and Andhra Pradesh, and the links that the Andhra Maoists were establishing with their Bihar counterparts,[33] the Union Home Ministry in New Delhi was alarmed. A Nodal Cell and a Joint Command of Operations were established, and in December 1991 more battalions of the central paramilitary forces were deployed in North Telangana and in Dandakaranya. Even the Border Security Force and the Indo-Tibetan Border Police were brought in. Full-scale counterinsurgency became the order of the day—the encircling and attacking of a village or a group of villages; setting up organized retaliation against the Maoists in the form of vigilante groups masquerading as rival mass organizations, for instance, in Bastar, the Jan Jagran Abhiyans; and use of rehabilitation funds to build a network of informers targeting Party leaders for assassination. In North Telangana, many comrades were killed in this manner, but their funeral processions attracted thousands, even tens of thousands of people. The Party's armed squads fought back, and it was decided that the lands that had been occupied but left fallow would be cultivated again.

What followed, as the CPI(ML)(PW) had anticipated, was a banning of the Party and its mass organizations, this on May 21, 1992, when the government realized that the Naxalites were indeed a political "force to reckon with and if . . . allowed to grow, the movement with its expanding mass base would sweep the ruling politics completely." The open political activity of SIKASA ceased; after 1992, with "barbaric repression," Maoist/Naxalite politics could only be clandestine, and even this "was crushed with an iron heel."[34]

Infiltration of police agents into the Party and its mass organizations was also a matter of grave concern, and the fear and suspicion that this possibility aroused also brought on some unintended consequences, very tragic ones that caused deep anguish, not only among the Maoists but also among those who placed high hopes in them. In February 1992, Sarala, a young woman wanting to take part in the revolutionary movement, got in touch with an armed squad of the Party in Nizamabad. She was later suspected of being an informer and was killed by one of the Party's activists, but upon further investigation, it was found that her intentions were bona fide; she was without blemish. This evoked a sense of deep anguish within the Party. However, seeking pardon from Sarala's family and the people didn't diminish the damage that had already been done. The Party surely needed to take account of all the consequences—immediate, medium and long term—of its violent actions, easy to suggest but hard to practice, especially in the face of the state's growing lawlessness.

In fact, the CPI(ML)(PW) was left with no other option but to resist state lawlessness with its own brand of unruliness and disorder. On January 30, 1993, the Party kidnapped a tribal Member of the Legislative Assembly and seven government officials, promising to set them free if the government released one of its leaders, Kranti Ranadev, from Warangal jail. The police put all the pressure they could on the political establishment to treat this as purely a law-and-order problem. But, given the manner of functioning of the political establishment, expediency ultimately prevailed, and the APCLC, whom the Maoists trusted, was allowed to intervene on the terms set out by the Maoists, to get the hostages freed, even though the release of Ranadev had to await some legal formalities, and the APCLC was left to ensure that these were completed. The police, of course, viewed the swap as a setback, and demanded, and got, "more powers, more resources, more infrastructural facilities."[35]

But in July 1996, in a High Court judgment on a TADA case involving Naxalites, Justice M. N. Rao commented that even as "left-wing extremism is viewed as a problem by the administration, it is increasingly perceived as a solution to their problems by the alienated masses." The judgment, recognizing Naxalites as contributing to a solution of the people's problems, called for an immediate cessation of police encounters *and* violence by the Naxalites, and asked for a meaningful search for a permanent solution.[36] Subsequently, a Committee of Concerned Citizens made concerted efforts to bring the government and the Naxalites to peace talks.

In spite of these developments, however, in December 1999, the government executed the infamous "Koyyur encounter" where three Central Committee members of the CPI(ML)(PW), Nalla Adi Reddy (Shyam), Arramreddy Santosh Reddy (Mahesh) and Seelam Naresh (Murali), were picked up in Bangalore, brought to Hyderabad, tortured and killed, and their bodies thrown in a Karimnagar forest to make it appear as if they were killed in a real encounter, the police even killing a militant from a nearby village to make its version seem more credible. When the CPI(ML)(PW) retaliated by killing the state's home minister in a landmine blast in March 2000, the state government offered to initiate the "peace process"!

The preconditions for the initiation of the peace process put forward by the CPI(ML)(PW) insisted that the government in office, with whom the Party was going to talk, having taken an oath of office to stand by the Constitution and the law, must adhere to that pledge made to the people. But the Party was castigated by so-called public intellectuals as presenting "unreasonable demands and preconditions." Basically, whenever the Maoists have come to talks, they have viewed this as an opportunity to articulate some of the real issues, those relating to "land to the tiller" and livelihoods. There's liberation, too, which the Maoist movement is fighting for, but this involves the "overthrow of the existing exploitative and oppressive system to bring in an egalitarian social order," which, of course, cannot be the subject of talks.[37]

MASS ORGANIZATIONS AND THE "MASS LINE"

The mass organizations, however, cannot retain their mass character when they are banned and repressed, The RSU was virtually pushed underground following the first round of state repression in 1985. A number of its student leaders were murdered in cold blood; its "Go to the Village" campaigns, organized jointly with the RYL, ceased. Its successes in student body elections and its public meetings on campus became a thing of the past. The RSU now attracted only the most intrepid; it held its meetings in closed-door classrooms with barely a score of students in attendance. The civil liberties activist K. Balagopal, one of the most insightful analysts of the movement, claimed that it was the authoritarianism of the CPI(ML)(PW) that had undermined its mass base,[38] but one must also acknowledge that the state's counterinsurgency had instilled the fear of death in the minds of the movement's supporters and they withdrew from active participation in the Party's mass organizations.

Balagopal's criticism of the CPI(ML)(PW) for its authoritarian mode of functioning, however, needs a different kind of probing. The Party makes it clear that the orientation of its mass organizations will be "according to the strategy of the protracted people's war [PPW]."[39] Thus "their purpose is to serve the war." The forms of mass organization and mass struggle then have to change in tune with the advance or retreat of the armed struggle. The Party stresses how the armed struggle and the mass struggle need each other to mutually advance in tandem, stating that even when the mass organizations were forced underground, people's participation continued to grow, which I think is not the case, for this does not correspond to the reality of North Telangana from the latter half of the 1980s to 2003.

State repression ultimately suppressed the mass character of the Party's mass organizations. The Party policy is basically to ensure that the mass organizations linked to it facilitate and ensure that the political consciousness of the masses is brought to a level where the people accept the "revolutionary positions" adopted by the Party. The Party claims that it does this by following the "mass line." Still, there are elements of an authoritarian mode of functioning, indeed, of undemocratically controlling the mass organizations, that has been written into the very constitution of the Party. We quote the relevant Article thus:[40]

> The party fractions shall be formed in the executive committees of mass organisations. Party fractions will guide the executive committees of the mass organisations adopting suitable method in accordance with the correct concrete situation. Fraction will function secretly. The opinions of party committee/member guiding the fraction *shall be considered as final opinion* [emphasis ours]. If fraction committee members have any difference of opinion, they will send their opinions in writing to the concerned party committee/higher committee. The concerned party committees shall guide fraction committees of different mass organisations at their own level.

Thus, this Article effectively gives the Party the right to violate the autonomy of the non-Party leaders of the mass organizations. Mao had this to say about cooperating with non-Party persons:[41]

> ... There is an article in the Administrative Programme of the Shensi-Kansu-Ningsia Border Region which stipulates that Communists should co-operate democratically with non-Party people and must not act arbitrarily or keep everything in their own hands. It is directed precisely at the comrades who still fail to understand the Party's policy. ... A Communist must never be opinionated or domineering ... and lord it over others. ... Communist Party ... members should be among the people and with them and must not set themselves above them. Members of the Assembly and Comrades, this

Communist Party principle of democratic co-operation with non-Party people is *fixed and unalterable* [my emphasis].

Setting oneself above non-Party persons and, in effect, issuing Party directives to them is "commandism" and failing to gain the support of non-Party leaders of the mass organizations is practicing "isolationism." Indeed, the Party will do well to remember that during the Cultural Revolution, the Chinese Maoists held that privileges derived from one's position in the Party are no less damaging than those originating in private property rights over the means of production. In fact, this failure on the part of the Party to adhere to Maoist principle has cost the Party dear.

Without mass support, an objectively weaker guerrilla army could never ultimately defeat the objectively stronger Indian armed police and army. It is here that the intelligence advantage counts—the Party's web of intelligence that derives from forging close relations with the people and infiltrating the Indian state's ranks. If the guerrilla army was able to successfully set up ambushes, concentrate and disperse the guerrillas as and when required, know when to avoid engaging the state's armed police and when to throw oneself into such confrontations, and how to beat a retreat when that armed police launched a mopping-up campaign, all these were largely due to the Party's intelligence advantage that comes from being close to the people.

But this intelligence advantage can be sustained if and only if the Party follows the "mass line." Maoism, like Leninism, is skeptical of the efficacy of mass spontaneity. At the core of organization is Party leadership. The leadership of the CPI(ML)(PW) not only had to embody a superior understanding of Maoism but correctly apply it under Indian conditions, for which it also had to correctly grasp the dynamics of Indian society. It was only then that it could formulate the correct "line," a set of programs and policies that prove their validity beyond the shortterm. The question has been how the leadership should arrive at the correct line. Mao's classic exposition is as follows:[42]

In all the practical work of our Party, all correct leadership is necessarily "from the masses, to the masses." This means: take the ideas of the masses (scattered and unsystematic ideas) and concentrate them (through study turn them into concentrated and systematic ideas), then go to the masses and propagate and explain these ideas until the masses embrace them as their own, hold fast to them and translate them into action, and test the correctness of these ideas in such action. Then once again concentrate ideas from the masses and once again go to the masses so that the ideas are persevered in and carried through. And so on, over and over again in an endless spiral, with the ideas becoming more correct, more vital and richer each time.

Maoism is thus against the imposition of Marxist-Leninist formulae without a detailed knowledge of the situation on the ground. As seems evident, the very formulation of the correct line requires the Party to rely on mass participation, and in doing so, avoid the errors of "tailism" (going by whatever the masses want irrespective what the Party has in mind) and "commandism" (enforcing what the Party believes is the right thing to do or achieve irrespective of the level of the people's consciousness).

But as parts of North Telangana and Dandakaranya turned into guerrilla zones, and life in these zones turned precarious in the face of intense state repression, what took a back seat was the application of the mass line. At the core of the state's repressive apparatus directed against the Maoists were the Special Intelligence Bureau (SIB) of the Andhra Pradesh Police and their "armed hatchet-men called 'Greyhounds'." The former have been "the plainclothes sleuths and murderers deployed to apprehend and kill Naxalites, their sympathisers, and whoever else is perceived as obstructing the anti-Naxalite operations of the police." The latter, a specially trained and equipped anti-guerrilla police force, had been created specifically to eliminate the Naxalites, "not by the process of any known law but by the lawless norms of arbitrary power." The National Human Rights Commission had proved totally ineffective; the executive magistrates' inquiries were worthless; and the authorities heaped nothing but scorn upon the investigations of the APCLC. The Naxalites of the CPI(ML)(PW) responded with landmines, for these, they felt, were an effective means of retribution. How else could they have come down with a heavy hand on the repressive apparatus of the state that was "committing more and more gruesome acts to eliminate" them and was "doing so as a matter of deliberate political policy"?[43]

Nevertheless, despite the brutal state repression, and consequent difficulties in practicing the mass line, one of the main achievements of the CPI(ML)(PW) in the guerrilla zone of North Telangana was that it transformed class-power relations. A section of the workers, the poor peasants and landless laborers, Dalits and the tribal people had stood up. They now had a voice of their own, with the courage to speak out, speak out against the oppression and the exploitation, fight against their domination.

THE GUERRILLAS AND THE PEOPLE

The Maoist guerrillas fought heroically. The Padkal encounter[44] of September 1993 is one instance; the collective memory of it is part of Naxalite folklore.

A five-person armed squad in a shelter in Padkal village in the Sirnapalli area of Nizamabad district was surrounded by armed police who initially took two of the women comrades hostage but soon killed them in an act of vengeance. The three remaining comrades battled it out. One of them was fatally injured, but squad commander Swamy and his comrade Kranti continued to retaliate. It was now one o'clock in the afternoon; they'd been in combat since last evening. The Director General of Police came and asked them to "surrender, promising safe passage." Kranti surrendered, but Swamy, nevertheless, single-handedly battled the enemy. The injured comrade, unable to bear the pain anymore, pulled the trigger on himself. It was now seven pm. The police set the house on fire. Swamy took a dead policeman's AK-47 and with a burst of firepower charged out of the shelter and escaped. He had not had a drop of water in twenty-four hours; the people gave their "*anna*" (an affectionate and respectful epithet) water but, terrified, asked him to leave. Covering himself with cow-dung, Swamy hid all night in a garbage dump. An elderly woman found him in the morning, fed him, and then informed him that the police had killed Kranti. She helped him hide all day, then disguised and took him by a safe route into the forest as night fell. We are reminded of what Mao wrote in *On Guerrilla Warfare*: "Many people think it impossible for guerrillas to exist for long in the enemy's rear. Such a belief reveals lack of comprehension of the relationship that should exist between the people and the troops."[45]

The close relation between the people and the guerrillas of the CPI(ML) (PW) was also evident in the building and rebuilding of the Martyr's Columns. There has been a running battle between the police and the people as regards these columns. The people build them, and then the police break them, but the people restore the columns, provoking the police to demolish them again. In the last week of July, Martyr's Week—Charu Mazumdar was martyred on July 28, 1972—public meetings have been held at these memorials, the guerrillas planting mines at the approach roads to the columns to prevent the police from disrupting the proceedings. And, in the wake of "encounter" killings, when the APCLC brought each of them to light, people marched to the police station to claim the martyr's body, not allowing the police to surreptitiously dispose of it, and then took out massive funeral processions with cries of "*Amar rahe* . . . (the comrade's name)," "*Johar Amarajeevi* . . . (the comrade's name)" and "Comrade . . ., *Lal Salaam*" filling the air.

GUERRILLA WARFARE IN THE ABSENCE OF BASE AREAS

With growing armed resistance, the balance between the populist participatory politics of the mass organizations and guerrilla warfare shifted inevitably in the direction of the latter. The beginning of the new millennium witnessed the formation of a People's Guerrilla Army (PGA) in December 2000. Armed conflict between the state's paramilitary forces and the guerrilla army now became the principal from of struggle in the guerrilla zones—in North Telangana and in Dandakaranya. The guerrilla forces were now no longer merely organized as people's militia and guerrilla squads; platoons and companies were put together under decentralized command. The counterinsurgency forces now aimed to wipe out the platoons and companies of the PGA with ever larger encirclement and suppression campaigns, and the PGA, in turn, launched tactical counteroffensives. The PGA retreated with the advance of the enemy, raided the enemy and captured weapons when the enemy camped, in North Telangana and Dandakaranya, for it had to rely mainly on the enemy for its supply of arms. But what ultimately determined the guerrillas' staying power in North Telangana and Dandakaranya was the extent to which they could get the support of the people. To what extent did the people keep the guerrillas informed of enemy troop movements, feed and house them, sabotage the enemy's military advantage, join the guerrilla forces?

It must be said of the CPI(ML)(PW)'s mass organizations—unlike those of the parliamentary left or the other mainstream political parties who organize mass support to bring progressive reform—that their popular mobilizations were, indeed, intended to precipitate a crisis of the state, to progressively weaken state power.[46] The state came down on these mobilizations "with the kind of brutal insensitivity that successive governments . . . exhibited in Andhra Pradesh" over more than three decades after the Emergency was lifted in 1977, beginning with the crackdown, as we have seen, in Sircilla and Jagtial taluks in Karimnagar district in October 1978. In response to this, increasingly, in retaliation, the CPI(ML)(PW) enhanced its military power. The state, in turn, readjusted its tactics, more brutal and deadlier than before, and thereby provoked a modification of the CPI(ML)(PW)'s response. What ensued was a sequence of moves and countermoves, where the Party anticipated the state's moves in advance, in keeping with its perspective of building a guerrilla zone. "Encounter" killings and cases of "missing" went up; the Maoists responded with kidnappings of state officials and mainstream party politicians. Police camped in the villages; the Party's platoons raided some of these camps. The combing operations of the security forces were stepped up; the landmines, remotely controlled by the guerrillas, instilled the fear of death in the marauders. More Greyhounds and fortified police stations came into existence; platoons and companies of guerrillas with more sophisticated armaments were organized. The spiral proceeded upwards.

In such a situation, what the Party desperately needed was the establishment of "base areas," self-administered, liberated areas, miniature "New Democratic" republics of the revolutionary forces, albeit under siege, but serving as places of refuge and remobilization for the guerrilla army. What are the ideal locations for base areas? First, the area chosen must have a history of peasant struggles against colonialism and "semi-feudalism." Second, preferably, the area chosen should be one where political instability has been the norm. Third, the area must be able to exert political influence over important adjoining provinces.[47] Fourth, areas at the confluence of more than two provincial boundaries are preferred for obvious reasons. Fifth, the terrain must be favorable for the guerrillas from the military point of view. Sixth, the area must be favorable and big enough to practice economic self-sufficiency.

Indeed, one can now infer as to why the old Bastar district of Madhya Pradesh was chosen by the CPI(ML)(PW) in 1981 as a possible favorable site for the establishment of a base area. The Bhumkal Rebellion of 1910 might have been an important determinant, besides the favorable terrain, economic self-sufficiency, the contiguity with Khammam and Warangal in North Telangana, provincial boundaries to the east, the south and the west of the district, and at a part of the southern tip, with both Andhra Pradesh and Orissa.

Nevertheless, the problem, from the Maoist perspective of progress in the PPW, is that they have not been able to turn any of the guerrilla zones into base areas. It will be impossible to advance the ongoing guerrilla war or the further spread of guerrilla zones without the establishment of base areas. In the plains areas, which are less suitable for guerrilla warfare and the establishment of guerrilla zones, the higher guerrilla units of the guerrilla army have been unable to continue their operations and have gradually had to move to the forest and hilly areas. Some of the existing guerrilla zones are potential candidates for transformation into base areas, but "the enemy" must be defeated there and the organs of political power have to then be established, a formidable task in the face of severe repression. The counter-insurgency is, of course, intended to turn existing guerrilla zones back into "White Areas" where the writ of a relatively stable, reactionary government runs. And even if the Maoists were to turn one of the guerrilla zones into a base area, there is no guarantee that it will remain one. That is, it can revert back to a guerrilla zone or even a White Area. From the Maoist point of view, if they create and sustain a few base areas, the PPW will be able to sustain itself over a long period; in the absence of base areas, the Maoist guerrilla army will not last long or grow. In guerrilla parlance, the base areas are its essential "rear."

There has been another aspect of the imperative to establish base areas, the sustenance of mass support. Difficult as it surely is, it has been imperative for the Party and its mass organizations to undertake economic development in the midst of the revolution, for the workers, the poor, and landless peasants, and the semi-proletariat cannot be expected to put up with their abysmal living conditions over decades. But this can only take place on a relatively stable basis with the establishment of base areas, which the Party has not been able to bring about, and the longer this adverse situation persists, the greater the chances of a withering away of the movement's support base. However, within the guerrilla zones in North Telangana and Dandakaranya, the Maoists have carved out their own domains in particular stretches, which they call "guerrilla bases," and it is these that serve as a sort of "rear," and where, in a very rudimentary form, "New Democracy" and the Maoist model of base-area development has been practiced.

The primary unit of people's power in the guerrilla base has been the *gram rajya* (village administration) committee. At a higher level, there have been Area Revolutionary People's Committees. Difficult as it surely has been to undertake economic construction in any guerrilla base in the midst of the class war all around in the guerrilla zone, the rudimentary Janathana Sarkars (people's governments) set up over there have taken up the responsibility to develop the productive forces (the material means of production and human capabilities) in agriculture, irrigation, fisheries, and small industry, and undertake development programs in the areas of health, education, etc., all of this activity through the establishment of cooperatives and mutual-aid arrangements.

MAOIST RESISTANCE IN RETROSPECT, 2003

How then, in retrospect and in terms of the perspective outlined earlier, should "Spring Thunder," Phase II, of Maoist resistance, covering the period 1977–2003, be looked at? Viewed in this light, there are three distinctive goals, independence, development, and revolution. Independence is not merely what it has meant for Indian big business and its political representatives—expansion of the Indian state's room for maneuver in the world capitalist system, with some bargaining power vis-à-vis the ruling imperialist powers. Development/modernization of the capitalist kind has been steered by the Indian big business–state–multinational bloc since 1957. But, from a "New Democratic" perspective, both real independence and genuine development require a revolution, defined by the aspirations of the exploited, the dominated and the oppressed classes. These yearnings were expressed in various forms right from the colonial period in the many peasant and tribal people's rebellions, which eventually metamorphosed into an ongoing revolution in the wake of Naxalbari, promising the poor peasants and tribal people equal access to farmland, forests, and the commons—to them *and* the workers, hitherto unparalleled relative equality.

In Maoist parlance, what the Naxalites set out to bring about is "New Democratic Revolution." The main targets of such a revolution are "imperialism," caste-based "semi-feudalism," and "comprador" big business. Their defeat is expected to make capitalism more compatible with democracy, and thus create the ground for transition to socialism. The path chosen for the struggle to attain "New Democracy" is "Protracted People's War," involving first a gradual area-wise political winning over of the vast Indian countryside, followed by the same, albeit rapidly, in the cities. In 1995, the CPI(ML) (PW) added another target. Patriarchy had to be confronted head on and overcome in the course of the "New Democratic Revolution."

"Spring Thunder," Phase II, was a period when the rebels of Phase I, defeated but still refusing to submit to injustice and exploitation, acquired a level of intelligent, dignified commitment to their cause, becoming thereby, more difficult to subjugate; they were now ready to go on even in the face of impossible odds. Indeed, by the beginning of the new millennium, the CPI(ML)(PW) had put together a People's Guerrilla Army. Unlike during "Spring Thunder," Phase I, the Maoists now had well-founded, dependable political organizations, the CPI(ML)(PW), CPI(ML)(PU), which merged with the former in 1998, and the MCC. But the Indian state, Indian big business, and the MNCs, and the political regime were far from being structurally weak, and the international context was no longer opportune. With the collapse of the Soviet Union, the sidelining of Maoist development strategy by the post-Mao Chinese Communist Party, and Washington's resort to naked imperialism, a real revolution in any country in the periphery of the world capitalist system now seemed hard to even conceive of, let alone bring about, compared to the "1968" period when the feasibility of radical change was palpable.

Looking back over the period 1977–2003, the retreating survivors of "Spring Thunder," Phase I, had regrouped in the form of CPI(ML)(PW) and MCC and staged a major resurgence. This renewal came about through the building of a network of people's support in some backward areas where the local structures of the Indian state were relatively more vulnerable. It was the combination of their mass organizations and people's guerrilla armies, to the extent that the two could complement each other while facing severe state repression, which accounted for the sustenance of the PPW, a long, painstaking process that got off the ground in the new millennium. Its viability depended on the unification of the two revolutionary forces, the CPI(ML)

(PW) and the MCC, which finally came about in 2004 after a resolution of the thorniest issues that had kept them divided. Maoist resistance had bred state terror, which in turn had bred fresh resistance, and unified resistance was slated to bring on extreme state terror. There have been moments of little triumphs interspersed as these have been with the many traumas that the Maoists and their supporters have experienced, and a long, thoughtful and restrained view of history seemed to be now, in 2003, asserting itself.

A political geography of the Maoist movement in 2003 would include the following areas, grouped in different ways, keeping in mind that the two main Maoist parties, the CPI(ML)(PW) and the MCC, were trying to build their respective areas of influence into contiguous domains of struggle with each area influencing the other:

- In Dandakaranya—the forest area situated in the border and adjoining tribal districts of the states of Andhra Pradesh, Chhattisgarh, Maharashtra and Orissa—on the Andhra-Orissa border, parts of the border districts of Andhra with Orissa, Khammam, East Godavari, Vishakhapatnam, Vizianagaram, and Srikakulam, and parts of those of Orissa with Andhra, Malkangiri, Koraput, Rayagada, Gajapati, and Ganjam; and in Maharashtra, parts of the districts of Chandrapur and Gadchiroli, contiguous with the districts of Adilabad and Karimnagar in North Telangana, and also Bhandara;
- in Telangana and Andhra Pradesh, especially in parts of the districts of North Telangana—Nizamabad, Adilabad, Karimnagar, Warangal and Khammam—and, apart from the districts bordering Orissa, in parts of seven other districts, East Godavari, Guntur, Prakasam, Kurnool, Mahbubnagar, Nalgonda and Medak;
- in Chhattisgarh, the then districts of Dantewada, Bastar and Kanker;
- in Bihar, parts of the districts of Rohtas, Aurangabad, Gaya, Arwal, Jehanabad, Patna, Nalanda, Nawada, Jamui, and Munger;
- in Jharkhand, parts of the districts of Garhwa, Palamu, Lohardaga, Gumla, West Singbhum, East Singbhum, Bokaro, Dhanbad, Giridih, Kodarma, and Chatra; and,
- in Orissa, besides parts of the districts bordering the then Andhra Pradesh, parts of the districts of Sundergarh, Mayurbhanj, Sambalpur, Jajpur, Kandhamal, Nayagarh, and Nabarangpur.

There was an absence of Maoist politics or little of any significant consequence in Punjab and Haryana, in Tamil Nadu, Karnataka, and Kerala, in Gujarat, Rajasthan, Uttar Pradesh, and in Uttarakhand, Assam, and the rest of the Northeast. In West Bengal, quiet underground work—the long, patient organizational work that precedes the firing of the first shots, as Ho Chi Minh would have put it—amongst ordinary adivasis and *moolvasis* (lower backward castes) in the Lalgarh and surrounding blocks of the district of West Midnapore was underway, beginning in the late 1990s.

In the areas of feverish activity, with Andhra Pradesh as the fountainhead, the movement went through ups and downs, recovering but again suffering serious losses. A serious setback came in Andhra Pradesh in 2001–03—success of the counterinsurgency—from which the movement did recover, but only partially, and then, beginning January 2005, it suffered a devastating reversal. We might well ask: With the Party forced to focus more on the military rather than the political, was the entry of new cadre over time, especially after 1990, marked by a lower level of understanding of "correct" Maoist political practice, the main cause of its added vulnerability? Did this enable the APSIB, the Andhra Pradesh police's elite intelligence unit, to successfully infiltrate the Party's political structure? No one will ever know for sure, but the systematic elimination of the top leadership of the Andhra Pradesh State Committee of the Party from 2005 onward suggests that there may be an element of truth in this hunch. What explains, apart from the fear of brutal state repression, the inactivity, the quiescence of the Party's mass base in Telangana and Andhra Pradesh? Repeatedly, reformist illusions prevailed in election after election. The electorate seemed to have been time and again building castles in the air—that if the government in power had failed, the opposition when it came to power in the next election would serve the people's interests and advance the "development" agenda. Even now, the Maoist movement is yet to recover in Telangana and Andhra Pradesh.

5

India's "1989"—"Financial Aristocracy" and Government *à Bon Marché*

The law locks up the man or woman
Who steals a goose from off the common,
But leaves the greater villain loose
Who steals the common from the goose.
—FIFTEENTH-CENTURY ANONYMOUS
FACT-OF-THE-MATTER VERSE

We have broken the hillsides
We have crushed stones
We have built projects with
our blood as granite.
Whose is the toil
and whose is the wealth?
—A STANZA OF THE POEM
"SONGS OF JUSTICE" BY CHERABANDA RAJU

Globally, "1968" was a decade of rebellion marked by demonstrations, social unrest, and violence directed against ruling establishments *and* against established Communist (with a capital C) and social-democratic parties, and, in the Third World, against parties that had led the nationalist movements. "New Left" revolutionary humanism was in the air; political expediency evoked derision; youth, in political ferment, accused the established left of conniving with the establishment and neglecting the truly wretched of the earth. In sharp contrast, November 9, 1989, the day German Democratic Republic government officials opened the Berlin Wall, marked the beginning of a period of capitalist triumphalism—"1989"—a chapter that lasted, internationally, until the Great Financial Crisis of 2008. "Regime change" had already been accomplished in Hungary and Poland, and the reunification of Germany was formally concluded in October 1990, leading to the disintegration of the Soviet bloc. The formal dissolution of the Soviet Union itself followed in December 1991, inaugurating the reconstruction of Russia on capitalist lines.

Principally, "1989" marked the victory of the U.S. ruling class in the Cold War with the Soviet Union, which was the main aim of U.S. foreign policy ever since 1917. The Soviet bloc had barely disintegrated when the Gulf War (August 1990–February 1991) provided the U.S. ruling class the opportunity of "repairing the tarnished image of a giant with feet of clay that the United States had received as a legacy of the Vietnam war," and it did this by bombing Iraq, "a third world country back into the pre-industrial age." This was an implicit threat to all other nationalist third-world countries to fall in line, for the "elimination of the Soviet Union as a source of support for anti-imperialist aspirations"[1] now meant that the earlier Cold War constraints no longer applied.

Moreover, with the collapse of the so-called socialist bloc, Leninism, already considerably tarnished by Stalinist practice, stood further discredited in the public eye. In addition, social democracy's anti-communist role in Western Europe became fully irrelevant. In the third world, the parties that led the national liberation or independence movements had by now been thoroughly discredited, and they quickly climbed on to the new bandwagon in town—capitalist triumphalism. Eastern Europe and the countries of the former Soviet Union witnessed a drive to privatize state property. In Russia, for instance, privatization of state-owned industrial enterprises and mines, forests, and a whole range of natural resources, including oil and gas, was accomplished even before a proper bourgeois state and independent judiciary were in place.[2] Overnight, big business oligarchs appeared where just yesterday there were no capitalists, this through a grab-what-you-can-for-yourself process. The capitalists in the making, it seemed, even drafted many of the privatization decrees themselves, eventually managing to legalize the private grabbing of state/public property. A Russian proletariat was also created, overnight. The workers who earlier "owned" their jobs, and had rights to housing, healthcare, childcare, and education for their children, lost all such guarantees.

China, in sharp contrast, didn't suffer such "shock therapy"; in Deng Xiaoping's now famous phrase, "mozhe shitou guo he," the transition was supposedly about "crossing the river by feeling for stones!" Not quite, though.[3] China's "1989" began much earlier, in 1978, with the Third Plenum of the Eleventh Central Committee of the Communist Party of China (CPC) in December of that year, after which, in 1980 the communes began to be dismantled. In 1982, the industry linked to them was turned into "township and village enterprises." Meanwhile, in 1979, it was decided that the "four modernizations" (of agriculture, industry, defense, and science and technology) needed an "open-door" policy, and this led to dramatic increases in foreign trade and investment, and the setting up of special economic zones in Guangdong and Fujian provinces, close to Hong Kong and Taiwan respectively, and then the turning of all coastal areas into export enclaves. From 1984 onward, the state sought to commoditize all labor services. The "iron rice bowl," wherein workers not only had presumptive rights to their jobs, but also rights to housing, medical care, education, childcare, and so on, was taken away. In 1992, the privatization of public enterprises took off, and, in 2002, capitalists became eligible for membership in the CPC.[4]

The contrast with China after 1949 in Mao's time couldn't have been starker. Maoist China had a definite view about how to get to socialism, what needed to be done to meet the basic needs of everyone in a poor country, and how those who had been at the receiving end were to have the liberty to express themselves. It did its best to feed, clothe, and house everyone, keep them healthy, and educate most of them. Development was to be on an egalitarian basis; all were to be in it together and everyone was to witness better times together.

In Western Europe and Japan, and in the third world, "1989" strengthened the trend toward emulation of Anglo-American neoliberal economic policy across the board—in greater trade and financial openness, privatization of public enterprises and service functions, strong intellectual property rights, active promotion of "financialization" (a gravitational shift of economic activity from the production of goods and non-financial services to finance), corporate governance, capital adequacy norms for banks, redefinition of the "prudent" portfolio of pension-fund assets, and an indifferent, often hostile, attitude toward trade-union rights, the minimum wage, and environmental standards. In the political realm, money and wealth hijacked elections and violated the integrity of liberal-political democracy. So, for example, in the United States, the Republican Party's money from the rich and the corporations beat the Democratic Party's money from the rich and the corporations, or vice versa. For the electorate, it was more than ever a choice between Tweedledum and Tweedledee.[5]

India's "1989" began in 1991 and has gone on much beyond 2008; the Great Financial Crisis didn't crash the Indian economic apple cart. It was multifaceted but the importance of the opening of the energy, mining, telecommunications, civil aviation, infrastructure (ports, highways, etc.), banking, insurance, and other sectors to private capital needs to be highlighted. So also is the need to emphasize the transformation of the character and composition of Indian big business that was brought about as a result. Money, the standard of all things and the measure of one's worth, has had many more avenues for profitable deployment than it ever had before in independent India.

In what follows, I will, among other things, profile the triumphs of the "financial aristocracy" in India's "1989." This section of Indian big business has been getting its wealth not by production alone, but by pocketing the already available wealth of others, including public/state wealth. These accounts are not intended to disparage individuals; indeed, in my view, the business behavior of the financial aristocrats I profile, their modes of acquisition and their pleasures, are normal and socially necessary for the functioning of capitalism. I would like to emphasize that the various ways by which India's financial aristocrats have gotten control of public/state assets are mostly legal. Money and finance are fungible, and so I wouldn't even try to make too much of a distinction between their "black" and "white" forms. I try to bring out the fact that the present phase of accumulation of capital in India has a lot to do with the pocketing of the already available public/state wealth and the wealth of others, and that the various ways of doing this have mostly been made legal.

MONSTROUS INCOME INEQUALITY

The monstrous inequalities of capitalism in India have been plain for all to see in the new millennium. The numbers, at least as far as incomes are concerned, have been presented in a working paper, "Indian Income Inequality, 1922–2014: From British Raj to Billionaire Raj?" by the celebrated author of *Capital in the Twenty-first Century*, Thomas Piketty, and his colleague Lucas Chancel.[6] India has the highest recorded increase in the share of the top 1 percent in national income over the past three decades, from 6.2 percent in 1982–83 to 21.7 percent in 2013–14. Indeed, the latter figure is the highest level recorded since the establishment of an income tax in 1922, overtaking the British Raj's record of the share of the top 1 percent in national income, which was 20.7 percent in 1939–40.

While incomes of the bottom 50 percent of the adult population (above twenty years of age) over the period 1980–2014 grew at 89 percent, and that of the middle 40 percent (individuals above the median income and below the top 10 percent earners) by 93 percent, those of the top 10 percent, the top 1 percent, the top 0.1 percent, the top 0.01 percent, and the top 0.001 percent grew at 394 percent, 750 percent, 1,138 percent, 1,834 percent and 2,726 percent, respectively. Indeed, India has recorded an immense gap between the growth of incomes of the top 1 percent (a growth rate of 750 percent) and the growth rate of incomes of the full adult population (187 percent). While the incomes of the bottom 50 percent grew in China over the period 1980–2014 by 312 percent, those of the bottom 50 percent in India grew by only 89 percent. Further, while the growth of incomes of the middle 40 percent over the same period in China was 615 percent, the corresponding figure for India was just 93 percent. Indeed, the growth of incomes at the very top of the income distribution in India (that of the top 0.001 percent) was 2,726 percent; the corresponding figure for China was lower, 2,546 percent.

Both China and India have recorded appallingly unequal growth over the last three decades, but China's growth process over the period 1980–2014 has been relatively much less unequal than India's. The bottom 90 percent of its population captured 56 percent of the national income growth compared to what India's bottom 90 percent gets, a mere 34 percent. Indeed, in India, the middle 40 percent seems to have benefitted the least (as compared to China, France, and the United States) from the total national income growth over this period. It is not India's middle class (the middle 40 percent), but merely the top 10 percent of the population (80 million adult individuals in 2014)—"Shining India"—that has inordinately benefitted from the growth of national income (it captured 66 percent of that growth). India has been "shining" by and large only for the rich.

Data, however, never really speaks for itself. Moreover, in this case, it is largely derived from tax declarations, which, one suspects, are often falsified. And in the case of the very rich who control corporations, the distinction between their income as individuals and the income of the enterprises they control is at least in part artificial. For instance, much of their consumption expenses, and personal ones at that, is passed off as company expenses. So the Chancel–Piketty estimates of income inequality may be considered merely the lower bound of the prevailing inequality.

As regards the top 1 percent, much of their income probably comes from profits from business, dividends and interest from stocks and bonds, rent from land and buildings, and salaries and bonuses deriving from management control in business enterprises, the latter more like property income rather than income from work. Moreover, over the last three decades, real wages have fallen relative to labor productivity, thus increasing the share of property incomes over incomes from work in value added. And, even within property incomes, the eschewing of antitrust action to reduce monopoly power has concentrated profits in the hands of the big oligopolies to the relative detriment of small businesses.

Of course, the access of big business to undervalued assets of the public sector, of mineral and forest resources, of land, and of the allocation of the spectrum for telecom should not be forgotten. The larger picture is of a financial aristocracy lording over a process of corporate-led jobless growth. As the eminent macroeconomist Amit Bhaduri explains quite simply, the basic recipe of such growth is that if ten persons each producing two units are displaced from the petty-commodity production economy and five find employment in the corporate sector with a labor productivity of eight units, employment and livelihood possibilities have halved, but output has been doubled. To incentivize such corporate investment, natural resources, including land, are transferred to the corporate business enterprises cheap. And there is a tacit understanding that the public-sector banks will be lenient in the event of loan defaults by politically influential sections of big business. The corporate business houses return the favor through handsome donations to the political parties that have enabled them to acquire the undervalued assets and even default on payments due to the public-sector banks. In the process, contesting elections become prohibitively expensive for persons or parties that do not have access to such donations. Corporate-led jobless growth and corporate-led democracy then rule the roost.[7]

That income inequality has attained and even exceeded levels prevailing during the British Raj is the tragedy of India ruled by a bourgeoisie that has been the product of the long degenerative process of colonialism, including the last quarter of the nineteenth century and the first half of the twentieth, when the country witnessed a decline in real per capita income and millions were the victims of man-made famines even as the moneybags thrived. Governments at the union level in the "1989" period have all been on the right of the political spectrum, bent upon ripping apart what they perceive to be any threat to the prevailing model of appallingly unequal growth. The liberty of capital to accumulate wealth has undermined the freedom of those who earn their livelihoods from work. Political equality has been undermined by the overarching domination of wealth.

GROWING "BLACK" ECONOMY

Moreover, we also need to keep in mind what has already been in place much before "1989." Indeed, the eminent economist, Professor D. R. Gadgil wrote this way back in 1949:[8]

Trade and finance in India have always been confined to a narrow range of communities; and large-scale industry has, for the most part, fallen under the control of a small section of financiers. . . . [B]ecause of the concentration of economic power and the integration of financial control, industrialists have found it easy to act in concert. . . .

. . . It has always been known that financial communities in India had developed tax evasion into a fine art. . . . Tax evasion by the rich may . . . have to be taken as a chronic feature of the Indian economic situation. . .

Following in this tradition of economic thought, in a remarkable book,[9] Professor Arun Kumar of Jawarharlal Nehru University, New Delhi, estimated the size of India's "black" economy as approximately 40 percent of its official ("white") gross domestic product (GDP) for the financial year 1995–96. Earlier, one of Cambridge University's foremost economists, Professor Nicholas Kaldor had estimated the size of India's black economy as 2–3 percent of its white GDP for the financial year 1955–56, and a Direct Taxes Enquiry Committee (Wanchoo Committee) had arrived at a figure of 7 percent of white GDP for the late 1960s.

From Kaldor's estimate of 2–3 percent of official GDP for 1955–56 to Arun Kumar's estimate of 40 percent of white GDP for 1995–96, it was a sixteen-fold increase in the relative size of the black economy. As per Kumar's estimates for 1995–96, around four-fifths of India's black gross domestic income is generated through *legal* economic activity, and overwhelmingly this tends to be property income rather than income derived from work. And, it must be remembered that these estimates exclude capital gains. What this suggests is that as the proportion of the black economy in India's official GDP has risen, so has the class distribution of income changed more and more in favor of those who derive their incomes from the ownership of capital. A more recent estimate of the size of India's black economy, again by Arun Kumar, puts it at 62 percent of GDP in 2012–13.[10]

To illustrate, consider one of the means by which black income is generated—the underreporting of production. An example presented in Kumar's book pertains to the evasion of taxes through non-declaration of part of total output in the production of liquor (alcoholic beverages). Since all costs of production and other costs are accounted for in the declared part of total output, the sales revenue from the undeclared part of output is an off-income-statement profit on which no income taxes are paid, and on which no dividend has to be paid to the shareholders. Note that since the undeclared output is also sold at the same price as the declared output, what would have been excise duty, sales tax, and octroi to be collected and handed over to government is now privately appropriated as profit. Such underreporting of production has been and still is (reportedly) one of the most profitable avenues for the "industrialists," politicians, and government officials involved.

Kumar's analysis suggests that growing illegality within a triad composed of powerful sections of the polity, the bureaucracy, and the police, taken together, and the judiciary, along with business, is the cause of the trend increase in the size of the black economy. Further, the concurrent increases in the relative share of the tertiary sector (very high for an economy with such a low per capita GDP) and the share of property incomes in gross domestic income are interlinked with the increasing share of the black economy in total gross domestic income. In the example outlined above, the generation of black income in the alcoholic beverages industry would not have been possible without the connivance of sections of the polity, the bureaucracy, the police, and the judiciary, and payments made to them.

MOVING THE MARKETS AND THE ECONOMY

What about the footprints of the black money stashed abroad, retraced to make the money reappear "white"? Surely officials in the Department of Revenue, Central Board of Direct Taxes, know that high net worth individuals and companies appoint "portfolio managers" to manage their funds parked overseas and that these funds are "invested" in a portfolio of assets, financial and non-financial, of which a bank deposit is just one type. And in today's financial world deposits in Swiss banks can be moved quickly into other assets in other tax havens and offshore financial centers, perhaps even brought back for another round of business in India.

The government's White Paper on black money[11] mentions such means of return flow of capital as "foreign direct investment through beneficial tax jurisdictions, mobilization of capital by Indian companies through global depository receipts, and investment in Indian stock markets through participatory notes." The latter, participatory notes (PNs as they are called)—an instrument which permits a foreign investor to invest in Indian securities but remain anonymous to Indian regulators—are an easy route to money laundering. But they have still been allowed, and the Working Paper doesn't even recommend doing away with them. It also doesn't disapprove of the preferential routing of foreign investment through Mauritius and Singapore, even though this route is used by foreign investors to avoid payment of taxes and also to conceal the identity of the ultimate investors from the regulatory authority, which knows very well that resident Indians are using this route to invest in their own companies.[12]

In the period since 1993, the Indian stock market, with its relatively small market capitalization and limited number of shares that are traded, has been extraordinarily volatile. For instance, from 2003–04 to 2007–08, net capital inflows (in search of better yields) far in excess of the current account deficit on the balance of payments took the markets to a new high, triggering the "wealth effect," the expansion of liquidity and, in turn, consumer credit, the *Le Grande Bouffe* (self-indulgent, elite consumption), and the release of "animal spirits" to boost private investment, leading to high economic growth until 2007-08. But net capital inflows turned abruptly into outflows with the outbreak of the great financial crisis in September 2008. Nevertheless, with the first signs of an ebbing of the crisis, and with easy monetary policy in the developed capitalist world, the emerging markets, including India, once again became "the favorites." There followed a repeat of the wealth effect, liquidity, booming consumer credit, *Le Grande Bouffe*, "'animal spirits,'" and so on, leading to high growth, but capital inflows subsided again with the Eurozone's crisis. The fate of the Indian economy has thus become a function of abrupt changes in the direction of net capital flows, and the Indian government, realizing this pattern, does all it can to please the financial markets, for it is these (metaphorical) financial shopping centers that have the power to engineer booms and busts with volatile inflows and outflows of capital.[13]

Ever since they were invited to invest, the government has always been doing all it can to satisfy the demands of foreign institutional investors (FIIs), turning the country into a tax haven as far as listed equity capital is concerned. The year 2013 marked twenty years since the FIIs started playing the Indian markets. As active portfolio managers, they move the markets, but as yet there seems to be no study by the Securities and Exchange Board of India (SEBI), which tells the public about the different categories of FIIs, how active each of these are, details of their typical portfolios, their respective inflows and repatriation of funds, their use of PNs, their associations with private equity firms, Indian institutional investors, and promoter-dealer networks. In the world of globalized finance, however, investment portfolios for the major centers are combined, for the markets (stock, bond, money, real estate, government securities, forex, and commodities) tick almost round the clock from Sydney and Tokyo on Monday morning to New York and Chicago on Friday at 5 p.m., via London, Frankfurt, and other important financial centers in between (and the digital books are passed at the appropriate times). So tracking the so-called sharp practices and discovering the footprints must be exceedingly difficult. Periodically, leaks of stolen financial data are highlighted in the media. For instance, from offshore accounts in the British Virgin Islands and other tax havens, the "Offshore Leaks" were publicly divulged in April 2013; from the HSBC's Swiss subsidiary in Geneva, the "Swiss Leaks" were disclosed in February 2015; from Mossack Fonseca, the Panamanian legal and other corporate services firm, the "Panama Papers" were opened up in April 2016; and from the Bermuda law firm Appleby and other entities, the "Paradise Papers" were made public in November 2017. Each of these leaks suggested widespread tax evasion by the wealthy and the powerful, and there was a storm in the media, but the dust soon settled down until the next exposure.

CACUS-LIKE RETRACING OF FOOTPRINTS

Questions as to how the financial aristocracy—which got rich not by production alone—and more generally, Indian big business, actually got their wealth, how the structure of the system is biased in their favor, rarely, if ever, seem to be posed in the media, even in 2013 when a Google search with "India corruption" threw up 66.7 million results! India's billionaires are all "entrepreneurs" and "innovators" par excellence, that is, going by how they are portrayed in the business media! It is reminiscent of New York University Professor Bertell Ollman's recounting of Marx's response to the ancient Roman myth of Cacus:[14]

> Cacus was a Roman mythological figure who stole oxen by dragging them backwards into his den so that the footprints made it appear that they had gone out from there. After quoting Luther's account of the story, Marx exclaims: "an excellent picture, it fits the capitalist in general, who pretends that what he has taken from others and brought into his den emanates from him, and by causing it to go backwards, he gives it the semblance of having come from his den."
>
> Capitalists present themselves as producers of wealth, providers of jobs, donors and public benefactors. The press (their press) usually refers to them as "industry." Is this an accurate description of who they are and what they do? . . .The footprints are there for all to see, but if we limit ourselves to what is immediately apparent . . . we will arrive at a conclusion that is the exact opposite of the truth.
>
> . . . In the case of the capitalists, only by examining how they got their wealth from the surplus labor of previous generations of workers [and from all kinds of business exploits in connivance with "friends in high places," I might add] (history) and how our laws, customs and culture are biased in their favor (structure) can we see it is not the capitalists who are serving society but the rest of society that is serving them.

Now, in official parlance, corruption simply refers to payments in kind or in monies over and above official emoluments—"gratification"—that a holder of public office or a state employee receives for services rendered. And black money, again in official-speak, refers to "assets or resources that have neither been reported to the public authorities at the time of their generation nor disclosed at any point of time during their possession."[15] So, for example, only the value of the "gratification" alleged to have been "earned" by A. Raja—when he was Minister for Telecommunications and Information Technology in 2008—for deliberately issuing licenses to create 2G subscriptions for cell phones in a dubious first-come-first-served manner, based on 2001 prices, rather than in an open auction process, is "corruption." But such "gratification" could, at most, only be a small fraction of the billions of rupees of revenue foregone by the state.

The presumptive loss of Rs 176,645 crore (10 million = 1 crore), an astronomical figure—as estimated by the Comptroller and Auditor General (CAG) of India[16]—that this sale of part of the wireless spectrum entailed for the public exchequer, and the corresponding windfall gains to the private parties who got the licenses, essentially stemmed from the sale of a small part of a scarce natural resource, the wireless spectrum. The latter needed to be sold because of the prior privatization of the telecom service function. In February 2012, the Indian Supreme Court found the grant of the 2G licenses "unconstitutional and arbitrary" and quashed all of them. The court is right that the then telecom minister Raja "virtually gifted away an important national asset," for soon after the grant of licenses, some of the license holders, Unitech Wireless, Swan Telecom, and Tata Teleservices, sold a chunk of their equity stakes to Norway's Telenor, United Arab Emirates' Etisalat, and Japan's NTT Docomo, respectively, reaping huge capital gains.

The question being raised relates to the appropriation of national resources by Indian big business and the MNCs, which leads to the process of accumulation of private wealth in real estate, the stock market, mining, and allocation of property rights over natural resources and the spectrum. The process of conversion of agricultural and other lands to real estate has been a source of acquisition of immense personal wealth by very powerful real estate developers. Foremost among them is the DLF group—its patriarch is Kushal Pal Singh who inherited its riches—one of the country's most valuable real estate companies, which acquired agricultural lands on the outskirts of New Delhi cheap and converted them into expensive real estate.

More generally, the process of capitalist development as it relates to forests and mining, large dams, special economic zones (SEZs), transformation of the urban landscape, and the private appropriation of common property resources by corporations is at the core of what the financial aristocracy has been up to in India today. Part of this has been ably documented by Perspectives, a non-funded, independent study group of some students and teachers of the

University of Delhi and New Delhi's Jawaharlal Nehru University, in two reports, *Abandoned: Development and Displacement* (2008) and *Communities, Commons and Corporations* (2012).[17] The identities of the beneficiaries and the victims of the process of capitalist development as outlined in these books tell a lot about the identity and the nature of India's ruling classes.

For instance, chapter 2 of Perspectives' *Communities, Commons and Corporations* tells the story of the impending ruin of coastal communities and eco-systems as a result of corporate "plunder" in the district of Kutch, engineered by a partnership of the Adani group, led by billionaire Gautam Adani, and politics-as-business, led by the Bharatiya Janata Party's (BJP) then chief minister of Gujarat, Narendra Modi, now (2018) in office as the Prime Minister of India. How capitalism handsomely rewards the most blatant anti-social behavior even as it severely punishes those who put in place the shared use of common resources is evident.

PRIVATE ENTERPRISE AT PUBLIC RISK

The accumulation-by-dispossession story brings to mind parts of Marx's description of the "financial aristocracy" and its nexus with the upper rungs of the polity during the July Monarchy (July 1830 to February 1848) in his *The Class Struggles in France, 1848–1850*. Sample this:[18]

> It was not the French bourgeoisie that ruled under Louis Philippe, but one *faction* of it: bankers, stock-exchange kings, railway kings, owners of coal and iron mines and forests, a part of the landed proprietors associated with them—the so-called *financial aristocracy*. It sat on the throne, it dictated laws in the Chambers, it distributed public offices, from cabinet portfolios to tobacco bureau posts. . . .
> . . . The ruling class exploited the *building of railways* in the same way it exploited state expenditures in general and state loans. The Chambers piled the main burdens on the state, and secured the golden fruits to the speculating finance aristocracy. . . .
> . . . Cheap government, *governement à bon marché*. . .
> . . . [T]he finance aristocracy . . . get rich not by production, but by pocketing the already available wealth of others. . .

Marx is here speaking of a capitalism during the period of the July Monarchy in France where the "financial aristocracy" had triumphed over the industrial bourgeoisie. The former not only had a free rein over the banks, the stock market, railways, minerals, land, water and forests, but controlled the state and nakedly used state institutions to promote its interests.

However, this is not to draw any kind of parallel with India today, except that the period from the early 1990s onward has witnessed the rise of a "financial aristocracy" which has been increasingly calling the shots in the corridors of power.

In France, an 1842 public-private partnership (PPP) built the railways. The government secured the land, mainly through expropriation, bore the costs of putting much of the infrastructure in place, the bridges, the tunnels and the track bed, while companies controlled by the financial aristocracy put in place the rails, the stations, and the rolling stock and got the operating leases that guaranteed their dividends, essentially skimming their profits off from state expenditure. Nevertheless, the French railways did get built, and the successors to the financial bourgeoisie of the 1840s, with Louis Napoléon at the political helm from 1851 to 1870, for all their stock swindling, saw to the building of the first steamship fleets, the Suez Canal, etc. In sharp contrast, there are as yet no assets of comparable worth that the Indian financial aristocracy has developed to offset the wealth of the nation that they have secured for themselves.

In India today, public-private partnerships are the norm in infrastructure projects—in airports, ports, power, railways, and highways. An example is the National Highways Development Project (NHDP) since 2000, one of whose major undertakings has been the construction of the so-called Golden Quadrilateral (four to six lane express highways connecting the four major metros) and the North-South and East-West Corridor, and the greenfield, modernization, and expansion projects of the Hyderabad, Mumbai, and Delhi international airports. In the field of railways, a dedicated freight corridor project, linking the ports of western India and the ports and mines of eastern India to Delhi and Punjab, has been approved in the Rail Budget of 2014–15. In this project, besides engineering, procurement, and construction contracts, PPP with the build-operate-transfer form of project financing is envisaged, under which "special purpose vehicles" (SPVs) will receive "concessions" from the Indian Railways to construct *and* operate sections of the facility.

Generally speaking, in PPP arrangements for the development of physical infrastructure, especially in the NHDP, the government provides more than the required amount of land for the project, permits commercial exploitation of the additional area, transfers some of its existing assets, changes the rules of the game to favor the SPV (the government even takes an equity share in it) that develops, builds, and operates the asset for the contracted period, and gives income tax and import duty concessions. But, besides these, there is also a provision called "viability gap funding," under which the government, at its discretion, provides a capital subsidy (grant) of up to

40 percent of the project cost to ensure the asset's economic viability from the point of view of its private developers/financiers. No wonder billionaires such as Gautam Adani, G. M. Rao, and G. V. K. Reddy have been thriving.

Take, for instance, the PPP for the Indira Gandhi International Airport (IGIA), in which the SPV is the Delhi International Airport Private Ltd (DIAL), which is controlled by the G. M. Rao-headed GMR Group, and in which the public sector Airports Authority of India (AAI) has a 26 percent equity share holding.[19] Frankly, with regard to almost everything—the structure of the joint venture, the leasing of land and transfer of the existing assets, the concession period and its extension, the right of first refusal, the commercial exploitation of land, the post-contractual allowance to DIAL to levy a development fee, and the aeronautical and other airport charges—the cabinet, Ministry of Civil Aviation, and the AAI decided and ruled in favor of the GMR group.

In effect, the government granted DIAL the sole right to operate the airport for a period of sixty years with the highly favorable terms and conditions frozen. DIAL also has the right of first refusal for a second airport planned within a 150 km radius of the IGIA, and there is a provision that increases the chances of DIAL bagging the development and operational contract for any such second airport. An overwhelming part of the total land area of the IGIA has been handed over to DIAL at a lease rent of Rs 100 per annum! Indeed, of this area, the portion available to DIAL for commercial exploitation, is, on a conservative basis, valued at Rs 24,000 crore. Even as it was initially decided that the project would be financed mainly through equity and debt, it was later decided to fund a significant part of the project cost from a development fee charged to passengers, which came to around Rs 3,415 crore or 27 percent of the project cost. In effect, this was "viability gap funding" through the back door, and it was a huge capital subsidy (grant) that greatly enhanced DIAL's expected profit rate. Thus, with the GMR-led consortium's equity contribution of a mere Rs 1,813 crore, it got control of a brown-field airport for sixty years, and commercial rights to a portion of land valued at Rs 24,000 crore for a pittance, from whose exploitation DIAL could potentially earn an estimated Rs 163,557 crore.

HOW MONEY BEGETS MORE MONEY

Basically, finance capital is socially "bribed" to accumulate private wealth,[20] whether by the M–C–M' route or by the M–M' course. In the former, M–C–M', money begets more money via production, whereas in the latter, M–M', the same happens with no relation to production. Let's look at their Indian *avatars* (incarnations).

Mukesh Ambani, chairman and managing director of Reliance Industries Ltd (RIL), is among the world's top billionaires. He inherited the largest share, 45 percent of the equity capital, in RIL. His influence runs far and wide. He is a former member of the board of directors of the Bank of America and of the international advisory board of the Council on Foreign Relations. He heads a business empire that was gradually integrated backwards, from textiles to polyester fibers to petrochemicals, petroleum refining, and upstream into oil and gas exploration and production. His father, Dhirubhai Ambani, was one of the most adept of India's moneybags as far as thick-as-thieves relations with government and political parties in power went. He could influence a whole host of rules and regulations related to industrial and import licensing, import duties, and quantitative restrictions on imports of polyester filament yarn.[21] And, in a financial environment (right from the early 1980s) where insider trading was the norm, with his mastery of the stock dealer–business promoter combination, given its privileged access to price-sensitive information, its web of non-bank financial firms, the accumulation of wealth through destabilizing stock prices was trouble-free.

Such stock market conduct in what was truly a laissez-faire setting guaranteed that the dominant promoter-dealer combinations could maximize their profits or minimize their losses any which way they chose. Indeed, looking at the structure and conduct of the stock market as a whole, in a long-term sense, the switching of funds from the early 1980s on, significantly shaped structural change in the real economy, preparing the material ground for neoliberal consolidation in the 1990s and the emergence of quite a few financial aristocrats whose route to enrichment was of the M–M' type.

A tracking of one such career, that of AB (his real name is disguised) and his financial business group, is intriguing. AB is the principal founder and promoter of the BM Group (BMG), along with ZM, a minority partner, the head of a prominent Indian big business group. Beginning from the latter half of the 1980s, over time, especially after 1992, BMG gradually established itself in a wide range of across-the-board financial services, from stock broking/dealing to auto-financing, investment banking, wealth management, fund syndication, mutual funds, life insurance, private equity, and real estate funding to commercial banking in the first half of the first decade of the new millennium. Various joint ventures with multinational finance companies—for instance, with a well-known U.S.-headquartered global investment banking and securities services firm for more than a decade, a notable global auto-financing company for a decade, and a London headquartered investment, insurance, and banking firm in insurance—made it possible to take on various business rivals. Financing against securities (as collateral), investment banking, and wealth management has been BMG's forte.

Indeed, from the time India's central bank, the Reserve Bank of India (RBI), bestowed BMG with a commercial banking license, with a wide array of bank and non-bank financial activities in its business portfolio, the group has been engaged in a whole range of financial activities across the board. These span a wide spectrum from commercial bank-style taking of deposits from the public to raising capital for clients through underwriting and issuing securities, market making, assistance in M&As, raising funds for leveraged buyouts, venture and growth capital, and placing loans to broker/dealer arms, secured by stocks/bonds, for their speculative trading and carrying of securities. The BMG is also engaged in investment portfolio management and private banking for high net worth individuals.

The group is organized, by and large, with BM Bank (BMB) as a bank-cum-holding company, possessing more than a dozen different entities, wherein a significant part of the bank's total credit to financial companies is to its own subsidiaries and associates, the risk of contagion thus running both ways. Among the country's banks, Indian and foreign, given the manner in which BMG is structured, BMB has the highest profit from capital market-related transactions, both in absolute terms and as a proportion of total consolidated profit. In India today, the regulators, the RBI and the SEBI, do not seem to take seriously the regulatory agenda of Glass-Steagall, itself dead in the United States long before Bill Clinton repealed the act in 1999. But in the wake of the great financial crisis, shouldn't the affiliations of BMB and its various subsidiaries and associates, given the nature of their business, be a matter of concern? Should the investment banking and securities entities be allowed to "gamble" with a significant part of the public deposits of BMB (we are referring to the speculative trading and carrying of securities by subsidiaries and associates with the use of bank credit)? Should a significant proportion of the subsidiaries'/associates' loans be secured by stocks and bonds? Should the bank act as an agent of its non-bank subsidiaries in placing loans to brokers and dealers? Should it help its private equity arm raise funds for leveraged buyouts, and venture and growth capital?

The process of financialization that is discussed here actually got resuscitated from the early 1980s onward. This had a lot to do with Ambani's RIL—and later, Reliance Asset Management Company (a public limited company since 1986)—with its significant reliance on capital raised from the stock market that triggered that bourse's active revival, leading, by the early 2000s, to the emergence of financier aristocrats like AB. Unlike the latter, however, it was RIL's exploits in the real part of the Indian economy that got

Mukesh Ambani to the top of the heap. It is time to look at that company's foray in the upstream oil and gas business.

The Panna–Mukta oil field and the Tapti gas field, discovered and developed by the public sector ONGC, was handed over to a partnership of Enron Oil & Gas India Ltd (incorporated in the Cayman Islands) and RIL, with the ONGC tagged along in what became a three-party consortium for the main benefit of the two private partners.[22] (Enron later sold its stake to British Gas Exploration and Production India Ltd [also incorporated in the Cayman Islands] for $350 million in an offshore deal.) But what about the KG–DWN–98/3 deepwater block (also referred to as the KG–D6 block), which was claimed to be RIL's discovery of India's biggest natural gas reserve, and the world's largest gas discovery of 2002, that took the company's share price into the stratosphere? It transpires that the KG–D6 gas reserves are a mere 1.93 trillion cubic feet (tcf)[23] and not the 5.3 tcf claimed for the D1–D3 development area in March 2004 or the vastly inflated 11.3 tcf attested to in October 2006.

Like the Panna–Mukta–Tapti fields, RIL has made hay with the award of highly favorable production-sharing contracts for the development of the country's largest natural gas reserves in the Krishna–Godavari (KG) basin where the government has borne practically all the risks and the private contractor gets the lion's share of the profits. Moreover, the latter was permitted to vastly inflate capital expenditure over the estimates initially agreed upon ("gold plating"). Indeed, the Ministry of Petroleum and Natural Gas and the Director General of Hydrocarbons seemed to have been more interested in protecting the private contractor's cost recovery and share of profit than the public interest.[24] The more basic question, however, is: Shouldn't the blocks in the KG basin that were awarded to Reliance have been the public sector ONGC's, for the KG basin's potential was first made evident by the latter way back in 1983?

In 2004, the government approved RIL and its minority partner Niko Resources Ltd's (Niko's) initial development plan for natural gas from block D-6 in the Krishna-Godavari basin, according to which the consortium would supply 40 mmscmd (million metric standard cubic meters a day) of natural gas based on an investment of $ 2.4 billion. In the same year the consortium won an NTPC tender to supply natural gas over a period of 17 years at a price of $ 2.34 per mBtu (million British thermal units), as also a contract with Reliance Natural Resources Ltd (of the Anil Dhirubhai Ambani Group) on the same terms. As per the production sharing contract, the consortium had the right to recover all approved-costs before sharing returns with the government. But, in 2007, a decision was taken by the then union petroleum minister Murli Deora to increase the price to $ 4.24 per mBtu for extracting

80 mmscmd of gas at a capital cost of $ 8.8 billion (permitting a vast infla-
tion of capital expenditure, disproportionate to the enhanced throughput).

Indeed, with the assurance of windfall profits, British Petroleum picked
up a stake of 30 percent in the consortium, from RIL in July 2011, at $7.2
billion. But despite the windfall gains from the price increase, the consortium's leader, RIL, failed to meet the throughput target. Despite this failure,
the consortium was granted a price of $8.4 per mBtu from April 2014,[25]
and this was claimed to be a market-determined price, although there is no
"international gas price" and, in North America, the price was then around
$ 4 per mBtu.

In effect, Murli Deora and, later, Veerappa Moily, as successive petroleum and natural gas ministers, enhanced the consortium's cost recovery
and inordinately hiked the price of the natural gas to give the consortium
windfall gains in profit, and, in all these alleged manipulations, they stand
accused of trampling upon the public interest.[26] In upstream oil and gas, can
it then be said that the government has aided RIL's accumulation by making
it easy for the company to "pocket" the national wealth?

SPECTRUM ARISTOS

Likewise, huge personal fortunes have been made from the privatization of
the telecom service function, so much so that the Telecom Minister A. Raja's
dubious "first come first served" 2G spectrum license allocation in 2008 even
attracted real estate magnates like Sanjay Chandra (son of Ramesh Chandra)
of Unitech (one of India's top real-estate groups by market valuation) who
floated Unitech Wireless, and (then) billionaires Vinod Goenka and Shahid
Balwa of DB Realty who promoted Swan Telecom. Soon after they got their
2G licenses, even though they didn't satisfy even the basic criteria of prior
telecom experience, they sold a significant part of their equity capital to
multinational telecom companies reaping huge capital gains. Swan Telecom
reportedly paid Rs 1,537 crore for its license, but soon thereafter sold 45
percent of its equity capital to the UAE-headquartered Etisalat for Rs 4,200
crore. Unitech Wireless paid Rs 1,661 crore for its 2G license, but went on to
sell 60 percent of its equity capital to the Norwegian multinational telecom
company Telenor for Rs 6,200 crore! But, as already mentioned, later, the
Supreme Court became a spoke in the wheel of such wheeler-dealers.

Bharti Tele-Ventures (now Bharti Airtel) was the first private operator
to launch cellular telecom services in India—aided by the deliberate initial
restriction to enter that was placed upon incumbent public sector telecom
entities—and gain a first-mover advantage. (The public sector MTNL's entry
into mobile telephony was stalled for quite some time, and only when it was,

later on, allowed to come in as a player did tariff rates came down significantly.)[27] Bharti snatched the pecuniary benefits flowing from the significant advantage the new mobile user derived from being connected to the already existing large public-sector network of fixed-line users, which made access of new mobile users to the network that much more valuable. Besides, with huge investments from Warburg Pincus and Singapore Telecom and a series of takeovers of firms that had bagged licenses in different telecom circles, the purchaser of an Airtel connection expected a quantum growth in the size of the overall network to increase the value of his/her connection, but it was Airtel that derived most of the pecuniary benefits of this value enhancement.

Moreover, the incumbent private operators now resorted to peculiar maneuvers—companies like Bharti and Hutchison–Max (Hutchison–Essar) bid high to bag licenses and then got the regulator to change the rules of the game in their favor. And then, the Cellular Operators' Association of India, which represented them, got the Telecom Regulatory Authority of India to adopt a pricing formula that allowed them to snatch rents (excess profits). Also, in the initial years, when the bulk of the network was composed of public-sector fixed-line users, tariff rules were stacked in favor of the mobile operators. And, as mentioned, mergers and acquisitions have been one of the most important aspects of the dynamics of accumulation in the industry. One of the biggest has been Vodafone's February 2007 acquisition of the controlling interest of 67 percent from Li Ka-Shing (Li Ka-Shing was the then chairman of Hutchison Whampoa) in Hutchison–Essar for U.S.$11.1 billion in an offshore deal that circumvented payments of capital gains tax to the government of India, and the subsequent July 2011 buy-out of Essar's 33 percent stake for $ 5.46 billion. Such has been the route to unprecedented private accumulations of capital in the telecom sector.

"WHERE MONEY, FILTH, AND BLOOD COMINGLE"

With huge capital gains, Essar has successfully exited from telecom, but the Essar group—headed by Shashi and Ravi Ruia, among the country's top billionaires—also has a prominent stake in mining, steel, oil, and electricity. Interestingly, in the mineral-rich region of south Chhattisgarh, following the provincial government's creation in June 2005 of an armed private vigilante force—called Salwa Judum (SJ)—to cut off the villagers from the Maoists, companies such as Essar Steel and Tata Steel allegedly began to contract with SJ for "protection and 'ground-clearing' services."[28] In Dantewada, Bastar, and Bijapur districts, in the context of large-scale acquisition of land by corporations, entire villages were evacuated and villagers forcibly herded into camps, from which those who escaped were branded Maoists and hunted down.

Indeed, in all of this, according to a 2009 draft report authored by Sub-Group IV of the Committee on State Agrarian Relations and Unfinished Task of Land Reforms, set up by the Ministry of Rural Development, New Delhi, SJ was "supported with the fire power and organization of the central forces." But more to the point, the draft report—though it was quickly officially disowned and withdrawn from the ministry's website—drew attention to what it called "the biggest grab of tribal land after Columbus" in the making as being initially "scripted by Tata Steel and Essar Steel who want seven villages or thereabouts each to mine the richest lode of iron ore available in India." In Dantewada and Bijapur districts, backed by the security forces, between June 2005 and 2009 SJ razed 644 villages, hounding the inhabitants into police camps, and forcing many more to just run any which way they could to save life and limb. Around 350,000 adivasis were displaced—47,000 were forcibly herded into roadside camps, 40,000 fled across the state border into Andhra Pradesh, and 263,000 sought shelters in the forests. Perhaps this was the largest and most brutal displacement so far in independent India.

In a capitalist system, the underlying basis of the dispossession of people from their lands is what potentially brings the highest rate of return from the private profitable use of those lands or from speculation based on the holding of those properties. Such dispossession usually takes place by the application of the law *and* the threat or actual use of force. In law, the state reserves to itself the right to acquire private property by exercise of "eminent domain" and "public purpose," this even on behalf of and for the benefit of certain private entities, by decreeing that any activity of the state and almost any activity of those private entities serve the "public interest." In the event of resistance to the handing over of the properties, the state threatens or uses force to acquire them. These are the means by which land was "liberated" from obstructions for its use by the state or for what was deemed its most private profitable use. One of these obstructions was "customary rights" (for example, community ownership of common lands, customary tenures, and so on), which were put an end to because they interfered with the capitalist process.

The Land Acquisition Act (LAA) of 1894 was the culmination of a series of colonial laws related to land acquisition from 1824 onward, the year 1863 marking the first incorporation of the provision for government to acquire land on behalf of the private sector, ostensibly for the "public purpose," the latter, itself quite all-encompassing. The colonial period, with its "development" projects, land settlements, Forest Acts of 1865, 1878, and 1927, de-proto-industrialization, and forced commercialization of agriculture, spawned a vast segment of displaced persons by the time India became independent in 1947. This near destitute segment of the Indian people got multiplied to become a huge contingent of marginalized people in the wake of further displacement as a result of the development projects of the post-independence period.[29]

The LAA of 1894 and the Forest Act of 1927 remained in independent India under Article 372 of the Constitution, which smoothed the incorporation of colonial era laws. Indeed, the LAA of 1894 was amended in 1962 to give greater powers to the state to characterize a whole range of infrastructural and industrial projects as serving the "public purpose," and in 1984 to make it even easier to acquire land for private companies. Any activity of the state was now deemed to serve the "public purpose," as also almost any activity of private companies. No wonder that there have been many resistance movements in recent times against acquisition of land,[30] especially when the state has sought to grab lands for and on behalf of private corporations. Prominent among these have been the movements led by the

- Bhumi Uchhed Pratirodh Committee in Nandigram in East Midnapore district of West Bengal, when the Communist Party of India (Marxist) [CPM]-led state government announced that it would acquire around 25,000 acres for an SEZ to be developed by the Salim Group of Indonesia;
- Krishi Jomi Bachao Committee in Singur in Hoogly district of West Bengal, when the CPM-led state government acquired 997 acres of land and leased it to Tata Motors to set up a car factory;
- Niyamgiri Suraksha Samiti in Lanjigarh and Niyamgiri in Kalahandi and Rayagada districts of Odisha, where the Biju Janata Dal-led state government decided to lease the mining of bauxite in the Niyamgiri (Kalahandi district) and other protected forests (Rayagada district) to a subsidiary of the MNC Vedanta Resources and a state-government mining company;
- POSCO Pratirodh Sangram Samiti in Jagatsinghpur and in the mining areas of Keonjhar and Sundargarh in Odisha, where the Biju Janata Dal-led state government sought to acquire land for POSCO of South Korea for captive iron ore mines, a steel plant and a private port;[31]
- MahaMumbai Shetkari Sangharsh Samiti in Raigarh in Maharashtra, when the Congress Party–Nationalist Congress Party-led state government approved a project of RIL in 2005 to set up an SEZ there across 14,000 hectares of land and Reliance began the process of acquiring the land.[32]

It is these and other anti-land-grab movements that forced the union government to repeal the LAA of 1894 and bring in the Right to Fair Compensation and Transparency in Land Acquisition, Rehabilitation and Resettlement Act, 2013, on 1 January 2014. But even this new law has not marked the end of the colonial legacy of land acquisition under the principles of "eminent domain" and the so-called "public interest."

BLACK GOLD FOR A SONG[33]

Besides land grabbing, the resources under the ground have also been up for snatching. A leaked draft performance audit by the CAG brought to light irregular and arbitrary allocation of blocks of already explored coal deposits to public and private-sector firms between 2004 and 2009 instead of openly auctioning them to the highest bidder.[34] It was known to the then Prime Minister Manmohan Singh—who was also officiating as Minister of Coal during the relevant period—that there was going to be a substantial difference between the price of coal as supplied by the public-sector enterprise Coal India Ltd and the cost of production of coal from the (to be) acquired captive mines of merchant power plants (set up by independent power producers), cement, and steel plants, but he didn't agree that the Indian state as the legal owner of the natural resource on behalf of its citizens should make sure that a significant part of such benefit accrues to them. He allowed the windfall gains of what was reckoned by CAG to be approximately Rs 10.7 lakh crore (Rs 4.80 lakh crore to the private companies), to be snatched by the companies. CAG had based its estimate on the difference between the price of coal and its cost of production at the then current prices (March 31, 2011) in the captive mines, multiplied by 90 percent of the geological reserves.[35] Indeed, when the prime minister was officiating as Minister of Coal, going by the date of allotment of the blocks of already explored coal deposits, significant windfall gains accrued, among others, to a number of Indian big business and multinational subsidiaries—Tata Power, Tata Steel, Essar Power, Hindalco, Adani Power, GVK Power, ArcelorMittal, BALCO, and Sterlite Energy (the latter two part of the Vedanta Resources business group).[36]

Essentially, Prime Minister Manmohan Singh allowed the already discovered coal deposits to be given to private-sector companies, including subsidiaries of ArcelorMittal and Vedanta Resources, controlled by billionaires Lakshmi Mittal and Anil Agarwal, for a song. The windfall gain of Rs 4.8 lakh crore to the private companies represents a loss to the citizens of India; this money "could have been spent for their benefit but was diverted to private pockets." Now, even if no bribe was paid, the loss to the people as a result of this privatization of the already discovered coal deposits remains. Indeed, it constitutes a regressive redistribution of wealth from the citizens of India to a whole host of private companies, including MNCs like ArcelorMittal and Vedanta Resources.

BRED ON PRIVATIZATIONS WORLDWIDE

Both Lakshmi Mittal and Anil Agarwal, whose initial wealth was inherited, have increased it phenomenally through privatizations—sale of state-owned assets at "throwaway" prices in the neoliberal era. One of Vedanta's prized purchases was 51 percent of the equity capital of the highly profitable Indian public-sector enterprise BALCO in 2001. Sterlite Industries, a subsidiary of Vedanta Resources, which acquired BALCO, funded both the Congress Party and the BJP. Indeed, in 2003, P Chidambaram, a corporate lawyer and prominent Congress Party politician, was a non-executive director on the board of Vedanta, which has its largest mining and non-ferrous metals business portfolio in India, besides Zambia and Australia, the Indian part essentially based upon acquisition of state-owned assets. The company's Indian business portfolio also includes commercial power generation and iron ore mining. Besides BALCO, Vedanta's aluminum business in India also encompasses the Lanjigarh Alumina project in Odisha. Even after the Dongria Khond adivasis of the Niyamgiri Hills have in their gram sabhas rejected the bauxite mining proposal, the company is still bent upon mining bauxite in the Niyamgiri hills, this despite the fact that it will destroy the habitat of the Dongria Kondh tribes.[37]

Lakshmi Mittal, the chairman and CEO of ArcelorMittal, the world's largest and most globalized steel company, brought India back into his business coffer in 2005 with a memorandum of understanding (MoU) that the then Mittal Steel would set up a 12 million tonne per annum (mtpa) steel plant in the province of Jharkhand. Then again in 2006, after the merger of his company with Arcelor, he committed, in another MoU, to set up another green-field steel plant of the same capacity in Orissa, and once more, promised a six mtpa plant in Karnataka, in all, pledging 30 mtpa fresh steelmaking capacity in India. But such words-of-honor apart, Mittal's business record is not one of green-field creations but acquisitions.

The latter, underway since 1989, first involved the takeover of state-owned steel plants at rock-bottom prices, including in Eastern Europe and in countries that were formerly part of the USSR. In Romania, in order to gain membership of the European Union (EU), state-assets were sold to foreign capital, like the Sidex Steel Works that the UK's then Prime Minister Tony Blair did a lot to ensure transfer to Mittal's Ispat International, promising in a quid pro quo to, in turn, help Romania gain its much-prized EU membership, which it got on January 1, 2007. More generally, the deals were really "sweet"—the sellers retained pension and environmental liabilities and Ispat International (this Mittal family-dominated firm later acquired the family holding enterprise LNM Holdings NV and merged with International Steel

Group in 2004 to form Mittal Steel) got tax loss carry-forwards from historical losses, besides favorable government and World Bank loans to further
sweeten the leveraged buyouts. Upon accomplishing a significant "original"
accumulation of capital via such acquisitions, Mittal then took advantage of
the long structural crisis that the steel industry was going through to takeover distressed steel companies in North America and Western Europe.

Essentially, neoliberal policy worldwide, of which privatization was a vital
component, the transition to capitalism in Eastern Europe and the former
Soviet Union, and political connections in Britain,[38] from which the Mittal
international business empire was controlled, and ruthless "entrepreneurship," explains Lakshmi Mittal's metamorphosis into "The Metal King" of
the world. In the aftermath of the Great Financial Crisis, however, Lakshmi
Mittal's net worth has plummeted. In India, ArcelorMittal, despite virtually
abandoning its steel project plans, has been trying to exploit lucrative iron-
ore mining leases in the Chiria and Gua areas of Paschim Singhbhum district
of Jharkhand. There's much more at stake in the Saranda forest region of the
same district, where the armed forces of the state claim to have "flushed out"
(the official discourse) the Maoists—the counterinsurgency over here was
called "Operation Anaconda"—in order to make the area safe for the exploitation of the huge deposits of iron ore which are the object of attraction of
companies such as ArcelorMittal.[39]

BIG BUSINESS AND POLITICS-AS-BUSINESS

Basically, with the rise of a financial aristocracy, the distinction between the
political and the economic, the "public" and the "private," is increasingly
blurred. Politics has also become a form of business, and a very lucrative
one at that. Take the two major political parties, the Congress Party and the
Bharatiya Janata Party. Their declared sources of funds are not even a fraction
of their expenses, that is, if one looks at these over an electoral cycle. In the
present neoliberal era, wherever and whenever they are or have been in power,
they have helped the financial aristocracy in plundering the nation's wealth of
natural resources, aided the "big bulls" in engineering the rise of the stock and
real estate markets through various means, all to amass private fortunes.

There has been a veritable orgy of corruption and graft, influence
peddling, bribery and embezzlement, all following the deregulation and
unfurling of "economic freedom" for the moneybags from July 1991 onward.
Buying the votes of parliamentarians, purchasing the appointment of particular individuals as union ministers, shopping for the pens of senior media
persons,[40] in effect, paying for "'justice," snapping up the support of some
NGOs and social activists, not to forget "laundering" of black money, and

snapping up mines, forests, land, water, and spectrums at throwaway prices, all these maneuvers have been subject to market principles. Yet Team Anna, and a number of other decent people, still believe that the system can be reformed by Lok Pals and Lok Ayuktas, this commission and that legislation.[41] What does one do when the system is rotten to the core? Its managers produce a White Paper on black money, and the business press and TV debate it. Some may even announce a "fast unto death" if some bill to set up another investigatory authority is not passed or their demand for some special investigation team to probe their charges of corruption against ministers, including the prime minister, is not met. But, sadly, things have gone far past such devices to reform the system.

The "February Revolution [of 1848 in France] aimed directly against the finance aristocracy"; it *"complet[ed] the rule of the bourgeoisie* by allowing, besides the finance aristocracy, *all the propertied classes* to enter the orbit of political power." But is bringing the so-called "industrial bourgeoisie" back into the circuit of power the answer to the problems of the Indian people? Who are the Indian industrial bourgeoisie's most powerful constituents today? The IT and pharmaceutical "entrepreneurs"? The Azim Premjis, Shiv Nadars, Cyrus Poonawalas, N. R. Narayana Murthys, Pankaj Patels, and K. Anji Reddys? But can the IT entrepreneurs contract with the who's who of Wall Street's financial conglomerates and gain as arbitrageurs of India's cheap "human capital" without the banks, the stock exchange, the realty firms, and the SEZ developers? According to a government report of 2008, 62 percent of the total number of India's SEZs were IT/IT-enabled services SEZs. So aren't the IT and ITeS entrepreneurs beneficiaries of the process of accumulation by dispossession?

What about the pharmaceutical magnates? In the pharmaceutical industry, aren't these magnates simply arbitrageurs of India's cheap "human capital," those who grasp the *base* technologies and, occasionally, even develop the *key* technologies to bring in huge profits from the export of medicines to the Triad countries? Could these entrepreneurs have become billionaires without the stock market and the whole financial architecture of modern capitalism? Viewed from the system's own inner logic, the financial aristocracy is as necessary as the industrial bourgeoisie. So it's not merely about bringing the industrial bourgeoisie back into the orbit of political power. Characteristically, the typical Indian big business house combines trade, production, and finance, and thus has a financial, industrial and mercantile character, all rolled into one.

The infamous Radia tapes and subsequent leaks suggest that one of India's most wealthy and powerful "industrial" business houses funded its lobbyist to maneuver to get its nominee appointed as union minister for communications and information technology. And, earlier, such maneuvers as the removal of Mani Shankar Aiyar as union minister for petroleum and natural gas in January 2006 and his replacement by Murli Deora, allegedly at Washington's behest, for the latter didn't want the planned Iran–Pakistan–India gas pipeline project to materialize. Of course, in feudal times state offices were bought in quite an undisguised manner and without any loss of face. In those times, a state official using his public office for the purposes of private gratification was not unusual, indeed, this was expected of him.[42]

Nevertheless, in twenty-first-century India, the then prime minister, Manmohan Singh, didn't think that there was anything unusual going on and would have continued to accommodate A. Raja in office if it were not for court strictures. Truly, the distinction between the "political" and the "economic," the "public" and the "private" got blurred as the financial aristocracy increasingly called the shots. Business and politics have been so closely intertwined. But even as we say this, we need to acknowledge that A. Raja, the politician, seemed to be merely a willing instrument of his wealthy and powerful clients, financial aristocrats, just as Murli Deora was of his principals in Washington DC.[43]

THE ARISTO—A NEO-REALIST DEPICTION

How then may the typical financial aristocrat be pictured in neo-realist terms? There are those Indian aristos who headquarter their companies in Amsterdam, own and control them from London, globally integrate mine, manufacture, and trade in different parts of the world, including India, stash the family wealth in the Dutch Antilles, and hire the palace of Versailles for the wedding of their daughter. Grounded in global markets and accumulation on a world scale, they are at their best with a political leadership and a state bureaucracy steeped in neo-liberalism. The "commanding heights" of policy formulation—the Prime Minister's Office and the Ministry of Finance—have to be "captured." So the aristo's foundation funds academic think-tanks, "world-class" universities, and the right kind of NGOs to spread the word about "good governance" and to shape the agenda of "social activism." "[W]hat better way to parlay economic wealth into political, social and cultural capital, to turn money into power?"[44] The governing principle is market valuation. Therefore, you don't put all your political, social, and cultural eggs in one basket. The Hindutva-nationalists—the Sangh and its Parivar—no longer mouth the doctrine of Swadeshi (economic nationalism). Moreover, for the aristo, what can be worthier than restoring the grandeur of Vedic culture, bringing back that Golden Age in the present epoch of globalization?

Whether national or multinational, the Family and the Business are the two defining symbols of the Indian financial aristocrat's world. All his (it's a patriarchal and enclosed extended-family life) decisions are guided by the concrete interests of his Business and those of his Family. That which is good for them is all that ultimately matters. The aristo is gentle, good-natured, understanding, even loving when it's a matter of the enclosed family, but he is predatory otherwise. Key politicians, judges, regulators, businessmen connected to the Family and those who are dependent on his Business (they will enjoy his patronage as long as they accept subordination), police officers, media persons, stock market dealers, all basically imbued with the profit motive, are "in his pocket." He has an air of arrogance and superciliousness, he's impenetrable, impervious, his gaze cold and harsh. He will even buy up a bundle of news and current affairs TV channels if the opportunity presents itself. And he will sell a controlling stake of shares if an offer that promises immense lucre comes along. With equity capital (shares), at times, and quite often, valued on the stock market quite independently of the value of a company's assets, the aristo feeds gluttonously on "miscalculations" in the market for corporate control. His struggle is pitted against rival Families and Businesses. He is part of the tiny minority of Indians who hold tremendous wealth *and* power. His "temple to the new India" is an obscene symbol of the gross inequality that stares anyone in the face in India today. Philanthropy and corporate social responsibility are "in" if they're good for the image of the Family and the Business, and they are, for he's definitely not the drab kind of businessman operating in the realm of legality; indeed, if an Aristo has gained the upper hand, it is through his utter defiance of all codes, legal and moral.

But what of the footprints that bothered Cacus? It all depends where the aristo has been the predator. If it's in Chhattisgarh or Jharkhand where he's grabbed mining rights, or at the Ministry of Mines in New Delhi, where a minister pontificates on good governance but changes the rules of the game for a price, perhaps a minister knows better. In this setting, predators don't need to bother about such things as "footprints on the sands of time." Are we being harsh and cynical? No, this is a world where predators go unpunished; it's at the intersection of business and politics, the latter, politics-as-business. And, a lot of the lucre revolves around capital-gains opportunities.

FINANCIAL CAPITAL AND SUB-IMPERIALISM

Wealth fundamentally originates in the exploitation of labor and the appropriation of nature in the process of production, but goes through all kinds of markets to become commodities, money, stocks and bonds, and other financial instruments, and back into money, commodities, and so on, with the hindmost appropriated by the financial aristocracy and other sections of big business. In this Age of Financial Capital, with a relatively independent financial complex sitting on top of the world's real economy and its national units, and significantly influencing the structure and behavior of those real economies and the corporations therein, the latter are being driven more and more to mobilizing their cash reserves for financial speculation and entrepreneurship.[45]

In the specific setting of "accumulation by dispossession" in the "non-capitalist areas,"[46] the creation of huge capital-gains opportunities begins with the state virtually driving peasants and tribal forest dwellers out of their habitats. The state then under-prices its sales of the grabbed lands and other natural resources to big businesses, the very resources they covet for their industrial, mining, real-estate, or infrastructural projects. For mining, the state hands over lucrative leases for a pittance (that is, the extractive rents of the increasingly scarce minerals are appropriated by the mining capitalists who are required to pay mere symbolic royalties to the *rentier* state). Having gained ownership over scarce natural-resource assets, the market valuation of which turns out to be a multiple of the undervalued prices at which they were bought, massive capital-gains opportunities are almost guaranteed, and the political brokers who fix the original deals get their cut.

The capital-gains opportunities come not merely from the bonanza of actually getting the natural resources dirt cheap. There is also an element of pure speculation, for instance, betting on expectations of such bonanzas in the future, which spurs further inflation of the financial-asset values. Indeed, the whole dynamic of "accumulation by dispossession" in the "non-capitalist areas" that promises cheap natural-resource hoards on the asset side of big-business balance sheets seems to be at the root of the unbridled greed and the political violence escalating into a "war against one's own people" where the victims uncompromisingly resist their dispossession. There are also the big money-backed electoral contests for political power; the fraud; the looting; the incapacity to recognize the value of older, nature-revering cultures; and the abuse of tribal habitats and ecosystems.

All this *political* expression of the "accumulation by dispossession" is somewhat reminiscent of Rosa Luxemburg's description of it in 1912 in her magnum opus, *The Accumulation of Capital*.[47] During the late nineteenth and early twentieth centuries, following the consolidation of giant corporations and oligopolies in the last quarter of the nineteenth century, there was a relentless drive among rival imperialist powers to acquire colonies to serve, among other things, as captive markets, as new sources of raw materials and labor, and as fresh investment opportunities. An analogous expansion of big capital into some of the "non-capitalist areas" of India is underway in our times, albeit not as extensive, and much more compact, but with a similar political expression and manifestation of the inhumanity of capitalism as in Luxemburg's times.

Driven by the dynamic of "accumulation by dispossession," the Indian state and big business, Indian and multinational, have been advancing their power, their influence, and their mutual interests in the "non-capitalist areas" within the country's borders. The process has been utterly disruptive and traumatic for the victims who have been left with no other option but to resist. The most striking "event" of this kind, the largest and most brutal displacement so far in independent India, happened in Dantewada and Bijapur districts of Chhattisgarh between June 2005 and 2009. The political expression of "accumulation by dispossession" in some of the "non-capitalist areas" of the country is an integral part of Indian "sub-imperialism."[48] It is just as ruthlessly inhumane as the "imperialism"[49] Luxemburg was trying to throw light on in her times, especially when the victims uncompromisingly resist the dispossession.

6

"The Near and the Far"— India's Rotten Liberal-Political Democracy

Once again they are coming to our village—
the eagles talking like parrots,
the hordes of blood-sucking vultures.
Guard!
Guard the green shoots of your dreams,
The flowering hopes in the corridors of your eyes.

That, once more, was the Telugu poet Cherabanda Raju ("Chera"), this time, in 1971, warning the villagers when the parliamentary political parties came soliciting for votes. The "blood-sucking vultures" that seized and profited from what the laboring poor turned out, came alongside the "eagles talking like parrots" with the promise that they would "eradicate poverty." *Garibi hatao* was the catchphrase, and a very electrifying one at that. Those who were plastering the walls of Telangana towns with slogans taken from Chera's poems had only meager resources at their command, unlike the "blood-sucking vultures" who had Indira Gandhi's promise of *garibi hatao* put up everywhere.

The hundreds of millions of people unable to make ends meet were easily taken in, unguarded as they were when those professional manipulators pulled the wool over their eyes. After all, the poor wanted what Mrs. Gandhi was saying to come true. But what if Chera's poems were to have made it across all the walls of Andhra Pradesh, exposing Mrs. Gandhi's hoax, her false mask of a messiah? The power of Chera's poems brought on persecution by the state. He was arrested under the Preventive Detention Act in 1971, under the Maintenance of Internal Security Act in 1973, and was implicated in the Secunderabad Conspiracy Case in 1974.[1] His poetry was banned. What an astoundingly dishonest garb of democracy!

Fast forward to May 2014. "Numbers" seem to have had the power to "sanctify." The context is very different, but I cannot keep my mind off that quote—"numbers sanctify"—from Charlie Chaplin's *Monsieur Verdoux*. Consider that the alleged mastermind of the 2002 anti-Muslim pogrom in Gujarat was soon to be sworn in as India's prime minister, at the head of a government in which his party, the Bharatiya Janata Party (BJP), the political party promoted by the Hindutvavadi Rashtriya Swayamsevak Sangh (RSS), won a majority in the Lok Sabha, the lower house of Parliament, with the Congress Party reduced to a shadow of itself. If one were to go by the BJP's presidential-style campaign, Modi ostensibly earned his place as India's prime minister based on his "performance" in Gujarat. What a travesty of democracy and secularism!

Cutting out all the claptrap, in this national election to India's 16th Lok Sabha, the truth is that the BJP's money beat the Congress's money, and, moreover, the BJP had the numbers advantage that it derived from the religious–communal polarization it engineered. According to the *Hindustan Times* of April 13, 2014, going by the estimate of "media buyers and sources close to the BJP's campaign," the party was supposed to end up spending about Rs 50,000 million on all media—print, television, outdoor, Internet and radio—"to block out all other political parties." A former Chief Operating Officer of Rediffusion Y&R, a media buying agency, is quoted as saying that "The BJP's spending is at least four times that of the Congress." Add to the Rs 50,000 million media blitz all the other election-related expenses of the BJP, especially those on private aircraft and helicopters, and the figure would have exceeded what Barack Obama spent on his 2012 presidential campaign, according to Siddharth Varadarajan,[2] a former editor of *The Hindu*. Surely all this influenced the electoral outcome, and is, more ominously, swaying the policies of the BJP-led government in office, not to forget the adverse effects on the character and integrity of Indian democracy itself. It is wealth that won the day. What then of India's liberal-political democracy? This concern is compounded by the fact that during the election campaign Modi spoke so strongly against corruption, even as private corporations bankrolled his soliciting of votes that cost them a fortune.

Money is now the standard of all things, the measure of one's worth; the shrewd party that commands the most money does, in the main, possess the greatest power. At no other moment from the time of the transfer of power in 1947 has capitalism in India been more incompatible with democracy, that is, if the latter is understood as governance in accordance with the will of the people—especially workers, poor peasants, the oppressed nationalities, women, Dalits, and tribal communities. The reason is the much deeper nexus than ever before between the political and the economic, between power and profit, at the local, provincial, national, and global levels. The growing relative influence of the big moneybags over public affairs and policy is in proportion with the increasing concentration of income and wealth in Indian society. More important, what is deemed to be good for these moneybags is now claimed to be good for India.

The dominant classes and their political representatives—the financial aristocracy, the industrial business tycoons, the MNCs, the rich landowners, a section of the rich peasants, controllers of the government machinery in the bureaucracy and the polity, leaders of the conventional political parties—have perfected the art of disguising the outward facade as the real. Authoritarian governance is made to appear as democratic rule. How can democracy flourish in a society that is so deeply marked by profound inequalities in the distribution of income and wealth, and manifest with caste and religious–communal prejudices? It cannot, so there is the periodic charade of choosing members of the political establishment, those financed and co-opted by the dominant classes, who will then govern the country, the states, the municipalities, and the panchayats,[3] the latter, where they exist, for the next five years. More than ever before, governments today are of the markets, by the markets, and for the markets—the market that as one poet put it, knows all about prices but nothing about values. What goes in the name of democracy is the initiation of so-called consensus, obtained through the orchestration of the media to secure the advantage of one or the other of the parties that represent the interests of the dominant classes, and then via elections, legitimizing such consent.

Moreover, when big money, from private corporate and individual wealthy donors, finds its way to big parties, the Congress and the BJP, it is not just a matter of governments of the markets, by the markets, and for the markets, but the parties are likely to be rendered beholden to big money, and, depending on their clout, they may be emboldened to extract big money from corporations and wealthy individuals, and the money footprints would be difficult to trace. When Mrs. Gandhi took to the promise of "distributive justice" to winning elections, as she did in 1971, she even made political donations from corporations illegal and much of these flows had to be credited below the counter, but after she changed track in 1980, it was just a matter of time before corporate donations were legalized again, this in 1985.

Wealthy non-resident Indians (NRIs), with their "post-box companies," were the first beneficiaries of the treaty with Mauritius—the so-called Convention for Avoidance of Double Taxation and Prevention of Fiscal

Evasion—entered into in August 1982, with Pranab Mukherjee, the then union finance minister, left to manage the "manna from heaven" on behalf of Mrs. Gandhi. The above-the-counter donations of individual private corporations in the 1990s and 2000s, however, showed almost matching amounts to the big two parties, exactly as corporations playing safe would have liked to have it, only that a great deal of the money reportedly changed hands below the counter, not surprising in a business culture where so much commerce is transacted off the books. And one must keep in mind that the "bourgeois" parties wither if they are left out of power for more than five years, for it is the discretion to allocate and direct the flow of state funds that sustains them, which explains their businesslike penchant to come together in coalition governments irrespective of the content of the politics, or for individual politicians to get on to the political horse that promises the best short-term prospects.

MONEY TO THE DEFENSE OF "DEMOCRACY"

Indeed, the minority Congress Party-led coalition government headed by P. V. Narasimha Rao that is credited with launching India's "1989" during its tenure in power from 1991 to 1996 survived a no-confidence motion in Parliament on July 28, 1993, when ten Members of Parliament (MPs) belonging to the Jharkhand Mukti Morcha and the Janata Dal cast their votes to defeat the motion and ensure the survival of the government. But later it came to light that these MPs had been bribed to do so. In the words of Fali S. Nariman, a distinguished jurist and senior advocate of the Supreme Court:[4]

> The CBI [Central Bureau of Investigation] filed criminal cases against them saying they had received bribes to do so. [But] [s]ince under Article 105(2) of the Constitution of India, no Member of Parliament can be made liable to any proceedings in any court with respect to any vote given by him in Parliament, the Supreme Court dismissed all cases against them.
>
> Our founding fathers had not anticipated that 50 years down the road in parliamentary democracy there would be shameless sons selling votes for monetary gain.

They—these "founding fathers"—could have, if they had been sensitive enough to discern that in the five years since the interim government with Jawaharlal Nehru (as the vice-president of the Viceroy's Executive Council) assuming the powers of prime minister took office in September 1946, the Congress Party's membership had zoomed, mainly because it was now the new center of patronage in the country and the perquisites of office seemed irresistible. Disgusted, the party's socialist stalwarts, J. B. Kripalani, Ram Manohar Lohia, and Jayaprakash Narayan, quit between 1948 and 1950, taking their followers with them. Later when a majority Communist Party of India (CPI)-led government in the new state of Kerala tried to implement the very land reforms, via the Land Reforms Bill of 1959, that the Congress Party had advocated in its Karachi resolution of 1931, and sought to upgrade the salaries and working conditions of teachers in private educational institutions and secularize the syllabi, via the Education Bill, an anti-state-government furor was engineered and the state government was dismissed by Nehru's central government.[5] The primary objective of the Indian Constitution, of securing justice, economic, political, and social, stated in the preamble itself, seemed to have been conveniently forgotten by Nehru, who was the most prominent among those hallowed "founding-father" figures.

Earlier in the 1950s, the life insurance business was nationalized, giving the government control over a huge pool of money. But soon, in 1958, it came to light that, because of political connivance, the public-sector Life Insurance Corporation of India bought worthless shares (at above-market prices) of some financially distressed businesses of an influential stock-market speculator, Haridas Mundhra, and suffered heavy losses. Public–private bed fellowship, which had been the Company Raj's preferred mode of conducting business, thus made a comeback in the early years of the "sovereign, socialist, secular, democratic republic" of India. Towering intellectuals like P. C. Mahalanobis in the Planning Commission provided the legitimacy of expertise to all the Nehruvian tall talk of distributive justice. Later, Mrs. Gandhi, in her tenure as prime minister, went a step further in her creation of Congress 2.0, a family concern. With sycophantic politicians by her side, she called on top bureaucrats to be "committed," and showed her readiness to reward "committed" judges with promotions to top slots in the judiciary. Her son Sanjay, who took over the party's youth wing, was allowed to create a parallel substructure of power, run parts of the government as his personal fiefdom, ruthlessly ordering mass sterilization and slum demolition during the Emergency.

SANCTIMONIOUS PREACHING OF FREEDOM AND EQUALITY

Curiously, the Emergency, when the fundamental rights of citizens were suspended, has been relegated to the exception not the rule, so it might be reasonable to examine what has gone by in the name of the rule—in the Constitution and the law itself. The "founding fathers," it may be recalled, didn't become the members of the Constituent Assembly on the basis of universal adult suffrage; they came from the provincial assemblies that had been elected by a very small section of what would have been the electorate on the basis of universal adult franchise, mainly those who owned property, and with separate such electorates based on religion. And some of them were the nominees of the princes. Moreover, as Nehru's biographer Michael Brecher wrote: "One of the striking features of India's 'new' Constitution is the continuity with British–Indian practice. Approximately 250 articles [out of 395] were taken either verbatim or with minor changes in phraseology from the 1935 Government of India Act, and the basic principles remained unchanged."[6]

In 1950, the Constitution of India gave legal expression to the imagined resolution of a number of class, caste, and religious–political contradictions, to capitalist relations of production, relations of social equality and non-discrimination, and to a limited extent, secularism in matters of state, even as the cumulative social struggles and movements of the past had not, as yet, completely ushered in capitalist relations of production, social equality and the separation of religion from politics. One may recall what the practical revolutionary Damayanti tells her radical guru Jali in Leo H. Myers' novel, *The Near and the Far*, set in an imaginary 16th century India: "India has always been full of holy men preaching the religion of freedom and equality, but without producing any practical results."[7] The Indian Constitution very lucidly, in Part III, lays down what should have been inviolable, namely, the fundamental rights, and then, in Part IV, what is not enforceable in court, the Directive Principles of State Policy, which is supposed to be "fundamental in the governance of the country." Indeed, "it shall be the duty of the State to apply these principles in making laws." The Constitution derived its inspiration, Justice V. R. Krishna Iyer majestically claimed, "from the Magna Carta, the French Revolution and the American Declaration of Independence."[8]

So, some "holy men preaching the religion of freedom and equality" sought to give the Constitution of India a conscience, that is, if one considers "the confluence of Part III and Part IV,"[9] as Justice Krishna Iyer neatly put it. But where does all this stand in the company of the progeny of the East India Company—Indian big business, the Indian state, and the subsidiaries of the MNCs? In Myers' novel, when the practical revolutionary comrades Damayanti and Mohan join the struggle to bring "freedom and equality," members of their own privileged class seek their defeat. Likewise, in India today, the coming of age to political consciousness of the Dalits and the "tribes" has brought on more severe repression by the ruling caste–class combine against them. Even today, a Dalit or "tribe" knows that she/he could be beaten, raped, or killed at the whim of a middle- or upper class–caste person and virtually nothing will be done about it.[10] In addition, expression of support to the Maoist revolutionaries brings on the repressive power of the Unlawful Activities (Prevention) Act against such solidarity.

Even as the various articles guarantee the seven fundamental rights, they are followed by clauses that impose "reasonable restrictions" on them. So, even as Article 22 (1) and (2) protects the citizen against arrest and detention, Article 22 (3) (b) takes away such protection if one is arrested or detained under a preventive detention law, and this became a reality when the Nehru government enacted the Preventive Detention Act immediately after the Constitution came into force, imprisoning thousands without trial. Under this Act, people were put into prison not for violating the law, but to "prevent them from doing something which they may do and which the government does not want them to do."[11]

What followed was a series of legislative monstrosities, the Maintenance of Internal Security Act (MISA) in 1971, the National Security Act (NSA) of 1980, the Terrorist and Disruptive Activities (Prevention) Act (TADA) of 1985, the Prevention of Terrorism Act (POTA) of 2002, and then the amendments of the Unlawful Activities (Prevention) Act (UAPA) of 1967 in 2004, 2008, and 2012, all further restricting the fundamental rights to freedom of expression, association, and assembly. Frankly, all these black laws have been rooted in the colonial Criminal Law (Amendment) Act (CLA) of 1908. With the CLA, the colonial state first defined "unlawful association" in order to impose a ban on some political organizations, and Indian governments after 1947 similarly used such powers to "curb dissent caused by widespread abuses of state power and the structural inequalities that plague Indian society." Indeed, the First Amendment of the Constitution, in 1951, soon after it came into force on January 26, 1950, itself marked the beginning of the process of abridging the freedoms of expression, assembly and association, thereby attenuating and impairing liberal-political democracy.[12]

"BATTLE OF DEMOCRACY"

To understand liberal-political democracy, one first has to situate it within a larger process called democratization. The latter is a long and arduous popular struggle to check *arbitrary rule*, replace it by a just and rational order, obtain a share for the people in the very making and running of that order, and interminably continue the struggle for qualitatively more just and rational orders.[13] Thus, the oppressed people who fought for their freedom against a slave-owning oligarchy, as in the slave revolt led by Spartacus, may be said to have made a significant contribution to the process of democratization. The latter involves the question of power, first and foremost, the destruction of established systems of power, to create a just and rational order. Liberal-political democracy is one such just and rational order, which Barrington Moore, Jr., defined as a system with the following essential rules and institutions:[14]

- Universal adult franchise;
- Parliament and state legislatures that make laws and hence are more than rubber stamps of the central or state cabinets;
- Laws that, at least on paper, do not discriminate (other than to overcome historical handicaps) on account of birth or inherited status;
- Bourgeois private property rights;
- Secularism, freedom of speech, and right to peaceful assembly; and,
- Elected civilian control of the Armed Forces.

Justice must be at the heart of such an order; "we" must ensure that the implicit "social contract" is honored by those who rule and govern. The fact, however, is that, in practice, the "freedom" necessary for the development of capitalism, expressed in the form of "bourgeois private property rights," namely, the freedom to possess, accumulate, and freely buy and sell private property, overrides the political rights, such as the freedom of speech, press, association, and assembly. The latter rights, essentially collective in essence, are often, in fact, revoked in situations where the "bourgeois private property rights" seem to be threatened, especially when the process of the accumulation of capital is put in jeopardy.

Now, *political* emancipation, which liberal reformists claim to be the fruit of liberal-political democracy, implies equal citizenship and democratic decision-making, but, in practice, under capitalism, do we really have all citizens freely and equally determining the terms of their cooperation in the public realm? Frankly, the concrete realization of this idea is not even possible under capitalism with its class distinctions and exploitation of the majority. Under capitalism, a majority of the people effectively remain excluded from active participation in the political process because they are compelled to spend most of their waking hours engaging in the struggle to satisfy their vital survival needs. The people can articulate freely their needs and preferences and convert these into political demands only when they are also economically emancipated, which is only possible with the institution of egalitarian principles governing the processes of production, distribution and accumulation. But to get there, they must first win the "battle of democracy."

In the absence of such advance of the process of democratization, the Indian ruling classes—with practically the bulk of the resource base and apparatus at their command—through the mainstream political parties and the media, successfully manage to claim to represent the "general interest," even though in reality they merely express their own *particular* interests based on property, inheritance, caste status, dominant nationality, and the Brahmanical version of Hinduism. In this way, they perpetuate, albeit under the guise of democracy, the *arbitrary rule* of privilege and property that is being witnessed in India today.

Three key underlying premises are:

(i) Liberal-political democracy is not entirely the product of capitalism *per se*. It is a product of democratization. In the Chartist movement of the 1830s and 40s in Britain, ordinary people—not capitalists and their political representatives—played a major role in the coming into being of liberal-political democracy, which happened later with the institution of universal suffrage and the winning of civil liberties. Over time, capitalism entered into a marriage of convenience with democracy, but, as the example of Chile in the first half of the 1970s shows, when a government, elected in accordance with the will of the majority of the people, begins to act in accordance with that will, in this case to do away with the old order and build a new one, capitalism dissolves its marriage with democracy and overthrows that government to establish a brutal military dictatorship.[15] Capitalism becomes incompatible with democracy when the people decide that capitalism has to go.

(ii) Democracy implies government in accordance with the will of the people. But, under capitalism, the economy has an *autonomous* existence,[16] and if the results it produces, like it does in India, such as mass poverty and gross inequality, inadequate employment, wages insufficient to satisfy even one's basic needs, acute insecurity of livelihoods, and near absence of any social security, despite state intervention, become unacceptable to the majority of the people, then capitalism will become incompatible with democracy. But, although the state has never been able to resolve or satisfactorily ameliorate the contradictions that give rise to such dismal economic results, it is made out that if the ruling party cannot perform the task, the opposition, when it comes to power, will. The people are manipulated to falsely believe that the results of the economy are determined by government and all that is required is "correct" policy.

(iii) Civil liberties and democratic rights, even when they are unambiguously part of the law of the land, invariably must be wrested from authority; they are never granted without a fight.

ABSENCE OF DEMOCRACY'S NECESSARY ECONOMIC CONDITIONS

It is the very people who have to spend most of their waking hours working in order to satisfy their vital survival needs whose democratic rights are perennially violated.[17] It is, indeed, a shame, a disgrace that the government, instead of being a model employer implementing labor law, refuses to treat a large section of those who are at the forefront of delivering certain essential social services—a large proportion of whom are women—as regular workers. There are hundreds of thousands of *anganwadi* workers in the Integrated Child Development Services (ICDS) program and their assistants providing pre-school education and nutrition to children below the age of six, who were paid (in 2013) honorariums of a mere Rs 3,000 and Rs 1,500 per month (around $50 and $25 per month, at Rs 60 per $). Those workers who cook and serve the mid-day meal in the schools were paid honorariums of Rs 1,000 per month ($16 to $17 per month) in 2013. "Para" teachers in the Sarva Shiksha Abhiyan ("education for all" program), graduates with a B.Ed. degree, were paid between Rs 3,000 to Rs 5,000 per month ($50 to $83 per month) in 2013, which was roughly one-tenth of a regular teacher's salary. And even the Accredited Social Health Activists (ASHAs) of the National Rural Health Mission (NRHM) who have been helping to bring down the country's pathetic maternal mortality rate, are being paid a pittance.[18] Taken together, more than a million government service-delivery jobs have been created over the last two decades, but all these workers have been denied employee rights by the government.

What about workers employed in the private sector, including Indian big business enterprises and the MNCs? Take the case of the workers in Maruti–Suzuki's Manesar factory in Gurgaon. "Lean manufacturing" involves measures to extract the maximum effort from the workers. In July 2012, contract and temporary workers comprised more than 75 percent of the total number of workers at the Manesar factory, rendering the workers vulnerable and thereby pliable to the management's dictates. Chapter 2 ("Dehumanization of Workforce") of a recent People's Union for Democratic Rights' report entitled "Driving Force: Labour Struggles and Violation of Rights in Maruti Suzuki India Ltd" provides a vivid account of the work schedule, the intensity of work, the conditions of employment, including wages and promotion, the plight of contract workers, mechanization, supervision, and management at the Manesar factory. To resist such a highly exploitative labor regime what was required was an independent—*not* a stooge—labor union, but the management actively prevented the workers from organizing themselves, resorting to suspensions, terminations and registration of false cases, more so when such a union got registered.

What about the workers in the hundreds of auto-component supplier factories linked to the main auto-assembly plants—the first and second tier sub-contracting auto-component suppliers, along with those in the small-supplier workshops that form the third tier in the auto-components supply chain? All these workers have been organizing and fighting against "unregulated, predatory labor relations" and, indeed, the "industrial terrorism unleashed under neo-liberalism." Worst of all are the conditions of workers in the third tier of the auto production chain who are not even unionized and where

> Everybody is a temp . . . there is no appointment letter, and there is no pay slip either . . . work is for two shifts of 12 hours each and workers are paid only for eight hours a pittance . . . wages are cut against rejects apart from workers being humiliated and beaten up . . . overtime is mostly unpaid, if paid, it is single . . . there is no holiday . . . this is the bottom of the production chain.[19]

And, if this isn't enough, let's look at the garment/apparel manufacturing cluster in Kapashera on the Delhi-Gurgaon border. Organized as buyer-driven global commodity chains, "oligopsonistic" (few large buyers with significant market power) firms like Gap and Marks & Spencer—among the big names on high street—have been at the center of sweatshop scandals involving violations of Indian labor laws and their own "ethical trading initiative" at their subcontractors' factories in this area, which is home to many a garment manufacturing sweatshop. The term "sweatshop" conjures up images of the conditions under which industrial laborers toiled against their will (they had little choice) in nineteenth-century England. William Blake's "Satanic Mills" were horrifying. The workday was long, the pay was abysmally low, and the conditions of work were unhealthy and unsafe. Tragically, the existential condition of the Indian garment manufacturing workers in Kapashera and Gurgaon in twenty-first century India is not very different.

What about the call center employees, the "new, proletarianized middle class," one might ask? The January 2007 newsletter of *Gurgaon Workers News* reported about a call center—right opposite the Hero–Honda factory in the Gurgaon–Manesar–Dharuhera industrial belt—with its proletarianized middle class employees working ten-hour night shifts, earning Rs 12,000 to Rs 14,000 a month, a fraction of what their counterparts in the United States and Western Europe got. Moreover, their office work is subject to Taylorized principles, that is, a continuous "assembly line" of calls, close monitoring by sophisticated management information systems, and ruthless exploitation just like their counterparts in the motorcycle factory across the road.

BONDAGE IN A "DEMOCRACY"

Gurgaon in the state of Haryana is south of south Delhi, but if one moves west of west Delhi one gets into the district of Jhajjar in Haryana, with the districts of Rohtak and then Jind to its north, where all along the country-side one can begin to understand the reality of Scheduled Caste (SC) and other most-backward caste laborers, including those who are seasonal migrant wage laborers from eastern Uttar Pradesh and Bihar. In the context of endemic underemployment and seasonal unemployment, forms of labor attachment are still prevalent, besides, of course, the intertwining of such relations with caste oppression and dependence stemming from essential consumption-related debt, which together lay the ground for (a sort of) involuntary servitude.

It took twenty-five years after the Constitution of India came into force for the Indian Parliament to enact the Bonded Labour System (Abolition) (BLSA) Act. The British rulers had instituted the Indian Slavery Act in 1843, which outlawed many economic transactions associated with slavery, this, even before the Crown took over the rule of India from the British East India Company in 1858. When the Slavery Act was in draft form, a section of the zamindars complained in a memorandum to the colonial authority that, according to "our" Shastras, slaves were "our" inalienable property to be bought, sold, or given away as gift! How on the dot the pioneer social reformer Jotiba Phule (1827–1890) was in unmasking such a culture of oppression.

Zamindars were the backbone of the Raj, yet the British went ahead with the enactment of its anti-slavery law. In practice, however, the zamindars and other rich landowners continued to practice an amalgam of the archaic and the modern—hereditary debt servitude. Aware Indians will have heard of *Adiyar* in Kerala, *Vetti* and *Bhagela* in Telangana and Andhra Pradesh, *Harwaha* in Bihar, *Hali* in Madhya Pradesh and South Gujarat, *Padiyal* in Tamil Nadu. These are more than merely forms of debt-bonded labor, based as they are on custom and brute force, and thus immensely varied. And, there are numerous reports about the large number of bonded laborers working in brick kilns, stone quarries, and so on. Why has Article 23 (prohibition of forced labor) and the BLSA Act been allowed to go for a toss, this despite the Bandhua Mukti Morcha and Asiad cases?[20]

Many of these bonded laborers are SCs and Scheduled Tribes (STs), and the Constitution has instituted many safeguards for them. Their acute unfreedom is something Indian democracy should feel ashamed of. Despite the Protection of Civil Rights (PCR) Act of 1955 and the Scheduled Castes and Scheduled Tribes (Prevention of Atrocities) Act of 1989 (in brief, the

Atrocities Act), such atrocities are a frequent occurrence. Both the British colonialists and Indians viewed the "tribes" of central and eastern India, and Indians by and large still view them, in racist-prejudicial terms as a non-Aryan black race. This racial prejudice is something most people prefer to maintain a silence about. The Chhattisgarh and union governments have not even thought it prudent to implement the Fifth Schedule and the Provision of Panchayats (Extension to Scheduled Areas) Act (PESA), 1996, in Bastar, one of the strongholds of the Maoist movement.

DEMOCRATIZATION AND THE VIOLENCE OF THE OPPRESSED

All this emphasizes the fact that under India's underdeveloped capitalism, most people effectively remain excluded from active participation in the political process because they have to spend most of their waking hours engaging in the struggle to satisfy their vital survival needs, and even here their democratic rights are perennially violated. It is nevertheless true that the exercise of universal adult franchise and inter-party electoral competition has put progressive legislation on the official agenda. But even here one needs to give the threat of violence by the oppressed and actual resort to violence by them its due.

The Naxalbari peasant armed struggle brought the agrarian question to the center of politics in West Bengal in the late 1960s and early 1970s. Later, public memory of the upsurge of anger and despair among the poor peasantry, their hopes of justice in a new order played an indispensable part in the institution of land reform by the CPI(M)-led Left Front government to prevent the landlords from forcibly evicting their tenants and ensuring the latter a guaranteed share of the net output of the crop. And, more recently, "the passage and implementation" of the Scheduled Tribes and Other Traditional Forest Dwellers (Recognition of Forest Rights) Act, 2006 (in brief, the Forest Rights Act), which "aims to provide secure land tenure to Adivasis," is—according to the well-known civil liberties activist and social anthropologist, Nandini Sundar—"officially conceded as arising out of the need to undercut the core constituency of the Maoists."[21]

The proposition that the Maoist movement is part and parcel of the process of democratization in India and has made a significant contribution to that endeavor is, of course, sure to be challenged by the academic and political establishment. Nevertheless, contrary to the ruling ideas emanating from that establishment, one might say that the violence of the oppressed has made and can make an important contribution to justice by democratic means. Yes, India's liberal-political democracy requires the violence of the oppressed to deliver justice, especially where the SCs and STs are concerned.

DESIGNATED "BACKWARD" IN ORDER TO MOVE FORWARD

But apart from the SCs and STs, as far as the social reality of the upper "backward" and intermediate castes were concerned, the class structure had, by the latter half of the 1960s, cut across the caste hierarchy. A significant section of the upper Other Backward Classes (OBCs)—actually, castes deemed to be socially and educationally "backward"—had made it to the ranks of the upper and middle classes. An upper OBC businessman and/ or politician, for instance, a Yadav from Bihar or Uttar Pradesh, could no longer be brushed aside, and certainly not those intermediate-caste businessmen and politicians just above the OBCs—the Jats of Haryana, western UP and Rajasthan, the Marathas of Maharashtra, the Patidars of Gujarat, the Kammas and the Reddys of Andhra Pradesh, and the Lingayats and the Vokkaligas of Karnataka. More than ever before, the class structure of Indian society had ascended over the caste hierarchy, at least that part of the latter above the lower shudras and the SCs. But, at this very point in time when the class structure had begun to overshadow the caste hierarchy, the Mandal Commission[22] insisted that the *shudra* caste identity be taken as *the* criterion of backwardness in Indian society.

The Commission drew on the legacy of Ram Manohar Lohia and one of the central tenets of Indian socialist thought. Indian socialists, in sharp contrast with the first and second generation of Indian Communists, regarded the caste system as the main roadblock of the movement toward an egalitarian society, and therefore became the strongest votaries of positive discrimination in favor of the SCs and OBCs, the latter, the Shudra jatis, articulating the principle of "'preferential opportunities." Lohia's anti-caste program demanded "'sixty percent of the leadership posts in government, political parties, business and armed services, by law and by convention, to the backward castes . . .'"[23] The election of a large number of OBC MLAs, especially Yadavs, a less socially and educationally backward *jati* among the OBCs, from the latter half of the 1960s onward, owes a bit to Lohia's stand regarding caste. But their political rise principally owes to the fact that the land reforms of the 1950s and 1960s had taken a section of the tenants who had occupancy rights and came from the intermediate and backward castes of "cultivators," into the ranks of the rich landowners.

Besides the new landholding Yadavs, Kurmis, and Koeris, many of whom flocked to the socialist parties, there were the intermediate-caste Jat landholders, but their pole of political attraction was Chaudhury Charan Singh, who brought landholding Yadavs (Ahirs), Jats, Gujjars, and even Rajputs on the same platform. Indeed, Mulayam Singh Yadav, the Samajwadi Party patriarch, first became an MLA, in 1967, on the Chaudhurys' party (the

Bharatiya Kranti Dal) ticket. Be that as it may, in the circumstances of 1977 the Janata Party brought "Kisan" (farmer) and backward-caste "quota" politics on the same platform. The result, among other things, was the Mandal Commission's report, which came in only after the fall of the Janata government, but was picked up, dusted, and released only after the Janata Dal (JD) came to power in 1989. By then, the backward and intermediate caste landowners had enriched themselves twice over on the government bounty of the Green Revolution package. They had even emerged as regional power brokers negotiating deals that propped up or toppled coalition governments at the Centre.

Lumping together, on the one hand, the Lok Dals of the Chaudhurys of UP and Haryana, the former, managed by Charan Singh's son, Ajit Singh, and the latter by Devi Lal, and, on the other, the many "socialist" old-timers who had gone their own ways after the breakup of the Janata Party, the JD, with V. P. Singh, a former Congressman as its party president, was a peculiar combination. It is significant that the latter, the day after being sworn in as prime minister in December 1989, in his address to the nation, singled out Lohia and Jayaprakash Narayan to highlight what he stood for. And, despite Devi Lal, what followed was the V. P. Singh government's implementation, with Sharad Yadav to the fore, of the Mandal Commission's main recommendations, and from then on, right through the 1990s and into the new millennium, all political parties in the Hindi belt, including the BJP, were obliged to give a significant number of tickets to OBC and intermediate-caste landholders or to their nominees.

Strangely, some scholars got so carried away that they called the political rise of the backward-caste rich peasants and large landholders India's "second democratic upsurge"! In reality, this was the further advance of a section of the Yadavs and the Kurmis, or more narrowly, the elite among them. Just like Charan Singh used the kisan identity to advance the interests of the intermediate-caste rich peasants and large landholders, so Mulayam Singh Yadav and Laloo Prasad Yadav used the large OBC base to advance the interests of the elite among the Yadavs, so much so that Nitish Kumar, a powerful Kurmi politician, broke with the latter to form the Samata Party in 1994, which allied with the BJP. In all this political maneuvering, the most backward castes among the OBCs have been denied their rightful place and share at the political high table. Ram Manohar Lohia's hopes of a "second democratic upsurge" have been buried in the ground.

Looking back at this reassertion of caste just when class was overshadowing it, one is reminded of a favorite Marx quote: "The tradition of all dead generations weighs like a nightmare on the brains of the living." What were essentially class contradictions were asserting themselves in terms of caste contradictions, for there is a common genre in the two sets of relations. As the eminent sociologist Ramkrishna Mukherjee put it: The "class structure has cut across the caste hierarchy," giving rise to new "political alliances and antagonisms."[24] Indeed, in the political arena, it was the erstwhile "socialists" who were among the first on the bloc to get on to the bandwagon of "Mandalization," periodically, opportunistically shifting their political ties, metaphorically speaking, today with the ruling party, tomorrow with the main opposition party, and the day after tomorrow, trying to cobble together a Third Front.

CONSOLIDATION OF THE HINDUTVAVADI RIGHT

Such politics was turning Parliament into an "endangered institution," as Sumanta Banerjee put it.[25] But the opening of the two locks, one, the lock of the markets, the other, the lock of the Babri Masjid at Ayodhya, both by the Congress Party, unleashed havoc.[26] Indeed, in November 1989, the Congress-led Rajiv Gandhi government allowed the Hindu consecration (*shilanyas*) of a Ram temple within the precincts of the Babri Masjid, when just a month before the Sangh Parivar had provoked the Bhagalpur riots in the course of the Ram Janmabhoomi campaign to collect bricks (shilas) for the proposed Ram temple, and violent incidents were still occurring there.

The subsequent consolidation of the Hindutvavadi Right as a result of the Ram Temple movement that demolished the Babri Masjid in December 1992, followed by the January 1993 pogrom against Muslims in Mumbai, brought the BJP to the forefront of Indian politics. The party, which had just two seats in Parliament in 1984, came to power at the Centre in 1998. After consolidating its position at the Union level and taking advantage of what U.S. imperialism set in motion after 9/11, the BJP unleashed another pogrom against Muslims, this time in its stronghold, Gujarat, in February–March 2002, with its then prime-minister-in-waiting, Narendra Modi, at the helm. Massacre, mutilation, rape, and violent ousting were sanctioned by the Sangh Parivar and the governing power elite at the state level, and permitted by state, including police, officials—shocking official complicity. Such complicity was witnessed in the anti-Sikh pogrom of 1984 as well, this time sanctioned and permitted by the Congress Party, including the Congress's union home minister at the time.

Now, let alone the fact that justice for the victims of the pogroms not only has been rare, but salt has been rubbed into their wounds. Even as the Srikrishna Commission of Inquiry that investigated the causes of the Mumbai pogrom held that the Shiv Sena Pramukh Bal Thackeray "like a veteran General commanded his loyal Shiv Sainiks" to spearhead the pogrom against Muslims, when Thackeray passed away in November 2012, the Congress-led government of Maharashtra accorded him a state funeral.

How does one explain such blatant attempts at extermination of "the other" or the coming into being of such devils of established violence, such demons of rapacity, in a democracy? There are no definite answers, but Indian national-chauvinists have always identified the Brahmanical version of the Hindu religion with the nation; it was and is *the* symbol of Indian nationalism. Even Gandhi promised Ram Rajya, the mythical Golden Age of the Ayodhya-born god Ram. But it needs to be made clear that his vision of Ram Rajya had nothing in common with the utterly uncivilized, sectarian mission of a Brahmanical Hindu Rashtra. Nevertheless, it is interesting how the interweaving of reality with myth comes to significantly influence the course of history. Be that as it may, anti-democratic forces invariably wrap themselves in the national flag. For them, secularism has never meant the separation of state and religion; it doesn't even mean that the state will maintain equidistance from all religions. Muslims are considered second-class citizens; in the eyes of national-chauvinists, simply "Pakistani agents."

Are the pogroms of 1984, 1993, and 2002 signs of the gangrene setting in within the veins of liberal-political democracy in India? Did this begin in the 1980s? Rather than cutting a long story short, it may be better to go back in time to 1947—the moment of the transfer of power and the partition of the country—in order to move forward? The Raj was never overthrown, for the colonial army, the bureaucracy, which were the so-called ICS steel frame, and the police that had repressed the real fighters for India's freedom, all these venerable institutions of late colonialism remained in place. Indivar Kamtekar, a brilliant historian whose scholarly work is an original reinterpretation of the 1940s and the transfer of power, holds that "Independence" was a handing over "at one stroke" of "the entire territory and state apparatus" of the Raj "to the leaders of the Congress and the Muslim League" in a "single negotiated transaction."[27] He argues that British rule was so powerful only because of its Indian collaborators—government personnel, business luminaries, landlords and rajas (princes). And, to add insult to injury, the courageous soldiers and officers of the Indian National Army were refused admission into the ranks of what became the Indian Armed Forces. What was the fate of the 20,000 mutineers of the Royal Indian Navy (who took part in the 1946 RIN Mutiny), one might want to know? Why is it that even the left-nationalist historians don't pose such a question?

BRAHMANICAL COMMUNALISM TO HINDU RASHTRAVAD

Partition was the biggest and the severest blow to the prospect of secularism in the Indian subcontinent.[28] It was at this time that Gandhi really stood out in his frontal opposition to Brahmanical Hindu communalism, his deep concern about and revulsion against those who organized the massacres, first and foremost, those that took place in India. And this exemplary courage to stand by his principles cost him his life, for his striving to bring about Hindu–Muslim unity was anathema to those who wanted to subject Muslims to a Brahmanical Hindu Rashtra. The tragedy, however, was that Brahmanical communalism, now transformed into Hindu Rashtravad, reaped significant gains, and across the border, Muslim communalism, which had metamorphosed into Pakistani nationalism (and later, with the rise of Bengali and other nationalisms, came to be expressed in the idiom of Islamic fundamentalism) won the day. In India, the Brahmanic form of Hindu nationalism completely overshadowed its Shramanic rival.[29] The consequence—what devastation, what trauma, and the magnitude of it all? As Kamtekar would put it: "If the elation of many Congress politicians in 1947 was visible at one extreme," at the other was the exceptional trauma of the "women abducted during the partition riots, and then claimed by the governments of India and Pakistan even when their families rejected them."[30]

Nevertheless, surely there must have been persons like Salim Mirza (memorably played by Balraj Sahni) and his youngest son Sikandar (played by Farooq Shaikh) in M. S. Sathyu's 1973 movie *Garam Hawa*, one of the most poignant films ever made on the Partition, and one that deeply moved a lot of people on this or that side of the border. And, of course, such satirical short stories as *Toba Tek Singh* by Saadat Hasan Manto, with those haunting last lines: "There, behind barbed wire, was Hindustan. Here, behind barbed wire, was Pakistan. In between, on that piece of ground that had no name, lay Toba Tek Singh."[31] As the well-known historian and public intellectual, Dilip Simeon, puts it: This "madman from the Lahore asylum, tortured by the prospect of 'repatriation', who fell in the no-man's land on a freshly drawn border, his head pointing to Pakistan and his feet toward Hindustan, and who attained sanity when India went insane," remains "the most poignant symbol of nationhood."[32]

But talking of pseudo-secularism, something the BJP leader Lal Krishna Advani loves to pontificate about, when in power, the BJP *and* the Congress, vis-à-vis Muslims, seem to have been following a similar implicit policy to what the British practiced after they crushed the anti-colonial armed rebellion of 1857—that in matters of recruitment into government service (of course, at that time, the army was the largest employer), suspect all Muslims as possible "traitors."

Clearly, when one tries to make sense of the present, one needs to look at the interplay of continuity with change. As Kamtekar holds, come

"Independence," the same British-created Constituent Assembly, now with only a handful of Muslim members left in it, retained a majority of the Articles of the Government of India Act of 1935. And, to paraphrase what Perry Anderson has written in a three-part essay in the *London Review of Books*[33]: The detested Section 93 now appeared as Article 356, to be used against the duly elected communist state government of Kerala in 1959. In the Constitution, even mention of the word "federal" was kept at bay. The first-past-the-post system of elections led to a cornering of representation at the constituency level, first benefitting the Congress, and then the BJP.

SATURATED WITH BLOOD AND VIOLENCE

What, however, haunts is the question of how liberal-political democracy came to be saturated with blood and violence. Independent India has witnessed severe state repression of the oppressed nationality movements in Kashmir and parts of the Northeast,[34] aided by laws such as the Armed Forces (Special Powers) Act (AFSPA), which give the armed forces immunity from prosecution for rape, abduction, torture, and summary execution in the course of counterinsurgency. In the present phase of the national movement in Kashmir, for the period from 1989 onward, human rights groups estimate that 8,000 to 10,000 Kashmiris[35]—the state government is said to have admitted to a figure of 3,744 in the J&K legislative assembly—were subjected to enforced disappearance and subsequently killed in fake encounters. Provisions in laws like the AFSPA, the Central Reserve Police Force Act and CrPC 197 (where official sanction of prosecution is required) give legal immunity to army, paramilitary and police officers for their actions, which means that they know that they are never going to be prosecuted and so they believe they have a license to rape and kill (in fake encounters) in the discharge of their official duties.

The Kashmir question, centered on the right to national self-determination, cannot be dealt with here, but to cut a long story short, the last nail that the Indian political establishment hammered into the coffin of liberal-political democracy in Kashmir was the rigging of the 1987 state assembly elections there. The Muslim United Front would have electorally defeated the Congress Party–National Conference combine if the election had not been rigged. Many of the victims of this political fraud became the leaders of the Kashmir liberation (azaadi) movement. In the initial years, 1988–1992, the movement, led by the Jammu and Kashmir Liberation Front (JKLF), a secular organization, seemed to have unequivocally taken a stand for the independence of J&K from the occupation of India and Pakistan. But for this stand of the JKLF, it had to bear a heavy cost in terms of human lives and sustenance; Pakistan pitched its support for JKLF's rival, the Hizbul Mujahideen.

The government of India wanted an enemy that was pro-Pakistan and Muslim fundamentalist, and Pakistan, in effect, assured it that this would be the case. The JKLF's elimination was thus a matter of time. The Kashmir "problem" came to be presented to the public as having been created by Pakistan with the aid of Muslim fundamentalist forces in Kashmir. Firing upon mass processions and demonstrations; taking revenge on the local public in reprisals for militant attacks on the Indian armed forces; mass killings during "crackdowns," in which an area is cordoned off, all men are made to gather in one place, "informers" then identify the persons support-ing or participating in the movement, the identified persons are picked up and taken away, and many of them are killed—this is how the Armed Forces have been dealing with the movement for azaadi, backed by laws such as the AFSPA and the J&K Public Safety Act.[36]

In February 2013, the former union home minister, then the union finance minister, P. Chidambaram, delivering the K. Subrahmanyam Memorial Lecture in New Delhi, is reported to have said:[37] "[I]f the Army takes a very strong stand against any dilution or any amendment to AFSPA, it is difficult for a civil government to move forward." Does this suggest that in India's liberal-political democratic setup, civilian control of the armed forces is weak? The executive of the Indian state can't discipline the army, as is evident from Chidambaram's statement, but what is more significant for our purpose over here is that no Member of Parliament has yet considered the issue important enough to be raised in Parliament.

Frankly, there is a consensus among all elected politicians in govern-ment and in the opposition as regards the privilege of immunity given to the armed forces. Indeed, there is an eerie silence in the rest of the country when it comes to the question of safeguarding the democratic rights of the people of Kashmir. As for the commercial media, its hailing of the "patrio-tism" of "our" army in Kashmir has masked genocide. Given New Delhi's use of military force in the Kashmir Valley over the last (almost) three decades, Kashmiri Azaadi is, indeed, a cry from the heart of the Kashmiri people for freedom from Indian oppression. The threat of, and resort to, state violence is intended to smother aspirations of sovereignty and force this oppressed nationality movement to accept forms of severely circumscribed autonomy.

To put the above in perspective, when it comes to safeguarding Brahmanical Hindu Rashtravad (Hindutvavadi nationalism), the Indian ruling classes and their political representatives don't seem to care a damn for liberal-political democratic niceties. Indeed, it is the tyranny of the Indian state and the rottenness of India's liberal-political democracy that have brought into existence the fighters for *azaadi* and the terrorists among them in Kashmir and parts of the Northeast, saturated as these areas have been over considerable periods of time in the post-independence period with blood and violence. So too has the Indian state's profound unwillingness to bring justice to the victims of the anti-Muslim pogroms been the mainspring of the coming into existence of terror in the name of the defense of Islam.

DEMOCRACY UNDONE

This leads to the conclusion that, without mincing words, India's liberal-political democracy is rotten. A core symptom of Indian liberal-political democracy's rottenness is the regime's constant violation of the conscience of the Constitution, "the confluence of Part III and Part IV" that was supposed to give it a sense of what is right and wrong. India's caste-ridden, Brahmanical-Hindu communalist, underdeveloped capitalism can only produce and reproduce a liberal-political democracy that is rotten. Justice remains a far cry. The main reason why India's liberal-political democracy is rotten is because the process of capitalist development from colonial times to the present has essentially been a *conservative modernization from above*. Moreover, the caste system and discrimination on the basis of ethnicity, nationality, and religion inhibit any stable, long-lasting unity of the oppressed and the exploited aimed at *progressive modernization from below*.

A question however remains: If India's liberal-political democracy is rotten to the core, what accounts for its stability? For one, the financial aristocracy, the other Indian big business luminaries, the MNCs, and the rich landowners—the dominant coalition—have the rich peasantry and sections of the middle class, especially the senior bureaucracy, entrepreneurs, professionals and private sector managers, under their ideological hegemony. The competitive electoral process ensures that the main political parties continue to seek to establish their authority over the working class, the middle and poor peasantry, and the large rural and urban marginalized sections of the population through a mixture of representation, co-option, and manipulation, including divide and rule along caste, ethnic, nationality and/or religious-communal lines, along with the waging of psychological wars to capture the minds of the oppressed and the exploited. In the last decade and a half, the political parties at the helm of the "political shell" of Indian capitalism have changed hands—from the BJP-led NDA to the Congress-led UPA with the support of the parliamentary left, and then from the Congress-led UPA, in its second innings, sans the parliamentary left, to a BJP-led NDA once again. But this shuffling of the parties in power has made little difference as far as advancing the process of democratization is concerned.

Barrington Moore's essential defining rules and institutions notwith-standing, the essence of India's bourgeois liberal-political democracy in practice has little to do with "freedom" in general, or even civil liberties and democratic rights, or secularism for that matter. It is free competition among two or more political parties for votes and political office, the counterpart of free competition for profits in capitalism's economic sphere. And, as in the economic sphere where the reality is one of oligopoly, market power, and restrictive trade practices, so also in the political sphere, the party that commands the most money and naked power is most likely to be voted into political office. It may be better to refrain from over-idealizing bourgeois liberal-political democracy.

What then of the crying need for economic emancipation as a necessary condition for political emancipation? In a world in which India's elite, like its counterparts elsewhere, has embraced the cynical view that all culture, ideas, and expressions are no more than mere commodities in the capitalist marketplace, the idea that economic emancipation is a necessary condi-tion for political emancipation has been diminished and devalued to the status of just another commodity in the marketplace of ideas. This brings me back to what the revolutionary Damayanti tells her radical guru Jali in Leo H. Myers' novel, *The Near and the Far*, about India's many holy men "preaching the religion of freedom and equality, but without producing any practical results." And when Damayanti and her comrade Mohan—in the political setting of our times, the late revolutionary Anuradha Ghandy and her comrade and husband Kobad Ghandy, left to wither away in prison as an under-trial—actually joined the struggle to bring "freedom and equal-ity" (and comradeship, the basic principles of democracy), members of their own privileged class sought their defeat, this in the name of *ahimsa* (non-violence) and *loktantra* (democracy).

--- 7 ---

Maoist! "Spring Thunder," Phase III

> ... humanity has the means to eliminate its age-old division into exploiter and exploited, but it seems as far as ever from achieving the elusive goal ... In the underdeveloped countries, ... the absolute need for revolutionary change is growing ... and movements giving practical expression to this need are taking shape ... But free development according to their inner logic is precisely what is being denied to these revolutionary movements. The barriers of course are being erected and continuously strengthened by the entrenched and enormously powerful classes ...
>
> —PAUL M. SWEEZY[1]

India's new financial aristocracy, callous, heavy-handed, insisting on operating on its own terms, has rendered an already rotten liberal-political democracy more degenerate, with a precipitous decline in standards. It wants to make as much monopoly profit as possible, grow as rapidly as possible, both with no hindrance from society and the state. By the early years of the twenty-first century, the capitalist tenet "grab what you can for yourself" gripped India's political and business elite like never before, and the accumulation of wealth by any and all available means became the norm. With the opening of the mining sector and infrastructural development on very lucrative terms to Indian big business and the MNCs, private corporations signed umpteen memoranda of understanding (MoU) with state governments and got hold of enclaves for development as special economic zones (SEZs). But both the MoU signatories, the state governments and the corporations, were apprehensive, because, in many cases, the project areas happened to be either where the Maoist movement was active or where it was taking root.

Map 3: Political Geography: "Spring Thunder," Phase III (2004–2013)

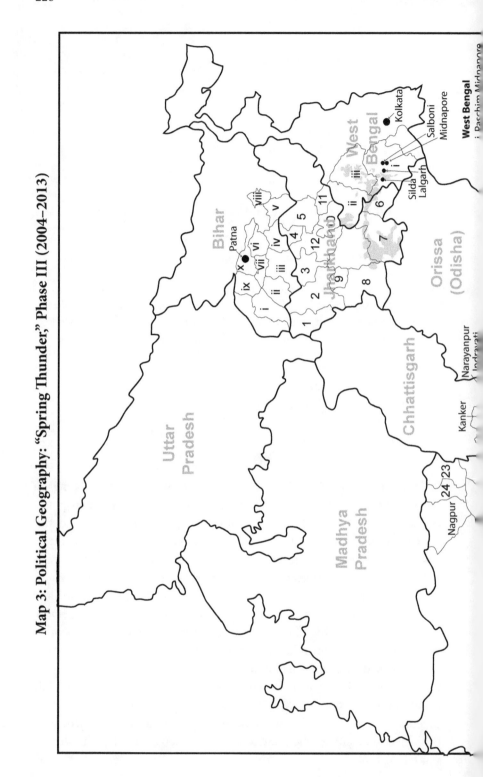

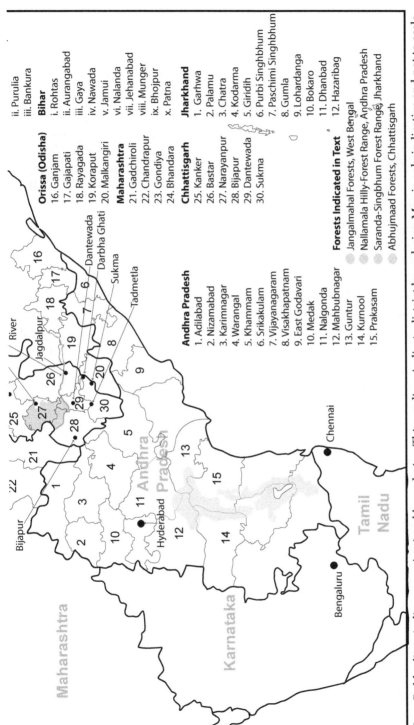

Andhra Pradesh
1. Adilabad
2. Nizamabad
3. Karimnagar
4. Warangal
5. Khammam
6. Srikakulam
7. Vijayanagaram
8. Visakhapatnam
9. East Godavari
10. Medak
11. Nalgonda
12. Mahbubnagar
13. Guntur
14. Kurnool
15. Prakasam

Orissa (Odisha)
16. Ganjam
17. Gajapati
18. Rayagada
19. Koraput
20. Malkangiri

Maharashtra
21. Gadchiroli
22. Chandrapur
23. Gondiya
24. Bhandara

Chhattisgarh
25. Kanker
26. Bastar
27. Narayanpur
28. Bijapur
29. Dantewada
30. Sukma

ii. Purulia
iii. Bankura

Bihar
i. Rohtas
ii. Aurangabad
iii. Gaya
iv. Nawada
v. Jamui
vi. Nalanda
vii. Jehanabad
viii. Munger
ix. Bhojpur
x. Patna

Jharkhand
1. Garhwa
2. Palamu
3. Chatra
4. Kodarma
5. Giridih
6. Purbi Singhbhum
7. Paschimi Singhbhum
8. Gumla
9. Lohardanga
10. Bokaro
11. Dhanbad
12. Hazaribag

Forests Indicated in Text
Jangalmahal Forests, West Bengal
Nallamala Hilly-Forest Range, Andhra Pradesh
Saranda-Singbhum Forest Range, Jharkhand
Abhujmaad Forests, Chhattisgarh

Note: Bolder lines indicate state/national boundaries. Thinner lines indicate district boundaries. Map is only indicative and not to scale.

Source: Map adapted from www.d-maps.com using information in Census of India.

"ACCUMULATION BY DISPOSSESSION"—ANDHRA PRADESH
SHOWS THE WAY

Among the state governments, the one in Andhra Pradesh, then headed by
Chandrababu Naidu of the Telugu Desam Party (TDP), had, with the backing of the World Bank, become a showcase of the way to embark upon the
neoliberal path of capitalist development. The Congress government headed
by Y. S. Rajashekara Reddy (YSR) that followed went a step further. Over the
years, the channeling of the agrarian surplus of the coastal districts into real
estate, the production, distribution, and exhibition of cinema, finance, the
alcoholic beverages business, the mafia, and transport had brought to the
fore a new class structure of the provincial ruling classes. The mafia entered
real estate and the politicos quickly followed.

Compulsory land acquisition through the plea of "public purpose"
and the principle of "eminent domain," both under the Land Acquisition
Act (LAA) of 1894 (as amended in 1984), and the notion that the state is
the trustee on behalf of the people of all natural resources, were used, nay
abused, by the state with a vengeance. Indeed, in the case of the Polavaram
dam project on the Godavari River, which was to adversely affect 150,000
persons in the Scheduled Areas,[2] more than half of them Adivasis, the government didn't even bother to consult, let alone seek the consent of, the
Mandal Praja Parishads, the panchayats, as required under the Provisions
of the Panchayats (Extension to Scheduled Areas) Act, 1996 (PESA), this
despite considerable opposition from the victims. Indeed, in East Godavari
district, the government began purchasing lands to resettle the displaced,
land that had been illegally occupied by influential non-tribal persons in
violation of Regulation 1 of 1970. The government was thus rewarding those
who had usurped tribal lands. But much of the displacement was going to
be in Khammam district where the government could not replicate such
stratagems, and it was here that considerable tribal unrest and agitation was
in store.[3]

There were also the SEZ projects, especially the multi-product ones, for
which the developers were demanding nothing less than 10,000 acres for a
single project, entailing massive displacement of people. And, these developers wanted the lands

> as close as possible to a four-lane highway, electrified railway line,
> shipping harbour, airport and a metropolitan city if possible. . . .
> [O]nce industry comes up, the land surrounding it will appreci-
> ate considerably in value, and can be the nucleus of a profitable real
> estate business that has nothing to do with the stated purpose of the

land grant. If the area is close enough to a metropolis, it may well turn out to be in fact the actual and not the subsidiary purpose of the whole affair.[4]

This was not all. Apart from the land grabs for the SEZs and the Polavaram project, there was a huge bauxite mining deal in the making. High-grade bauxite is found in a vast area stretching from the districts of Rayagada, Kalahandi, and Koraput in southern Orissa to Visakhapatnam district in northern Andhra Pradesh. But these are Scheduled Areas, and the grant of mining leases to private corporations has been prohibited, this following the Supreme Court's 1997 ruling in *Samatha vs. State of Andhra Pradesh*.[5] Moreover, the resistance of the Adivasis to Utkal Alumina International's project in Kashipur block in Rayagada district was remarkable, and the government of Andhra Pradesh was apprehensive of a repeat of such uncompromising opposition in the Visakhapatnam Scheduled Area. Of course, it then planned that a public enterprise, the Andhra Pradesh Mineral Development Corporation, would take on the job of mining the ore and selling it to a private corporation, thereby subverting the Supreme Court's *Samatha* ruling. But the resident Adivasis were going to be displaced and the water source serving the valley all around was going to be severely polluted, and the authorities were apprehending considerable tribal unrest and agitation.[6]

Essentially, a big-business bonanza was in the making in Andhra Pradesh, but what big business and the government were paranoid about was: what if the Maoists organized the victims of the "accumulation by dispossession" in the "non-capitalist areas"?[7] The Congress Party had dislodged the incumbent Chandrababu Naidu-led TDP government to come back to power in Andhra Pradesh in 2004, and even at the Centre, the BJP-led alliance, which claimed that it had made India "shine," was voted out of power. The new chief minister of Andhra Pradesh, YSR, had called Chandrababu Naidu a stooge of the World Bank when he was in the opposition, but now he began to steal a march over his political rival in an even more relentless promotion of neoliberal capitalist development. The Maoists had, however, identified "surplus lands" (lands above the legally specified ceiling) all over the State and were demanding their takeover by the state government for redistribution among the poor and landless peasantry. More importantly, they even pinpointed surplus lands on the outskirts of the state capital, Hyderabad, held by certain individuals and enterprises, waiting to be turned into expensive real estate. Clearly, they were the big spoke in the wheel, holding up the process of "accumulation by dispossession" in the "non-capitalist areas" of Andhra Pradesh.

HUNTING DOWN THE ANDHRA MAOIST LEADERS

YSR, however, had to keep an election promise to initiate peace talks with the Maoists. But did he intend to stop the cold-blooded murder of Maoists? The ban on the Communist Party of India (Marxist-Leninist) (People's War) [CPI(ML)(PW)]—it was soon to become the CPI(Maoist) in September 2004 after merger with the Maoist Communist Centre—and its mass organizations, in force since 1992, was lifted, and the Party responded by ceasing its attacks on the "instruments and partisans of the establishment."[8] The Party could now (for a while) propagate its politics openly. But were the police going to stop torturing the kith and kin of Maoists to reveal their whereabouts? Was it going to refrain from viewing the provision of food and/or shelter to the Maoists as a crime? Were the police officers going to stop viewing any radical social-political activism by the mass organizations as Maoist inspired? Not able to catch the Maoists, would the police now stop picking up and killing members of the mass organizations as surrogates of those in the underground? Were the police going to desist from killing Maoists taken into custody? Or stop infiltrating the political structure of the Party? And, importantly, would there be a resolution on the thousands of acres lying fallow in north Telangana, land that had been seized by the CPI(ML)(PW)'s Rythu Coolie Sangham (peasants and laborers association) but were not being allowed by the state to be cultivated by the poor peasants and landless laborers to whom these acres were allotted by that organization?

The Maoists seemed to have trusted the state more than what the past practice of the Andhra Pradesh Special Intelligence Bureau (APSIB) and the Greyhounds warranted. The talks, however, made no headway, and, in the meantime, YSR revealed his cards; the police then resumed their nasty acts. On January 8, 2005, Lakshmi, an executive committee member of the Andhra Pradesh Chaitanya Mahila Samakhya—the women's mass front (women have always been in the forefront of radical left movements, right from the time of Telangana in the 1940s)—was picked up, brutally tortured, and killed. But the most ruthless repression that the Maoist movement in Andhra Pradesh would ever witness began after the Maoists assassinated Narsi Reddy, a Congress Party member of the Legislative Assembly on August 15, 2005. The police then let loose organized private gangs—called Narsa Cobras, Kakatiya Cobras, Nallamala Cobras, more venomous than the real reptile—to decimate the mass organizations and deprive the Party of its mass base.

The main target of this counterinsurgency operation was, however, the Party leadership, which was sought to be physically eliminated. Thus began a hunt that was to witness the killing, in cold blood, of many of the leaders of

the Andhra Pradesh unit of the Party, among the most outstanding the Party
had nurtured and developed over the years. The following is an incomplete
list of the Telugu Maoist leaders "hunted" down:

- Settiraju Papaiah, alias Somanna, a member of the Special Zonal
  Committee of north Telangana, was allegedly abducted by the APSIB in
  Bangalore on June 29, 2006, brutally tortured, killed on July 1, his body
  thrown in the forests of Warangal.
- Burra Chinnayya, alias Madhav, state secretary of the Party, and seven
  of his comrades were killed on July 23, 2006, when the Greyhounds
  and a special police force of a battalion size attacked the headquarters
  of the State Committee in the Nallamala forests. The attackers had pre-
  cise information; it is said that they even knew the exact tent in which
  Madhav was an occupant.
- Raghavulu—a member of the State Committee of the Party, who came
  from a poor peasant family and grew up as a cattle-herd boy—and eight
  of his comrades were killed on November 8, 2006, in a forest area in
  Cuddapah district.
- Chandramouli, a Central Committee member of the Party and a
  member of its Central Military Commission, and his wife Karuna, a
  barefoot doctor, were cold-bloodedly murdered in the Eastern Ghats on
  the Andhra-Orissa border on December 29, 2006, when they were on
  their way to the Party Congress.
- Patel Sudhakar Reddy, alias Suryam, Vikas, a Central Committee
  member, and his comrade, Venkatayya were picked up in Nashik (in
  Maharashtra) on May 23, 2007, airlifted to Warangal, brutally tortured,
  murdered the next day, their bodies thrown in the Lavvala forests.

In an interview published in July 2007, the Party General Secretary,
Muppalla Laxman Rao, more popularly known as Ganapathy, admitted that
in Andhra Pradesh, "the enemy has the upper-hand from the tactical point
of view."[9] The Party fought back, as was evident from the stunning attack
on two platoons of the Greyhounds by a company of its People's Liberation
Guerrilla Army (PLGA) on June 28, 2008, in the Sileru River on the Andhra-
Orissa border. But practically, an important section of the top leadership
of the Party in Andhra Pradesh was brutally eliminated. What lies behind
this severe setback suffered by the Party? One hypothesis, based mainly on
the police tracing of the Party leaders mentioned above, is that the APSIB
seemed to have penetrated/infiltrated into the Party's political structure.

Surely the votaries and beneficiaries of "accumulation by dispossession"
in the "non-capitalist areas" of Andhra Pradesh must have heaved a sigh of

relief. For the victims, however, the damned of the earth in Andhra Pradesh, especially the Adivasis, displaced and driven away by the SEZs, the many infrastructure projects, the Polavaram dam in the making, and bauxite mining, they were deprived of what would have been uncompromising leadership in their resistance to the "development of underdevelopment" that such ventures have invariably inflicted on them.

The main political expression of "accumulation by dispossession" in the "non-capitalist areas" has been political violence, which has escalated into a war of the state against its own people when and where the victims have uncompromisingly resisted the process. Besides such political violence, there has also been fraud, looting, an incapacity to recognize the value of older, nature-revering cultures, and abuse of tribal habitats and ecosystems. All this aggression that enables "accumulation by dispossession" in the "non-capitalist areas" is an integral part of Indian sub-imperialism.[10] What follows is an account of this sub-imperialist aggression of the state and uncompromising Maoist resistance to it.

MAOIST RESILIENCE IN BASTAR

The Maoists suffered a severe setback in Andhra Pradesh, but they had already earlier created, what in guerrilla parlance is called, a rear, in Dandakaranya, the forest areas situated in the border and adjoining tribal districts across the northern and northeastern Andhra Pradesh border, in the states of Maharashtra, Madhya Pradesh (later divided into two states, Madhya Pradesh and Chhattisgarh) and Orissa. The old Bastar district of the then state of Madhya Pradesh had emerged as one of their most formidable strongholds. Consequently, the central paramilitary forces had become a permanent feature of the landscape of the old Bastar district, which in November 2000 became part of the new state of Chhattisgarh.

Bastar, as it was then known, has since been divided into six administrative districts—Sukma, Bijapur, Dantewada, Bastar, Narayanpur and Kanker. (See map pp. 226–27) The CPI(ML)(PW) had, early on, envisaged the creation of a guerrilla zone in the old Bastar district. The Dandakaranya Adivasi Kisan Mazdoor Sanghatan (DAKMS), the Dandakaranya Krantikari Adivasi Mahila Sangh (DKAMS), and the guerrillas had challenged the status quo there—rich Adivasi landholders and village headmen, and the non-Adivasis who had grabbed Adivasi land and, over time, become rich landholders, even as they retained their earlier identities as traders and contractors. The Maoists had also organized the ordinary tribal people to resist the oppressions of forest, revenue, and police officials. Over time, thousands of acres of forest land and rich landholders' patta land (land with a title deed) were seized and distributed among the poor and landless peasants in those areas of the old Bastar where Maoist writ could be enforced.

With the security forces coming in to defend the status quo that the Maoists had challenged, vast tracts of Bastar turned into a guerrilla zone. A section in the zone, on the northern side of the Indrāvati River in Narayanpur district—Abujmaad (Maad, in brief)—turned into a guerrilla base for the People's Guerrilla Army. Thus, on the one hand, there was a tribal peasant movement led by the DAKMS and the DKAMS that had a guerrilla army (the PGA) and a political party to back it, which ensured the tribal people's rights over the forests and tracts of agricultural land. On the other hand, there were the Adivasi and non-Adivasi rich landholders, the former village headmen, traders, contractors, and state officials, backed to the hilt by the central paramilitary and provincial armed police and the mainstream political parties, the Congress, and the BJP. Into this economic and political scenario came Indian big business and the MNCs. "Grab-what-you-can-for-yourself" capitalist development was rearing to take off.

The dynamic of "accumulation by dispossession" had intensified the corporate land grab in the old Bastar region and some of the other districts of Chhattisgarh. Tata Steel, planning to set up a five million tonnes per annum steel plant in Lohandiguda (Bastar district), and Essar Steel, a 3.2 million tonnes per annum plant in Dantewada, allegedly tried to rig gram sabha (village council) consent in Lohandiguda and Durli (in Dantewada district) blocks. The Swiss MNC, Holcim, and its French counterpart, Lafarge, were eyeing the huge limestone deposits in Bastar, Rajnandgaon, and other districts of the state. Hindalco was waiting in the wings to get hold of bauxite deposits in Jashpur, Kanker, Bastar (the new district), and other districts. A. Jindal company was awaiting a lease on coal deposits in Sarguja and other districts of northern Chhattisgarh. The Australian mining corporation, Broken Hill Properties was on the lookout for a lucrative business offer that might come its way, and Caterpillar was waiting in the wings to sell mining equipment.[11] Unfortunately though, for Indian big business and the MNCs, the Maoists happened to be here.

The legacy of Gunda Dhur, the inspirational Adivasi hero who had fought against British colonialism, is evoked for inspiration by the Maoists. In the local public imagination, there's still something mysterious about Gunda Dhur, the leader of the Bhumkal Rebellion of 1910. The memory of this revolt is particularly important for the Gondi Maoists, because the adverse impact of colonial land and forest administration policies on the tribal peasantry of Bastar was its proximate cause.[12] The zamindars and tribal headmen had then mostly collaborated with the British colonialists,

for they had gained from the land revenue system that the latter had instituted. And, the transfer of power in 1947 brought almost nothing in terms of
recompense for the Gondi peasants. Moreover, the electoral opportunism of
the mainstream political parties is felt by the Gonds even today; these children of the Indrāvati do not seem to trust the present set of political fixers
anyway, whether of the Congress Party or of the BJP.

STATE-BACKED, STATE-ARMED PRIVATE VIGILANTE FORCE

In 2003–04, the then Union Home Minister, the BJP's L. K. Advani, assured
support to so-called "people's resistance groups" to wean away the villagers from the Maoists.[13] The following year, 2004–05, grants were disbursed
to "Nagarik Suraksha Samitis" (citizen defense outfits) and the like for
"security-related expenditure," and to the state police for honorariums for
"Special Police Officers" (SPOs).[14] The central government and its provincial counterpart in Chhattisgarh were thus able to create the wherewithal
for the launch of Salwa Judum (meaning "purification hunt," in Gondi)—a
state-backed, armed private vigilante force to cut off the villagers from the
Maoists —in June 2005. At the provincial level though, the capitalist tenet
grab-what-you-can-for-yourself also influenced the outcome. In Jason
Miklian's account of the role of Salwa Judum in the counterinsurgency:[15]

> . . . Salwa Judum leaders function as *local warlords* [my emphasis],
> demarcating Dantewara assets and territory among themselves. They
> built their strength by redirecting funding provided by the state gov-
> ernment for IDP [internally displaced person] camps into personal
> coffers and by funding personal armies with the *money received from
> mining companies who contract them for protection and 'ground-clear-
> ing' services* [my emphasis].
> . . . Salwa Judum is in many ways a complete success, operating
> exactly as its founders intended as *a land and power grab masquerad-
> ing as a local uprising* [my emphasis].

Disease metaphors have been having a field day. Maoism is purportedly
a "contagion," an "infection," a "contamination," and a "deadly virus" in the
"discourse of counterinsurgency."

But the close bond between the Maoists and the tribal people in Bastar
has been cemented and nurtured since the 1980s. And 2010 marked the cen-
tenary year of the Bhumkal Rebellion. "Accumulation by dispossession" was
leading to a loss of traditional livelihoods, and to displacement and ecological degradation, and the tribal people were looking to the Maoists (indeed,

they too were the Maoists here) to stand by them in the defense of their villages, their rights to *jal–jangal–zameen* (water-forests-land), their ancestral property, and the provision of a modicum of security in their lives.

Iron ore from the Bailadila mines is exported to Japan cheaply compared to the price that the sponge iron manufacturers of Chhattisgarh pay for a lower-quality grade of ore. Essar Steel's pipeline, 267 kms long, carrying beneficiated iron ore in the form of a slurry all the way from Bailadila through the states of Chhattisgarh, Orissa, and then Andhra Pradesh to the port at Visakhapatnam (Vizag) makes it cheaper, but at a further cost to the Gonds in terms of the scarcity of water and a significant drop in the ground water level. The tribal people are being deprived of the land under their feet, their ancestral land; the minerals in the ground below are being taken away; and the forests with which they enjoy a symbiotic relation are being cut down. In such circumstances, "to rebel is justified."

The Salwa Judum operation, a huge land grab, initially scripted by Tata Steel and Essar Steel, had a devastating impact on the Gondi peasants.[16] In Dantewada, Bastar, and Bijapur districts in Chhattisgarh, in the context of large-scale acquisition of land by corporations in what is a mineral-rich region, entire villages were evacuated and villagers forcibly herded into camps, from which those who escaped were branded Maoists and hunted down. In the face of such devastation, where was the Maoist resistance? Frankly, from June 2005 for about eight months, the Maoists and the PLGA, including its militias at the village-level, couldn't prevent the killings of hundreds of ordinary Gondi peasants, the razing of hundreds of villages, the forcible herding of people into camps, and the sexual atrocities against women. Vast stretches of cultivable land lay fallow; collection of minor forest produce was totally disrupted; people didn't have access to the weekly *haats* (local markets); the schools had been turned into police camps. A complete trampling upon the rights of people and a total rupture of the social-cultural fabric of life were a stark reminder of rule under an occupation army. But, the Maoist guerrilla base in Maad remained intact.

It was only after eight months that the Maoists raised a Bhumkal militia, which then led the resistance at the local level and protected the people as they resumed agricultural cultivation and collection of minor forest produce. Mass rallies were organized under such banners as the All-India Adivasi Manch, the Bastar Sambhag Kisan Sangharsh Samiti, Jameen Bachao Sangharsh Samiti, and so on. Concurrently, with the reorganization of the people's militia and other wings of the PLGA, a "tactical counteroffensive campaign" got underway.

On July 16, 2006, the PLGA attacked the Salwa Judum–Special Police Officer-organized, security forces-protected Errabore camp in Dantewada to free the detainees there. On March 15, 2007, the PLGA attacked a police camp that had been set up in a girls' school in Ranibodli (in Bijapur police district) killing sixty-eight policemen, a significant proportion of them SPOs, and looted weapons, making sure that all the school girls in the hostel were safe. It is significant that after most of such attacks the Party appealed to the SPOs—who were locally recruited tribal youth—to quit their jobs and seek the people's pardon. In one such statement issued after the Ranibodli raid, Gudsa Usendi, the Dandakaranya Party spokesperson, appeals to the good sense of these desperadoes:

> . . .the government is playing a dirty and dangerous game of keeping you in the front and making you kill your own brothers and sisters, mothers and fathers. That's why we are asking you to quit this job.

Clearly, given the backing of the Party and the PLGA, the tribal masses could not be terrified into submission. But the Salwa Judum–SPO operation went on. On January 8, 2009, in the village of Singaram (Dantewada district), the Salwa Judum–SPOs displayed a level of savagery, indeed, barbarity, that was shocking. They took their hostages to a canal and butchered them, taking turns in raping the women before slaughtering them. But repression breeds resistance, and severe repression only hardens it.

OPERATION GREEN HUNT

> I've seen all this . . . , the rapes and beatings, jungles being combed by the police. We realized there's no way out but to fight, to take up a gun, and fight.
> —A YOUNG WOMAN GUERRILLA, SPEAKING OF
> PRIVATE VIGILANTE AND STATE REPRESSION[17]

In September 2009, the Union Home Ministry, with the joint command that it had organized to coordinate the counterinsurgency operations of the central security forces with the police forces of the seven affected states— Andhra Pradesh, Chhattisgarh, Jharkhand, Bihar, Orissa, Maharashtra, and West Bengal—where the Maoist movement was spreading, launched Operation Green Hunt (OGH). Significantly, Dantewada, the epicenter of what the Indian state calls "left-wing extremism," was where OGH began, in the Kishtaram-Gollapalli area. As expected, the Maoists responded with an intensification of their "tactical counteroffensive campaign."

On April 6, 2010, PLGA guerrillas the size of a small battalion ambushed troops of the Central Reserve Police Force (CRPF), including members of COBRA (Commando Battalion for Resolute Action), modeled on the lines of the Andhra Pradesh Greyhounds, between Tadimetla and Mukaram villages in Dantewada district, killing seventy-six of the state troops. In the statement issued after the attack, in a section entitled "why this counter-attack was carried out" the Party mentions, among other things, the barbaric acts of the state forces, the Singaram incident (the state atrocity mentioned above), in particular. The press release goes on to say:

> . . . Behind the April 6 attack on the CRPF in Tadimetla lays the anguish, sorrow, insults, exploitation and repression suffered by thousands of Adivasis of Bastar. This is incomprehensible to those hypocrites and empty phrase-mongers who repeat endlessly that Naxalites should give up violence.

There's a lot more detail that can be added, but suffice it to say that OGH was stepped up from January 2013. In a major incident in Edsametta village on the night of May 17, 2013, in Bijapur district, personnel of the COBRA fired unilaterally and indiscriminately, killing eight ordinary Adivasis, including four minors, none of whom were Maoists. This deliberate targeting of the support base of the Maoists is part and parcel of the state's counterinsurgency policy. It occurs so often, for instance, what the villagers of Sarkeguda, Kothaguda, and Rajpenta (in Bijapur district in southern Chhattisgarh) suffered on June 28, 2012, when 19 of them were gunned down, even when there was no exchange of fire. It is as if whoever supports the Maoists deserves to be killed, for according to state intelligence, these were among the villages that backed the Maoists.

Clearly, the supreme leader of Salwa Judum, Mahendra Karma, had to be confronted, and this is exactly what the Maoists undertook.[18] A daring ambush of an armed convoy of provincial Congress Party leaders by Maoist guerrillas on May 25, 2013, in the Darba Ghati valley in the Sukma area, 345 kms south of the state capital of Raipur, shocked the Indian state apparatus. The Z-plus and other categories of armed security personnel—entitlements of the "lords" of India's political establishment—were no match for the guerrillas. The main targets of the attack were Mahendra Karma, founder of the Salwa Judum, and Nand Kumar Patel, the chief of the Congress Party in the state and a former state home minister.

The convoy was returning from a "Parivartan Yatra" ("March for Change") rally in Sukma, and the Maoists knew not only that Karma and Patel were in the convoy, but even the route that it was to take. The assassinations were thus carefully planned and executed, though they took a two-hour-long gun battle with the state forces to accomplish, a clash in which many who merely serve or protect the oppressors, and do so because they have little choice, were either killed or injured. The Maoist guerrillas reportedly even provided first aid to some of these persons who suffered injuries.

RIGHTEOUS INDIGNATION AGAINST MAOIST VIOLENCE

Inevitably, in the aftermath of the incident, a chorus of righteous indignation against Maoist violence filled the waves, especially on TV, conveniently overlooking the fact that there are two reigns of political violence in Bastar. The first is state and state-sponsored terror, which, heartless and coldblooded, has constantly been outdoing itself in barbarity and callous indifference to human life. The second, the political violence of the oppressed, is driven by an urge to transcend the prevailing exploitative economic relations and overthrow the oppressive social and political order. This, the violence of the oppressed, is reactive; it stems from the continuing acts of violence of the oppressors.

More important, the violence of the oppressors and the violence of the oppressed seem to have had a profound effect on the political culture and social psychology of the oppressed. There's this almost natural fury of the tribal peasants, men and women, even those in the Maoist militia and the PLGA, for they have suffered so much at the hands of their oppressors, and there's a public memory of the exploitation, the oppression, the misery, the anguish that has been passed on over generations. There's a public memory of the collective resistance too, for instance, that of the Bhumkal Rebellion of 1910. These simple truths have to be repeatedly restated, for the intellectuals of the establishment want to blot them out. They want to leave them out of remembrance or consideration, just as they want to obliterate from public memory the reasons for the class war. What the Indian state had been executing was akin to a "strategic hamlets program"—isolation of the tribal peasants from contact with and influence by the Maoist guerrillas. This was the first phase of the anti-Maoist counterinsurgency, to clear the path for big business's "accumulation by dispossession" in the "non-capitalist areas," with OGH being the grand design of its second stage.

Interestingly, the then Indian Prime Minister, Manmohan Singh, was always rather upfront in stating the main reason for this war. Talking to a select group of editors on September 6, 2010, he pointed out that "Naxalite [Maoist] areas happen to be those areas which are the heartland of India's mineral wealth . . . If we are not allowed to exploit the mineral resources of this country, I think the growth path of this country will be adversely affected." This was repeated by him in a speech to Indian Police Service (IPS) probationers on December 24, 2010: "Naxalism [Maoism] today afflicts central India where the bulk of India's mineral wealth lies and if we don't control Naxalism, we have to say goodbye to our country's ambitions to sustain a growth rate of 10–11 per cent per annum." The Bastar region of Chhattisgarh happens to be one such mineral-rich area, but it is also where large parts have been turned into a guerrilla zone by the CPI(Maoist). These are tracts where the revolutionary movement is strong, but where the Party and its mass organizations are in power only as long as the guerrillas have the upper hand over the state's forces, and where power can revert back to the Indian state when the guerrillas are forced to retreat.

It is no wonder then that sections of the corporate media bay for the blood of the "left-wing extremists" and even equate the human rights groups with the latter. Far away from the scene of Maoist ambush, ensconced in the safety and comfort of their TV studios, the big guns, TV anchors and "talking heads," the Arnab Goswamis, boom in the aftermath of every such surprise guerrilla attack. They cannot stomach a successful ambush by the Maoist guerrillas. "This is a major setback for Operation Green Hunt; shouldn't it be overhauled and intensified?" Or, better still, "shouldn't the Army be deployed on the frontlines in Bastar?" That would certainly give the establishment a considerable tactical advantage but would turn out to be a huge strategic blunder.

The Maoist leadership has been uncompromising in safeguarding the Adivasi habitat. The public-sector Steel Authority of India Ltd (SAIL) had planned to mine iron ore from the Raoghat area, not far from Narayanpur town, in southern Chhattisgarh, but had to defer its plans in the face of people's struggles against such mining. SAIL however revived its mining project after government assurances of paramilitary protection of operations in 2007, and more recently, with the deployment of twenty-one more battalions of paramilitary forces. Plans are also afoot to revive a multipurpose dam project at Bodhghat on the Indravati River, which would displace 70,000 persons, wipe out hundreds of villages, and destroy the beautiful Chitrakoot waterfalls, but here too, expected unrelenting resistance is the cause of much official apprehension.

Meanwhile, the counterinsurgency operations have already gone high-tech with unmanned aerial vehicles, commonly known as drones, deployed to "remote sense" the locations (and relocations) of the "left-wing extremist" guerrillas. The government has deployed around 120,000 armed personnel, commandos, paramilitary, and police in Dandakaranya, and is proposing to locate an army training school in Maad, spread over 750 square km and encompassing ninety villages, which will entail the destruction of many habitations of the Maadia Adivasis. It can't stomach the fact that Tata Steel was forced to give up its plans to locate a 5 million tonne per annum steel plant in Lohandiguda in Bastar district in the face of concerted resistance of the tribal people there. Indeed, in November 2015, there were leaks of the government's plans to bring attack helicopters (helicopter gunships) into operation in the class war in southern Chhattisgarh, that is, in the whole Bastar region.

"CONSTRUCTION" IN THE MIDST OF DESTRUCTION

It is perhaps time to take a short break from destruction and say a few words about its opposite. It is remarkable that in the midst of the class war the Maoists are making efforts to govern in pockets of the Dandakaranya guerrilla zone where their writ runs—their guerrilla bases. In 2001, Punjabi writer Satnam spent time with the Maoist guerrillas and the people who support them in Maad and wrote about them in *Jangalnama*.[19] In January 2010, the well-known People's Union for Democratic Rights' activist Gautam Navlakha along with Swedish writer Jan Myrdal, visited this guerrilla base and wrote about life in this "Maoist heartland." They found the guerrillas alongside the people engaged in such activities as agriculture, education, and healthcare. The guerrillas have harnessed the "collective energy of the people in improving their material conditions."[20]

Navlakha throws light on Maoist politics and their organization of a Janathana Sarkar (people's government) there, albeit, in an embryonic form at the primary level.[21] At the village level, the primary unit of people's power is the gram rajya (village republic) committee. At a higher level, there are Revolutionary People's Committees (RPCs), elected bodies that govern three to five villages, Area RPCs, elected from the members of fourteen to fifteen RPCs, and divisional RPCs, elected from three to five ARPCs, all with the right to recall elected members. The people's power that is being mobilized is of the broad masses of the tribal peasantry, this after the Maoists have accomplished the following in the guerrilla zones:

(i)   significant increase in the labor rate for tendu leaf collection and for cutting bamboos;

(ii)   confiscation of the excess land of the *majhis*, *patels*, and *sarpanches* (who used to make landless tribal persons till those lands, either as seasonal wage or attached laborers) and the takeover of forest lands;

(iii) distribution of these lands among the poor and landless peasants, with the *pattas* (title deeds) given jointly in the names of male *and* female heads of the household; and

(iv)   the freeing of young tribal women from exploitation by tribal chiefs, rich peasants, forest department and police personnel, and from being reduced to "servicing" young tribal men in the village dormitory, the Ghotul.

The RPCs, according to Navlakha, can take credit for the following achievements:[22]

(i)   They have persuaded qualified doctors to train "barefoot doctors" who have then been able to treat the three most deadly illnesses—malaria, cholera, and elephantiasis—in these localities.

(ii) They have gotten party cadres to double up as teachers in the schools; textbooks have been prepared for students up to Class V, with one on the history of Dandakaranya under preparation.

(iii) They have organized cooperative farming and pisciculture, albeit in a small way, in which the land (and wells and ponds), commonly owned through the RPC, is collectively cultivated and the harvest is shared; where the land is under household ownership, poor peasants have been provided with seed, free of cost.

(iv) Generally, cooperation and mutual aid in the form of voluntary labor teams are the norm in the creation of productive assets.

Difficult as it surely is to undertake economic construction in the midst of the class war in a guerrilla zone, poor peasants and landless laborers cannot be expected to put up with their abysmal living conditions for long. Popular support will not last if the Maoists cannot assure the tribal peasants a modicum of security by preventing the grabbing of *jal–jangal–zameen* (water–forests–land) by the Indian state and their handing over to big business. Moreover, besides, *physical* security, there is the question of assuring the habitability of the natural environment as well as the security of the tribal peasantry in their *sociocultural* environment.

"SECOND SANTAL REBELLION"

The habitability of the natural environment and the security of the tribal peasantry in its sociocultural environment have to be an essential component of the Maoist agenda of "New Democracy." The state governments, backed by the Centre, however, seem to be bent on accomplishing just the opposite, benefiting big business in the name of "development." The neoliberal capitalist bug seemed to have also bitten the Communist Party of India (Marxist) [CPM]-led Left Front government in West Bengal. The repression let loose in Nandigram in East Midnapore district when the peasantry resisted an impending land grab was appalling, especially the March 14, 2007, incident of police firing which killed fourteen persons.

In 2008, the state's then Chief Minister, Buddhadev Bhattacharjee, allotted 4,500 acres of land at Salboni in West Midnapore district to the Sajjan

Jindal business group for a proposed steel plant. He sweetened the offer by arranging the assignment of SEZ status to the project, thereby bestowing a host of fiscal and other concessions to it. This when his government's land reform program of allotting *pattas* (title deeds) for cultivable forest land and forest land under cultivation to tribal peasants had been kept in cold storage. Here too, however, the government was apprehensive, for the Maoists had been working underground amongst ordinary Adivasis and moolvasis in some parts of the district since 1998.

Indeed, in a dramatic flash, the CPI(Maoist) lit a prairie fire on November 2, 2008, when the chief minister, along with two central government ministers and a host of officials, was returning after a foundation stone-laying ceremony at the site of the proposed steel plant by the Sajjan Jindal business group at Salboni. Maoist guerrillas detonated a land mine that narrowly missed its target. The political message of the land mine was loud and clear. The Maoists and their Santal comrades were against any government that considered the demands of big business more important than the essential needs of ordinary people. It was not, however, merely the loss of their "ancestral land." Its unilateral transfer from the government to big business, without their consent, was an affront to their dignity; their notion of honor had been violated. The deeply felt resentment of ordinary Adivasis and moolvasis only grew, sharpened by the political consciousness of some of them who were in close contact with the Maoists since 1998.

The provincial intelligence bureau perhaps knew this, and the police unleashed a reign of terror in the Lalgarh area, to the west of Salboni. Even school kids were beaten and charged with "waging war against the state," among other things. But worse was to come. In a midnight swoop on November 6–7 on the villages in Lalgarh block, the police kicked and beat— with their lathis and butts of their rifles—a number of women, among whom were Chintamani Murmu and Panamani Hansda. Chintamani was badly injured in the eye and Panamani suffered multiple fractures in the chest. The Adivasis, mainly Santhals, have been subject to police oppression over generations, but now, with the Maoists by their side, their sense of dignity could no longer be crushed. The policemen, the jotedars (landlords), the usurers, all of them were the "notorious *dikus* (intruders), parasites." There was an ethnic aspect of class exploitation in these parts. November 7 was Russian Revolution anniversary day. The CPM that led the sarkar (government) which colluded with the *diku*, masqueraded as a revolutionary force in a big show of strength, even as, here in Lalgarh, the real thing was brewing with the tribal people outraged at the CPM-led Left Front government's sellout of their "ancestral land."[23]

At first more spontaneous, by mid-November 2008 the Pulishi

Atyachar-er Birudhhe Janasadharan-er Committee (People's Committee against Police Atrocities), the PCAPA, was formed to lead the mass struggle in Lalgarh and the adjoining areas. (Apart from Lalgarh, the uprising spread to Binpur, Jhargram, Belpahari, and Jamboni blocks over the first month since the outbreak on November 7, 2008.) A twelve-point charter of demands was drawn up, among which was that the Superintendent of Police of the district and those responsible for the atrocities on the women should hold their ears and crawl with their nose facing the ground in apology and that the chief minister too should also tender an expression of regret. Significant on the list, apart from the call for the removal of police camps, was the demand for the withdrawal of the false cases and charge sheets filed since 1998 against people who had been framed as Maoists.

What was really heartening were the direct forms of people's democracy in practice. Each village now had a gram (village) committee with five women and five men on it; two persons, a man and a woman from each village, were a part of the central coordinating committee; taking and ratifying decisions were done in an utterly democratic manner; officials had to sit on the ground on hand-woven mats on equal terms to negotiate with the committees. All this brought into sharp focus the contrast with the practice of rotten liberal-political democracy by the mainstream political parties in India. The other aspect was that, in Jangalmahal (literally, the "jungle estates," tribal blocks in West Midnapore, Purulia, and Bankura districts of West Bengal), the CPM-led Left Front government had abysmally failed on the "development" front. The public distribution system had collapsed, the primary health centers were almost non-functional, and even potable water was not easily accessible. In sharp contrast, the PCAPA-led mass movement, with meager resources at its command, was able to run health posts with doctors from Kolkata coming in once a week, construct and repair embankments, dig ponds, set up tube wells, teach the local language in some schools, much of all this through *shramdaan* (voluntary labor).

With modes of direct participatory democracy, the movement spread further—to Goaltore, Salboni, Nayagram, even Garbeta, a CPM stronghold. Students came out in solidarity. The traditional local leadership of the Santals, the Majhi Madwa, and the Jharkhandi political parties, who came to take advantage of the mass outrage to convert it into a vote bank, were asked to back off. The CPM's "divide and rule" tactics failed, but the Party repeatedly made the charge of Maoist involvement to justify what was on the anvil—state and state-sponsored terror. Nevertheless, the spread of the struggle, the road blocks and the bandhs, the attacks on CPM offices, and so on, ultimately forced the government to remove the police camps, which had occupied school buildings among other places.

Very soon, within a month, ten of the twelve demands were met. Even the chief minister was forced to apologize. But the two main demands, the apology of the Superintendent of Police and his men who had committed the midnight raids and the excesses remained, as also the demand for the dropping of the cases/charge-sheets filed against so-called Maoists since 1998. The struggle thus went on, and, indeed, practically the entire state machinery was kept out of operation in the areas of struggle for months. In keeping with the changing dynamics of the situation, the PCAPA and the CPI(Maoist) together, in tandem, seemed to have struck an astute balance between political mobilization, armed actions, and social welfare/"development" activity.

However, the situation was on edge. In progressively taking over CPM strongholds, the Maoist leadership was working toward banishing the ruling leftists from the area. But in doing so, it was precipitating a crisis of the state. That moment came on June 14, 2009, when the target was the "White House," the "palatial" (in sharp contrast to the deprivation all around it) house of Anuj Pandey, the CPM Zonal Secretary. He was in control of Dharampur, whether it was getting work in the National Rural Employment Guarantee Scheme, below-the-poverty-line ration cards, or deciding who would be the beneficiaries of welfare programs like the Indira Awas Yojana. He was in the saddle, and locally he directed the CPM *harmads*, armed goons who enforced the Party's writ. That is why the Maoists chose to destroy the "White House," for it was a symbol of the "*Ancien Régime.*" The grand finale was when Maoist leader Bikash, an AK-47 slung over his shoulder, made a public declaration that, indeed, the Maoists were leading the movement.

Perhaps the CPI(Maoist) knew of the impending entry of the Joint Forces, jointly decided upon by the then Congress Party-led government at the Centre and the CPM-led West Bengal government. The occupation of Jangalmahal by the Joint Forces brought about a sea change in the Lalgarh movement, especially in the balance between mass political mobilization and alternative development activity, on the one hand, and armed resistance, on the other. With the entry of the Joint Forces in the manner of an occupation army and the conduct of the CPM harmads in the manner of local collaborators, the CPM began recapturing its territorial strongholds. But even as the Maoist guerrillas and the Sidhu-Kanhu militia (the latter, of the PCAPA, and named after two of the four Murmu brothers who had led the Santal Rebellion of 1855) resisted the Joint Forces and the CPI(M) harmads and even carried out ambushes and landmine explosions, the tempo of mass political mobilization and social welfare/development activity by the PCAPA became a real challenge to sustain.

The Santal Rebellion of 1855 was brought on in the wake of the tribal people being once again cheated of their lands. It began at the end of June of that year and was marked by a "festival" of acts of defiance over a period of four months before martial law was proclaimed in November and the rebels were brutally crushed by January 1856. In what the PCAPA has called the second Santal rebellion, however, the resistance took a fresh turn with the PLGA raid on a camp of the Eastern Frontier Rifles at Silda (in West Midnapore district) on February 15, 2010. Condemnation of the Maoists in the commercial media assumed hysteric proportions. Three months later, the Gyaneshwari Express train was sabotaged, on May 27–28, 2010, leading to its derailment, and with an oncoming goods train hitting the loose carriages, nearly 150 passengers died, and predictably, the Maoists were blamed,[24] this to buttress the "discourse of counterinsurgency." As in Bastar, disease metaphors—"deadly virus" and so on—of colonial vintage had a field day, for both the West Bengal and the central governments didn't seem to want the public to know the truth.

BROTHERS AND SISTERS OF SIDHU AND KANHU

Whenever there is a Maoist attack, the police raid our villages. . . For how long will we suffer this oppression . . . ? All of us are Maoists, let the police arrest us. Today we have come out.
—ARATI MURMU, A WOMAN WHO WAS ASSAULTED BY
THE POLICE, AND HAD GONE TO BLOCK
THE LALGARH POLICE STATION[25]

During the occupation, the media dutifully published the versions fed to it by the police in Midnapore and Jhargram. However, one needs to hear the voice of the PCAPA, through *Letters from Lalgarh*,[26] a set of six dispatches written by the PCAPA to various organizations and intellectuals in Kolkata over the period March–September 2010. At the time of publication, 2013, all the signatories of these letters had been killed or were in jail. Indeed, a month before the first letter was penned, Lalmohan Tudu, the president of the PCAPA, was cold-bloodedly assassinated on February 22, 2010 (as per a statement of the PCAPA) when he went to meet his daughter who was to appear in the state board examinations scheduled to begin the next day. Sidhu Soren, who led the Sidhu-Kanhu militia, and four of his comrades were killed on 26 July 2010 while they were asleep in the jungles of Metala (again, according to a statement of the PCAPA). Umakanta Mahato, a member of the central committee of the PCAPA, falsely accused in the sabotage of the Gyneshwari train, was allegedly cold-bloodedly assassinated by Joint Forces personnel, accompanied by CPM men, on 27 August 2010, in the forests of Parulia while returning home (according to the testimony of

Sabita Mahato, wife of Umakanta Mahato). It seems as if it was the implicit policy of the West Bengal and central governments to annihilate the leaders of the PCAPA.

A more comprehensive account of life in the midst of the occupation would speak of the pathetic role of the judiciary at the local level, the role of the harmads as collaborators of the Joint Forces in the occupation, schools turned into police camps, the PCAPA's attempts to continue the implementation of their development programs in the midst of the occupation, as also, their mass mobilization in the form of rallies and meetings, and the role of women in the resistance. The latter, for instance, the 35,000 women entering Jhargram on July 20, 2010, demanding that the perpetrators of the rapes in Sonamukhi be punished, the formation of the Nari Ijjat Bachao Committee (Committee to Safeguard the Dignity of Women), women leading a campaign to demolish liquor shops in Ramchandrapur, Chandabila, Nekradoba, Piyalgeriya, Barodehi and other villages, all this in the midst of the occupation, is remarkable.

But, politically, the PCAPA was naive. It first characterized the Trinamool Congress (TMC) as "part of the ruling clique responsible for sending the Joint Forces into Jangalmahal," but later, when TMC leader Mamata Banerjee took the initiative to organize an "anti-terror forum" and a rally in August 2010 in Lalgarh to oppose the CPM and its harmads, the PCAPA softened. It wholeheartedly cooperated with the "anti-terror movement-struggle which . . . [had] been formed with the initiative of the Trinamool leader Mamata Banerjee, intellectuals and human rights organizations."[27] Indeed, the PCAPA went all out to make Mamata Banerjee's rally in Lalgarh a success. It was here that she made all the tall promises—to withdraw the Joint Forces, punish the harmads and the police officers responsible for the atrocities committed, and institute enquiries into the killings—that eventually won her the Jangalmahal seat in the 2011 state assembly elections. What followed was the formation of TMC's own harmads, the Bhairav Bahini, a strengthening of the intelligence serving the counterinsurgency, and the capture, brutal torture, and assassination of the Maoist politburo member and the Party's main leader of the Lalgarh uprising, Mallojula Koteswara Rao, a member of the Politburo of the CPI(Maoist), who was popularly known as Kishenji.

What explains the terrible blunder committed by the Maoists and the PCAPA in allowing Mamata Banerjee and her TMC to gain a foothold in Jangalmahal, which ultimately led to a severe setback for the resistance? Surely, temporary, conditional alliances must be made at certain junctures in the course of a "protracted people's war" (PPW). In such politics, one has to utilize a conflict of interests, even if temporary, among one's adversaries.

The question, however, relates to the handling of a whole set of contradictions in the course of an alliance with a temporary, unstable, thoroughly unscrupulous and conditional associate.

The CPI(Maoist)'s characterization of the CPM as "social fascist" was ridiculous, even though the latter was acting as a collaborator of the Joint Forces. The Maoists should have made a distinction between CPM-harmad combatants and CPM non-combatants, and refrained from unleashing political violence on the latter. The killings of CPM non-combatants in Jangalmahal in the course of the occupation, as repeatedly alleged by the CPM itself, seems to have unnecessarily escalated the antagonistic contradictions between the CPI(Maoist) and the CPM in West Bengal to a multiple of what this hostility might otherwise have been, and ultimately, the TMC took advantage of the situation to steal a march over the CPM in Jangalmahal in the state assembly elections of April–May 2011.

As regards the TMC, the PCAPA should never have accepted the leadership of Mamata Banerjee when the TMC joined the anti-terror forum. Conceding the leadership to Mamata Banerjee gave the TMC the opportunity to wean away some of the PCAPA's cadre and mass base. And, given the track record of parties like the TMC as regards the sharp contrast between their electoral manifestos (promises) and their conduct as soon as they come to power, a party like the CPI(Maoist) and its mass organization, the PCAPA, whose cadre and leaders risked their precious lives, should never have had any positive expectations from the TMC. Nevertheless, peace talks, if these could have been forced on the TMC-led government that came to power, would have been beneficial to the people, to the extent that some concessions for the people could have been extracted from the mouth of the tiger, the Indian state, and would have given the resistance movement time to recuperate and reorganize in Jangalmahal.

With respect to the establishment, its insensitivity in the face of tribal anger and despair knew no bounds, this despite the expression of outrage at the sight of Joint Forces personnel carrying the dead bodies of young Maoist guerrillas, killed while they were asleep in the jungles of Ranjja in June 2010, hung animal-like, hands bound, legs tied, from bamboo poles, the security-force jawans conveying the bodies just like colonial hunters coming back from a *shikar* (hunting animals, mainly for sport) once did, with their prized dead game. The PCAPA comment is salient: "Those who were killed were our sons and daughters; they turned Maoists to resist (the) atrocities of (the) harmads. The way their dead bodies were carried after hog-tying them puts any civilized society to shame."[28] But worse was to follow.

Was the claimed encounter on November 24, 2011, in the Burishol forest in West Midnapore district in which Kishenji was supposed to have been killed, real? Frankly, given the complicity of the media bosses and some senior journalists with official mendacity, the truth about the circumstances of his death is not yet known in the public realm. A press statement from Abhay, spokesperson of the Central Committee of the Party, dated 25 November 2011, unambiguously stated that Kishenji was killed "after capturing him alive in a well planned conspiracy."[29]

The renowned radical Telugu poet Varavara Rao who accompanied Kishenji's niece Deepika to bring the body back to Kishenji's home town of Peddapalli in Karimnagar district of Andhra Pradesh is reported to have said: "In the last 43 years, I have seen so many bodies killed in so-called encounters but have not seen a body like this one. . .There is no place on the body where there is no injury."[30] According to CDRO (Coordination of Democratic Rights' Organizations) activists who saw the body before the commencement of the post-mortem, "on the back side of the head, part of [the] skull [and] brain [were] missing;" the right eye had come out of the socket; the lower jaw was "missing;" there were four stab wounds on the face; knife injuries were observed on the throat; there were hand fractures and two bullet injuries under one of the arms; "one-third of the left hand index finger was removed;" there were signs of enrooted bullets through the lungs; the right knee was hacked; the foot of the left leg was "totally burnt;" in all, "there were more than 30 bayonet-like cut injuries on the front of the body." And, while there were "bullet, sharp cuts and burn injuries," surprisingly there were "no injury marks on his [Kishenji's] shirt and pant corresponding to [those on] his body parts."

A press release ("Killing the Talks and Faking an Encounter," Kolkata, 2 December 2011) by the CDRO—based on the observations of a CDRO fact-finding team that visited the spot in Burishol forest where the alleged encounter took place on November 24—states that "the extent of the damage caused to the body against the rather undisturbed surrounding of the spot where the body lay raises our suspicion about the official version." Indeed, "right next to where his [Kishenji's] body lay on the ground is a termite hill" that "remains undamaged by all the alleged exchange of fire." Even nearby, "not a single termite hill was damaged and [there was] no visible sign of burn or fire due to heavy rifle and mortar firing!" Clearly, the veracity of the official story must be seriously doubted (in fact, there are versions of it that contradict each other!), and it is telling that no independent judicial inquiry headed by a sitting or retired Supreme Court or High Court judge was appointed to investigate into the circumstances surrounding Kishenji's death.

Frankly, Kishenji's killing is very much part and parcel of the established criminal practice of state terrorism, and it is tragic that, despite an active civil liberties and democratic rights movement that doesn't allow such utter contempt for the law to go unchallenged, the state ultimately went scot-free even when it allegedly committed a cold-blooded murder. When will the state terrorists be stripped of their impunity and brought to justice? In early 2011, a bench of justices Aftab Alam and R. M. Lodha of the Supreme Court, responding to two public interest litigations related to a fake encounter in which Cherukuri Rajkumar ("Azad"), CPI (Maoist) politburo member and Party spokesperson, and journalist Hemchandra Pandey were allegedly shot dead in Adilabad district on the night of July 1–2, 2010, by the Andhra Pradesh police after being picked up at or near Nagpur, said: "We cannot allow the republic killing its own children."

Like the Azad fake encounter case, the Kishenji one too seems to be part of the genre where impunity breeds contempt for the law. Such scorn for the legal code is by now ingrained in the wielders of repressive power—recidivists in the coercive apparatus of the Indian state. Kishenji's elimination was really vendetta killing by such recidivists, for he combated state terror to the very end. And, even in this "battle," unlike many of the officers of the repressive apparatus of the Indian state, he respected the dignity of "prisoners of war." The fair treatment and release of the former Sankrail police station Officer-in-Charge Atindranath Dutta who was taken hostage by the Maoists in October 2009 bears this out.

ETHICS OF THE VIOLENCE OF THE OPPRESSED

Coming back to the chorus of righteous indignation against Maoist violence, it is necessary to analyze what has been happening and why, since Naxalbari in 1967. Given the fact that ordinary people, especially Adivasis and Dalits, have suffered so much at the hands of their oppressors, from colonial times to the present, there surely is a widespread emotional need to avenge deeply felt wrongs, and there must be many frustrated and tortured people who are ready to sacrifice their lives to avenge themselves or their fellow victims. It is perhaps incorrect to condemn their motives or their violent actions. Indeed, it can even be said that the CPI(Maoist) is doing the right thing. It has mobilized these people in a collective struggle to change the very conditions which have driven some of their fellow men and women to engage in violent acts of revenge.

In the context and circumstances, and, given the fact that the Indian Constitution and the law have failed to bring justice to the victims,[31] the violence of the oppressed, led by the Maoists, is a necessity. Or, to put it differently, in the context and circumstances the use of violence is a *necessary evil*. Moreover, the violence of the oppressed is serving the cause of justice. And, given that the law and the Constitution have let the victims down, it is morally justified. The oppressed have been left with no other way but to challenge the violence that reproduces and maintains their oppression.

Nevertheless, there are dehumanizing aspects of the violence of the oppressed. Often, violence and non-violence are contrasted as mutually exclusive ways of confronting oppression, and the Maoist way is claimed to be exclusively violent. This is far from the truth. At the heart of the political activity of the Maoists is organizing and convincing people, not only of the need to fight against oppression, but of the need for a new society free of oppression, and most of this political activity involves a non-confrontational meeting of minds. The Maoists are trying to bring about the liberation of the oppressed, *not for* them but *with* them, and in a more committed manner, and so reflection and action are not divorced from each other. Solidarity with the oppressed has meant fighting at their side in the liberation struggle. In the best tradition of the philosophy of non-violent resistance, Maoist practice is based on the "notion of witness," whereby a small number of highly committed revolutionaries, by force of example, involving a great deal of sacrifice, and taking huge risks, engage in a pedagogy *with* the oppressed, learning about oppression and its causes. From this reflection comes a realization of the need for engagement in the struggle for liberation, a collective fight for freedom and justice.

In their violent political resistance, however, the Maoists need to take account of the entire set of consequences. It is heartening to find that in the fight against the oppressors and their hired combatants, the Maoists are now sensitive to the injuries and deaths that they inflict on those who serve or protect the oppressors but do so because they have little choice. Yet the revolutionaries need to be persuaded, as for example, the People's Union for Democratic Rights has tried, to specify certain limiting conditions for the deployment of violent means, like the Common Article 3 of the Geneva Conventions and Protocol II relating to non-international armed conflict. Cruelty and brutality must never be a part of the means of revolution. Revolutionary upheavals almost inevitably lead to "excesses," but these cruel and brutal overindulgences must never be condoned or sanctioned by the revolutionary leadership. Moreover, another consequence of violent means is that the mass base of the Maoists then comes under attack and the Maoists are often unable to protect their supporters.

PERSISTENCE OF REVOLUTIONARY MOBILIZATION

How does one explain the persistence of revolutionary mobilization over half a century? The Maoist movement in India is—alongside the one in the Philippines—one of the world's longest surviving peasant insurgencies.

Alpa Shah, a social anthropologist who has carried out long-term ethnographic research in a Maoist guerrilla zone in Jharkhand, has come to
the conclusion that it is the "relations of intimacy" that have been built
between the Maoist organization and the people in its areas of struggle that
are crucial to understanding the growth, development, and persistence of
revolutionary mobilization.[32] These relations of intimacy are grounded in
Maoism, which stems from Marxism–Leninism, and is principally concerned with how to bring about a just and egalitarian society even when
the material conditions are unfavorable for this to happen.[33] Alpa Shah's
explanation is the most authentic among the scholarly works on the subject that I have read. Moreover, it matches closely with what I came to
believe in the mid-1980s after spending a week in Maoist areas of struggle
in the then Gaya district of Bihar, and I have found no reason since then to
alter my views. It may then be helpful to go over Alpa Shah's explanation
of what accounts for the persistence of Maoist revolutionary mobilization
in India.

Regarding the Maoist organization, Shah holds that

> an enormous effort was made to supersede and negate the specifici-
> ties of caste and class divisions among all the people brought into the
> revolutionary fold. This involved, in particular, paying great attention
> to treating lower castes and tribes with respect and dignity as equals.[34]

With respect to relating to ordinary people, she writes:[35]

> In everyday life it is often the small things that mattered in the rela-
> tive reach of the Maoists in comparison to that of the Indian state:
> for instance, the tone of the voice in which one was spoken to, the
> way one was greeted, the way one's house was entered, whether one
> sat on the floor like everyone else or required a chair to be found. In
> contrast to the state officials, the Maoists (whose leaders were also
> outsiders—often high-caste Bihari men) had made it a point to be
> gentle and kind in everyday interactions. . . . They did not want spe-
> cial treatment and even insisted on doing things that no villagers
> would expect of their outside guests—like washing their used plates
> and cups and helping with household chores. Unlike the personnel
> of the Indian state, the Maoists had over time become 'apna,' 'one of
> our own' . . . because of their ability to treat the villagers as equals,
> overriding differences of caste. They had built relations of respect and
> dignity, but equally important, relations of joking and teasing.
>
>   . . .

... not only was it common practice for high-caste Maoist leaders to eat from the same plate as low castes or for them to make a point of eating beef or rats to undermine quintessential markers of 'untouch-ability,' it was also significant that villagers exploring inter-tribe or caste unions (prohibited in the villages) found a space of freedom for their exploration in living with the Maoists.

It would seem to be appropriate to paraphrase Alpa Shah and say that it is Maoism that has

> guided the creation of relations of intimacy which enabled the Maoist guerrillas to be accepted by the local people as one of them. . . . In the case of the Maoists, these relations of intimacy manifest themselves in the creation of new subjects beyond the caste and class divides of rural India, nurturing spaces of freedom which contest established rules of endogamy, of hierarchy and traditional conventions. These are spaces of freedom which have proved attractive to historically marginalised and discriminated populations.[36]

To all that Alpa Shah says above, I would add that here one finds com-radely love based on human solidarity, and when this takes place between high-caste Maoist leaders, albeit those who have declassed and "decasted" themselves, and historically marginalized and discriminated persons shar-ing joy and sadness, understanding and knowledge, and even humor (what Shah calls "relations of joking and teasing"), both sides are enriched. The relation is one of care and concern, and respect stemming from knowing one another, and motivated by care and concern. As the Maoists teach the people, they are also being taught by them. All this has been possible because the Maoist leaders have consciously, in appropriate social settings, chosen to substitute "friendship" for "leadership."

It might be pertinent to also mention that, like the social anthropologist Alpa Shah, a sociologist, Juhi Tyagi, who has also carried out ethnographic field research on the Maoist movement in three North Telangana districts, has found that the resilience of the Maoist movement derives from the fact that the *sanghams* (village-level units of the Maoist mass organizations) have been instrumental in enhancing the class consciousness of poor peasants and landless laborers. The Maoists have also empowered these village-level units to act autonomously in struggles at the local level. Indeed, they have created what Tyagi calls an effective "organizational field"—units of their mass organizations like the RCS, SIKASA (translated from Telugu as the Singareni collieries workers' federation), and the Viplava Mahila Sangham (revolutionary women's association) working in concert to build class consciousness and jointly struggling to achieve shared goals.[37]

WHERE IS THE MAOIST MOVEMENT GOING?

The Indian state, however, wants to snap these "relations of intimacy" of the Maoists with the wretched of the Indian earth. The counterinsurgency has deliberately blurred the distinction between combatants and non-combatants in order to make the people who support the Maoists believe that the PPW is a "no-win" strategy, and ensure that, in their own interest, for survival and a return to "normalcy," they will distance themselves from the revolutionaries. The PPW, counterinsurgency strategists know, is predicated upon a symbiotic relation of the guerrillas with the people. These strategists also know that the Maoists principally seek the political (rather than the military) defeat of their enemies. So the counterinsurgency engages in "low-intensity warfare" (LIW)—prolonged military attacks that are kept below the gravity of conventional warfare, and are combined with political, economic, ideological and psychological antagonisms. The LIW strategists know that the logic of the revolution is principally centered on the political (rather than the military) defeat of the enemy, and so they seek to distort and pervert that logic, turning the revolution against itself. The revolution is sought to be delegitimized and isolated—for instance, through recourse to "strategic hamlets" to separate the guerrillas from the people. The Maoist movement is, in turn, bent upon overthrowing the Indian state, this through a combination of protracted armed struggle, mass mobilization, and strategic alliances with the oppressed nationalities. Neither of these possibilities—that is, what the Indian state and the Maoists are respectively bent upon achieving—however, stands a chance at this juncture.

In the process of taking on the might of one of the most powerful capitalist states and ruling classes among the underdeveloped countries of the world, the Maoist movement has become increasingly more militarized. Moreover, the Indian state has been striving to limit the movement exclusively to armed confrontation. Consequently, the movement is finding it increasingly difficult to win widespread legitimacy among the people, without which it cannot succeed. The absence of "base areas" handicaps the movement in more ways than one. Principally, without base areas, the Party's mass-line politics does not even have a chance of being popularly perceived as a superior form of representation to the establishment's rotten liberal-political democracy. Nevertheless, one possibility that "Spring Thunder," Phase III, throws up is "simultaneous uprisings in a wide range of geographic and social settings, that is, many Dantewadas, Lalgarhs all over the country"[38] in opposition to "accumulation by dispossession" and sub-imperialist aggression, creating great turmoil that might bring about "a crisis in the affairs of the ruling order"[39] and herald a critical leap forward.

In 1967, the Naxalites/Maoists launched a protracted struggle to remove the predatory Indian ruling classes and their political brokers from power, those to whom the British colonial rulers had transferred power in 1947. But, fifty years later, they are nowhere near that goal. The revolutionaries have been trying to imitate the Chinese Communist Party's PPW path to liberation, but the truth is that, even in 2017, the Maoist guerrillas are just a relatively small armed force (compared to the state's armed police and military) operating on the margins of Indian society. Their political voice is yet to resonate far and wide in that society. The Maoist movement has just not been able to deal with the broader sweep of the "present as history." The present all-encompassing political challenge centered on fighting "semi-fascism" remains unaddressed in the face of the ongoing compulsions of the PPW. As it is, the Maoist movement has been forced into ebb tide in the towns and cities, and in the plains of the countryside. Admittedly, "Red Areas" may not presently be feasible in these settings, but "Pink Areas" may at least be worth striving for, through a judicious combination of legal and semi-legal tactics. Although India is still mainly rural, for every 100 rural persons, there are now (as per Census 2011) 45 urban persons. In the political struggle to influence public opinion in India's liberal-political democracy, the Maoists have been left far behind. The virtual non-existence of radical politics in the towns and cities, and in the plains areas, shuts out the possibility of the Maoists becoming a dominant and powerful left force, and, in these dark times, the most effective anti-fascist force.

The movement has witnessed many setbacks, and many mistakes have been made by the revolutionists. Looking back, these impediments to progress were only to be expected in the thick of taking on one of the most formidable and ruthless of the counterrevolutionary forces in the semi-periphery of the world capitalist system. The Maoists are nowhere near winning over the majority of the oppressed and the exploited in rural India. The movement has not yet made significant inroads into the worlds of the highly exploited workers and the urban poor in the towns and the cities. The main obstacles to revolutionary change still have not been addressed with any measure of success—the caste system, which is fundamentally antithetical to any meaningful unity of the exploited and the oppressed; the divisive cards of religion, ethnicity, and nationality, played by the political parties of the ruling classes to divide the masses; and, the soldiers/police who are not unwilling to use force against their fellow citizens. It is only when the soldiers and the police reckon that the oppressed and the exploited might win that they may join them, as happened during the French and Russian revolutions.

Nevertheless, the Indian state has not been able to put down the movement; indeed, if one takes a long view, the movement has been through ups and downs, but it has, so far, managed to recover from the severe setbacks it suffered. But fifty years have gone by, and the costs of being forced to maintain the status quo are proving to be extortionate for the poor. The costs of going without a revolution are accumulating at an atrocious rate, including the tragedies of the victims of *Hindutvavadi* (deriving from a militant political Hinduism) semi-fascist politics, backed by a "secular state" that has gone "rotten at the heart," to which the narrative will now turn.

8

"Rotten at the Heart"— The "Secular State"

Mark you this, Bassanio,
The devil can cite Scripture for his purpose.
An evil soul producing holy witness
Is like a villain with a smiling cheek,
A goodly apple rotten at the heart:
O, what a goodly outside falsehood hath!
—ANTONIO, IN AN ASIDE TO BASSANIO,
IN WILLIAM SHAKESPEARE'S
THE MERCHANT OF VENICE

On his way to winding up his three-day visit to India, in New Delhi on January 27, 2015, the then U.S. President Barack Obama surprisingly deviated from his main agenda to drive home a message about Indian secularism. Some analysts called this move Obama's "parting shot." Referring to the Indian Constitution, he said: "Your Article 25 says all people are equally entitled to the freedom of conscience and have the right to freely profess, practice and propagate religion." And then, he went on to emphasize that "upholding freedom of religion is the utmost responsibility of the [Indian] government." Indeed, nine days later, at a high-profile National Prayer Breakfast on February 5, 2015, in Washington, perhaps surmising that his reference to the Indian Constitution didn't seem to have had the desired effect, Obama appealed to Gandhian ideals, calling attention to "acts of [religious] intolerance [in India] that would have shocked Gandhiji, the person who helped to liberate that nation."

Coming from a U.S. president, this exhortation was unexpected; in the recent past, U.S. presidents have invoked Christianity to justify

Washington's naked imperialist policy. The Hindutvavadis were, however, caught with their khaki-shorts down; Obama's reminding their *sarsangh-chalak* (supreme leader)-styled Narendra Modi, India's Prime Minister, of his failure to uphold the constitutionally guaranteed fundamental right to freedom of religion was, they felt, cheeky and ill-mannered. Modi, too, was embarrassed by Obama's remarks, and it took him quite a while to address the question of freedom of religion, which he did, eventually, bringing into focus the Indian ideology of secularism, twelve days after Obama evoked Gandhian ideals. This was in a speech at Indian Secularism's "national celebration" of the elevation to Catholic sainthood of a priest and a nun from Kerala on February 17, 2015 in which Modi proclaimed his government's commitment to "positive secularism," namely, "equal respect *and* treatment for all faiths, appeasement of none," as the Bharatiya Janata Party's (BJP) patriarch L. K. Advani would surely have added. According to Modi, the Indian Constitution's principle of "positive secularism" has its "roots in the ancient cultural traditions in India," which are "in the DNA of every Indian," and now "the rest of the world too is evolving along the lines of ancient [Early] India."[1]

The problem with this cultural rhetoric is not merely that these tall claims are fake, but also that the "secularism" deriving from Vedic times and "values" has no resemblance to what is understood as secularism in the post-Enlightenment world of today. Modi's revivalist "positive secularism" oozes with Hindu religiosity, even as the "secular" Indian state sets itself up as the underwriter of all faiths with its chief executive affirming the glory of Hinduism.

Modi was, of course, only mouthing the usual Hindu nationalist discourse that claims an unrivalled spirituality and tolerance in Early India, as also of Hinduism today. The reality in this respect has been the exact opposite of such assertions. Indeed, the attacks on five churches in Delhi during November 2014 to January 2015, when the Union Territory of Delhi was under president's rule and the Union Home Ministry under Rajnath Singh was responsible for the maintenance of law and order there, are reminiscent of the destruction of Buddhist monasteries, in connivance with the state, during the Sunga and Gupta periods (second century BC to seventh century AD) in Early India.

But coming back to the sense that Modi ascribes to Indian secularism, one must note that as India becomes more "secular" in the "positive" sense, it becomes more Brahminical-Hindu, with Brahminical religion being claimed as a way of life of all Indians. And when Modi wants the rest of the world to "evolve along the lines of ancient [Early] India," he sees the need for Christianity and Islam, the world's other major religions, to be "secularized" along the lines of Brahminical Hinduism, into a "pluralistic" and "tolerant" way of life. He believes that the other states of the world can be truly "secular" if they embrace India's uniquely Hindu way of life!

The claim that Brahminical Hinduism offers a "pluralistic," "tolerant" way of life does not correspond to the reality of Hindutvavadi cultural policing in the service of Hindu orthodoxy, attacking those who expose its self-serving myths, a more recent instance of which is the assassination in February 2015 of the Communist Party of India (CPI) leader Govind Pansare, author of *Shivaji Kon Hota?* (Who Was Shivaji?). Earlier, in August 2013, Narendra Dabholkar, a rationalist and founder-president of the Maharashtra Andhashraddha Nirmoolan Samiti (Committee to Eradicate Superstition, Maharashtra), was murdered, and again, in August 2015, M. M. Kalburgi, a scholar of Kannada folklore, religion and culture, and a critic of Hindu idolatry, was killed. The assassinations of Pansare, Dabholkar, and Kalburgi have been widely suspected to have been the handiwork of Hindutva-nationalist outfits. Indeed, with Hindutva-nationalism on a new high in the political and cultural realms, the struggle to defend science and reason is going to be a long and hard one.

SHUDDHI AND *GHAR WAPSI* IN HISTORICAL PERSPECTIVE

Moreover, there is no evidence that Prime Minister Modi is walking back his talk, for that would have necessitated the union government taking legal action against the likes of the president of the Vishwa Hindu Parishad (VHP), Pravin Togadia, and even against the *sarsanghchalak* of the Rashtriya Swayamsevak Sangh (RSS), Mohan Bhagwat. It is these xenophobic men who have trampled upon the religious faith of Hindus by portraying Indian Muslims and Christians as enemies. With one of his pracharaks as prime minister, Bhagwat has perhaps been counting on being assigned the role of *Raj Guru* (the prince's counselor) and in fulfilling the RSS's mission of "regenerating Indian society in order to restore the nation's vitality," and what could be better than the "*ghar wapsi*" (bringing them all back home) exercises. After all, the prodigal who converted to Christianity or Islam needs to be brought back to the "ghar," the Hindu religion, and the nation, which is claimed to be that of the Hindus, but only after a "*Shuddhi*" (derived from *Shuddhikaran*, a purification rite) ceremony, for these Others are deemed to have been defiled by Christianity and Islam, and therefore they need to be cleansed before bringing them back to the "ghar" in the *jati* (caste) quarters of their origins.[2]

It would perhaps be proper to trace when the Shuddhi being talked about in the twenty-first century actually began. The results of the Census of British India of 1871–72,[3] more specifically those on caste and religion, put the figure of the "twice-born" castes roughly at around 10 percent of the total population of 238.8 million, whereas Muslims and the so-called untouchables, taken together, were—again, very roughly—at least twice that number, precipitating communal paranoia among the upper-caste leaders of the so-called twice-born castes. The political need to hammer out a pan-Hindu identity by bringing on board the *shudra jatis*, the "Untouchables" and tribal people (many of whom were by then "semi-Hindooised"), came to the fore with the Shuddhi movement launched by the Arya Samaj (founded in 1875, the year the results of the 1871–72 Census were made public), led by Swami Dayanand Saraswati.

Later, his main follower, Swami Shraddhanand, who in 1923 founded the Bharatiya Hindu Shuddhi Mahasabha, pushed the Shuddhi agenda with a missionary zeal, leading to flash points with Muslim politics (the All-India Muslim League had, in fact, been formed in December 1906) and his consequent assassination on December 23, 1926. At the Gauhati Session (December 26–28, 1926) of the Indian National Congress, and in *Young India* (December 30, 1926), M. K. Gandhi moved and wrote condolence motions, which, in parts, read:[4]

> Swamiji . . . was a man of action, not of words. . . . He was a warrior. And a warrior loves to die not on a sick-bed but on the battlefield. . . . I cannot therefore mourn over his death. He and his [*sic*] are to be envied. For though Shraddhanandji is dead, he is yet living. (*Young India*, December 30, 1926)
>
> . . . Let us not shed tears of sorrow but chasten our hearts and steel them with some of the fire and faith that were Shraddhanandji's. (Speech at Gauhati Congress, 1926)

In this tribute to the Shuddhi warrior, Gandhi comes across as more of a Hindu patriarch in the tradition of Shraddhanand than as one of the main leaders of the national movement! Perhaps this is not surprising, given that the Hindu Mahasabha at the all-India level was formed in 1914, V. D. Savarkar's *Hindutva: Who Is a Hindu?* was first published in 1923, and the RSS was founded in Maharashtra in 1925, all three giving a definite ideological content to the communal-hate politics that was already in motion.

VIOLATION OF FREEDOM OF RELIGION

Today, a number of states—for instance, Odisha, Arunachal Pradesh, Gujarat, Madhya Pradesh, Chhattisgarh, Himachal Pradesh—have laws on conversion from one religion to another, all ostensibly to safeguard "freedom of religion," more so in the wake of the voluntary conversion of a large number of Dalits to Islam in the village of Meenakshipuram in Tirunelveli district of Tamil Nadu in February 1981, alarming the Arya Samaj, the VHP, and the BJP. The premise underlying these laws is that most conversions are taking place through use of force, inducement, allurement or fraudulent means, a claim that has "hardly any material base." The reasons are actually "socio-economic," which cannot be criminalized and made actionable. The supposition of these laws, however, casts aspersions on the religious minorities and renders them "vulnerable to intimidation and violence." Priests and nuns are assaulted, in some cases even murdered, and paradoxically, the so-called Freedom of Religion Acts aid the social and political legitimization of such crimes.

Conversions happen for socioeconomic reasons, but instead of providing basic social welfare services to the vulnerable, the state colludes with elements who "unleash terror on priests and nuns" trying to "provide the deprived with education, medicine, clothes and food."[5] And, to top it all, the Supreme Court, to which the constitutional validity of the Freedom of Religion Acts of Madhya Pradesh and Orissa went in appeal, refused to read Article 19 (1) (a) (right to freedom of speech and expression) alongside Article 25 (1) (freedom to freely profess, practice and propagate religion); it decreed that there is no fundamental right to conversion.[6]

FUSION OF RELIGION AND POLITICS—HINDUISM AND HINDUTVA

Surely, the freedom to profess, practice, and propagate one's religion should be part of the freedom of speech and expression, but acts ostensibly framed to ensure freedom of religion deny this fundamental right, especially in the case of religious conversion from Hinduism, which is invariably deemed to be due to force or fraud. To understand why such laws find legitimacy, we need to trace the roots of the ascendency of Hindutva as an ideology. It can be said that Hindutva stems from the political tradition of inculcating a mass nationalist spirit in a Hindu idiom, pioneered in modern India, in the 1890s, by Bal Gangadhar Tilak. He was instrumental in turning the hitherto household worship of the Hindu deity Ganesha (or Ganapati) into a grand public event, Sarvajanik Ganeshotsav, as also Shiv Jayanti, the birth anniversary of Shivaji, into a magnificent commemoration of the seventeenth century Maratha warrior as a ruler who—in a spurious reconstruction of history—is said to have defended both the nation and the Hindu faith. The Sarvajanik Ganeshotsav and the Shiv Jayanti became celebrations of national *and* Hindu glory, designed to inculcate a mass nationalist spirit in a Hindu

idiom, in the process exacerbating Hindu-Muslim ill-will with the urging of
cow protection and boycott of Muharram processions.[7]

Not unexpectedly, 100 years later, on December 11, 1995, the Supreme
Court passed a judgment that "allows candidates to invoke the Hindu
nationalist idea of India as a Hindu nation in election campaigns."[8] The
case relates to a by-election in December 1987 for the Vile Parle constituency in North-West Mumbai in which Prabhakar Kunte of the Congress
(I) lost to Ramesh Prabhu of the Shiv Sena—the "army" of Shiva, pillar
of the Maharashtrian establishment—Kunte alleging that Prabhu and his
party leader, Bal Thackeray, used illegal tactics in appealing to the electorate in the name of religion and intimidating the voters. Besides virulent
communal-hate[9] propaganda, one of the main slogans raised by the Sena
in its election meetings was: "The protection of Hinduism is protection of
the country."[10]

The Supreme Court didn't, however, heed the writing on the wall. In
Justice J. S. Verma's opinion, in *Dr Ramesh Yeshwant Prabhoo vs Prabhakar
Kashinath Kunte and others* (1996 SCC (1) 130), "the promise to make India
into a Hindu rashtra" could not "be counted as an appeal to religion for
votes because Hinduism is not a religion but a way of life of all Indians."
"Hinduization of Indian culture" posed "no threat to the constitutional
promise of secularism because 'secularism in the Constitution is merely
a reaffirmation and continuation of the Indian [i.e. Hindu] way of life.'
Secularism, in this reading, only requires a perpetuation of Hinduism."[11]

This apart, some well-meaning secular intellectuals really believe that
Hinduism, including its dominant Brahminical variety, as a faith *and* a way
of life, teaches tolerance, and is therefore good. But, unlike Justice Verma,
who used the terms Hinduism and Hindutva interchangeably and presented
Hindutva as Hinduism, the Indian way of life,[12] these intellectuals argue that
Hinduism has nothing to do with Hindutva (Hindu nationalism), which is
bad. They advocate the endorsement of Hinduism, a "good," to fight/oppose/
expose Hindutva, a "bad." "Good" Hinduism must be used to fight "bad"
Hindutva.

Certainly, Hindutva is not a religion; it is an ideology that its proponents
deploy in order to acquire political power and establish a Hindu Rashtra,
and in this endeavor they use the beliefs, symbols, and values of Hinduism
to advance their cause. But the religiosity of Brahminical Hinduism coupled
with its "iconography, allegories and millenarianism (Ram Rajya)" used
by the Hindutvavadis in their political mobilizations bring Hinduism and
Hindutva together, portraying both, in the eyes of the public, very favorably.
The Hindutvavadis consciously cultivate Hindu sensibilities—very effectively—to advance their cause.[13]

But in consciously or unconsciously endorsing such political use (abuse?) of Hinduism by the proponents of Hindutva the Supreme Court's "Hindutva judgment" really tampered with the heart of secularism and liberal political democracy. The rot had, however, already set in much earlier. We need to then turn to Hindutvavadi terrorism, and then to Delhi, 1984, Mumbai, 1993, and Gujarat, 2002, the three major communal-hate pogroms in the "secular, democratic republic" of India, and view all of these with an historical eye.

HINDUTVAVADI TERRORISM AND STATE COMPLICITY

It was V. D. Savarkar, when he headed the Hindu Mahasabha during 1937–42, who urged Hindutva nationalists to join the British-Indian Army in order to "militarise Hinduism" to take on the Muslims in the civil war he was anticipating after the British left. In the princely states too, the Hindu Mahasabha focused on establishing its influence in their armies, and at the time of Partition, obtaining access to armaments to attack Muslims.[14] Savarkar wanted the caste-Hindu middle classes to get into uniform, learn discipline, acquire expertise in the use of arms, be ready to spill blood, attain "masculinity," and become Rambos (exemplary radical Right militants) in leading the *squadristi* of the Hindutva-nationalist movement.

But, before Savarkar, it was B. S. Moonje,[15] among the foremost of the Hindutvavadi leaders from the early 1920s to the start of the Second World War, who looked to fascist Italy as a source of inspiration and helped establish, in the 1930s, direct contacts with fascist leaders there, this in order to militarize the Hindutva-nationalist movement "according to fascist patterns." Moonje's scheme of the Central Hindu Military Society and the foundation of its Bhonsala Military School was a concrete manifestation of the attempt to achieve this objective, as also the evolution of the concept of internal enemy "along explicitly fascist lines."[16]

However, we need to get back to Savarkar, for it his portrait that adorns the Central Hall of the Indian Parliament—for the section of the establishment calling the shots in the corridors of power, paying homage implies *Heil Swatantryaveer Savarkar!* Yes, Savarkar even "supported Hitler's anti-Jewish policy," drew a strong parallel "between the Muslim question in India and the Jewish problem in Germany," and mooted the idea "that being a Hindu was a matter of race and blood, not only a matter of culture," "strikingly similar to the racial myths elaborated in Germany."[17]

Contemporary involvement of Hindutvavadi militants in a series of terrorist acts—bomb blasts in Malegaon (in 2006 and 2008), on the Samjhauta Express (in 2007), at Hyderabad's Mecca Masjid (2007), at the Ajmer Sharif

Dargah (2007), and Modasa (2008)—including an ex-army major and a serving Lt. Colonel in one of these operations, and evidence of RSS sanction at the highest level for these crimes, seem to be a clear indication of progress on Savarkar's project. The confessions of Swami Aseemanand—who headed the Vanvasi Kalyan Ashram's religious wing, the Shraddha Jagran Vibhag— in December 2010 to a magistrate, and in interviews (four of them, between January 2012 and January 2014) given to Leena Gita Raghunath, the latter cited in an essay penned by her,[18] directly point to the fact that the terrorist acts were sanctioned by Mohan Bhagwat, the current chief of the RSS and the Sangh's general secretary at the time. Raghunath writes:

> According to Aseemanand, both RSS leaders [Mohan Bhagwat and Indresh Kumar, the latter "now on the organization's powerful seven-member national executive council"] approved [sanctioned his proposed plan to bomb "several Muslim targets around India"], and Bhagwat told him, "You can work on this." Indresh added, "You can work on this with Sunil [Sunil Joshi, Assemanand's accomplice, an RSS pracharak]. We will not be involved, but if you are doing this, you can consider us to be with you."

A disclosure by Rohini Salian,[19] the then special public prosecutor, that she had been asked by an officer of the National Investigative Agency (NIA) to go "soft" on the Hindu extremists accused in the 2008 Malegaon bomb blast case, and also that she wanted to seek discharge of the nine Muslims arrested and charge-sheeted for the 2006 Malegaon bomb blasts but the NIA was not in favor of her suggestion, suggest that the BJP leaders bossing over the NIA wanted the public prosecutor to protect the Hindutvavadi extremists accused. Worse, such moves suggest that this directive of the political bosses is not grounded in law; they are tampering with the judicial process, not allowing it to get to the truth of the matter and punish those who have committed the terrible crimes. The Hindutvavadi extremists accused in the bomb blasts mentioned earlier are deemed, according to the leaders of the Sangh Parivar, to be "patriots."[20] And so the NIA seems to be creating the grounds for dropping all the charges against the Hidutvavadi extremists. It had already done this in the 2008 Malegaon bomb blasts case, and has even discharged some of the accused after believing their statements, in effect, taking on the role of the judiciary in examining and discarding the evidence gathered by the previous investigating agency.[21]

Basically, as far as India is concerned, there are three kinds of terrorism. The first is the terror perpetrated by the state. The second is the terrorism of those among the Muslim victims who feel defeated, humiliated, and crushed by state terrorism and the forces of Hindutva-nationalism with active state complicity, and see no possibility of justice from the courts. And the third is Hindutvavadi terrorism, which is, partly, at least, a consequence of the second kind of terrorism, as also the state's tendency to let Hindutvavadi terrorism ride, even though it is aware of the careful planning that has gone into its making.[22]

Indeed, even the demolition of the Babri Masjid, codenamed "Operation Janmabhoomi," and executed on December 6, 1992, was an elaborately planned and meticulously executed operation. But while "credit" has so far been given to the leaders of the RSS, the VHP, and the BJP, one must now also give brownie points to the retired military officers (their names are not in the public realm as yet) who trained a thirty-eight-member squad, a "Laxman Sena," to demolish the Mosque, as a *Cobrapost* probe has revealed,[23] and to which Central Bureau of Investigation officials have confirmed that "there is no new revelation in it" and that all the disclosures had already been included in the charge-sheet that the agency has filed.[24] Be that as it may, the vandalism of the Laxman Sena put into orbit the devils of violence and rapacity in two of independent India's worst communal-hate pogroms.

COMMUNAL-HATE POGROMS

Religious-communal hate politics, a characteristic feature of power struggles in India since the 1890s, was given an ideological content with the founding of the Hindu Mahasabha in 1914 and the RSS in 1925. Hardly unexpected, religious-communal violence became a tragic facet of Indian politics from the 1920s onward and grew steadily in the wake of Partition. The Great Calcutta Killings of 1946, communal clashes all over north India and Bengal, the genocidal "cleansing" of the Punjab, both in Pakistan and India, must be mentioned, as also that, in the Partition riots, taken together, 500,000 persons of all communities died and 14 million were subjected to forced migration. And, in the aftermath of Partition, the massacres of Muslims in what was hitherto the state of Hyderabad under the Nizam in the wake of the Indian Army's "Police Action" in September 1948, as also of Hindus in East Pakistan in 1949 and 1950, all these tragic happenings need to be broached.[25]

The "Classified and Confidential Detailed Report of Pandit Sundar Lal, Qazi Abdul Ghaffar, and Maulana Abdulla Misri on the Aftermath of the Police Action [Military Invasion] by the Indian Army of the Hyderabad State in September 1948"[26] has a "very conservative estimate that in the whole state at least 27 thousand to 40 thousand people lost their lives during and after the police action." It mentions, in particular, the worst reprisals against

Muslims in Osmanabad, Gulbarga, Bidar, and Nanded districts, which had been the main strongholds of the Razakars militia, where the number of people killed "was not less, if not more than 18,000." In the town of Latur, "the home of Kasim Razvi" (the politician who headed the Razarkars militia), "which had been a big business centre, with rich Kuchhi Muslim merchants, the killing continued for over twenty days. Out of a population of ten thousand Muslims there were found barely three thousand still in the town. Over thousand had been killed and the rest had run away with little else besides their lives and completely ruined financially." As the well-known lawyer and historian A. G. Noorani puts it:[27]

The Sundarlal Report is of more than historical importance; it is of current relevance, for *the massacres*, coupled with the *national indifference to them*, had left scars in the minds of Muslims in the State, Hyderabad city in particular [italics, our emphasis].

DELHI, 1984, BOMBAY, 1993, AND GUJARAT, 2002

The roots of Hindutva-national chauvinism appear to run deep, beyond the bounds of the Sangh Parivar. The Congress Party, which lays claim to the idea of "composite nationalism" and its associated ideal of "composite nationhood," has also virtually endorsed Hindu communal-hate themes, most visibly, in Delhi, 1984 and Bombay, 1993. One has only to make a comparison of the reign of terror let loose against the Sikh community in Delhi following Mrs. Indira Gandhi's assassination in 1984,[28] the Shiv Sena-led pogrom against Muslims in January 1993 in Bombay[29] under a Congress government in the state of Maharashtra, and the one in Gujarat led by the RSS and its Sangh Parivar organizations, including the BJP, from February 27 to mid-May 2002[30] when a BJP government was in power.

The attacks on members of the Sikh community in Delhi and its suburbs in November 1984, "far from being a spontaneous expression of 'madness' and popular 'grief and anger' at Mrs. Indira Gandhi's assassination as made out to be by the authorities, were the outcome of a well-organized plan marked by acts of both deliberate commission and omission by important politicians of the Congress (I) at the top and by authorities in the administration." Following the announcement of Mrs. Gandhi's death, three vicious rumors were circulated—that Sikhs celebrated the prime minister's assassination, that "train-loads of hundreds of Hindu dead bodies arrived at Old Delhi Station from Punjab," and that the water supply was poisoned by the Sikhs, which shaped the public mind in acquiescing in the attacks and murders that followed.

The Bombay pogrom too was "pre-planned." The religiosity of the *maha aartis* (songs praising, and lamps offered to, a Hindu deity in mass ceremonies) used for propaganda and mobilization by the Hindutvavadis often were "open provocations," but the police did nothing. In Gujarat on February 27, 2002, in the aftermath of the Godhra tragedy, the then Chief Minister of Gujarat, Narendra Modi, connived with the VHP to immediately brand the tragic episode as a Pakistani Inter-Services Intelligence conspiracy, the Union Home Minister L. K. Advani following suit. The former then allowed the VHP to take the dead bodies of the *kar sevaks* to Ahmedabad by road in a procession to incite Hindu passions, and even supported a bandh called by the VHP, both to incite religious hatred against Muslims.

In Delhi 1984, the arsonists that systematically set fire to Sikh houses, shops, and *gurudwaras* (literally, doors to the guru, places of worship for Sikhs) were led and directed by well-known Congress (I) leaders and workers who identified the Sikh houses and shops, even using voters' lists to identify Sikh households. In Bombay in January 1993, the Hindutvavadi marauders had "carefully prepared lists of houses, businesses, and vehicles of Muslims, and they precisely targeted them," just like their counterparts in Gujarat in 2002 had, according to Human Rights Watch, "computer printouts listing the addresses of Muslim families and their properties, information obtained from the Ahmedabad municipal corporation among other sources."

At the height of the pogrom in Delhi, 1984, October 31 to November 4, "the police all over the city uniformly betrayed a common behavioural pattern, marked by (i) total absence from the scene; or (ii) a role of passive spectators; or (iii) direct participation or abetment in the orgy of violence against the Sikhs." In Bombay in December 1992, after the demolition of the Babri Masjid, the public anger of Muslims was countered by police brutality; in January 1993, when the pre-planned attacks on Muslims took place, the same police "looked the other way." Most likely, "there were unwritten indications from the top not to intervene," just like in Gujarat in 2002. Here, the Chief Minister, Narendra Modi, at a meeting at his residence in the evening of the day of the Godhra tragedy, advised (ordered?) senior bureaucrats and the top guns of the police that "this time the situation warranted that the Muslims be taught a lesson . . . it was imperative that [the Hindus] be allowed to vent their anger" (according to the Indian Police Service officer, Sanjiv Bhatt, who was present at this gathering).

In Delhi, 1984, soon after the assassination, at a high-level meeting at the prime minister's official residence, a senior police officer "expressed the view that the army should be called as otherwise there would be a holocaust. No attention was paid to this view." The delay in calling out the army and "a deliberate design to keep (it) ineffective" when it did come in, was unpardonable—Prime Minister Rajiv Gandhi held charge of Defense and Narasimha Rao was the Home Minister. Among other tragedies, on November 2, 1984, every train "was left at the mercy of gangsters who dragged out Sikhs from the incoming train compartments, lynched them, threw their bodies on the platforms or the railway tracks and set on fire many." In Bombay in January 1993, the Army "was restricted to meaningless flag-marches"; in Gujarat in 2002, there was a deliberate two-day delay in deploying the Indian Army to restore law and order.

In Delhi, 1984, certain Congress (I) leaders—even MPs like Sajjan Kumar, Dharamdas Shastri, and H. K. L. Bhagat—"played a decisive role in organising the riots. . . . It is difficult to believe that Prime Minister Rajiv Gandhi was unaware of the activities of (these) important and well known members of his party for full five days (for October 31 to November 5)." In Bombay in January 1993, the Union Defence Minister Sharad Pawar was trying to settle political scores with the Chief Minister of Maharashtra, Sudharkarrao Naik, and vice versa, with both openly leveling charges against each other, even as the Shiv Sena "openly claimed 'credit'" for the pogrom. In Gujarat in 2002, more sinisterly, the VHP leader Ashok Singhal viewed what his forces had done as "a matter of pride" and "a befitting reply to what had been perpetrated on the Hindus in the past 1000 years" and his compatriot Pravin Togadia was proud of the "Hindu awakening," even as Prime Minister A. B. Vajpayee blamed the Muslims when he rhetorically asked, "who lit the fire?"

In one respect, Bombay, 1993 and Gujarat, 2002 were different from Delhi, 1984. In Bombay in January 1993, for instance, in the "targeting of isolated Muslim homes and businesses, there was a clear attempt to bring about a *geographical division of the city on communal lines*" (my emphasis), just as in Gujarat in 2002 the Hindutvadi attackers targeted—looted and burnt—Muslim properties and establishments, even those with Hindu names, leaving the Hindu-owned ones unscathed, a clear attempt to bring about a similar *spatial division of the city along communal lines*.

Delhi, 1984, as the historian Dilip Simeon puts it, "set a new standard for the normalisation of brutality and lawlessness in the Indian polity."[31] Indeed, the powers-that-be allowed this "brutality and lawlessness" to "rage for several days," and this "new standard" ruled the roost in Bombay in January 1993. As the Lok Shahi Hakk Sanghatana–CPDR Report put it: the "Shiv Sena-led mobs" went on "an unprecedented spree of murder, loot, and arson for 10 days as the chief minister, defence minister, police, paramilitary, and Army watched on, and as the prime minister doled out assurances to delegations in Delhi." Such a standard of brutality and lawlessness had indeed become the new normal, for in Gujarat in 2002, too, such attacks lasted three days with total state complicity, and continued sporadically until mid-May 2002.

In the aftermath of 9/11 and with Washington's declaration of the global "war on terror," the Sangh Parivar was emboldened in Gujarat in 2002 to prove that it could be more sinister, more evil and wicked than the Congress and the Sena had been in Mumbai in January 1993. A case in point was the nine-month pregnant Kausar Bano's killing at Naroda Patia in Gujarat in 2002; whatever the highly-paid lawyers defending the Hindutva brigade might have argued, the barbarity, the savage cruelty, nothing could have been more sinister than that.

The alleged mastermind of the pogrom is now India's prime minister. So far, the Indian courts, despite *prima facie* allegations of gross criminal misconduct against Narendra Modi and other powerful persons, for instance, in Zakia Jafri's case,[32] have been reluctant to initiate criminal court proceedings against the accused because of their high rank and the power that they wield. Now that Modi is in the prime minister's chair, the chances that the principle of equality before the law will be upheld in this matter are minuscule. This is an outrage, given that even the initial charges against Modi are of gross criminal misconduct—promoting enmity between Hindus and Muslims, making statements that led to harm to Muslims, acting in a manner prejudicial to inter-religious harmony, engaging in acts that promoted national disintegration, and in unlawful activity with the intent of causing harm to Muslims.[33]

RETROGRESSION IN THE INDIAN STATE AND IN BRAHMINICAL HINDUISM

Is the executive of the Indian "secular state" grounded in the constitution and the law when it sends a message to the bosses of the law-and-order machinery to turn a blind eye to terrible mass crimes taking place in front of their very noses? When it considers the killers to be patriots and those who want to bring these xenophobic liquidators to book, "desh drohis" (betrayers of the nation)? Can the Indian state be characterized as "secular" when the executive demands of the public prosecutors (whom it appoints) and the investigative agencies protect the Hindutvavadis accused of committing the terrible crimes? What about the two major political parties, the Congress and the BJP? The former once promoted enmity between Hindus and Sikhs, and the latter, between Hindus and Muslims, and both acted in a manner that was prejudicial to interreligious harmony, engaged in unlawful activity with the intent of causing harm to Sikhs, in one case, and Muslims, in the other.

A great deal of importance has been given to Delhi 1984 in the above narrative because—and this comes out so well in Uma Chakravarty and Nandita Haksar's *The Delhi Riots: Three Days in the Life of a Nation*, where the oral testimonies speak for themselves—many of those who experienced Delhi, 1984, had either been through the trauma of West Punjab 1946–47 or had inherited the memory of it all. Then it was unfortunate the country was divided; all of a sudden they found themselves in a *gair mulk* (an alien land). But here and now, Delhi, 1984, the horror of it all, the devils of violence, the demons of rapacity, the crimes against humanity come back to haunt them once more, in their own *mulk*, turned into a tyranny but masquerading as a democracy.

A state is secular if it (i) guarantees individual and corporate "freedom of religion," (ii) treats the individual as a citizen irrespective of his/her religious affiliation, (iii) does not constitutionally identify itself with any particular religion, and neither promotes nor interferes with any religion, in other words, "separation" from religion.[34] As far as the Indian constitution is concerned, it safeguards, in Article 25, freedom of conscience and free profession, practice, and propagation of religion, relating to condition (i) above. Article 15(1), in maintaining that "The State shall not discriminate against any citizen on grounds only of religion, race, caste, sex, place of birth or any of them," and Article 16 relating to equal opportunity in public employment or office, relate to condition (ii). And Articles 25 to 28,[35] among other things, suggest that the state must treat all religions alike, with no specific religious preferences, it being obvious then that the state cannot establish or practice any religion, and thus these articles relate, somewhat, to condition (iii). Indeed, in *Keshavananda Bharati vs. State of Kerala* [(1973) 4 SCC 225], a full bench of the Supreme Court ruled that secularism is a part of the "basic structure"[36] of the constitution.

Nevertheless, religious organizations have influenced the functioning of the state in matters of civil law and in education. If the state in India was secular, it would have, by now, seven decades after independence, phased out all religious, caste, and community codes, and brought in a universal, secular, uniform civil code. Indeed, beyond the principles of the constitution and modern jurisprudence, the traditional concepts of "rule" and "law" seem to apply quite a bit—in the commitment of infractions, in many a case, the penalties that apply depend upon one's class, caste, ethnic, gender, and/or religious identity. The traditional concepts of rule and law seem to have been applied not merely by quasi-judicial *khap* panchayats (of caste-clan elders) in the North Indian countryside, but even by the union executive and the Supreme Court in the capital. For instance, (i) In the immediate post-independence period, Kashmir's largely Hindu army was absorbed in the Indian Army, but Hyderabad's Nizam Army, largely Muslim, was disbanded, leading to the loss of livelihoods of 20,000 persons, an instance of discriminatory treatment of the Other.[37] (ii) In a hearing in the Supreme Court on July 28,

2015 on Yakub Memon's petition in the 1993 Bombay bomb blasts case seeking a stay on his execution, one of the judges, Justice A. R. Dave, who refused to stay the death warrant, "recalled verses from the Manusmriti" to justify his stand.[38] The Manusmriti goes by an archaic notion of law as dharma or caste duty that takes into account a person's so-called karma, rebirth, and caste status in the assignment of punishment for crime. In such a conception of law, a Muslim, deemed to be a complete outcaste, deserves the worst.

In the case of Yakub Memon, the law has, in effect, allowed the criminal justice system to induce the accused with an implicit promise of protection against the death penalty if he gave himself up and stood trial, and it has then overlooked the "mitigating circumstances" of his cooperation with the Intelligence agencies and executed him. The March 12, 1993, Bombay bomb blasts was the direct consequence of the December 6, 1992, demolition of the Babri Masjid and the January 1993 anti-Muslim pogrom in Bombay, in both of which there was state collusion/connivance, with the perpetrators guaranteed to go scot free. The utterly tragic consequences notwithstanding, these blasts nevertheless reverberated with a powerful political message. Even the Shiv Sena's *pramukh sher* (leading tiger), Bal Thackeray, who, in January 1993, "like a veteran General, commanded his loyal Shiv Sainiks" to attack the Muslims and "ensure that 'not a single *landya* (derogatory Marathi word for Muslims) would survive to give oral evidence,'"[39] now put his tail between his legs and sought even more heavily-guarded state protection in his den, Matoshree.

There can be no doubt that religious mysticism, mythological beliefs, and the portrayal of "Hindu civilization" as a "golden age" but "Muslim civilization" as "despotic tyranny" seem to affect the ways in which some of the modern ideals that permeate the constitution are interpreted, this with the blessings of the Indian judiciary. The judgment by the Lucknow Bench of the Allahabad High Court in the case of the Babri Masjid–Ram Janmabhoomi at Ayodhya on 30 September 2010 is

> based on the belief that lord Ram was born under the central dome of the masjid . . . built in 1528. . . . On the night of 22–23 December 1949 some 50 people led by three persons entered the mosque and installed three statues under the central dome . . . police should have acted under Section 145 of the Criminal Procedure Code (CrPC) . . . to clear the mosque of the idols . . . (but) (in)stead the UP government attacked the mosque and prohibited the removal of the idols (thereby) condon(ing) . . . the crime . . . a catena of (subsequent) judicial orders . . . effectively converted the masjid into a temple. On 19 January 1950, civil judge Bir Singh restrained Muslims from removing the

idols through a temporary injunction which was confirmed by the
Allahabad High Court on 26 April 1955. Later on, . . . the Rajiv
Gandhi government manoeuvred and manipulated things in such
a way that on 1 February 1986 the district judge of Faizabad threw
open the mosque to Hindus, transforming it into a temple. In 1989
all the suits were transferred to the Allahabad High Court to be heard
together. On 14 August 1989, the high court ordered the continuance
of the status quo as it was on 1 February 1986. . . .

. . . [Meanwhile,] a political movement was organised for the demolition . . . The Indian state had a few years to mobilise its machinery
to prevent the illegal act of demolition. But the state defaulted. On 6
December 1992, few thousands of people gathered at Ayodhya, led by
the top leaders of the Bharatiya Janata Party and other Hindu fundamentalist organisations, several of whom addressed the mobs calling
upon them to demolish the mosque. The armed forces of the Indian
state were present in strength. When the mobs stormed the mosque
and razed it to the ground, the armed forces exulted along with the
mobs. The Indian state facilitated the demolition of the mosque. . . .

. . . [Following the demolition,] (i)nstead of handing over the place
to Muslims to rebuild the mosque, the central government acquired
all the areas in dispute in the suits pending in the Allahabad High
Court along with certain adjacent areas. . . .

. . . The judgment of the Allahabad High Court of 30 September
2010 . . . put the final seal on the acts of installation of statues and
demolition of the mosque.

. . . [Clearly,] (t)he sequence of omissions and commissions committed by the executive and judiciary manifests a consistent tendency
that, when the dispute is between the views and faiths held by some
fundamentalist forces among Hindus and the views and faiths
expressed by other religious elements, they take a stand in favour of
Hindu fundamentalists.

. . . (O)ne seeks remedial measures from the judiciary when the
executive or even the legislature itself commits illegal acts. But what
does one do when the judiciary itself commits unlawful acts?[40]

Appeals against the HC judgment are now in the Supreme Court. Will
the Modi government, if and when it gets the required support in the Rajya
Sabha, make a law for the construction of the Ram temple as proposed in the
BJP's manifesto? As A. G. Noorani puts it, if such a law comes to pass and
then a temple rises on the debris of the demolished mosque, "(i)t will rise on
the ruins of secularism and the rule of law as well."[41]

What then of the Indian brand of secularism? Gandhi had an equal regard for all religions; obviously, to do so, he would have, presumably, carefully studied all religions. If he did, in the matter of caste, how could he have had equal respect for Hinduism and Buddhism? In the matter of personal law regarding divorce, how could he have had an equal regard for Islam and Christianity? Can then one have equal regard for the content of all religions? Perhaps Gandhi chose to abstract from all these specific matters of concern and only focus, in the abstract, on the humanist element of all religions. Indeed, the notion of Indian secularism bandied about by the establishment as a constitutional feature, *sarva dharma samabhava* (equal regard for all religions) within the state's jurisdiction, is said to derive from Gandhi's ideal. But can one consider the caste system in Hinduism a humanist element of that religion, or can one reckon that aspects of Muslim personal law related to divorce by repudiation is humanist?

Clearly, a state claiming to be secular must go by Enlightenment thought. It must conduct a concrete analysis of the concrete situation regarding all the religions in its jurisdiction. Being neither religious nor against religion, such a state must then actively critique religion and the anti-humanist elements of religions, and it must encourage and support those struggling for reform within the various religious communities.[42]

POLITICAL RELIGION, RELIGIOUS POLITICS

A critique of the dominant religion in India would reveal that it has been used, nay abused, as an ideology to perpetuate gross injustice on a large section of the population. Even in the twenty-first century, the lower shudras, the Dalits, the *Adivasis*, and the lower caste, Dalit and adivasi converts to Christianity, Islam, and Sikhism, taken together and constituting a majority of the population, are the victims of appalling oppression and discrimination justified on the basis of traditional concepts of "rule" and "law." Dalits, Adivasis, and the lower shudras, including those among them who converted to Christianity, Islam, Sikhism and Buddhism, are socially marginalized and spatially isolated from the three upper varnas and the upper shudras, and the poor among them remain the most intensely exploited and oppressed victims of the class–caste structure condoned by the Manusmriti. Truly, Brahminical religion as an ideology has contributed to the implantation of an exceptionally durable and extraordinarily vicious caste–class system of domination, oppression, and exploitation.

A radical critique of Brahminical Hinduism as a political religion and of the character of religious communal-hate politics might provide a clue to understanding the Indian state's apparent complicity with (i) those who vandalized the five churches in Delhi during November 2014 and January 2015; (ii) the VHP's forced *ghar wapsis* (re-conversions); (iii) the Hindutvavadi terrorists who are deemed to be patriots (*deshbhakts*); and, (iv) those who organized and executed the pogroms against Sikhs and Muslims. It seems as if the executive of the Indian state cared not at all about Article 14 (equality before the law, and the state treating people in the same circumstances alike), Article 15 (prohibiting discrimination on grounds of religion, race, caste, sex or place of birth), Article 25 (freedom of conscience, and freedom to profess, practice, and propagate one's religion), and, indeed, Article 21, the right to protection of life and personal liberty.

In the commission of the infractions and the mass crimes that have been alluded to, the penalties—or the lack of any, where there is official impunity—have been determined by the class and religious identities of the offenders and the victims. As Uma Chakravarti puts it in the case of Delhi, 1984, "the long road to justice has led nowhere."[43] All this leads to the question: Is there an *institutional* bias that favors Hindus and is prejudiced against Christians, Muslims, and Sikhs in India? What the latter have been up against are the commissions and omissions of powerful persons in authority who hold supremacist beliefs and points of view stemming from religious-communal hatred.

DEVIL CITING THE SCRIPTURES

Overall, the facts suggest that the "secular state" in India, by its political use of Brahminical religion, has a strong tendency to retrogress toward a Hindutvavadi state. Brahminical religion, taking advantage of the Indian state's ideological affinity with it, has been a party to a tendency toward that religion's de facto reversion to a state religion, even as the state uses "positive secularism" as an ideology to buttress its legitimacy. To return to the verse from *The Merchant of Venice* with which this chapter opened, with Antonio in an aside to Bassanio, who needs to borrow money from Shylock to be eligible to become a suitor to Portia. Antonio is here describing Shylock as a man who looks good on the outside (a "goodly apple") but is evil within ("rotten at the heart").

Just as Shylock in *The Merchant of Venice* is an "evil soul producing holy witness," so also the Indian state wants to appear spiritual and tolerant on the outside, committed to "secularism," in Modi's words, devoted to "equal respect *and* treatment for all faiths." But, just like Shylock is like a "goodly apple rotten at the heart," so also, in practice, the Indian "secular state" (i) aids the Hindutvavadi forces in not allowing Muslims and Christians to propagate their religion beyond their own laity (that is, blocks conversions); (ii) treats Muslims and Christians as second-class citizens; and (iii) is wedded to Brahminical religion and the ideology of Hindutva and promotes the interests of that religion and that brand of "semi-fascist" politics, as it did in Delhi 1984, Bombay, 1993, and Gujarat, 2002. It's time then to try to understand the "semi-fascist" tendency at work—"authoritarian democracy," complicity of the state in the *mala fide* acts of the Hindutva-nationalist movement, and so on. Even today, "patriotic" Hinduvavadi scoundrels are forcing Muslims to chant "Bharat Mata Ki Jai" (Hail the Victory of Mother India), attacking Muslim and Christian clergy for religious conversions, provoking the lynching of cattle traders and beef eaters, and attacking young Muslim men married to or in love with Hindu women after falsely accusing them of feigning love in order to convert the women to Islam, the accused Muslim men labeled "love jihadis"!

9

"Little Man, What Now?"
—In the Wake of Semi-Fascist and Sub-Imperialist Tendencies

You can't have ideas like mine and expect to be left alone.
—PIER PAOLO PASOLINI, THE ITALIAN POET, FILMMAKER,
NOVELIST, AND POLITICAL JOURNALIST, SHORTLY
BEFORE HIS ASSASSINATION,
NOVEMBER 2, 1975

Overburdened by anxiety over the sway of Hindutva-nationalism after February 2002, compounded by isolation at a workplace breeding mistrust and back-stabbing, its management steeped in the values of the *Dharmashastras* (patriarchal caste-Hindu law books), I was compulsorily retired "in the public interest." When I think of those times, I invariably remember the character Pinneberg, the "little man" or "nobody" from the German novelist Hans Fallada's 1932 *Little Man, What Now?* The novel hit the stands just before the Nazi Party took over. "Nothing lasted but being alone"—those words from its final chapter say a lot about the solitariness upon rejection of those who "don't belong." In 1935, Fallada was classified by the Nazi regime as an "undesirable author." That was more than eighty years ago, but now, "master criminals" are running amuck once more in twenty-first century India.

It seems reasonable to assume that liberal-political democracy in India, however rotten it may be, is not about to be discarded, for capitalism in its neoliberal form and India's nascent "sub-imperialism" are not threatened. They do not, as yet, need the application of the ultimate safeguard—fascism. Two processes, running parallel to each other over the last two decades, neo-robber baron capitalist development and Indian big business and the state's nascent sub-imperialist tendency, on the one hand, and the reactionary Hindutva-nationalist movement, on the other, have congregated once again, since 2014, at the national level. They are now greatly strengthened compared to such convergence at the time of the Bharatiya Janata Party (BJP)-led National Democratic Alliance (NDA) government during 1998–2004.

The consequence of this can be *semi*-fascism—fascism hyphenated with a semi—not full-blown fascism, mainly, but not wholly, because there is no need to dispense with electoral democracy, given bipartisanism (concurrence of the Congress and the BJP) as far as both neoliberal economic policy and strategy and nascent sub-imperialism are concerned. Indian big business has no reason to endorse an overthrow of electoral democracy and support the institution of a one-party dictatorship. Despite the Maoist movement, the ruling establishment is not threatened by revolution from below, and hence, there is no imperative for instituting a full-blown fascist regime.

CLUES FROM HISTORICAL FASCISM

Any analysis aiming to understand contemporary semi-fascism in the making must revisit historical fascism, especially in Germany and Italy.[1] It can be argued that the rise of historical fascism emanated from the impact of the imperialist First World War on the economic and social structures of some of the defeated developed capitalist nations. The Kingdom of Italy joined the Entente in May 1915, urged on by Mussolini's paid war propaganda, and after secret negotiations with Britain and France, bargained for territory if victorious. But although in the victorious camp in 1918, with the wretchedness of life in the trenches, and poverty, misery, and degradation at home for the majority, Italy's fate was much like that of the defeated Central Powers. So the context was the war, the "defeat," the reparations (in the case of Germany), hyper-inflation (in Germany but not in Italy), deep despair, and imagined-threatened disintegration of the nation-state.

Adding to this was the buildup of a reactionary mass movement anchored in paramilitary formations, the subsequent emergence of a one-party regime with a *Führer* or a *Duce* as the supreme symbol of authoritarian leadership, a repressive regime that was violently nationalistic, racist (racist anti-Semitic, in the case of Germany), intolerant of opposition, hostile to civil liberties and democratic rights. And before fascism came to power there was its principal adversary, a formidable labor movement, with one wing led by social democrats, and the other, smaller, but headed by communists with revolutionary objectives. The independent labor movement was among the first targets in both Italy and Germany, in both cases replaced swiftly by a fascist all-inclusive labor movement directly integrated into both party and state. Fascism presented itself as an authoritative alternative in the form of militant, demagogic nationalism[2] and violence (with the use of "storm-troopers/Blackshirts" in active complicity with the state) against all those whom it singled out—communists, social democrats, the labor movement, and in Germany, the Jews, the gypsies, and the Slavs. Mussolini eventually fell in line with anti-Semitic racism, from 1938 onward.

When the reactionary mass movement (fascists mobilized the masses from below) and party upstaged the other right-wing nationalist parties, cartelized big business came eagerly on board. In both Germany and Italy, the fascists came to power by "constitutional" means, and only then did they refuse to play the liberal-political democratic game. Upon coming to power, Hitler and Mussolini smashed all opposition and blocked all channels to re-formation of a legal opposition in their respective regimes. The crux of the transition from liberal-political democracy to fascism was the permanent suppression of legal opposition by doing away with the very rights of political opposition—freedom of the press and speech, freedom of association, freedom to vote and seek public office. The important point is that the reactionary mass movement heralding "national renewal," whether in Germany or Italy, did not by itself produce fascism. The Great Depression, monopoly capitalism mired in stagnation, and deep economic, political, social, and cultural decline in Germany (in Italy, the fascists came to power before the Great Slump), and importantly, serious undermining of the very structure of capitalist rule, led to the rise and consolidation of the fascist regime. And with the coming to power of fascism, the strong state and one-party system followed, and then, imperialist strategy. Monopoly capital and the state came together to aggressively extend their influence, their power, and their mutual interests beyond the national borders.

There is just one more thing that needs to be mentioned. With the establishment of a strong state and a close state–big business bloc, and with some sections of big business losing favor (in Germany, the Jewish capitalists were expropriated), some parvenus backed by powerful fascist politicians entered the ranks of big business. Personnel of the top levels of big business were absorbed into the state apparatus—the separate channels through which the ruling class exercised its political *and* economic power in liberal-political democracy now tended to converge into one under fascism. Nevertheless, in return for support from big business, the Nazis restored a number of oligopolies held or controlled by the state, those in banking, mining, steel, ship-building, and shipping lines to big private capitalists favored by them.[3]

This move served the purpose of consolidating Nazi power with the support such privatizations garnered from certain favored plutocrats. The Nazis also built one of the most formidable industrial public-sector conglomerates in the world at the time, the Reichswerke Hermann Göring.

This bare account of historical fascism suggests that it would be best if fascism/semi-fascism is theorized as a process, keeping in mind the various aspects/elements just mentioned, for then one can avoid the pitfall of permanently fixing its meaning based on its historical forms in Germany and Italy. As a process, following the gaining of control of the executive of the state by fascists, it might be useful to discern the process and tactics of "bringing into line" (in German, *Gleichschaltung*)—and thereby ensuring political conformity—the bureaucracy, parliament, the judiciary, the military, local and provincial governments, the media, culture, and educational institutions.

The semi-fascist tendencies in India today can be better understood against this background.

MONSTROUS POLARIZATION AS THE "NATURAL ORDER" OF SOCIETY!

Capitalism is based on exploitation—private appropriation of part of the product of the labor of others and of natural resources—and this generates inequality. Neo-liberalism exacerbates such inequality. It is a package of policies coupled with an ideological framework. The policies include free trade, privatization, financial openness, the elimination of government regulations on capital, and fiscal conservatism leading to reductions in social programs, all these appended with a facade of social and governance issues, such as, for instance, fighting corruption. The ideology assigns primacy to economic growth, believes in the dynamism of the market and the private sector, and celebrates inequality. India embarked on such neoliberal economic policy two and a half decades ago, leading to big business's "accumulation by dispossession," backed by the state's sub-imperialist aggression in the "non-capitalist areas," which brought on Maoist "Spring Thunder," Phase III.

India's moneybags took full advantage of the freedom to accumulate wealth by all available means. The "financial aristocracy" benefited the most from this opportunity, for it multiplied its wealth not by production alone but by pocketing the already available wealth of others, state property and the commons, leading to the monstrous class polarization seen in India today.

Even learned economists seem to be mystified by the economic system, as shown by an examination of the false solutions they propose to solve the problems of the 56.1 percent of the population who are at the bottom of the steep economic hierarchy. Basically, their diagnoses of the problems are oblivious of the real world of classes, wherein ownership entitles a few to substantial shares of the output. Despite a trend annual rate of growth of real national income/product of around 6 percent (official statistics seem to overestimate services sector growth) over two and a half decades since 1991, the distribution of that income—which is not merely a passive consequence of production and exchange—has prevented the increment of aggregate income from raising the standards of living of the masses. Hardly anyone, even in the economics profession, ever mentions Marx's labor theory of value and his analysis of exploitation. Didn't he also say something about the loop between the ruling classes and the ruling ideas?

Any wonder then that the three-fifths of the population whose lives are ruled by external economic compulsion cannot understand the world around them and are subject repeatedly to false promises. One might surely be dismayed by the many visible strains of irrationality. The extent of mystification and superstition all around the three-fifths of the population, who constitute the poor, the miserable, and the degraded, needs to be explained. Perhaps, in the face of the conservativeness of the administrative, professional, scientific, and technological sections of the middle class, the reactionary ideological influence of establishmentarian media and educational institutions, and the pernicious hold of mercantile, credit, and "semi-feudal" capital over the lives of the petty commodity producers, one at least has a clue as to why so many in India today are utterly confused and misinformed, why Hindutva-nationalism as an ideology has grown in strength.

Class–caste distinctions and Hindutvavadi morality are openly flaunted, especially by the nouveau riche, who unlike its older counterpart, relates to money as if it can buy anyone and anything. This is not at all surprising, for neo-robber baron capitalist development has paved the way for the making of fortunes by the privileged where there were not many such avenues earlier, and with low income taxes and a lack of a social code regarding the extent of permissible relative poverty, the billionaire–casual wage worker income ratio on the order of 10^6 (a million to one!) is seen as part of the "natural order" of society. Indeed, the nouveau riche also defines "quality," and does it very carefully for those who come from Dalit–*bahujan* (the latter, literally, the majority of the people, irrespective of the lower sub-castes assigned to them) social backgrounds, this in order to preserve that "natural order."

PROPENSITY OF OVERPRODUCTION

The relative immiserization and the monstrous class polarization that India has witnessed over the last two and a half decades are consequences, not of any "natural order" of society, but of the working out of the very nature of capital as self-expanding value. Marx put it wonderfully well when he wrote: "The real barrier of capitalist production is capital itself." With the sharp deceleration of real GDP growth (the more recent official numbers are suspect), what is now unfolding is the contradiction between the capacity to produce and the capacity to consume. The process of accumulation is predicated upon an increase in the rate of exploitation, but at the same time, the realization of the additional surplus is dependent upon additional purchasing power of the mass of consumers. Both are essential to spur investment and economic growth in a capitalist system. But relative immiserization has reached a point where it is holding down growth of the relative purchasing power of the masses, weakening consumption and adding to overcapacity, thus lowering expected profits on new investment, and thereby dampening the propensity to invest.[4]

The neoliberal path of capitalist development followed over the last two and a half decades is suffused with a realization problem, and the captains of big business and the MNCs at the top of the social-class pyramid, the main beneficiaries of the skewed distribution of the surplus, are now trying to maintain their higher rates of profit by holding back on investments that would otherwise have expanded the stock of productive capital. A successful process of accumulation requires a rise in mass consumption, but when the capitalist class does not concede a sufficient rise in the incomes of the regular and casual workers and the petty commodity producers, the addition to productive capacity turns out to be more than what the increase in consumption can possibly sustain. In such a situation, and with self-imposed caps on civilian government spending, militarism and nascent sub-imperialism, besides financialization, the offsetting tendencies, come to the fore.[5] A system's tendencies are a function of its nature or character, and in this sense, the sub-imperialist and semi-fascist tendencies of the Indian political-economic system are a function of that system's nature and character. These tendencies will manifest themselves to the extent that the "interfering conditions" are weak or absent.

NASCENT SUB-IMPERIALISM

India has some of the most powerful and wealthy captains of big business in the semi-periphery of the world capitalist system. However, in the process of advancing their power, their influence, and their mutual interests beyond the country's borders, the Indian state and Indian big business are dependent upon U.S. imperialism, a dependence that deepened following the collapse of the Berlin Wall and the demise of the Soviet Union. The Indian regime began to alter its foreign policy, ultimately leading to a strategic alliance as a junior partner with U.S. imperialism. Yet, in emphasizing U.S. imperialist agency, one should not forget that India's nascent sub-imperialism is also the global face of Indian big business. Indeed, India's nascent sub-imperialism springs from the very nature of its semi-peripheral underdeveloped capitalism, which is steered by the Indian big business–state–multinational bloc.[6]

Sections of Indian big business and the subsidiaries of the MNCs have gained unprecedented prosperity over the last two decades, derived from high rates of exploitation at home and the growth of exports of IT and IT-enabled services, pharmaceuticals, etc., mainly from arbitraging cheap "human capital" and from super-exploitation of those who produce surplus value or the surplus product. A relatively significant outward foreign direct investment, including to the developed capitalist countries, mainly through cross-border mergers and acquisitions, must also be acknowledged.[7]

There has thus been a rise of the "financial aristocracy," which is increasingly calling the shots in the corridors of power, and the consolidation of oligopolistic market structures in the modern industrial and services sector, reinforced, no doubt, by the MNCs. Indian big business, now that it has been exposed to two decades of constant pressures from foreign institutional investors, this in the presence of competition from and collaboration with MNCs, and competition from imports, and despite being technologically dependent on Western and Japanese monopoly capital, is now emulating its Western counterpart far more closely than is usually admitted.

FINANCIALIZATION, CONSUMERISM, AND MILITARISM

With the globalization of the country's financial markets—gross capital inflows and outflows as a percentage of GDP increased from 15.1 percent in 1990–91 to 53.9 percent in 2010–11—international financial capital is now a prominent structural characteristic of the Indian economy. Not to be left behind, Indian big business has jumped on the financial bandwagon. The registration of new non-government public and private limited companies in terms of sheer numbers, points to the extraordinary growth of "finance" vis-à-vis "industry." There were 40,459 registrations of companies (43.8 percent of the total of such registrations) in finance, insurance, real estate, and business services during 2012–13, compared to 14,146 (15.3 percent) in manufacturing in the same year (part of the trend in recent years), and cumulatively, as on 31 March 2013, 282,093 (32 percent of the total such companies at work on that date) in the former compared to 196,314 (22.2 percent) in the latter.[8] With various kinds of non-bank financial companies within the fold of the large business houses, inter-company investments financed by debt have made the process of "centralization of capital" (gaining managerial control over smaller capitals) less complicated.[9]

La Grande Bouffe, so characteristic of consumerism, is confined to the elite, which imitates the consumption patterns of its counterparts in the developed capitalist countries.[10] Much of this is ensconced in a corporate milieu wherein a considerable part of personal consumption is written off as business expenses, and the very rich siphon off part of the surpluses that they appropriate to tax havens. As the saying goes, "nothing is enough for those for whom enough is too little." Thorstein Veblen's concepts of conspicuous consumption and leisure, and pecuniary emulation,[11] these in the context of monstrous class polarization, are more relevant than ever before. Even as Indian semi-fascist leaders control people by bringing them under the sway of Hindutva-nationalism and other demeaning passions through shared devotion to *Bharat Mata* (Mother India)—with their flags, anthems (*Bande mataram*), loyalty oaths, symbols, and myths—consumerism in a corporate capitalist milieu, with its subliminal suggestions regarding the criteria of success and the ruthlessness with which affluence must be pursued, virtually declares war on nature.

Loyalty to particular brands, just like allegiance to Bharat Mata, is created through symbols and images, basically by manipulation through emotional appeal. However, at least with respect to historical fascism, the demeaning passions didn't last after its defeat, but consumerism, it seems, is worse in this respect. For those who indulge in it, they apparently fleetingly satisfy their basic compulsions, but they remain subjugated and confined, slaves of those urges. This is really echoing Pasolini, but it also raises a disturbing question: Is consumerism strengthening the incipient mass psychology of fascism? Certainly, the impression that wallowing in branded consumer goodies is equivalent to the attainment of political liberty and economic freedom, what Herbert Marcuse called "repressive desublimation," has gained much ground in these neo-robber baron capitalist times.

But now, in the throes of a "realization crisis" (a severe aggregate demand constraint), with the economy having generated capacity faster than the growth of demand, especially in consumer durables, including cars produced by the MNCs, the further opening of external markets in South Asia and beyond has become an imperative. To enable this, the government of India, via state enterprises/agencies, has been investing in infrastructural projects in South Asia as a means of expansion into neighboring-country markets. And with the state tending to increase military expenditure and import technologically superior hardware subject to the quid pro quo of gradual indigenization in India's own developing military-industrial complex, a coalition of interests involving India's defense ministry, military top brass, Indian private corporate sector (PCS) companies in the armaments business, and their multinational collaborators is solidifying.

The PCS has been making significant inroads in defense procurement with the government using the "offset policy"—under which foreign suppliers of defense hardware have to source a part of the contract value locally—to get the foreign companies to preferably set up joint ventures with Indian PCS partners. The public-sector enterprises and the ordnance factories under the Department of Defence Production are really the ones that have built the required technological capabilities over many years of learning-by-doing, but they are being progressively sidelined in favor of the PCS upstarts. The Indian PCS companies benefitting from the offset policy are mere junior partners of the foreign original equipment manufacturers. For instance, Dassault Reliance Aerospace Ltd, a joint venture of French military aircraft manufacturer Dassault Aviation SA and the Anil Dhirubhai Ambani business group's Reliance Aerostructure Ltd, was set up to discharge the "offsets" in the deal (in September 2016) between the French and Indian governments for the purchase of 36 Rafale fighter jets at a cost of €7.87 billion.

The question being asked is whether such deals might in the future lay the foundation for profitable military exports from India. The Indian state is a regional military power that has built a nuclear weapons arsenal, and besides, it even has a missiles and missiles delivery development program. And it has for a long time been fighting internal wars.[12]

"GREATER INDIA" AND WASHINGTON'S "PIVOT TO ASIA" STRATEGY

What is of crucial significance is Washington's "Indo-Pacific" (earlier dubbed "Pivot to Asia") strategy in the wake of China's rapid economic development over the last thirty-five years, Beijing's securing of international energy and raw material sources and surface transportation routes for the same, and her accompanying geopolitical ascendency, all of which have upset the long-established U.S. imperialist dominated order in Asia. The U.S.'s strategic alliances with Japan, Australia, and India are aimed at containing China through political, diplomatic, and military means, and Washington's three strategic partners are now being pressured to, in turn, forge strategic ties with each other. As a junior partner of the United States, the Indian Navy is fast becoming the chief policeman of the Indian Ocean, and the Indian military's dependence on the U.S. military–industrial complex is increasing, this via supply of military hardware and a homeland security deal with Israel too. Basically, India is being groomed for the role of a sub-imperialist power in South Asia and beyond by the United States. Washington has designated New Delhi as its "major defense partner," which is supposed to facilitate "technology sharing with India to a level commensurate with that of its closest allies and partners." This is also supposed to include "license-free access to a wide range of dual-use technologies," and "support of India's Make in India initiative," and assist in the development of an Indian military-industrial complex and its "integration into the global supply chain."[13]

Indeed, the fact that India is going to service the United States (U.S.) Seventh Fleet reflects the sea change in Indo–U.S. relations.[14] Way back in December 1971, when the Indian Army's and the Mukti Bahini's (the Bangladeshi "freedom fighters") victory in East Bengal was drawing near, the U.S. Navy dispatched a ten-ship Naval task force from its Seventh Fleet, then stationed off South Vietnam, to the Bay of Bengal to threaten the Indian armed forces. Earlier, in August 1971, India had entered a Treaty of Peace, Friendship and Cooperation with the Soviet Union, Article IX of which assured New Delhi that the Soviet Union would come to India's defense in the event of an external threat or an actual breach of security. And, indeed, cruisers, destroyers, and a submarine of the Soviet Navy apparently trailed the Seventh Fleet's task force into the Indian Ocean to ward off the U.S. threat.

But following the end of the Cold War and even before the collapse of the Soviet Union, New Delhi quickly signaled a somersault. During the first Gulf War (August 1990–February 1991), New Delhi permitted the refueling of U.S. military aircraft on Indian soil. The Logistics Exchange Memorandum of Agreement (LEMOA) with the United States, signed in August 2016, marked the completion of the somersault, for it lays the ground for the Indian and U.S. militaries to work closely together, allowing the use of their respective bases for refueling, maintenance, and replenishment of supplies. At a joint press conference at the Pentagon at the time of the signing of LEMOA, in late August 2016, the then U.S. Secretary of Defense, Ashton Carter, explained that LEMOA makes "easier *operating together* when we choose to." It makes the "logistics of *joint operations* so much easier and so much more efficient." His counterpart, the then Indian Defence Minister, Manohar Parrikar, concurred that LEMOA would ensure "logistics support to each other's fleet . . . for *joint operations*" (all italics, my emphasis). We do not know for sure, but it seems reasonable to surmise that LEMOA will enable *forward* deployment of military material and personnel from Indian military bases and ports.

The question naturally arises about the link between Hindutva-nationalism and India's nascent sub-imperialism. The bolstering of the semi-fascist project of the Hindutva forces really followed the U.S. "war on terror" in the aftermath of 9/11, and this provides the connecting link of India's nascent sub-imperialism with Hindutva-nationalism. What is relevant here is Hindutva-nationalism's expansionist thrust, its call for the "recreation" of *Akhand Bharat*, undivided India, geographically as it existed prior to Partition in 1947 as defining the country's geographical frontiers. This encompasses the territory of what the Hindutvavadis would equate with that of the ancient *Bharatavarsha*, "purified" culturally and embracing a hoary "civilizational heritage," and yet technologically modern.

The building of such castles in the air can be dismissed as part of the irrational and mystical outpourings of Hindutva, but even an Indian government under Congress-Party leadership eagerly played the role of the pawn that Samuel P. Huntington—in his influential book *Clash of Civilizations*—assigned to it, coming close to "US–Israel alliance against the largely Islamic 'axis of evil' nations" and positioning itself "as nuclear-armed bulwark" against China.[15]

In such a defense framework, smaller neighboring states are considered mere protectorates under India's security system. Further, it is the extension of India's "strategic neighborhood" to the entire area around the Indian Ocean region adjoining the Persian Gulf (the extension of the Indian Ocean through the Strait of Hormuz), East Africa, and Southeast Asia—the Hindutva-nationalist conception of "Greater India,"[16] defining the country's "ideological frontiers," This is, from Washington's point of view, the geopolitical significance of India. More plainly speaking, the junior partner's military presence at the core of the arc between Washington's military consolidation both in the Persian Gulf and in East Asia explains the geopolitical relevance of India to the United States.

Tragically, the ascendancy of Hindutva-nationalism—based, as it is, on a chauvinistic hatred of Muslims and an irrational and mystical appeal to *Akhand Bharat* and "Greater India"—will further the sub-imperialist urging. Readers will have noted what kind of nationalists these Hindutvavadis are, who, like their Congress counterparts, endorse and build upon a strategic alliance as a junior partner with U.S. imperialism. However, a sub-imperialist power, being both a victim and a beneficiary of imperialism, does exercise a degree of "tactical autonomy." It has to be consulted by its imperialist principal in matters of common concern with regard to its designated domain of external power. Thus, for instance, in Nepal, with both India and the United States seeking the military and political defeat of the Nepali Maoists, during 2001–04, Washington determined the nature and extent of intervention there. But, with the Congress Party's return to power, post-June 2004, New Delhi, wary of U.S. military intervention,[17] took the lead to determine the kind of involvement it thought best, and Washington, after some hesitation, apparently concurred with New Delhi's fresh set of tactics to end the revolution in Nepal.[18]

But with the BJP—accompanied by a foreign policy influenced by for-mulations of *Akhand Bharat* and "Greater India"—back in power at the center, if the sorcerer, metaphorically speaking, were to allow his apprentice to call up the nether world to cast a spell, he may not then be able to rein in what his apprentice would have unleashed. For instance, in September 2016, the then U.S. Secretary of State, John Kerry, apparently cautioned New Delhi against any Washington-style "war-on-terror" adventurism. Despite this, "the sorcerer's apprentice" claimed to have conducted an on-the-ground "surgical strike" targeting "terror launch pads" in the Pakistan-administered part of Kashmir, and then bragged that he had discarded the "shackles" of "strategic restraint" and called the bluff of Pakistani "nuclear blackmail."

India's then Defense Minister, Manohar Parrikar, even likened the Indian armed forces unit that had presumably undertaken the "surgical strike" to Hanuman, the mythical monkey-god in the Hindu epic *Ramayana*, who on being reminded of his prowess, instantly strode across the ocean to teach Ravana, the *rakshasa* (demon) king of Lanka, a lesson. And, like Ravana, the military top-brass of Pakistan, Parrikar boasted, had been left "bewildered," unable to react. But such adventurism, if it was really a "surgical strike," that is, if it struck deep into Pakistani territory, could have led to an escala-tion of Indo-Pak hostility resulting in all-out war. Both Pakistan and a UN Observer Group, however, denied that any such Indian operation had been undertaken. Indian establishment discourse has been falsely presenting an indigenous national liberation movement in Kashmir as Pakistan-sponsored Jehadi cross-border terror in order to delegitimize it, and the Indian public was made to believe that a "surgical strike" was conducted to preempt such terrorist infiltration. But, imagine what the consequences could have been if an Indian army unit had, indeed, struck deep into Pakistani territory in the form of a real "surgical strike."

Clearly, a careful and clearheaded analysis of the Indian sub-imperialist tendency is of utmost importance. But it's time to come to grips with the Hindutva-nationalist movement that brought the BJP to power at the center in 2014.

"STATE-TEMPLE-CORPORATE COMPLEX"

१२०० *saalo ki ghulaami ki maansikta Hindustaniyon ko pareshaan karti rahi hai.* (Colonial subjugation over 1200 years has plagued Indians.)
—PRIME MINISTER NARENDRA MODI IN HIS FIRST
SPEECH IN THE LOK SABHA, ON JUNE 11, 2014

Clearly, Narendra Modi was articulating the Hindutva perspective of Indian history, wherein the "Muslim civilization" period is depicted in terms of "despotic tyranny," this in sharp contrast to the earlier "Hindu civiliza-tion," portrayed as 2,000 years of a "golden age." But, apparently, there was not even a murmur of protest or argument in Parliament. The long-drawn struggle between (receding) "secular" nationalism and (advancing) Hindutva-nationalism seems to have moved decisively in favor of the latter.

The captains of Indian big business seem to have come on board, but, naturally, their contribution is based upon profit calculus. At the "Vibrant Gujarat" Summit held in January 2013, this is what Mukesh Ambani, CEO of Reliance Industries Ltd and India's richest billionaire, proclaimed: "In Narendra *Bhai* [brother], we have a leader with a grand vision." His brother Anil, CEO of the Anil Dhirubhai Ambani business group, went several notches ahead, hailing Modi as "king among kings"! And, he went on: "Narendra Bhai has the Arjuna-like clarity of vision and purpose." Ratan Tata, CEO of the Tata business group from 1991 to 2012, was all praise for Gujarat's "investment climate," attributing it to Modi's leadership: "Today when investors look for locations to make investments, they would be look-ing for locations which are investor-friendly. Gujarat stands out distinctly in the country and the credit for it goes to Modi."

This support for Modi is based on pragmatic business grounds rather than those of ideology. In the case of Ratan Tata, surely this is the case, but one needs to probe a bit deeper into what may be called the nationalistic Hindu religiosity[19] of the Indian capitalist class and the middle classes. Such religiosity accompanied by ostentatious rituals—yajñas, *bhumi pujas* (a prayer ritual at the inauguration of a new construction site) before the start of construction of projects, etc.—has made for a distinctly Hindu texture in the public sphere. Even the representatives of the then Left Front govern-ment participated in the *bhumi puja* performed by Tata Motors in Singur.

Some of the same gurus and swamis who have participated in and blessed the Hindutva-politics of the Vishwa Hindu Parishad (VHP) have had generous benefactors in Lakshmi Mittal (of ArcelorMittal) and Anil Agarwal (of Vedanta Resources). Corporate patronage and generous fund-ing of Hindu religious institutions is too well known, but land gifted or sold for a song by the Indian state to these institutions is not, besides promo-tion of the *Amarnath Yatra* (an annual pilgrimage to the Amarnath Temple in Jammu and Kashmir) that is said to bring spirituality and patriotism together. Reflecting over all of this and more in 2009, the philosopher of science and author of works on religion and Hindu nationalism, Meera Nanda,[20] discerned an emerging "State–Temple–Corporate Complex" that, she felt, will wield decisive political and economic power. All the national-istic Hindu religiosity that Nanda draws our attention to has contributed to the hegemonic rise of Hindutva-nationalism, itself a part of the global resurgence of rightwing ideology since the 1980s, and sections of Indian big business have embraced it.

POWER OF HINDUTVA AS AN IDEOLOGY

What accounts for the power of contemporary Hindutva? The BJP has its roots in the political project of Hindutva-nationalism, which reformulated Hinduism as Hindutva (literally, "Hinduness"), a social–cultural–religious fabric that has proved singularly appropriate to political mobilization. A Hindu is defined, in V. D. Savarkar's *Hindutva: Who is a Hindu?* (written in 1923) as "a person who regards the land of *Bharatvarsha* . . . as his father-land, as well as his Holy land—that is the cradle land of his religion," thus identifying *pitrubhumi* uniquely with *punyabhumi*, "(a)scribing sanctity to the land of one's birth," and thereby providing the link with nationalist discourse, but ensuring that Muslims and Christians are excluded from being identified as Indian nationalists.[21]

"Hindus" can thus claim to be the primary citizens of India because their religion and their ancestry are indigenous to *Bharatvarsha*. And, besides the unique identification of *pitrubhumi* with *punyabhumi*, a shared "Hindu Sanskriti" (culture based on Vedic foundations), a set of languages originating in Sanskrit, and the *Dharmashastras* (the Hindu law books laying down the social codes, including those related to caste and gender) are all appealed to, which together make for "cultural nationalism" and the imagined community of the "Hindus." This Hindutva-nationalism has been projected as synonymous with Indian nationalism, sidelining what was anti-colonial and "secular" in the latter.

There's just one more dimension that needs to be flagged in the above theorization of Hindutva—that Hindutva-nationalism is identified with a particular version of Hinduism. This is how Romila Thapar may put it, though her contention that "Hindutva is in many ways the anti-thesis of Hinduism" is perplexing. Of course, she says this from the secular perspective of opposition to the abuse of religion or the vile political use of religion. As she says in her celebrated essay "Syndicated Hinduism":

> The Hindu, it seems, is being overtaken by the Hindutvavadin, who is changing the essential nature of the religion. There is something to be said for attempting to comprehend with knowledge and sensitivity and not just the verbosity of glorification, the real religious expression of pre-modern Indian culture, before it is snuffed out.

She is here recalling the *Shramanism* (in relation to popular religious cults) that sprang up in the latter part of the first millennium BC, which "explored areas of belief and practice different from the *Vedas* and *Dharmashastras*" and "often preached a system of universal ethics that spanned castes and communities," in opposition to Brahminism. She is also referring to the *Bhakti* (devotion) cults from the seventh century AD, as also to "'folk Hinduism'—the religions of the Dalits, tribals and other groups at the lower end of the social scale." All these progressive trends are being snuffed out with the hegemony of Syndicated Hinduism that "draws largely on Brahminical texts, the *Vedas*, the epics, the *Gita* and accepts some aspects of the *Dharmashastras*"[22] and this is the version of Hinduism with which Hindutva-nationalism identifies. One might then say that Hindutva-nationalism, identifying itself with Syndicated Hinduism, actively promotes it, through the auspices of the VHP, as a guide to political and social life in India today—political Hinduism, if one might like to call it by that name.

The insidious spread of Syndicated Hinduism and Hindutva-nationalism in public life in India is not new. Even Jawaharlal Nehru, in his *An Autobiography* (also known as *Toward Freedom*, published in 1936) wrote: "Many a Congressman was a communalist under his national cloak." Madan Mohan Malaviya (1861–1946), who was president of the Congress Party in 1909, 1918, 1930, and 1932, espoused the ideology of Hindutva and was one of the initial leaders of the Hindu Mahasabha and its president in 1923. In the 1950s, Congressman K. M. Munshi (1887–1971) exploiting what he claimed to be collective memory of the "trauma" suffered by Hindus following the raid of Mahmud of Ghazni on the temple of Somnath, encouraged the turning of it into a political slogan.

Nehru would have been traumatized if he had even an inkling that, as events were to unfold after his death, it would be his grandson, Rajiv Gandhi, of all persons, who would decide to remove the seals from the Babri Masjid in February 1986, and in 1989, allow *shilanyas* (the laying of foundation stones in a religious ceremony) to take place there. Indeed, Rajiv Gandhi launched his campaign for the 1989 elections from Faizabad, the town adjoining Ayodhya where the Babri Masjid was located, calling for the ushering in of Ram Rajya (the rule of god Ram), the expression, unlike when Mahatma Gandhi used it, now clearly invoking Hindutva connotations. And so, the destruction of the Babri Masjid at Ayodhya on December 6, 1992, came to be justified as avenging the Somnath temple raid of 1025 AD, this, after nearly a thousand years! In 1998 at its Panchmarhi Convention to chart out a political strategy, the Congress Party even went to the extent of endorsing "soft Hindutva" themes in order to steal a march on the BJP.[23]

I think that Christophe Jaffrelot[24] has a point when he argues that the hegemony of the ideology of Hindutva must be seen in the extended process of socialization of generations of Hindus, through the Rashtriya Swayamsevak Sangh's (RSS) web of *shakhas* (daily local branch gatherings of members) and network of front organizations collectively known as the Sangh Parivar,[25] the creation and diffusion of which explains its hold in Indian society and politics. Indeed, the political fervor of Hindutva-nationalism seems to have moved women in a special way, with many making symbolic offerings of their *mangalsutras* (holy thread necklace worn to indicate married status) to the cause of "God Ram." And, in the 2002 pogrom in Gujarat, the Hindutva-nationalists managed to mobilize even Dalits and shudra jatis and adivasis as foot soldiers of the fascist militia. Remarkably, the BJP has not found the political difficulties of integrating the other backward classes (OBCs)—the shudra jatis—into the Hindutva fold insurmountable, for instance, in Gujarat, Rajasthan, Madhya Pradesh, and Chhattisgarh.[26] A more recent instance was in the 16th Lok Sabha elections, in Maharashtra, Uttar Pradesh, and Bihar,[27] in the latter two, the party even stealing a march over the Samajvadi Party and the Rashtriya Janata Dal, respectively.

The roots of the rise of Hindutva-national chauvinism should be traced to India's conservative modernization from above, the development of underdeveloped capitalism, and so they run deep, beyond the bounds of the Sangh Parivar. Such religious nationalism seems to have taken hold of the Congress Party too, at crucial moments, for instance, during the Delhi, 1984, and Bombay, 1993, communal-hate pogroms. And even though the memory of these pogroms brings forth, even today, feelings of deep anguish, torment, and despair, it is difficult not to express the thought that there was this mostly, silently complicit, majority Gujarati-Hindu population, Gujarat's *mitläufer*,[28] receptive to the Sangh Parivar's "storm-troopers" committing mass murder. The alleged mastermind of the pogrom is still India's prime minister, in power, no doubt, due to majority support from an expanded all-India Hindu *mitläufer* claiming (in 2014) that it voted for the BJP because it saw in Modi the vikas purush (man of progress) par excellence.

SUPREME SYMBOL OF AUTHORITARIAN LEADERSHIP

That such a person is the prime minister of India is, no doubt, the fulfillment of the classic fascist dream. The Hindutva-nationalist movement has finally got its supreme symbol of authoritarian leadership and what is being carefully polished is the RSS and *Führer/Duce* principle of *ek-chalak anuvartitva* (translated as obedience to one leader). In a sense, the Hindutvavadis are behaving as if they have achieved their own *swaraj* with Modi as their dictator. The figure of Modi representing strong authority and whose legitimacy derives from being the one who vanquished "the Other" perfectly matches the psychic desires of Hindutvavadis socialized in caste-Hindu families. Personality traits such as "puritanical rigidity, narrowing of emotional life, massive use of the ego defence of projection, denial and fear of ... [one's] own passions combined with fantasies of violence," as also, conspiratorial painting of "every Muslim as a suspected traitor and a potential terrorist,"[29] all these characteristics fit Modi very well for his role as a *sarsanghchalak* (supreme leader)-type prime minister. What is paranoid and obsessive-compulsive in the individual, is in a semi-fascist regime, normal and politically desirable (from the perspective of its supporters) for the functioning of such a system of government. Public events around Modi are being carefully choreographed, his exaltation of youth, his masculinity, how he relates to the masses.

The first thing Modi did after it was clear that his party had won a majority was to emphasize strength through unity leading to national renewal. The "truths" that are being cultivated about him are those that appeal to the fantasy—above all, the hearts and only then the minds—of youth. The promotion of a lavish cult of personality is on; any policy decision, if its legitimacy is to be upheld, is claimed to have a certificate of approval from Modi. In short, an arrogant, manipulating, stop-at-nothing, callous Hindutvavadi is being projected as the celibate, 56-inch-chested workaholic dedicated entirely to his mission of "development" and the nation. Following the success of the Hindutva-nationalist movement, then, isn't the semi-fascist regime gradually taking shape?

SEMI-FASCIST *GLEICHSCHALTUNG*

Before arriving at the gist of the semi-fascism in the making, it might be prudent to briefly touch upon some of the more recent developments following Hindutvavadi control of the executive of the Indian state after the BJP won a majority in the 16th Lok Sabha elections in April–May 2014. Here are some of the ways and means whereby the bureaucracy, parliament, and the state assemblies, the judiciary, the military, the media, culture, and educational institutions are being "brought into line." India's rotten liberal-political democratic regime is witnessing further degeneration following a strong dose of "*authoritarian* democracy."[30] Prime Minister Narendra Modi has been seeking and claiming "spiritual" connection with the people. Authoritarian democracy, in its Indian version, is being based on the premise that the Hindutva-nationalist movement has a broad popular consensus, enabled by the Sangh Parivar's cultural interventions to give "Hindu *sanskriti*" (culture) a national form. Conformity and homogeneity are sought to be achieved, followed by consent, with the people constantly being urged to rally behind Narendra Modi.

Intellectuals are being attracted and absorbed (co-opted), and then enlisted in the regime's cultural, educational, and research initiatives. They are not being asked to subscribe to the Sangh Parivar's ideology but to embrace the values of the Indian nation-state with which the Modi regime identifies itself. Pluralism and diversity are deemed dysfunctional; emphasis is being placed on coercion, not on consensus. The regime is endeavoring to implement the RSS's wish-list in the fields of education and culture.

The appointments to the chairpersonships of two of the most important social-science research bodies, the Indian Council of Historical Research (ICHR) and the Indian Council of Social Science Research (ICSSR), of persons of Hindutva-ideological persuasion, suggest that the Modi government merely wants likeminded ideologues and loyalists to head these bodies. Contrast these academic research appointments with the Modi government's refusal to approve the Nalanda University board's recommendation of the 1998 economics Nobel recipient Amartya Sen for appointment as the university's chancellor for a second term in office. The message is clear. Indeed, open, critical lectures and discussion on "controversial subjects" are being slapped with sedition charges, and in the universities, such events are being cancelled. As regards media, culture, and educational institutions, the process of "bringing into line" has been, metaphorically speaking, akin to Hindutva Chambers of Culture springing up to define what is a "good, acceptable" film, book, article, piece of social-science research, or TV newscast. Writers, filmmakers, social-science scholars, and journalists found wanting are made to bow before the respective Hindutva Chamber of Culture if they want to continue to practice their craft!

The affairs of the Modi government are being run in a manner wherein major interest groups address a vastly-strengthened Prime Minister's Office, which claims to resolve matters in the best interests of the "general will of the nation." Privatization is set to be a political tool to enhance the financial aristocracy's support for the Modi government and the BJP. One way or the other, it will facilitate the accumulation of private fortunes and business empires by the BJP's principal business collaborators. Heavily backed by Indian big business and the MNCs, the Modi government has discovered in the movement to a goods and services tax (GST) regime a way of initiating the de-federalization of the republic. With uniform GST rates for the republic, the freedom of the states in the realm of some indirect taxation, hitherto their prerogative, has been taken away. In the GST Council, in which GST rates are decided, a state government is only one member among many, and there is only one state-GST for each broad commodity group, applicable across all the states—a "serious encroachment on the federal structure."[31]

The greater infusion of money and wealth in the hijacking of the electoral process has made the government's "economic" ministries business-driven, and they are being run along business lines (for example, the Ministry of Environment and Forests "fast-tracking" environmental clearances). Economic policy is framed mainly through interaction with those who represent business interests. The "Make in India" policy is predicated upon an extension of low-wage arbitraging policy with changes in labor law and repression of independent trade unions to achieve low-cost-based international competitiveness.

The BJP's bid to build a Ram Temple in Ayodhya over the ruins of the Babri Masjid is once again set to move center-stage in 2019 to coincide with the 17th Lok Sabha (lower house of parliament) elections. Its three-pronged electoral strategy to bring about a "Congress-*mukt* Bharat" (an India "free" from the Congress Party) and upstage the regional parties, including its own coalition partners, has, so far, failure in Delhi and Bihar notwithstanding, fit the bill. The three principal instruments of the strategy have been, one, BJP's money beating all other parties' money; two, the adroitly rebranded *vikas purush* (development man), "56-inch chest, daring, charismatic, self-made" Modi, "brilliant orator," promising *achhe din* (good times) and *sabka saath, sabka vikas* (with everyone, everyone's progress); and three, practically the whole of the rest of the Sangh Parivar, in an aggressive assertion of identity based on religion, subtly and even luridly, urging all Hindus to take "revenge" through the ballot box. Taken together, the three instruments of the electoral strategy have been pitched in a manner that is whipping up Hindutva-national sentiment in the run-up to the vote in 2019.

Installing a loyalist yes-man like Ram Nath Kovind as president, that is, head of state and commander-in-chief of the armed forces, in effect, makes Modi the head of state as well as the head of government, with an even more narrow check on his power. Officers of the Indian Foreign Service and the Army are also being motivated to "synchronize" their postures with the Modi regime as foreign policy is being increasingly informed by the notions of *Akhand Bharat* and Greater India, leading to deterioration of New Delhi's relations with Islamabad and Beijing. The army chief, General Bipin Rawat, has been irresponsibly boasting that India is prepared to fight a two-front war against China and Pakistan simultaneously. And, to make matters worse, a third point of conflict with China, in the Doklam or Donglang Plateau (territory under dispute between Bhutan and China)—the earlier two concerning the McMahon Line in the northeast and India's claim to Aksai Chin in the northwest—has been provoked.

Concurrently, the Modi regime has been nurturing and supporting the Hindutva-nationalist movement even to the extent of being complicit in the movement's "patriotic" acts, such as attacking or lynching Muslim cattle traders, alleged cow-killers or "beefeaters" in the name of *gau mata ki raksha* (protection of the sacred cow). The so-called *gau rakshaks* (self-appointed cow protectors) have unleashed yet another form of *aatankwad* (terrorism)—*gautankwad*—which is very much in tune with the Hindutva-political culture of unlawful resort to violence and intimidation against Muslims and Dalits.

The BJP has been trying to push constitutional reform that will make it easier for the executive to undermine the independence of the judiciary. An opportunity to that effect came when the National Judicial Appointments Commission Act, 2014, and the Constitution (Ninety-Ninth Amendment) Act, 2014, came into force from April 2015. The NJAC would have been appointing and transferring judges to the higher Indian judiciary after replacing the collegium system, thereby, in effect, giving significant clout to the executive in the selection of judges, since, among other things, the Union Law Minister would have been one of its members. But a constitutional bench of the Supreme Court, by a 4 to 1 majority, upheld the collegium system (under which the judiciary itself selects judges) and struck down the NJAC and the Constitution 99th Amendment Act as "unconstitutional." Not to be outdone, the government has since been stalling judicial appointments under the collegium system and is demanding the power to reject any collegium-recommended name on grounds of "national security" risk, even as it is refusing to give in writing the evidence that it claims to have against such an appointee.

What is worrying is the fact that the BJP believes that all the other branches of the state must bow to a parliamentary majority; so the judges of the higher courts, the Chief Justice of the Supreme Court included, must preferably be comprised of persons who hold the government-of-the-day's overall view of the law and the Constitution, in effect, the ruling party's view of the law and the Constitution. If such a situation ultimately comes to prevail, this will lead judges, in the course of their work, to fall in line with the ruling party's overall view of the law and the Constitution in order to enhance their chances of rising higher in the judicial hierarchy. Surely, the independence of the judiciary will then be progressively compromised. And then, among other "illegalities," the resort to state terror to maintain control over the Other—whom the executive considers its "objective"/"necessary" enemy—will be freed of judicial restraint.

SEMI-FASCISM AND THE SEMI-FASCIST—THE GIST

Here then is the gist of the semi-fascism in the making: an "authoritarian-democratic" regime and a sub-imperialist power, with the regime maintaining a close nexus with big business, nurturing and supporting the Hindutva-nationalist movement to the extent of being complicit in its acts, and insisting on controlling its "necessary" enemies through the use of terror. India's semi-peripheral and sub-imperialist standing in the world capitalist system is conducive to semi-fascism. Unlike fascism, which does away with liberal-political democracy and institutes a one-party dictatorship, in effect, carrying out a political counterrevolution, a semi-fascist regime doesn't outlaw political opposition. It retains the legal framework of "free competition" for votes, which is the essence of liberal-political democracy. This is because India's liberal-political democracy is rotten; the electoral process has already been successfully hijacked with the power of money and wealth.

How then will it be possible to identify an Indian semi-fascist when you encounter one? Simple—his/her ideology of Hindutva-nationalism, his/her upper-caste, "Aryan" superior manner vis-à-vis lower castes and Dalits, his/ her reactionary right-wing views, his/her support for the state's sub-imperialist ventures and use of terror against its "necessary" enemies.

THE RISK OF NO LONGER BEING UNDERSTOOD

Disturbing and dreadful! This is reminiscent of what Pier Paolo Pasolini wrote in his last book of poems:[32]

> I am like a cat that's been burned alive
> Run over by a truck
> Hung from a tree by the kids in the street
> But with still at least six
> Of its seven lives . . . Death isn't
> Not being able to communicate
> But no longer being understood.

In today's age, reality is deliberately masked and perverted.[33] As Eric Hobsbawm hinted at in his *The Age of Extremes*, "Most young men and women . . . grow up in a sort of permanent present lacking any organic relation to the public past of the times we live in." What compounds the problem is the seeming existence of two presents, one dished out by capitalism's triumphant media through a vast simulator of disinformation that programs what people see and think, while the other, the true present, appears fugitive and elusive, at the borderline so to say. It is only occasionally that a Noam Chomsky, a Romila Thapar, or an Arundhati Roy is allowed entry. It is on such occasions that the tradition of intellectual opposition is permitted its bite. But with the way reality gets recessed through the big media, these opposition figures conveying the real present invariably appear transient, fleeting, almost like exiles or fugitives. It is in times like these, semi-fascist times in which the existence of a *mitläufer* is denied, and when Gujarat, 2002, is reaffirmed by a Zakia Jafri and a Teesta Setalvad, the establishment's intellectuals, hurl back: "It doesn't matter now." Already there are signs of Hindutva-Chambers-of-Culture lists of writers, filmmakers, social science scholars, and journalists classified as "undesirable," like Hans Fallada, the author of *Little Man, What Now?*, was in 1935. Truly, one runs the risk of no longer being understood.

──────10──────

History, Memory, and Dreams— Reimagining "New Democracy"

> . . . I pondered all these things, and how men [and women] fight and lose the battle, and the thing they fought for comes about in spite of their defeat, and when it turns out not to be what they meant, and other men [and women] have to fight for what they meant under another name. . .
> —WILLIAM MORRIS, IN AN OFT-QUOTED PASSAGE FROM *A DREAM OF JOHN BALL*[1]

> Men [and women] make their own history, but they do not make it as they please; they do not make it under self-selected circumstances, but under circumstances existing already, given and transmitted from the past. The tradition of all dead generations weighs like a nightmare on the brains of the living.
> —KARL MARX, *THE EIGHTEENTH BRUMAIRE OF LOUIS BONAPARTE*[2]

Indian society is changing and, within limits, as a consequence of Naxalbari and the other struggles of the "1968" period, underwent progressive change, but not exactly as the Maoists and the other '68ers had envisaged, namely, the creation of a decent human society. So also did the peasants' revolt in Kent in 1381 bring change, but not as one of the folk heroes of that rebellion had expected. The poet, novelist, textile designer, and socialist activist William Morris was attracted to the character of the English priest, John Ball, one of the folk heroes of that rebellion, precisely because the roving preacher articulated socialist ideas much in advance of his time.[3] The rebellion was about attaining liberty, but John Ball tried to raise it beyond that end, upholding the banner of social equality. This caught the attention of Morris, the narrator in the *A Dream of John Ball*, confronted with the injustices of capitalism in his own times, in England in the nineteenth century.[4]

Surely, we need to listen to the "small voices" of history and of contemporary times—the opinions and feelings of the exploited, the oppressed and the dominated—heed what they say, learn from them. The creation of a decent human society might ultimately come about after many defeats and setbacks, but only in a process of struggle by ordinary people, who may not yet be ready to emancipate themselves, but who can become capable of doing so by launching and sustaining revolutionary struggles. It is in these struggles that ordinary people would remake society and, in the process, remake themselves.

"1968" was a high point of the radical left, which rejected the capitalist system and expressed an abhorrence of the imperialism that was an integral part of it. The '68ers also made explicit their profound indifference to attempts at reforming capitalism. But more importantly, this left viewed the Soviet Union and its East European satellites as exploitative and oppressive class societies from which socialists can learn what not to do. China at the beginning of "1968," despite the setbacks it suffered and the retreats it was forced to make, was seen as trying to build a just and egalitarian society, even though the material conditions were not favorable to the attainment of such an outcome. All the more was it held up as worthy of emulation by a section of the left in India and was commended for the sheer effort it was making to move in that direction. Sadly, however, the post-Mao leadership of the Chinese Communist Party took a huge step backwards, and then began to move forward along the path of capitalism, developing the productive forces at breakneck speed. Today, there is no model of socialism that the Indian Maoists can hold up as worthy of taking as an example, and this leaves them and the Indian masses without a living source of inspiration.

India's present is the dreadful outcome of some two and a half centuries of the development of underdeveloped capitalism, that is, if one were to include the period of its passage to that system. Essentially, India was molded in the colonial period by a combination of political and economic forces to serve the needs of the development of capitalism in England and the expansion of the British Empire, these with disastrous social and economic consequences for Indian society. The process of colonization aggravated the already existing economic problems and social ills. The worst result has been the *extreme* polarization of Indian society—wealth, privilege, and power on the one hand, and poverty, misery, and frustration on the other. At the apex of the former in the post-independence period has been Indian big business, the product of a long degenerative process of colonialism, and therefore unequal to the task of playing a progressive historical role.

The consequence of this is the tragedy of independent India ruled by an Indian big business–state–multinational bloc with the support of large landholders in the countryside—678.8 million human beings (in 2011) have been relegated to irrelevance, unless they decide to enter history on their own terms. The process of capitalist industrialization since the 1920s was weak, and it couldn't advance without being dependent on foreign capital and technology. A symptom of its weakness is the fact that it has not led to the employment of even 10 percent of the workforce in modern, *contemporary* manufacturing industry. Modern industry couldn't advance without a continuous, systematic reliance on import of the latest vintages of technology. The consequence was Indian big business itself weakened and dependent, certainly not innovative, more a freeloading exploiter, unable to successfully industrialize the country and help put in place a proper liberal-political democratic regime. Worse still, the urban artisan was ruined by the process of de-(proto)industrialization, and so was the actual tiller of the land, the genuine peasant, by the various land tenure systems the colonial regime put in place and by the process of forced commercialization of agriculture.

Armed rebellions, people's wars, and revolutions in colonial and independent India, as we have seen, have not been a matter of choice or preference. They have been the result of internal contradictions between the exploited classes/oppressed people struggling for progressive change and systemic forces promoting the status quo. Wealth, privilege, and power have belonged to the ruling classes—the controllers of Indian big business, state assets, and the subsidiaries of the multinational corporations—and they have done and will do all they can to preserve that control, permitting only such reforms as they deem to be in their own interests.

There is another reason why to understand the Naxalite/Maoist movement and some of the other militant struggles of the "1968" period, as well as the persistence of the former over a period of five decades, making it one of the longest running peasant insurgencies in contemporary times, it is necessary to grasp the fact that some core traits of the colonial state and society have been embedded in the state and society of independent India. The British East India Company, on behalf of the British state, acquired India by force and established a colonial state to rule over it, which came directly under the British state in 1858. Coercion was the main governing principle, but over time, the British colonialists sought the support of a greater proportion of the propertied and professional classes, drawn from the so-called "twice-born" castes among the Hindus and the *ashraf*[5] among the Muslims, this to consolidate their rule. Local collaborators among these classes were a dime a dozen, so to call a spade a spade, there were the *external* colonizers, the British, and the *internal* colonizers, a significant section of the propertied and the professionals, all Indians. Indeed, it was the latter that made possible the two-centuries-long colonial occupation which could never have stretched that long solely on the basis of coercion.

So, political power didn't merely stem from the great inequality between the British colonialists and their Indian subjects, but also from the fact that there were local collaborators of the upper classes, subordinated by the British colonialists by means of persuasion and more of a share of the appropriated surplus, and who, in turn, were complicit in the subordination of the lower classes by means of coercion. The most compelling instance of this was "subinfeudation," wherein multiple intermediaries got a share of the surplus (in the form of rent) extracted from the genuine cultivators, those who actually tilled the land. There were those who were designated as *ryots*—and they too regarded themselves as cultivators—but in practice they lived off the labor of the genuine cultivators who were tenants without occupancy rights or simply tenants-at-will.[6]

After the Jallianwala Bagh massacre of 1919, it became a bit more difficult for the British colonialists to co-opt the bulk of the upper-class (those from the propertied and professional classes) nationalists. However, these nationalists, their associates, and an ideologically committed cadre under their control, regarded the masses (whom they mobilized) with suspicion. They even publicly dissociated from them when these "subalterns" resorted to tactics not a part of the Gandhian political repertoire, especially violent acts, and even called off popular movements when the masses disobeyed their directives.

Any wonder then that after the British colonialists transferred power to these upper-class nationalists, the masses—workers and petty commodity producers (of agricultural commodities, and other goods, and/or services), and their dependents—were treated by these worthies as subjects, not citizens, just like the British had done in the colonial period. The eminent historian Ranajit Guha puts it aptly: "How very similar this appeared to be to the distance which separated the colonized and the colonizer in the days of foreign occupation!" And he adds: "After the transfer of power the old traditional divisions not only surfaced again, but did so even more vigorously than before in some instances as the dominant groups paraded their newly acquired importance and the subordinate ones sulked in resentment."[7]

TAKING THE PERSPECTIVE OF THE "SMALL VOICES"

If taking the perspective of the exploited, the oppressed, and the dominated is essential to understanding the truth about colonial India, this has also been the approach adopted to unraveling the truth about India after

Naxalbari—by giving vent to the rebellious voices of the colonial period, throwing light on the radical nature of the albeit short-lived acts of insurgency of the oppressed peasantry which were crushed by the colonial army with its military superiority. All the so-called stratagems of "winning of hearts and minds" that followed were a sham. Mention must be made here of the Gudem–Rampa uprisings over the period 1839–1924 by the rebellious tribal people. The 1879-80 *fituri* [uprising], for instance, led by the daring Koya tribal hero, Tamman Dora, set out to vanquish colonial state power in the hills locality, dominated by outsiders who protected the local Indian exploiters—money-lenders, traders, and contractors.

Then there was the 1922–24 *fituri*, led by Alluri Sitaramaraju in Gudem. Sitaramaraju was a Telugu who, like the present-day Telugu Maoists, identified with the grievances and aspirations of the tribal people of the Gudem hills. And, like the Telugu Maoists of contemporary times in their People's War to overthrow the Indian state, Sitaramaraju wanted to use the hills as a base to launch an armed struggle against British rule. Like the Telugu Maoists of today, he too had close tribal associates, Gam Mallu Dora and Gam Gantam Dora, for instance, and tried to advance to a more sophisticated form of guerrilla warfare.

Interestingly, like the Telugu Maoists, he too had a policy of sparing, as far as was possible, the foot soldiers of the security forces, those who were forced to make a living by serving in the armed police forces of the state. And, just like in contemporary times when the entire political establishment is ranged against the Maoists, the Telugu leaders of the Indian National Congress, the main party of the political establishment of Sitaramaraju's times, threw their weight against the *fituri* that he led. The reasons too were similar. Just as the political establishment's hostility toward the Maoists stems from the fact that this establishment represents the interests of the dominant classes, the hostility of the Telugu Congressmen toward Sitaramaraju and his *fituridars* of the Gudem hills stemmed from the fact that those Congressmen represented the interests of the money-lenders, traders, contractors, and other exploiters, all elite Indians, protected by the colonial state, whose rule the *fituri* was bent on overthrowing.

It would not be honest to conclude that the many such uprisings in colonial India, short-lived acts of insurgency of the oppressed peasantry, are irrelevant and unimportant in the unfolding history of modern (and contemporary) India.[8] Indeed, just after Naxalbari, in the autumn of 1967, the Naxalite leader Charu Mazumdar said: "...hundreds of Naxalbaris are smouldering in India . . . Naxalbari has not died and will never die."[9] Certainly, in retrospect it can be said that he was not daydreaming, for the power of memory—of the armed peasant struggles of the colonial period—and the dreams unleashed gave the movement a fresh dynamic, and continues to do so even after fifty years have passed.

Mao famously said that a revolution "cannot be so refined, so leisurely and gentle, so temperate, kind, courteous, restrained and magnanimous. A revolution is an insurrection, an act of violence by which one class overthrows another." Like Mao, the Communist Party of India (Maoist) [CPI(Maoist)] poses the revolutionary question in terms of "armed revolution against armed counterrevolution." Presumably, certain internal contradictions of the system have developed to a stage wherein "People's War" has become the principal means of resolving them. The dominated classes are being organized to overthrow the oppressive Indian state and the unjust social order that it preserves. Such ideas about revolution, in their more generalized form, come from the collective memory of the French Revolution. Mao very likely also drew upon the collective memory of the French Revolution. The Russian and the Chinese revolutions were conceived as the beginning of a process of fundamental transformation of socioeconomic and political structures and institutions for the creation of a better world, with the basic changes in the socioeconomic reinforcing those in the political, and vice versa. Mao, of course, spoke of *uninterrupted* revolution. The outburst unleashes dreams and radical social demands; the future is thus, as yet, unachieved.[10]

From the time of independence in 1947, India has had the resources and the potential to achieve a high level of human development, yet the great majority of the country's people have remained desperately poor. Tragically, India remains among the most poverty-stricken countries in the world, with most of the population still inadequately fed, miserably clothed, wretchedly housed, poorly educated, and without access to decent medical care. Hundreds of millions have been the victims of Indian capitalism's irrationality, brutality, and inhumanity. It is no wonder that for fifty years, the one persistent message of the Maoists has been that India's deeply oppressive and exploitative social order is crying out for revolutionary change. Structurally bred on "rent" (monopoly profit)—the antithesis of what the classical economists regarded as profit—and constantly seeking monopoly positions and accumulating vast amounts of capital derived from "rent," Indian big business has directly contributed to rendering India's liberal-political democracy rotten. In such a setting, the New Democracy propounded by the Maoists should have stood a better chance, but in a propaganda-managed democracy the public doesn't even get to hear those small voices articulating New Democracy, nor have the Maoists been able to practice New Democracy in their guerrilla bases, for these areas of refuge are constantly under siege.

IN EMPATHY WITH "SMALL VOICES"

What must New Democracy be like in the twenty-first century? Mao first began to use the term "New Democracy" in 1939 when he was convinced that in the epoch of imperialism the Chinese bourgeoisie could not lead to victory the Chinese revolution, or any such revolution aimed at the overthrow of "semi-colonialism" and "semi-feudalism." His classic text, *On New Democracy*,[11] is dated January 1940. Such a revolution, Mao reckoned, could only be brought about by the "people," composed of the working class, the peasantry, the urban middle class, and the "national bourgeoisie" in a four-class alliance led by the Chinese Communist Party.

Importantly, as part of the process of modernization, the attack on Confucian values launched at the time of the May Fourth (anti-imperialist political and cultural) Movement of 1919–21 was to be continued, this to usher in a New (Democratic) Culture. In a letter of 1944, Mao wrote: "There are those who say we neglect or repress individuality [*ko-hsing*]; this is wrong. If the individuality which has been fettered is not liberated, there will be no democracy, and no socialism." He was thus calling for profound changes in the political culture then prevailing.[12] He would never have believed that those who didn't or couldn't pick up a gun weren't revolutionaries. For him, democracy and revolution were indivisible. Mao constantly solicited the support of the "people"; bringing "90%" (an overwhelming majority) of the population on the side of the revolutionary forces would minimize the tragic necessity of violence, he argued.

Empathizing with the political thoughts and feelings of the "small voices" of history and of the "present as history," voices that have been silenced in India's public life, some literally extinguished, it is apparent that Indian big business, all sections of it, will oppose the formation of a New Democratic state. All the more reason why any program of New Democracy should be much more socialist-oriented than capitalist-positioned, and in this light, it would be useful to re-imagine New Democracy in empathy with the "small voices" of history and the "present as history." Politics must be put in command; the New Democratic stage of development must keep the ultimate objective of socialism in mind. New Democracy must be pushed as far left as possible, in order to provide the most favorable terrain upon which socialism can then be launched. The main internal and external adversaries will be Indian big business and U.S. imperialism, respectively.

The historical process has permeated and significantly affected the narrative till now, but memory and dreams also must be allowed to also play their part. For those who strive to build an egalitarian and just society no matter how unfavorable the material conditions for the emergence of such a society, Mao's approach that a democracy cannot have bureaucrats, technocrats, or even a vanguard substituting for the people, deciding for them, seems critical. Ordinary people will have to take on public responsibilities and roles by rotation, judging their peers fairly and squarely. All socialists should have a strong antipathy toward state bureaucracies, with their hierarchical structures, rigid principles, secrecy, passive obedience, deference to authority, and careerism.

The Maoists trace the root cause of the rottenness of liberal-political democracy in India to what they call "semi-feudalism and semi-colonialism." Interestingly, however, they see no serious contradictions between the big landowners of the Indian countryside, on the one side, and the controllers of Indian big business, state assets, and the subsidiaries of the MNCs, on the other. How then are those big landowners "semi-feudal"? Their relations with their tenants and their workers have elements of "semi-feudalism," but their agricultural businesses are strongly oriented toward the national market for agricultural commodities, in some instances, even toward the international agricultural commodity markets. Their mode of business behavior is therefore capitalist, and it is misleading to analyze their class position within the ruling capitalist alliance as "semi-feudal."

One crucial historical difference between China and India is that the former was a semi-colony, while the latter was a colony. In a semi-colony the ruling classes and the state are relatively weak compared to the same in a colony. Indeed, as Hamza Alavi[13] argued long ago, the colonial state in India was overdeveloped in relation to the economic base in terms of its powers of control and regulation, and the bureaucracy, the military, and the polity in independent India have had a vested interest in maintaining this important feature of the state. This state, with its modern, largely public-sector transportation and communication infrastructure and its massive armed forces, police, and paramilitary has been able to put down or severely impede all people's revolts, from the Telangana armed peasant movement (1946–48) to the Naxalite/Maoist movement examined in this book.

What, then, of the peasant question (strictly speaking "peasant" includes those cultivators who have a claim, however tenuous, to a plot of land, and also to rural landless wage laborers) in contemporary times? At the heart of capitalism is the "commodification" of land (and other natural resources), the "proletarianization" of labor, and markets for money and finance. With these in place, the "economic sphere" gets separated out of the totality of the social process—"disembedded" was the word used by the Austro-Hungarian economic anthropologist and socialist Karl Polanyi.[14] But even as capitalism unleashes enormous increases in labor productivity, it undermines the sources of wealth—human labor and nature. The right of a human being to subsistence is denied; hunger becomes a whip to enforce discipline; workers are not merely exploited, they are degraded and de-cultured, reduced to mere toilers. With land and other natural resources reduced to commodities, the existential environmental dangers multiply.

Under capitalism, the exploitation of natural resources—oil and gas, coal, uranium, bauxite, iron ore, etc.—is managed by giant oil and mining companies supported by their home states and "safe" client host states, and a network of financial institutions, all of which drive the process of "accumulation by dispossession." Safe client host states and their "internal colonies" ensure cheap labor-power, low-cost, low royalty rate, high-profit minerals, and huge capital gains in the exercise of options, along with a predatory public administration, paramilitary, and armed police that overwhelm the indigenous peoples in these regions.

In the face of all the capitalist depredations laboring human beings and nature are made to suffer, however, human beings come together to launch a "countermovement" to socially protect labor; to preserve the habitability of the natural environment and the security of individuals in their sociocultural environments; to protect productive enterprise from the implications of treating money and finance as commodities; and to safeguard and advance the democratic ideals of liberty, equality, and fraternity (better expressed today as comradeship). The "counter-movement" gradually realizes that it has to struggle to change structures—the Maoists are trying to carry out a "New Democratic Revolution" (NDR)—not merely remove the worst politicians.

THE CLASSIC PEASANT QUESTION

> You take my life
> When you take the means whereby I live.
>
> —WILLIAM SHAKESPEARE,
> *THE MERCHANT OF VENICE*, ACT 4, SCENE 1

One might legitimately ask: What do the land (and resource) grabs have to do with the peasant question? Indeed, younger readers might ask: What is the peasant question? One of the clearest articulations of it came from the radical economist, Nirmal Chandra, who queried: "How can the mass of peasantry be drawn into a revolutionary movement spearheaded by the socialists, representing above all the proletariat?" And he goes on: "The difficulty, at bottom, stems from the fact . . . that the peasant possesses 'two souls,' one of the proprietor, and the other of a worker."[15]

At the heart of the peasant question is political strategy and tactics concerning the transition from capitalism to socialism, and in this, the most difficult problem is how to reconcile the needs of the oppressed for immediate improvements with the necessity of overthrowing the whole system, in order to do away with exploitation, oppression, and domination. For one, the internal terms of trade should never be allowed to be unfavorable to peasants. Reconciling reform with revolution is not an easy task, but in any articulation of the peasant question, this is necessary. In India, since colonial times, millions of people have been dispossessed, uprooted, and displaced.

Since colonial times, the means whereby the peasants lived have been taken away in the name of "improvement." In rural areas, many poor peasants who are still in possession of a small plot of land have lost their non-market access to the means of subsistence from what used to be the commons (shared pastures, fields, forests, fisheries, and irrigation systems). And with the coming of the agro-food corporations and their agents in the business of "contract farming," the peasants cannot decide what to produce, how to produce (some of the imposed techniques require environmentally destructive inputs), and for whom to produce. In addition, when they are dispossessed of their land by the projects of the "financial aristocracy," they are forced to join the ranks of the millions of "footloose laborers."

The classic peasant question focused on class differentiation of the peasantry in the process of capitalist development, the dénouement of which was supposed to be its differentiation into capitalists and proletarians. In between, the class categories were rich peasant, middle peasant, poor peasant, and landless laborer (Mao's conception of the Chinese peasantry in 1930) or big capitalist peasants, middle peasants, small peasants, semi-proletarians/tiny peasants, and the agricultural proletariat (Lenin for Russia in 1920), or some combination of the two for India today. One also has to take into account what the well-known Soviet agrarian economist and rural sociologist, Alexander V. Chayanov, stressed, namely, "demographic differentiation," which has also been propelling the peasant economy, and which in India has also manifested itself in the labor intensity of cultivation.

RADICAL LAND REFORM

In the land reform that is at the heart of New Democracy, following the allotment of individual household plots of land to the tillers, this after land is decreed to be no longer a commodity, the peasants will have to be urged, democratically, to form mutual aid teams where a small number of households will pool resources other than land—tools, implements, draft power, occasional labor—but still cultivate the land on an individual basis. Given the adverse land-person ratio, this will necessarily be followed—and the peasants will have to be convinced of the advantages—by the formation of elementary cooperatives, in which land as well as other resources are pooled, albeit, with individual ownership rights maintained. Incomes will then be based partly on property ownership and partly on labor time committed to cooperative production in ratios set to garner majority local support.

"Dividends" will have to be paid on the assets, including land made available, and one will have to anticipate the complaint of the middle and rich peasants that this was not as much as they would otherwise have received, that is, if they had cultivated individually by hiring in labor. When crop yields begin to increase because of more intensive use of labor in the cooperative mode, the conflict regarding how to divide the income as between the labor contributed and the assets pooled will become sharper. The resolution will possibly have to take the form of moving from something like a labor to capital share of 40:60 to 60:40, for, over time, it will be living labor that will be contributing more to the addition of assets.

A time would then come when the new assets created by labor overwhelm the original assets pooled at the time of the formation of the cooperative, when it then becomes appropriate to abolish the capital share of the net output, that is, move to "advanced cooperatives." The latter would entail a definite socialist advance, involving all peasant households being incorporated in such producer cooperatives, with common ownership of all productive resources. As the American farmer and author of *Fanshen* (which documented the Chinese land reform program of the 1940s), William Hinton puts it:

> When the new capital created by living labor surpasses and finally overwhelms the old capital with which the group started out, then rewarding old shareholders with disproportionate payments amounts to exploitation, a transfer of wealth from those who create it by hard labor to those who own the original shares and may, currently, not labor at all.[16]

THE CONTEMPORARY "PEASANT" QUESTION

While the New Democratic land reform will thus take the peasants toward the socialist path in its resolution of the peasant question, one also has to take account of the peasants who were forcibly thrown off the land. To the classic schema of dispossession through class and demographic differentiation of the peasantry, dispossession through displacement must be added, this to take account of the impact of the processes of "development" on the dispossession of the peasantry in contemporary times. The peasant question will thus have to be posed multidimensionally as a series of questions that New Democracy will have to resolve.[17]

One is the *question of landlessness, or near landlessness,* especially of Dalits and Adivasis. The colonial period, itself, produced a large segment of displaced persons when forest, river, and mineral resources were exploited, as also due to the processes of de-(proto)industrialization and forced commercialization of agriculture. The Adivasis, in particular, were forced to make an "illegal" living in the hostile environment created by the revenue, forest, and police departments. Already at the time of independence, there was a large contingent of displaced persons, and these people were further marginalized by the development projects that followed. Lower class and poor Adivasi people among the displaced are looked down upon as a law-and-order problem, and even when there is a resettlement and rehabilitation policy (usually considered as a necessary evil whose cost has to be minimized) for them and it is implemented, they have to wait for a long time before they get reintegrated into the wider society/economy.

Two is the *Adivasi/indigenous people's question* that will have to address the tribal peasantry's precarious existence in the forests. The Forest Acts since 1865 failed to record the rights of Adivasis and other forest-dwelling communities, rendering them, in effect, illegal occupants and illegal users of the forests. Their denial of the resources of the forests has only deepened their vulnerability, in many an instance reducing them to migrant workers. Nevertheless, any attempts by the state to seize the forests have invariably been met with fierce resistance, a whole series of Adivasi uprisings, and now, Maoist-led rebellion, bearing witness to this. Today, the prohibition of alienation of Adivasi lands in Scheduled Areas to non-Adivasis, as also the Forest Rights Act, 2006, and the Panchayats (Extension to Scheduled Areas) Act, 1996, are observed more in the breach. The Indian officials, foresters, and policemen who replaced their British counterparts in the post-1947 period have continued to treat the Adivasis as a colonial people.

Three is the *housing/homeless people's question* in the context of the launching of urban and infrastructural projects that displace the urban poor, more than once in the same city when "more valuable real estate" appears.

Four is the *informal workers' question* in the context of the casualization of work, subcontracting, modern putting-out arrangements, and the like.

Five is the *migrant question and the question of their "alien" cultural and political context,* these concerning both internal migrants and migrants from Bangladesh and Nepal in particular.

Six is the *question of mass hunger* amidst an abundance of food in the context of the increasing commoditization of food with freer trade (that renders peasants vulnerable to international price fluctuations), the diversion of land from food-grain cultivation to cash crops and exportable agricultural commodities, the diversion of grain to the production of biofuel in the developed capitalist countries, and direct cash payments to the "targeted" poor, this in the midst of a tendency of declining food consumption per person. The question of mass hunger is crucial if one goes by the significantly higher poverty estimates based on National Sample Survey figures of calorific intake per person per day obtained directly rather than based on estimates obtained by adjusting (for inflation) the set of 1973–74 nominal expenditure figures adequate to obtain the 2,400 calories per capita per day in rural India and 2,100 calories per capita per day in urban areas.[18]

Seven is the *ecological/environmental question* in the context of deforestation (the Chipko movement), large dam projects, mining, manufacturing, and electricity generation and transmission projects, tourist resorts, and wildlife sanctuaries, among others. In articulating this question, one cannot remain silent on the question of the underlying capitalist system, which is really at the heart of the problem. As Marx understood it, nature requires long cycles of evolution, development, and regeneration, whereas capitalism is governed by the imperative of short-term profits. In India, caste discrimination and the colonial–racial oppression of the Adivasis are also intimately implicated in ecological devastation. Adivasi community lands have been subject to severe ecological damage as a result of rampant deforestation, and as a consequence, their agriculture has deteriorated so badly that they are unable to meet even their food needs from the land, forcing them to migrate out in search of wage work, thereby exposing them to exploitation of the worst kind and an extremely hard life for tribal women in particular.[19]

SOVIETS FOR RESOLVING THE SEVEN "PEASANT QUESTIONS"

Overall, what needs to be stressed is the large number and proportion of petty commodity producers in the workforce, of which peasants are a significant part. They are subjected to appropriation by mercantile, credit, and primary landowning capital of the profit, interest, and rent, respectively (the latter, mainly in the case of tenancy in agriculture) in the value added of their economic activity, and are left to extract their own "wages," which, invariably, may not even be the imputed official minimum wages. This is what puts them in "the latent" part of the reserve army of labor, which makes for a huge overall reserve army of labor (the sum of the "floating," the "latent," and the "stagnant" parts thereof), whose size is more than the size of the active army of persons who make a livelihood by the sale of their capacity to work.

The point is that with such a significant "pivot" upon which the law of supply of and demand for labor works, as Marx put it, the tendency of real wages to increase is severely restrained. There are a relatively small number of owner-controllers of Indian big businesses, the state enterprises, and the subsidiaries of the MNCs, beneficiaries of the skewed distribution of the economic surplus, at the apex of the steep social-class hierarchy, at the bottom of which are a large number of casual laborers and the huge reserve army of labor. The way the classic peasant question has been transformed multi-dimensionally into the series of questions must be seen in that light, which suggests that the institutionalization of New Democracy is going to be exceedingly difficult and challenging. Among other things, this will require the putting in place of local institutions of direct democracy in the form of soviets (councils that the workers, peasants, and other petty commodity producers must elect in the course of the NDR) to grapple with these questions at the local levels.

And here, particularly, the concerns of women, Dalits, and Adivasis, as articulated by them, must be heeded. The CPI(Maoist)'s Central Committee member, the late Anuradha Ghandy, felt that Dalit, Adivasi, and women's liberations have to be a prominent part of the fight for New Democracy. For her they were a prerequisite for any kind of democracy,[20] for at present, as far as women, Dalits, and Adivasis are concerned, there is not even a partial fulfillment of three of democracy's aspirations—liberty, equality, and comradeship. Women are made to do much more than half the society's work and they "belong" to men; no wonder patriarchy is such a powerful ideology. An inclusive civil society can emerge only when caste, gender, and racial/ethnic/national hierarchies are dissolved.

What approach would New Democracy take toward the nationality questions in Kashmir and the Northeast, and especially in the context of the Indian state's violent suppression of the right to self-determination fought for by the nationality movements? Supporting the "nationalism of the oppressed" is not an end in itself. New Democracy must support the right to self-determination of the Kashmiris, not because it favors secession, but only because it stands for free, voluntary association. That is, the Kashmiris must be given the freedom to decide whether Kashmir should be a part of India or not, as distinct from being included in India by forcible association.

Lest this be misunderstood, it needs to be clarified that a socialist must oppose all oppressions—class, ethnic/national, caste/racist, and gender— for Marxism is a philosophy of equality. It is also a philosophy of the poor and the downtrodden, the proletarians; so besides women, Dalits, Adivasis, Kashmiris, and other oppressed nationalities, a New Democratic program must put the interests of the casual workers and the petty commodity producers, and their dependents, center stage. They are a majority of the Indian population that has been excluded from active participation in the political process because they have to spend most of their waking hours engaging in the struggle to satisfy their vital survival needs. New Democracy must institute egalitarian principles governing the processes of production, distribution, and accumulation so that this large section of the population attains a degree of economic emancipation—the universal right to decent livelihood, food, housing, education, and health—that allows it to actively participate in the political process and make real choices. Democratic institutions can be effective in India only if (the monstrous) inequality is combated and the spirit of comradeship begins to flourish.

All this will require, in the immediate, a particular Keynesian macroeconomic policy mix that ensures that higher labor productivity provides more goods and services for a better standard of living for all, which can happen only if it is accompanied by the expansion of employment at satisfactory wages. And, of course, the process of economic growth and distribution of income in favor of the poor, with the latter a part and parcel of the growth process itself. This must be integrated with a process of development that simultaneously systematically breaks the social barriers of discrimination based on caste, gender, religion, ethnicity, and nationality.[21] New Democracy will have a better chance of attaining such "development with dignity" because the political context and the institutional means to stimulate the economy and press for important socioeconomic changes would be in place.

WHAT IS THE STRUGGLE ABOUT?

New Democracy needs to be re-imagined as part of a longer, truly democratic, human needs-based "political transition period" on the road to a communitarian basis for socialism—a socialism-from-below.[22] The expropriation of the capitalists, difficult in itself, had been accomplished post-1917, in the former Soviet Union and in China. But the *power of capital* has nowhere been overcome, as István Mészáros (1930–2017), the Hungarian Marxist philosopher, constantly emphasized. The capital system has, so far, always got the better of partial human-emancipatory efforts. Capital as a social organic system has to be eradicated and a socialist social revolution must ultimately implant the foundation of "a society of equals," capable of taking deep roots. Revolution must be a "profound process of ongoing social transformation" in this direction.[23] This means political transitional forms on the road to socialism, like New Democracy, will have to be very carefully thought through.

Implicit in a communitarian basis for socialism, a socialism-from-below, is a view of democracy and democratization as a process. The basic principles of democracy, liberty, equality, and comradeship, the latter implying solidarity, mutual respect, trust, and support, are also democracy's aspirations. Democracy cannot come into being if these aspirations are not at least partially fulfilled, and it is in the militant mass movement during a revolutionary upheaval that such aspirations gain true recognition.

The human needs that have to be met for everyone are adequate food, clothing, and shelter; clean air and water; a safe environment; free, easily accessible medical care of the best standards available; household possessions, including a home; education that guarantees decent employment; recreation and leisure; friendship, love, and affection, which gives one a sense of belonging; and genuine democracy that comes only with liberty, equality. and comradeship, all these to ensure human dignity and esteem. Fulfillment of higher human needs such as work that is personally fulfilling and socially meaningful and the freedom to choose from within that repertoire of work what one really wants to do and to do it, including the opportunity for creative expression, must also be on society's priority list, so that one can ultimately fully realize one's individuality and potential. Meeting all the above-mentioned needs of everyone would require a complete reorganization of all existing socioeconomic and political institutions and structures. This can only be accomplished after removing the persons at the helm of Indian big business, the state apparatus, and the subsidiaries of the MNCs, as also the professional elite at their command, from their positions of ownership and/or control.

Certainly, one of the biggest challenges will then be that of democratic economic planning to ensure that one, the productive resources get distributed among the various lines of production; two, there is a constant, steady flow of materials through the productive process; and three, consumer goods and services emerge in quantities and qualities sufficient and in line with the human needs of everyone. Each production unit will be managed by the people who work in them, and will thus have complete autonomy, but its output will have to be consistent with the objectives of the national economic plan. Hopes must be placed in a younger generation socialized and educated in concerned, caring communities and the radically reorganized schools and universities. They will work together to achieve these and other difficult but worthwhile goals. All this is predicated upon the inculcation of a socialist-humanist culture, which can only come about if the process of such infusion begins in the very act of building the movement for New Democracy today. It is from this movement that the political institutions of New Democracy will take shape.

The New Democratic constitution must allow for multiparty political pluralism, wherein each party accepts New Democracy as essentially making the transition from capitalism to socialism more compatible with democracy and thereby aiding the transition to socialism-from-below.

One-party rule will not appeal to the people and will not be in their interest. Both government and religious bodies must be excluded from control over education, which must be democratically controlled by the people. Education must not be disseminated from above, for going by Marx's third thesis on Feuerbach, who will then educate the educators? While "freedom of conscience" must be safeguarded, simultaneously—to paraphrase Marx's words—conscience needs to be liberated from the specter of religion. The aspirations of democracy—liberty, equality, and comradeship—can never even be partially fulfilled without the secularization of Indian society. Indeed, the polarization of Indian society through the spread of the ideology of Hindutva is making matters worse.

New Democracy needs to combat the ideology and practice of Hindutva-nationalism, semi-fascism, sub-imperialism and its imperialist principles with all the "weapons" in its "magazine." In foreign policy, this certainly demands a rapprochement between India and China, and their alliance with Russia to thwart Washington's political maneuvers, especially the pitting of India against China, the basis for which was laid long ago by borderlines imposed by the British colonizers. In the immediate present, as part of an interim political program, how then may the forces of New Democracy take on Hindutva-nationalism and semi-fascism?

PARTISANS IN COMMON

Where are the weapons?
I have only those of my reason
and in my violence there is no place
for even the trace of an act that is not
intellectual.

—PIER PAOLO PASOLINI,
POET, FILMMAKER, NOVELIST, POLITICAL JOURNALIST,
IN AN AUDACIOUS AND INSPIRING POEM
WRITTEN IN 1964, ENTITLED "VICTORY"[24]

The proponents of New Democracy must bring together a wide range of partisans in common, including poets, filmmakers, litterateurs, and writers of political prose. Pier Paolo Pasolini, the unarmed partisan who once brought his creations to the magazine—poetry, cinema, literature, and political prose—famously said: "I have only those of my reason." The bard dreams on a gray morning that Italian partisans killed in the resistance against fascism return from their graves to see if those who survived made the world worth their martyrdom. What they discover is betrayal, an Italy inimical to justice, trivialized by the power of consumerism. With the high hopes they once had shattered, the partisans preach vengeance, retribution.

Don't you see nothing has
changed?
Those who were weeping still weep.
. . .
Those who have stolen from
the common good
precious capital and whom no law
can
punish, well, then, go and tie them
up with the rope
of massacres. At the end of the
Piazzale Loreto
there are still, repainted, a few
gas pumps, red in the quiet
sunlight of the springtime that
returns
with its destiny: It is time to make it
again a burial ground.

Piazzale Loreto is the square in Milan where, after Mussolini was shot dead on April 28, 1945, his body was hung upside down from makeshift scaffolding. And, among the partisans who descended "from their graves, young men whose eyes" held "something other than love," was Pasolini's martyred sibling, Guido, who had joined the Catholic partisans in the fight against fascism, and whom the poet saw off at the railway station, when, in 1944 at the age of nineteen, he left home to join the armed struggle against fascism, never to return. The left has never been the only partisan against fascism.[25]

The German-born American political theorist Hannah Arendt, who was no votary of identity politics, once said: "When one is attacked as a Jew one must defend oneself as a Jew." I am reminded of Shahid Azmi, the advocate who never turned his back on Muslim youth falsely implicated in criminal cases. He was my comrade in the Committee for the Protection of Democratic Rights in Mumbai. Having been through acute suffering at the hands of the police and the criminal justice system, he could empathize with the suffering of others like him. As my friend and comrade, Monica Sakhrani, put it, roughly something like this: "It would have been impossible for him to live with himself had he given up his work as their advocate," for which he was assassinated on February 11, 2010.

Some Muslims who feel the community has been defeated, humili-ated, and crushed by the forces of Hindutva-nationalism with the active complicity of the Indian state, and do not expect justice from the courts, do see terrorism as the only weapon that can strike back. From each crime of the Hindutva-nationalists and the complicit state, the explosive RDX is delivered. Nevertheless, one has to embrace humane values even in the struggle against state and state-sponsored terror. Just as the latter is criminal, so also is the terrorism of the insurgent Islamic groups fighting it. The desperate followers of the leaders preaching vengeance are "as much victims as those who perish in the attacks of which we read and hear." But let's make no bones about it. State and state-sponsored terrorism is the more dangerous, for it masquerades as justice. The fight against terrorism, "the cycle of senseless violence," will make headway only as part of the larger struggle to do away with the injustice that gives rise to it. In these dark times, Islamic and Hindu liberation theologies might also be the need of the hour. And, winning the political and legal battle to strip the state and state-sponsored terrorists of their impunity and bring them to justice is an integral part of that fight,[26] for which Shahid Azmi fought to the very end.

In his own way, Shahid Azmi had something in common with Pasolini. They were unarmed partisans who, nevertheless, fought against neo-fascism/semi-fascism in the making with other weapons. Pasolini fought with the weapons of poetry, cinema, literature, and political journalism, Shahid Azmi with the weapons of jurisprudence and the law. India's liberal-political democracy is rotten, and this makes the way easier for semi-fascism. All the more reason why those who have been struggling to further the process of democratization should be welcomed to bring their "weapons" to the "magazine." A Subbarao Panigrahi, like the guerrilla-poet in Srikakulam, with his *Jamukulakatha* (theatrical rendering of songs in a folk idiom), brutally "encountered" by the police, will surely be there, but so too must a Gandhi, like the Mahatma with his pacifist resistance, risking his life in Kolkata, Noakhali, Delhi, and what are now, Bihar and Haryana, in trying to prevent the anti-Muslim pogroms there, even ready to confront the Hindutvavadi mobs who were killing Muslims, assassinated by a Hindutva-nationalist intolerant of his multicultural, multi-religious, assimilative idea of Indian nationhood.

And all those who are committed to the habitability of the natural environment and the security of everyone in their sociocultural environments, implacably opposed to the monstrous class polarization that has been a consequence of the accumulation process following India's "1989," and the associated hijacking of the electoral process with the power of money and wealth. They too must be part of the "magazine." A twenty-first century United Front must include all sections of the left and must be one where non-party but generally leftwing persons feel at home. It brings to mind

Samir Amin's idea of a Fifth International[27] that draws its inspiration from the First International, the only International to recognize the plurality of the socialist tradition, and that's the principle a twenty-first century United Front should uphold. A much broader Popular Front, also the need of the hour, will include all those who regard semi-fascism as a priori intolerable.

In his final work, *Salò*, a very disturbing allegory of fascist repression and intolerance, Pasolini tried to track the roots of fascism (and "neo-fascism"), the socioeconomic and psychological conditions that gave rise to it. Above all, what made the self-proclaimed "Masters" representing the landed gentry, religion, and the law (the swelling book of rituals and rules), finance capital and its politics—all "lawless and without religion," and above all, consumed by the lust for absolute power—unleash the horrors of Mussolini's *Repubblica di Salò*. In the face of the Resistance, though, the Republic of *Salò* didn't last. So too, will any nation-state founded on Hindutva meet its doomsday.

SECULARIZATION AND DEMOCRACY

> The *democratic* state . . . does not need religion for its political completion. On the contrary, it can disregard religion because *in it the human basis of religion is realized in a secular manner.* The so-called Christian [or, one might add, Hindu, or Islamic] state, on the other hand, has a political attitude to religion and a religious attitude to politics. By degrading the forms of the state to mere semblance, it equally degrades religion to mere semblance [additions and italics, mine].
>
> —KARL MARX, *ON THE JEWISH QUESTION,*
> FEBRUARY 1844[28]

The truly democratic state is not anti-religion. Within the limits of reason it respects religion, but it certainly must have already critiqued religion, overcome, and gone beyond it,[29] even as it retains the human foundation of religion—the "heart of a heartless world, and the soul of soulless conditions"[30]—which it must realize in a secular way. This is the way one must grasp the *dialectical* relation between religion and the democratic state. Tragically, India's rotten liberal-political democracy and "secular state" are a far cry from such a dénouement.

I have had a Christian upbringing and so I have been searching for the "human basis of religion" in Christianity, but one might very well look for it in some of the Bhakti traditions of Hinduism. Consider the words of Saint Paul in 1 Corinthians 13 in the New Testament: "And now abideth faith, hope and charity, these three, but the greatest of all is charity." Here's an explanation of what St Paul meant:

Charity in the vision of St Paul doesn't mean giving alms, but is again a translation of the Greek 'agape,' which means something like acting according to your conscience with full consideration of the fate of your fellow man. That means, in one sense and perhaps above all, that every . . . [human being] is important—not only people as a whole, but every individual is important.[31]

Such a progressive interpretation of charity had its origin in the early Christian period, when Christianity was the religion of the oppressed, the persecuted, the damned, and the banished, when Paul met the same horrible fate—beheading—as that of John the Baptist. But, refusing to give reason its due, deliverance was always believed to come only in the hereafter. Be that as it may, the "human basis of religion" inherent in the notion of acting according to one's conscience with full consideration of the fate of one's fellow human beings—focusing on the personal, ethical side of the individual—is already ingrained in the mode of thought and the basic structure of feeling of revolutionary romanticism, in other words, already realized within revolutionary romanticism "in a secular manner." More generally, such a "human basis of religion" can be realized "in a secular manner" by a New Democratic state through a practice based upon the mode of thought and basic structure of feeling of revolutionary romanticism.

A LIBERTARIAN DEMOCRATIC CONSCIOUSNESS

Revolutionary romanticism, however, calls for a libertarian democratic consciousness, which requires a deep commitment to beauty, artistic freedom, and democratic rights, more generally speaking, and further, to craftspersonship, to un-alienated and creative work, to love, to sexual fulfillment in erotic love, to the unity of all working people, to their mutual and shared interests. A New Democratic Revolution may not be a democratic way of bringing about democracy, but it will certainly help in establishing the preconditions of democracy. As Barrington Moore analyzed long ago, England, France, and the United States underwent "bourgeois revolutions" from below to emerge as capitalist democracies, but Germany and Japan, restraining such revolutionary impulses, underwent the transition to capitalism through a conservative alliance between the pre-capitalist landowning classes and the rising capitalist class, and the result in both these countries was fascism.[32]

I am an old-fashioned socialist who continues to insist that wealth comes from the exploitation of human labor *and* the appropriation of nature. To paraphrase Marx but also to bring in the importance he assigns to ecology,[33] I would like to emphasize the point about capitalist wealth originating in the exploitation of labor and the appropriation of nature in the process of pro-duction:[34] "Capital is dead labor" and out-of-play nature "that vampire-like only lives by sucking living labor" and extant nature, "and lives the more, the more labor" and nature "it sucks."

At the heart of what I have been stressing about India's semi-peripheral underdeveloped capitalism is what I have called monstrous class polariza-tion—*islands* of wealth, luxury, and civilization in a vast *sea* of poverty, misery, and degradation. By no stretch of imagination can "the sea" enjoy equal citizenship and partnership in the process of democratic decision-making alongside "the islands." In the absence of economic emancipation of the majority, political emancipation is a far cry. The people's struggle for eco-nomic and political emancipation, indeed human emancipation, and how they can realize this goal is the problem of India.

The rotten liberal-democratic regime, however, couldn't care less. It seems to be taking on semi-fascist traits and assuming the position of a sub-imperialist power in South Asia, even as hundreds of millions of Indians continue to be relegated to irrelevance. What then of the prospects of New Democracy? Very dim, unless at some point the soldiers and armed police-men in the employ of the state reckon that the people might win, and so they join the masses in revolt. I hope to live to witness the times when those hundreds of millions of Indians relegated to irrelevance, heeding the "small voices" of history and "the present as history" decide to enter history on their own terms. Society, after all, is a human creation subject to human influence, and so, a society of equality, cooperation, community, and soli-darity is still possible.

Appendix: Caste

Caste is a Portuguese synonym for *varna*, literally meaning "color," but indicative of a hierarchical social order of four varnas—Brahmin, Kshatriya, Vaishya, and Shudra—in descending order of claimed "natural" superiority and purity (implying Shudra inferiority and impurity) that evolved and stabilized in Early India roughly over the period 600 BC–AD 700. Vedic religion was then in the process of attaining its Brahminical form, providing the social order with the principle of Varna as its ideological prop. If one were to go by Marxist historical analysis, that social order already had a ruling-class combine of affluent priestly and warrior classes, with the merchants (in the period 200 BC–AD 300) having pledged political allegiance to it. At the bottom of the caste hierarchy were the bulk of the actual producers of the society's wealth—the artisans and craftspersons, peasants, bonded landless laborers (*dasa-karmakaras*) and other manual toilers, servants—who made up the socially oppressed, the economically exploited and politically dominated classes.

The ideological principle and the social institution of Varna thus seem to have stemmed from the existing class structure corresponding to it. At least that seems to be broadly the Marxist perception in India.[1] Caste as an ideology appears to have reduced the role of violence *vis-à-vis* consent in the domination (enforced consent) of the ruling classes. And caste relations came to dominate precisely because they were also a part of the relations of production, with the economy a totally dependent sub-structure within the social formation.[2]

Remarkably, caste as an ideology and as an extremely conservative social institution has proved to be eminently flexible and adaptable in rationalizing and legitimizing prevailing systems of domination and exploitation right from its evolution in early India down to the present. Hence, a brief outline of caste—as a deep-seated social institution that has persisted through successive social formations—over the *longue durée* might be helpful. How has the caste system reproduced itself from generation to generation over millennia? The historian Uma Chakravarti has argued that patriarchal control over women's sexuality has been critical for ensuring upper-caste control over material and cultural resources and the denial of these resources to the lower castes, especially those relegated to the category of the Untouchables.[3] In contemporary times, in large parts of the Indian countryside, caste as a socio-religious institution has continued to determine access to and control of the means of production and has, partly at least, even structured the relations of production. The nexus of the dominant-caste *maliks* (akin to kulaks) with the state at the local and the provincial levels largely explains dominant-caste hegemony at these levels and permits maliks to pay their low-caste laborers a wage much lower than the statutory minimum and even violate their sense of dignity with impunity.[4]

Caste relations, based on the myth of upper-caste superiority and lower-caste inferiority, have evolved over successive social formations in early, medieval, early modern, and modern India, more rapidly over the last three centuries in India's petty-commodity, tribute-paying social formation and the contemporary, semi-peripheral, underdeveloped capitalist one. They encompass the antagonistic attitudes of the upper castes toward the lower castes, as well as the former's exploitative and discriminatory behavior toward the latter. Caste has manifested itself at the local level in the form of empirical entities called *jatis*, endogamous subgroups, historically associated with particular occupations, in each of the four varnas, nay five, for another, more degrading order than the Shudra, the Ati-shudra was demarcated from the Shudra, with the most degrading jobs assigned to this lowest varna. Indeed, it has been denied the right to live alongside the other varnas, and thus has been segregated from the rest as Untouchable.

Based as they were on a hierarchical occupational division of labor, the jatis (occupation-based caste groups) continued to grow in number with the extending division of labor, and in the traditional village economy they provided the mechanism for the non-market exchange of goods and services, centered on the landowning dominant caste in the *jajmani* (patron) system. Caste, in the form of jatis, came to constitute a rigid, rather closed social stratification system with little, if any, social mobility, and in which the differences between the jatis were maintained and expressed by gradations according to ritual status. The main characteristics of caste as jati have been the following:

- endogamy (marriage only within one's caste) and patriarchal control of the sexuality of upper-caste ("twice-born") women,

- restrictions over inter-dining,
- hierarchy based on the Brahminical Hindu principles of *Karma* and *Dharma* (the former claiming that one is born into a particular jati because one deserved to be born there, and the latter specifying a code of duties),
- notions of purity and pollution derived from the ancient "Hindu" scriptures (stressed by the French anthropologist Louis Dumont with regard to the Varnas) and thus the avoidance of pollution by the "pure" from the "impure," and
- hereditary occupational specialization based on interdependence and mutual obligations, with work itself related to rank and purity.

Importantly, especially in the countryside, in the petty-commodity, tribute-paying social formation and in present-day, semi-peripheral, underdeveloped capitalism, the relations of production have also—partly at least—been structured by caste relations, with landlords, not necessarily of the Brahmin or Kshatriya jatis, oppressing, dominating, and exploiting Shudra or Ati-shudra jati, landless laborers.

Nevertheless, with the onset of underdeveloped capitalism following the impact of colonialism, the hereditarily transmitted occupational structure began to disintegrate and break down. The jatis began to take up occupations not in line with their traditional ones, and with this, the acceptance of one's predestined recognized role and the practice of that role as one's dharma (duty) weakened. Moreover, with certain lower jatis stealing a march economically over jatis above them, the economically mobile jatis began to emulate the superior jatis ritually and culturally to legitimize the process of their upward social mobility, which the eminent sociologist M. N. Srinivas designated as Sanskritization.[5]

With these changes, economically mobile lower jatis seem to have enhanced their social status in the caste hierarchy. However, where an ati-shudra jati improved its economic standing, the corresponding convergence of its social status was denied. For instance, the Mahars, an ati-shudra (Untouchable) jati from the Ratnagiri district of the erstwhile Bombay province, were able to join the British Indian Army and thereby improve their economic standing. They viewed this new livelihood opportunity as a means of overcoming the social stigma of Untouchability, but a commensurate enhanced social status was vehemently denied them by the province's caste-infused society. Indeed, even B. R. Ambedkar (1869–1956), a Mahar who was arguably the most learned and progressive among the leading Indian politicians of his times, "experienced the pangs of Untouchability" in India's caste-ridden society; he always seemed to be getting the devious message that he "'must remain in [his] . . . assigned place.'"[6]

All the same, with a breakdown of the hereditary occupational division of labor, a crucial pillar of the caste system was enfeebled. And yet, the disadvantage inherited from the past and reinforced by the present caste relations remained. The lower shudra jatis and the Untouchables—the latter were bureaucratically designated as the Depressed Classes, and from the 1930s onward labeled as the Scheduled Castes (SCs)—continued to be reduced to servitude. Dehumanized and degraded, they suffered unimaginable humiliation and hostility. M. K. Gandhi designated them as Harijans ("children of God"), equals before the gods and goddesses of the Hindu pantheon, but social equality has eluded them. They opted instead for the name "Dalit" (meaning "broken," "crushed"), given to them by the low-caste, anti-Brahminical reformer, Jotiba Phule (1827–90).

Right through Indian history, the lower castes and the Untouchables have reacted to the terrible situation into which they have been forced. There have been a series of anti-caste interventions and reform movements right from ancient to contemporary times. The historian of Indian philosophy Debiprasad Chattopadhyaya's *Lokāyata: A Study of Ancient Indian Materialism* and his *Indian Atheism: A Marxist Analysis*[7] suggest ruthless persecution of all anti-Vedic and anti-varna individuals and groups, so much so that nothing remained of the Lokāyata works (its first text, *Lokāyata Shastra*, is dated to the fourth century BC), and the philosophy of Lokāyata (early materialism) had to be reconstructed from mostly denigrated references to its ideas in rival texts. Lokāyata's atheism, its opposition to Vedic rituals, and the four-tiered class–caste structure aroused the ire of the lawgivers, and this perhaps explains the ruling classes' total hostility to it.

Later, Buddhism challenged the Vedic social order and the religion that was its ideological prop, but the "combined ruling class of Brahmanas and Kshatriyas launched a major counteroffensive against the socio-historic threat to Vedic religion in the Sunga and Gupta periods, and this led to the revival of Vedic religion in the form of Brahminism. The class structure of *chaturvarnya* became more rigidly hereditary and endogamous than ever before through scriptural injunctions as well as state policy . . ." Vedic religion now appeared in its full-fledged Brahminical form. The *Manusmriti*, probably compiled in the first century AD, ascribed divinity to the absolute monarch and made it his duty "to enforce the rigid and hereditary *chaturvarnya* through *danda* or the coercive power of the state." The state-led Brahminical "strategic counteroffensive" was successfully completed by the seventh century AD.[8]

In modern India, the early twentieth century and the 1920s saw the political awakening of the Untouchables fighting for civil rights—the Namashudras in Bengal; the Adi-Dravida in Madras Presidency; the

Ad-Dharma in the Punjab; the Mahars in parts of Bombay Presidency (by the latter half of the 1920s, under the leadership of B. R. Ambedkar); and the Ezhuvas (Iravas) of Travancore under the leadership of Sri Narayana Guru. And, as well, the Non-Brahmin movements in Maharashtra, beginning with Jotiba Phule's Sathyashodhak Samaj (Society of Seekers of Truth), founded in 1873, and in Tamil Nadu, especially the Self-Respect Movement, led by E. V. Ramaswamy Naicker, alias "Periyar" (1879–1973).[9]

The colonial government was prevailed upon to introduce job quotas for the Depressed Classes (the Untouchables) in the administration, and these were extended proportionately in 1946, and continued in post-1947 India. Reserved seats for the SCs were also instituted for admissions in higher education. Such reservations (top-down grants) in government jobs and in higher educational institutions prompted the leaders of the Shudras to also make a bid for the same, and the Kaka Kalelkar Commission in 1955 made such a recommendation. Later, the Backward Classes Commission, chaired by B. P. Mandal, in 1978 also came to such conclusions, and in 1990, the V. P. Singh government decided to extend such reservations to the Shudra jatis, officially designated as Other Backward Classes (OBCs). But with these reservations, castes began to take on, even more than before, the character of interest groups.[10]

The joint electorates with reservations for the Depressed Classes in the colonial period were continued for the SCs post-1947, but inevitably this practice led to the selection of only those SC candidates who were acceptable to the caste Hindus. Invariably, radical Dalits, those who worked for the liberation of the Dalits, were sidelined. Similarly, the Dalit-led and the OBC-led political parties, given the electoral arithmetic, also chose only those Dalit and OBC candidates who were acceptable to the caste Hindus.

Identity-based politics became the name of the electoral game. Powerful Shudra and Dalit politicians, in a bid to carve out a larger role for themselves through gaining political power, organized identity-based fronts to share power with more powerful upper-caste politicians. However, all these aspects of caste in Indian politics must be seen in the larger context of a century and a half of the development of underdeveloped capitalism, as a result of which the class structure of Indian society has been increasingly overshadowing the caste hierarchy. Irrespective of their position in the caste hierarchy, the powerful and wealthy politicians of each caste believe that they must somehow come to exercise power in government, and they opportunistically use the primordial identity of their respective castes to advance their political and economic interests. In the process, Phule, Ambedkar, and Periyar's politics of combating Brahminism is sidelined; at most, such a radical agenda only gets lip service.

Phule, Ambedkar, and Periyar wanted a wider unity of the oppressed: Phule, a unity of the Bahujan Samaj (the masses), and especially the Shudra jatis and the Untouchables, Periyar, a coming together not only of all low-caste Hindus, Shudra jatis, and Untouchables, but also Christians and Muslims. But as Ambedkar realized, the "graded inequality" of the caste system creates divisions that destroy the very basis of bringing the "aggrieved parties" on a common platform. As he put it:[11]

> In a system of graded inequality there are the highest (the Brahmins). Below the highest are the higher (the Kshatriyas). Below the higher are those who are high (Vaishya). Below the high are the low (Shudra) and below the low are those who are lower (the Untouchables). All have a grievance against the highest and would like to bring about their downfall. But they will not combine. The higher is anxious to get rid of the highest but does not wish to combine with the high, the low and the lower lest they should reach his level and be his equal. The high wants to overthrow the higher that is above him but does not want to join hands with the low and the lower, lest they should rise to his status and become equal to him in rank. The low is anxious to pull down the highest, the higher and the high but he would not make a common cause with the lower for fear of the lower gaining a higher status and becoming his equal. In the system of graded inequality there is no such class as completely unprivileged except the one which is at the base of the social pyramid. The privileges of the rest are graded. Even the low is a privileged class as compared to the lower. Each class being privileged, every class is interested in maintaining the system.

Arundhati Roy, in her essay "The Doctor and the Saint," gets to the heart of the logic (of the "graded inequality") of the caste system when she writes:[12]

> The 'infection of imitation', like the half-life of a radioactive atom, decays exponentially as it moves down the caste ladder, but never quite disappears. . . .
>   . . . [This] means that Brahminism is practised not just by the Brahmin against the Kshatriya or the Vaishya against the Shudra, or the Shudra against the Untouchable, but also by the Untouchable against the Unapproachable, the Unapproachable against the Unseeable. It means there is a quotient of Brahminism in everybody, regardless of the caste they belong to. . . .
>   Brahminism makes it impossible to draw a clear line between

victims and oppressors, even though the hierarchy of caste makes it more than clear that there are victims and oppressors. (The line between Touchables and Untouchables, for example, is dead clear.) Brahminism precludes the possibility of social or political solidarity across caste lines. As an administrative system, it is pure genius. "A single spark can light a prairie fire" was Mao Zedong's famous message to his guerrilla army. Perhaps. But Brahminism has given us a labyrinth instead of a prairie. And the poor little single spark wanders, lost in a warren of firewalls. Brahminism, Ambedkar said, 'is the very negation of the spirit of Liberty, Equality and Fraternity.'

"Some closed the door," he wrote, "others found it closed against them."

As it is, alienation under capitalism divides working people and even induces loss of a sense of workers' potential as a collective of human beings, but in the presence of the "graded inequality" of India's caste system, which has had the effect of sealing off the various jatis from one another, such estrangement is reinforced. Moreover, when class differentiation, which, even by itself, is harsh enough to lead to very unequal access to wealth and income, healthcare and education, and a whole lot of other needs and opportunities, traverses caste and gender, as it does, the results and the experiences have been even more extreme. With reservations in government jobs and in admissions to higher educational institutions for SCs and OBCs, and with reserved seats for SCs, albeit with joint electorates, in parliamentary, state assembly, and *panchayati raj* ("assembly-of-five" governance at the local level) elections, however, over time, SC and OBC establishments have come into place, and they seem to have no fundamental political differences with the status quo. Dalit/OBC ministers in the Union and State cabinets, Dalit/OBC Members of Parliament and of the state legislative assemblies, and the Dalit/OBC officials in the civil bureaucracy, the police, and the judiciary who back these powerful politicians, are invariably persons who have been co-opted into the establishment that safeguards the status quo. Indeed, given the graded inequality of the caste system, fragmented at every level, and shaping access to economic and intellectual resources, the most acute contradictions are no longer between the upper castes (the foremost beneficiaries of the system) and the Dalits (the foremost victims) but between the latter and the jatis in the middle or even those more adjacent to the Dalits. The caste system has also deeply divided and degraded the Dalits. Sweepers, scavengers, and gutter and latrine cleaners, the most downtrodden of the lot, are treated as untouchables by other untouchables. So, while caste-Hindus treat the Dalits as pariahs, a subset of the latter treats the even more degraded untouchables in the same way.

Depressing, isn't it? India seems to be in a hopeless, irretrievable situation. Even as I have also been indicating the points at which the development of underdeveloped capitalism has destabilized the caste system, with the more recent rise of *Hindutva-raashtravaad* (political-Hindu nationalism in a Brahminical cultural idiom), a reassertion of upper-caste dominance seems to be underway, this with a vengeance. Toleration of the Dalits lasts as long as they keep to their assigned place/position; otherwise, extreme cruelty and brutality are unleashed. The interpenetration of casteism and communal hatred when it comes to Dalit conversions to Christianity or Islam, a closing of the gateways to inter-caste and Hindu–Muslim marriages (and breeding) by keeping a strict check on the sexuality of caste-Hindu women—these bugbears are intensifying. Speaking in the Constituent Assembly on 4 November 1948, Ambedkar remarked: "Democracy in India is only the top dressing on an Indian soil that is essentially undemocratic." Caste-ridden India is a disturbing place. It is, however, not a lost cause. The Dalit–OBC Question is all about Dalit–OBC liberation, which is essential to the liberation of all people, and impossible without it. Dalit–OBC liberation is all about bringing dignity to caste-disparaged people in the process of annihilating caste as an institution.

Notes

INTRODUCTION

1. The data are taken from the World Bank's 2017 report, *World Development Indicators*. The figures on prevalence of child stunting in India, Bangladesh, and China are for different years in the period 2008–15, and hence, they are not strictly comparable. India's figure on the prevalence of child stunting relates to the year 2015–16 and seems to be taken from the preliminary results of its "National Family Health Survey 2015–16."

2. Utsa Patnaik and Prabhat Patnaik, *A Theory of Imperialism* (New York: Columbia University Press, 2017), Table 7.5, 114 for the 1993–94 figures, and, Prabhat Patnaik, "Economic Liberalisation and the Working Poor," in *Quarter Century of Liberalisation in India: Essays from Economic & Political Weekly* (New Delhi: Oxford University Press, 2018), 55, for the 2011–12 figures, taken from an unpublished paper by Utsa Patnaik.

3. Rosa Luxemburg, *The Accumulation of Capital*, translated from the German by Agnes Schwarzschild (London: Routledge and Kegan Paul, 1951), 446.

4. It is not the market economy per se that transforms a non-capitalist region but significant entry of big business that brings this about, for big business comes with all the necessary political support to accomplish its mission.

5. Joan Robinson and John Eatwell, *An Introduction to Modern Economics* (New Delhi: Tata McGraw-Hill, 1974), 322.

1. NAXALITE! "SPRING THUNDER," PHASE I

1. *Thema Book of Naxalite Poetry*, edited and introduced by Sumanta Banerjee (Calcutta: Thema, 1987), 71–72.

2. Sumanta Banerjee, *In the Wake of Naxalbari* (Kolkata: Sahitya Samsad, 2008), vii. This remarkable book was first published by the Calcutta publisher Subarnarekha in 1980, and then by Zed Press, London in 1984 under the title *India's Simmering Revolution: The Naxalite Uprising*.

3. Ibid., chapter 4, 112.

4. Evocative, no doubt, but this metaphor, "spring thunder," should not be taken to suggest that the uprising was akin to the natural phenomenon of a thunderstorm. The volition, the motivation, and the reasoning of the poor peasants and the workers who were the protagonists of the uprising should be emphasized.

5.   Manoranjan Mohanty, *Red and Green: Five Decades of the Indian Maoist Movement* (Kolkata: Setu Prakashani, 2015), 80. Part I of this book reproduces the author's 1977 book, *Revolutionary Violence: A Study of the Maoist Movement in India*, which, alongside Sumanta Banerjee's *In the Wake of Naxalbari*, ranks as among the two finest accounts of the Naxalite movement in its first phase.

6.   The 1964 split in the CPI—hitherto émigré from October 1920 to December 1925, formally launched in India on December 26, 1925—led to the formation of the CPI (Marxist) [CPM]. The CPM, unlike the CPI, considered the ruling Congress Party as the main political representative of the bourgeoisie and the landlords, led by the big bourgeoisie, which collaborated with foreign capital. In contrast, the CPI considered the Congress Party as the main political representative of the *national* bourgeoisie, and hence a potential ally. Moreover, the CPI leadership had taken a national chauvinist position in the Sino-Indian border dispute, which was in sharp contrast to that of the faction which went on to form the CPM.

7.   Charu Mazumdar, Reference Archive, Documents, www.marxists.org/reference/archive/mazumdar/.

8.   Suniti Kumar Ghosh, *Naxalbari Before and After: Reminiscences and Appraisal* (Kolkata: New Age Publishers, 2009), 128.

9.   Ibid., 132.

10.   Ibid., quoting from page 120 of the book *Maoist 'Spring Thunder': The Naxalite Movement, 1967–1972*, by A. P. Mukherjee, the then Superintendent of Police in the Darjeeling Area.

11.   Ibid., 133.

12.   Banerjee, *In the Wake of Naxalbari*, 104–105, 107.

13.   Mohanty, *Red and Green*, 71.

14.   Ghosh, *Naxalbari Before and After*, 136.

15.   Ibid., 164, 381.

16.   David Arnold, "Rebellious Hillmen: The Gudem-Rampa Risings, 1839–1924," in Ranajit Guha (ed.), *Subaltern Studies I* (Delhi: Oxford University Press, 1981), 88–142.

17.   Banerjee, *In the Wake of Naxalbari*, chapter 5.

18.   Charu Mazumdar, "Srikakulam: Will It Be the Yenan of India?" *Liberation*, March 1969, at www.marxists.org/reference/archive/mazumdar/1969/03/x01.html.

19.   Banerjee, *In the Wake of Naxalbari*, 129.

20.   One recalls with horror the encounter killings in Andhra Pradesh prior to and during the dark days of the Emergency period (1975–77), a few of which were investigated in detail by a committee (set up by Jayaprakash Narayan, as president of the Citizens for Democracy) headed by Justice V. M. Tarkunde, due mainly to the painstaking work done by the civil-rights lawyer K. G. Kannabiran as member-secretary, and a group of committed civil-liberties activists.

21.   Sumanta Banerjee, "Mapping a Rugged Terrain: Naxalite Politics and Bengali Culture in the 1970s," in the volume *Discourses on Naxalite Movement, 1967–2009: Insights into Radical Left Politics*, edited by Pradeep Basu (Kolkata: Setu Prakashani, 2010), 1–14.

22.   *Frontier*, September 18, 1971, quoted in *Naxalbari Before and After*, 230.

23.   Lawrence Lifschultz, "The Problem of India," *Monthly Review*, 32:9 (February 1981), 19.

24.   Ashok Mitra, *Calcutta Diary* (Kolkata: Paranjoy Guha Thakurta, 2014; first published London: Frank Cass, 1977), 71, 43, 44, 47. In the Third Reich, such "encounter" deaths were glossed over with the vindication, "Shot while trying to escape."

Jan Myrdal, *Red Star over India: As the Wretched of the Earth are Rising—Impressions, Reflections and Preliminary Inferences* (Kolkata: Setu Prakashani, 2012), 16.

25. Dalit is a self-description of the outcasts/*ati-shudras* (those who have been relegated below the lowest *varna* in the caste hierarchy) as "the crushed" or "the oppressed." The official description is Scheduled Caste. The Appendix on Caste might be helpful.

26. The *Shudra jati* is the fourth *varna* in the caste hierarchy, a low caste. The Appendix on Caste might be helpful.

27. Our account of the movement in Bhojpur draws on *In the Wake of Naxalbari*, 342–346.

28. Our biographical note on Jagdish Mahato draws on Arun Sinha's "Class War in Bhojpur—I," *Economic & Political Weekly*, 13:1 (January 7, 1978), 10–11.

29. Banerjee, *In the Wake of Naxalbari*, 343.

30. Ibid., 344–45.

31. Ibid., 149.

32. In this and the next two paragraphs, I draw on a telephonic conversation with the revolutionary Telugu poet Varvara Rao on June 27, 2011.

33. Known for *Jamukulakatha* (theatrical rendering of songs in a folk idiom), he played a major role in extending the Srikakulam movement into the province of Orissa (Odisha since 2011), but, as already mentioned, was captured and "encountered" by the police in December 1969.

34. The Andhra State Committee of the CPI(ML) and later, after the breakup of the Party, the so-called Central Organizing Committee, in which KS played a major part in Andhra Pradesh, also learned from Charu Mazumdar's "People's interest is the Party's interest" (May 1972), indeed, from the critiques of Sushital Roy Chowdhury—editor-in-chief of the Party's English monthly *Liberation*, among his other responsibilities—in late 1970. Unfortunately Roy Chowdhury died of heart failure in March 1971.

35. Sircilla and Jagtial taluks in Karimnagar district were declared "Disturbed Areas" by the state in October 1978.

36. Lin Biao, in his 1965 pamphlet, "Long Live the Victory of People's War!," summed up the essence of such a strategy in the following words: "To rely on the peasants, build rural base areas, and use the countryside to encircle and finally capture the cities—such was the way to victory in the Chinese revolution." www.marxists.org/reference/archive/lin-biao/1965/09/peoples_war/ch03.htm.

37. www.marxists.org/reference/archive/lin-biao/1965/09/peoples_war/ch07.htm.

38. Mao Zedong, "Problems of Strategy in China's Revolutionary War," December 1936, Selected Works, Vol. I, www.marxists.org/reference/archive/mao/selected-works/volume-1/mswv1_12.htm.

39. Adivasis are tribal people who were the "original inhabitants" of the Indian subcontinent. The girijans (hill people) of Telangana and Andhra Pradesh are also adivasis, the majority of whom are forest dwellers. The official bureaucratic label is Scheduled Tribe. Throughout this book, I view the various adivasis—distinct tribes, for instance, Gonds in Bastar in the province of Chhattisgarh, or Santhals and Oraons in Jharkhand and the adjoining parts of West Bengal—as distinct communities of people, with their own dialects, customs, culture, and rules which structure how they act toward and in regard to each other. What distinguishes them from mainstream society, whether Bengali, Oriya, or Telugu, is internal social relations based much more on kinship bonds, frequent cooperation to achieve common goals, and maintenance of a certain distance from the state and mainstream society because

there is an historical memory of such contact—with state officials, traders, usurers, and contractors—as having brought oppression, exploitation, and degradation. A helpful introduction to tribes in modern India is Virginius Xaxa, "Transformation of Tribes in India: Terms of Discourse," *Economic & Political Weekly*, 34:24 (June 12, 1999), 1519–1524.

40. *Thema Book . . . ,* 32, 45–46.
41. Ibid., 104-105.
42. Ibid., 99.
43. Editorial Note, "Kista Gowd and Bhoomaiah: Plea for Presidential Clemency," *Economic & Political Weekly*, 10:43 (October 25, 1975), 1674.
44. Sumanta Banerjee, "Remembering My Old Comrades," *Frontier*, 49:45 (May 14–20, 2017), 8.
45. Shahid Amin's *Event, Metaphor, Memory: Chauri Chaura, 1922–1992* (Princeton, N.J.: Princeton University Press, 1995) and Subhas Chandar Kushwaha's *Chauri Chaura: Vidroh Aur Swadhinta Andolan* (New Delhi: Penguin Books, 2014) are two of the finest accounts, so far. We have drawn on a book review of the latter by Chaman Lal, "'Chauri Chaura' Revisited," *Frontier* (July 27–August 2, 2014), 9–12.
46. A. G. Noorani, *The Trial of Bhagat Singh: Politics of Justice* (New Delhi: Konark Publishers, 1996).
47. Bhagat Singh, "To Young Political Workers" (February 2, 1931), at www.marxists. org/archive/bhagat-singh/1931/02/02.htm.
48. Radha D'Souza, "Bhagat Singh: Eighty-Three Years On," a review of Chaman Lal's *Understanding Bhagat Singh* (Delhi: Aakar Books, 2013), *MRZine* (July 12, 2014), at https://mronline.org/2014/07/12/dsouza120714-html-2/.
49. Samar Sen's foreword to the first volume of *Naxalbari and After: A Frontier Anthology*, Volumes I and II, edited by Samar Sen, Debabrata Panda, and Ashish Lahiri (Calcutta: Kathashilpa, 1979).
50. Ghosh, *Naxalbari Before and After*, vi.
51. Sumanta Banerjee, in "Remembering . . . ," writes about his comrade Bhabani Choudhury, of the "rumblings going on inside him—the urge for solidarity with the poor, and at the same time his love for Rabindranath [Tagore] and Bengali literature (which were dismissed as 'reactionaries' by the philistine leaders of the Naxalite movement)" [page 6].
52. Charu Mazumdar, "Party's Call to the Youth and Students," *Liberation*, 2:11 (September 1969), translated from the original in Bengali, which appeared in the weekly, *Deshabrati*, August 21, 1969.

2. "1968" INDIA AS HISTORY

1. *Poems by Faiz*, Translated, with an Introduction and Notes, by Victor G. Kiernan (London: George Allen and Unwin, 1971), 123, 125. In line 5 of the verse I have quoted in the text, I have taken the liberty to substitute "they" for "there" in the original.
2. *The Manchester School*, 20:1 (January 1952), 83.
3. Paul M. Sweezy, *The Present as History: Essays and Reviews on Capitalism and Socialism* (New York: Monthly Review Press, 1953).
4. One of the most thorough accounts of the Emergency is David Selbourne's *An Eye to India: The Unmasking of a Tyranny* (Harmondsworth: Penguin, 1977).
5. The Nehru and Mrs. Gandhi years merit considerable coverage in Ramachandra Guha's *India after Gandhi: The History of the World's Largest Democracy* (London:

Picador, 2007), but for our purpose, a succinct summary of what Guha considers the work done by the former that is then undone by the latter appears on 518–19, 21.

6. On *Midnight's Children*, its author Salman Rushdie and his depiction of the wicked "Widow," Mrs. Gandhi, and her son, Sanjay, "Labia Lips," I have drawn on Katherine Frank's "Mr. Rushdie and Mrs. Gandhi," *Biography*, 19:3 (Summer 1996), 245–258.

7. Ranajit Guha, "Indian Democracy: Long Dead, Now Buried," *Journal of Contemporary Asia*, 6:1 (1976), 39–40.

8. Bipan Chandra, *Nationalism and Colonialism in Modern India* (New Delhi: Orient Longman, 1979).

9. Bipan Chandra, Mridula Mukherjee, and Aditya Mukherjee, *India after Independence* (Gurgaon: Penguin Books, 2008). For Jawaharlal Nehru, see chapter 13, 219–234.

10. Consider the case of P. Rajan, a student of the Regional Engineering College, Calicut, who, for his Naxalite leanings, was whisked away by the police from his hostel in the early hours of March 1, 1976, never to be seen again. His father, T.V. Eachara Warrier did all he could to trace the whereabouts of his son, but with *habeas corpus* suspended during the Emergency, all his efforts were in vain. Upon the lifting of the Emergency in March 1977, Warrier moved the Kerala High Court in a habeas corpus petition, and the case uncovered the fact that his son had died in "illegal police custody." (Rajan was not even produced before a magistrate at the time of his arrest) as a result of brutal torture ("What Happened to the Rajan Case?," *PUCL Bulletin* [October 1981], archived at www.pucl.org/from-archives/81oct/rajan. htm.) Rajan's body was never found. The former editor of the *Hindu*, Siddharth Varadarajan, after touchingly referring to the English translation of Warrier's Malayalam account *Oru Achchante Ormakal* (Memories of a Father), writes: "Years later, the driver entrusted with the task of getting rid of the evidence told *Matrubhoomi* that Rajan's battered, lifeless body was fed to pigs at the government-owned Meat Products of India factory in Koothattukulam" (June 28, 2015), at www.blogs. timesofindia.indiatimes.com/toi-edit-page/lest-we-forget-emergency-remember-a-fathers-lament-2/.

11. Ruth Glass, "Exit Mrs. Gandhi," *Monthly Review*, 29:3 (July-August 1977), 68–69.

12. Harry W. Blair, "Mrs. Gandhi's Emergency, the Indian Elections of 1977, Pluralism and Marxism: Problems with Paradigms," *Modern Asian Studies*, 14:2 (1980), 238.

13. Cited in the *New York Times Magazine*, April 4, 1976, and quoted in Andre Gunder Frank, "Emergence of Permanent Emergency in India," *Economic & Political Weekly*, 12:11 (March 12, 1977), 465.

14. Our brief account of Primila Lewis's unveiling of the character of a section of India's "most 'modern' gentry" draws on a review of her book, *Reason Wounded*, by Mary Tyler ("Beyond the Emergency," *Economic & Political Weekly*, 14:12/13 [March 24-31, 1979], 621, 623).

15. Madhav Gadgil and Ramachandra Guha, "Ecological Conflicts and the Environmental Movement in India," *Development and Change*, 21:1 (1994), 101–136.

16. I liberally draw on a personal e-mail dated 13 January 2016 from Ramachandra Guha answering my queries about the main activists of the Uttarakhand Sangharsh Vahini at the time and the kind of struggles they organized in the Chipko movement.

17. Gadgil and Guha, "Ecological Conflicts and . . .," 120–22.

18. Mary Tyler, *My Years in an Indian Prison* (Harmondsworth: Penguin, 1978), 213–14.

19. In an article *"Kala Swatantrya Din"* (Black Independence Day) in the magazine *Sadhana* (August 1972).

20. S D, "Maharashtra: Children of God Become Panthers," *Economic & Political Weekly*, 8:31–33, Special Number (August 1973), 1397.

21. "Dalit Panthers' Manifesto," Bombay 1973, at ir.inflibnet.ac.in:8080/jspui/bitstream/10603/14528/15/15_appendicies.pdf. For a comprehensive academic study of the Dalit Panther movement covering the period 1972–79, see Lata Murugkar's *Dalit Panther Movement in Maharashtra: A Sociological Appraisal* (Bombay: Popular Prakashan, 1991).

22. "Children of God . . .," 1395–98, and Special Correspondent, "Dalit Panthers: Another View," *Economic & Political Weekly*, 9:18 (May 4, 1974), 715–716.

23. *Bulletin of Concerned Asian Scholars*, 10:3 (1978), 8.

24. "Children of God. . .," 1395–1398.

25. The writers and poets went their own ways, in Dhasal's case, for instance, two novels, more poetry, literary awards, but politically, he even hobnobbed with the semi-fascist Shiv Sena, a pillar of the Maharashtrian establishment, penning columns for the Sena's daily, *Saamna*.

26. P. A. Sebastian, "Rape and the Law," *Economic & Political Weekly*, 15:11 (March 15, 1980), 549–550.

27. M. R., "Railway Strike: The Fall-Out," *Economic & Political Weekly*, 9:23 (June 8, 1974), 892–893. The Maintenance of Internal Security Act, 1971, included provisions for indefinite preventive detention, search and seizure without warrants, and other repressive powers. It was based on the Preventive Detention Act, 1950, that lasted till the end of 1969.

28. We have drawn upon an excellent analysis of what brought on the strike in the Indian Railways, this in a paper by Stephen Sherlock, "Railway Workers and their Unions: Origins of 1974 Indian Railways Strike" (*Economic & Political Weekly*, 24:41 (October 14, 1989), 2311–2322).

29. Ibid., 2311, 2321–22.

30. Ibid., 2322.

31. Labor is the value creating activity of human beings, whereas labor power is the capacity to perform labor under capitalism, which is a commodity that is bought and sold. The value of labor power is determined by the quantity of socially necessary labor required for the production of the historically and socially determined means of subsistence of the laborer and his/her family, that is, when the laborer owns no means of production and is forced to sell his/her labor power, for otherwise he/she and his/her family would be left without the basic means of sustenance.

32. Dev Nathan, "Structure of Working Class in India," *Economic & Political Weekly*, 22:18 (May 2, 1987), 799–809. The laws related to labor that we are referring to are the Factories Act, 1948; the Payment of Wages Act, 1936; the Minimum Wages Act, 1948; the Equal Remuneration Act, 1976; the Workmen's Compensation Act, 1923; the Employees State Insurance Act, 1948; the Maternity Benefits Act, 1961; the Employees' Provident Fund and Miscellaneous Provisions Act, 1952; the Bonded Labour System (Abolition) Act, 1976; the Industrial Disputes Act, 1947; and the Contract Labour (Regulation and Abolition) Act, 1970. See *Anonymous Struggles* (Delhi: People's Union for Democratic Rights, May 1983), 10–19.

33. My account of the "short-lived Dalli-Rajhara spring" draws on Ilina Sen's *Inside Chhattisgarh: A Political Memoir* (Gurgaon: Penguin Books, 2014) and the People's Union for Democratic Rights report, *Shankar Guha Niyogi and the Chhattisgarh People's Movement* (Delhi: PUDR, November 1991).

34. PUDR, *Shankar Guha Niyogi and the . . .*, 3.

35. Ibid., 4.

36. Sen, *Inside Chhattisgarh . . .*, 67.

37. PUDR, *Shankar Guha Niyogi and the . . .*, 10.

38. We estimate the sizes of the three different components of India's reserve army of labor with data drawn from the National Sample Survey Organisation's "Employment and Unemployment Situation at a Glance," NSS 27th Round (October 1972–September 1973)," *Sarvekshana*, 1: 2 (October 1977), 81–102.

39. An explanation of why I take roughly 50 percent of the number of self-employed in March 1973 to be petty commodity producers/service providers is given in my piece, "India's Labor-Market 'Pivot': Rough Estimates, Origins, and Implications," which can be found on sanhati-india.org/.

40. We are not adding on the lumpenproletariat, for which we do not have a reasonable estimate.

41. EPW Research Foundation, "Poverty Levels in India: Norms, Estimates and Trends," *Economic & Political Weekly*, 28:34 (August 21, 1993), Table 6, 1766. Scheduled Castes and Scheduled Tribes suffer from a higher extent and severity of poverty than the general population, with the latter much worse off than the former.

42. On the crisis in East Bengal, what was then East Pakistan, and later, Bangladesh, I draw on two articles in *Monthly Review*, 26:8 (January 1975), 26–45, the first, "Bangladesh: The Internationalization of Counter-Revolution," by a correspondent, and the second, "Supplemental Remarks," by Aijaz Ahmad.

43. "Supplemental Remarks" by Aijaz Ahmad, going by the reliable reports of the Bangladeshi radical intellectual, Badruddin Umar, 38.

44. Ramachandra Guha, *India after Gandhi: The History of the World's Largest Democracy* (London: Picador, 2007), 463.

45. For this, we draw on APDR's first declaration on September 9, 1972, two and a half months after its formation, in "About APDR," accessed at www.apdr.org.in/.

46. This reminds me of a more recent experience of the radical political prisoner, Arun Ferreira. In 2011, as Ferreira took a stride to freedom through the Nagpur prison door, cops of the C-60 commando force, at the helm of the counterinsurgency in Gondia and Gadchiroli districts in Maharashtra, abducted him, clearly in connivance with the police station and the prison authorities. They drove him to Gadchiroli, produced him before a magistrate in order to convert illegal police custody into its legal counterpart, and after five days in the "company" of policemen, Ferreira was sent back to Nagpur jail after implicating him in yet another case. Arun Ferreira, *Colours of the Cage: A Prison Memoir* (New Delhi: Aleph, 2014), 143–44.

47. Aswini K. Ray, "Civil Rights Movement and Social Struggle in India," *Economic & Political Weekly*, 21:28 (July 12, 1986), 1202.

48. K. G. Kannabiran, "Creeping Decay in Institutions of Democracy," *Economic & Political Weekly*, 27:33 (August 15, 1992), 1718.

49. Mohan Ram, "Parvathipuram Conspiracy Case," *Economic & Political Weekly*, 14:19 (May 12, 1979), 827–28. There was also the Nagi Reddy Conspiracy Case involving Tarimela Nagi Reddy and the other members of the Andhra Pradesh Coordination Committee of Communist Revolutionaries (APCCCR).

50. Harjot Oberoi, "Ghadar Movement and Its Anarchist Genealogy," *Economic & Political Weekly*, 44:50 (December 12, 2009), 42. Why, one might ask, were the British colonialists so brutal and so callous in their treatment of the Ghadarites, given the fact that the Ghadar revolution never really took off, nipped as it was in the bud by British intelligence agents? Well, what the Ghadarites had in mind was truly audacious—they wished for an *internationale* of colonized peoples; they

wanted to organize the very Indian troops which the British colonizers had sent to subjugate not merely the peoples of the Indian subcontinent, but also other peoples, such as in Egypt and Kenya. Moreover, their vision was that of an *azad* (independent) India of multiple *quams* (peoples), a secular, multinational, people's India. See Radha D'Souza, "Revolt and Reform in South Asia: Ghadar Movement to 9/11 and After," *Economic & Political Weekly*, 49:8 (February 22, 2014), 59–73.

51. "Theses on the Revolutionary Movement in the Colonies and Semi-Colonies," *International Press Correspondence*, 8:88 (December 12, 1929), at www. bannedthought.net/International/Comintern/Congresses/6/RevMovementInThe-Colonies-Comintern-1928-crisp.pdf

52. M. R., "New Uses of a Colonial Law," *Economic & Political Weekly*, 9:24 (June 15, 1974), 940–41. Manoranjan Mohanty, "Lessons of the Secunderabad Conspiracy Case," *Economic & Political Weekly*, 14:10 (March 11, 1989), 482.

53. Kannabiran, "Creeping Decay in Institutions of Democracy," 1719.

54. Neville Maxwell, *India's China War* (London: Jonathan Cape, 1970), 419.

55. Text of an Online Petition to the Government of India Demanding an Apology to the People of Mizoram for the Unwarranted Air Raids on Aizawl by the Indian Air Force on March 4–5, 1966, *Red Banner*, 2:1 (March 2011), 74.

56. "Verdict in Sikkim," editorial, *Economic & Political Weekly*, 14:42–43 (October 27, 1979), 1737–38.

57. While the zamindar had the right to collect rent from his tenure-holders on his estate, the latter in turn leased the lands they held under tenure to a second tier of tenure holders who in turn further leased to a third tier of intermediaries, and so on, down the line, until the multiple-times-leased land reached the actual cultivators. The tax revenue that the zamindar paid to the colonial authority and the sum of the net incomes of the zamindar and all the intermediaries constituted the surplus, that is, if one reasonably assumed that the actual cultivators barely managed to extract subsistence "wages" from what remained of the net output.

58. Elizabeth Whitcombe, "Whatever Happened to the Zamindars?" in *Peasants in History: Essays in Honour of Daniel Thorner*, edited by E J Hobsbawm, W Kula, Ashok Mitra, and Ignacy Sachs (Calcutta: Sameeksha Trust by Oxford University Press, 1980), 179.

59. These quotes are from the "Report of the Task Force on Agrarian Relations" (New Delhi: Planning Commission, 1973), cited in P. S. Appu, "Agrarian Structure and Rural Development," *Economic & Political Weekly*, Review of Agriculture, 9:39 (September 28, 1974), A-71. The author, P. S. Appu (1929–2012), a widely regarded authority on India's land-reforms program, was land reforms commissioner in the Ministry of Agriculture and the Planning Commission during 1970–75.

60. Ibid., A-72. The last sentence is from the conclusion of the Planning Commission's "Report . . . on Agrarian Relations."

61. One big exception was Kerala, where a CPI-led state government, and later, a CPM-led one too, succeeded in carrying through land-to-the-tiller policies. See Ronald J. Herring, *Land to the Tiller: The Political Economy of Agrarian Reform in South Asia* (New Haven: Yale University Press, 1983).

62. P. S. Appu, "Tenancy Reform in India," *Economic & Political Weekly*, 10:33–35, Special Number (August 1975), 1355, 1357.

63. A well-known North American scholar of India, Francine Frankel, in her *India's Political Economy, 1947–1977: The Gradual Revolution* (Princeton, N. J.: Princeton University Press, 1978), concluded that the goal of a "socialist pattern" of development could not be achieved because the political leadership did not mobilize and

organize the lower classes to achieve it. How could she have expected establishment politicians to undertake such a task, given their class affiliations?

64. *Calcutta Diary* by Ashok Mitra (Kolkata: Paranjoy Guha Thakurta, 2014; first published, London: Frank Cass, 1977).

65. Harry M. Cleaver, Jr., "The Contradictions of the Green Revolution," *Monthly Review*, 24:2 (June 1972), 81–82.

66. Abhijit Sen, "Economic Reforms, Employment and Poverty: Trends and Options," *Economic & Political Weekly*, Vol. 31, Nos. 35-37, Special Number, September 1996, Table 1, 2460.

67. Cleaver, Jr., "The Contradictions of . . .," 83.

68. Ibid., 81.

69. Ibid., 86–87, Tables 1 and 2.

70. These articles call upon the state to direct its policy to ensure "that the ownership and control of the material resources of the community are so distributed as best to sub-serve the common good" and also to make sure "that the operation of the economic system does not result in the concentration of wealth and means of production to the common detriment."

71. Ashok Mitra, *Terms of Trade and Class Relations: An Essay in Political Economy* (London: Frank Cass, 1977).

72. Sen, "Economic Reforms, Employment and Poverty . . .," 2459–2477.

73. Nirmal Kumar Chandra, "The Peasant Question from Marx to Lenin: The Russian Experience," *Economic & Political Weekly*, 37:20 (May 18, 2002), 1927.

74. Ranajit Guha, *Elementary Aspects of Peasant Insurgency in Colonial India* (New Delhi: Oxford University Press, 1983), 226.

75. Kathleen Gough, "Indian Peasant Uprisings," *Economic & Political Weekly*, 9:32–34, Special Number (August 1974), 1391 and 1403. Also see her "The Indian Revolutionary Potential," *Monthly Review*, 20:9 (February 1969), 23–36.

76. Gough, "Indian Peasant Uprisings," 1392–1395. Regarding the drain of wealth from Bengal in the initial decades of colonization, the nature of the private property rights in land in the countryside that the British colonialists introduced, deindustrialization in India in the nineteenth century, and especially in Gangetic Bihar, and other important aspects of the impact of colonialism on the Indian economy, see Professor Amiya K. Bagchi's *Colonialism and the Indian Economy* (Delhi: Oxford University Press, 2010), a collection of his scholarly papers on the subject, first published over a period of six years from 1973 onwards.

77. The Marxist historian Irfan Habib has estimated the value of the East India Company's imports to Britain paid for with the land revenue to be 9 percent of the gross domestic product in 1801 of the Indian territories it had colonized up to that year. See his "Colonization of the Indian Economy, 1757–1900," *Social Scientist*, 3:8 (March 1975), 28.

78. Two sections in Utsa Patnaik's "Aspects of India's Colonial Economic History" (*Economic & Political Weekly*, 49:5 (February 1, 2014), 31–39), a review article based on Amiya K. Bagchi's *Colonialism and the Indian Economy* (Delhi: Oxford University Press, 2010), "Property Relations" and "The Value of Land" are particularly enlightening in this respect.

79. They however gave more security of tenure to non-cultivating tenants, not to poor peasants who actually tilled the land.

80. B. M. Bhatia's *Famines in India: A Study of Some Aspects of the Economic History of India, 1860–1945* (Delhi: Asia Publishing House, 1963) has been a standard reference source on famines in India, especially the ones in the late 19th century.

81. Evident in Bihar, Orissa, and West Bengal, for instance, by 1953–54, and at the all-India level by 1971–72. R S Deshpande, "Land Policy Issues in the Development Context," in Asian Development Bank edited *Agriculture, Food Security, and Rural Development* (New Delhi: Oxford University Press, 2010), Table 2A.5, 69–73.

82. Arup Kumar Sen, "Indian Mutiny (1857): Popular Revolts against British Imperialism," in Immanuel Ness and Zak Cope (eds.), *The Palgrave Encyclopedia of Imperialism and Anti-Imperialism* (London: Palgrave Macmillan, 2015), 703–707. Also see Gautam Bhadra's interpretation of 1857 in his portrayal of "ordinary rebels," in *Selected Subaltern Studies*, edited by Ranajit Guha and Gayatri Chakravorty (New Delhi: Oxford University Press, 1988).

83. Suniti Kumar Ghosh, "Marx on India," *Monthly Review*, 35:8 (January 1984), 47–48.

84. Ranajit Guha, "Indian Democracy: Long Dead, Now Buried," 41–42. P. Sundarayya's account—he was one of the leaders—of the "Telangana People's Armed Struggle, 1946–1951" has been published in *Social Scientist* (1:7–10, 1973) in four parts, part one, the historical setting, part two, the first phase and its lessons, part 3, the struggle when it was pitted against the Indian army, and part 4, which covers the background to the decision to withdraw the struggle. The sharp differences that developed within the CPI over the Telangana armed struggle when the armed squads had to fight the Indian army are dealt with in Mohan Ram's "The Telangana Peasant Struggle, 1946–51" (*Economic & Political Weekly*, 8:23 (June 9, 1973), 1025–1032).

85. Guha, "Indian Democracy: Long Dead. . ." 40–41.

86. Ajit Roy, "'Revolution' by 'Consent': Indian Case Study," *Economic & Political Weekly*, 17:46/47 (November 13, 1982), 1880, quoting T. Nagi Reddy, *India Mortgaged: A Marxist-Leninist Appraisal* (T Nagi Reddy Memorial Trust, Anantapuram, 1978), 4.

87. Suniti Kumar Ghosh, "On the Transfer of Power in India," *Bulletin of Concerned Asian Scholars*, 17:3 (July–September 1985), 37.

88. Roy, "'Revolution' by 'Consent' . . ." 1879, 1880–81.

89. Elections were constrained by several limiting conditions/qualifications, including property ownership.

90. Ghosh, "On the Transfer of Power in India," 34, 36, 37.

91. In Chittagong, revolutionaries led by Surjya Sen seized the local armory on April 18, 1930, issued an independence proclamation in the name of the Indian Republican Army, and fought a pitched battle on April 22 in which 12 of their comrades died.

92. Indivar Kamtekar, "The Fables of Indian Nationalism," *India International Centre Quarterly* (Monsoon, 1999), 44–54.

93. Our accounts of the Gujarat and the Bihar movements selectively draw on (1) John R. Wood's "Extra-Parliamentary Opposition in India: An Analysis of Populist Agitations in Gujarat and Bihar" (*Pacific Affairs*, 48:3 (Autumn 1975), 313–334), and (2) Ghanshyam Shah's *Protest Movements in Two Indian States: A Study of Gujarat and Bihar Movements* (Delhi: Ajanta Publications, 1977).

94. An "external" emergency was already in force, and as we have seen, it was being used against uncompromising radical opponents.

95. Balraj Puri, "A Fuller View of the Emergency," *Economic & Political Weekly*, 30:28 (July 15, 1995), 1739.

96. Ibid., 1741.

97. Ibid., 1741. Puri quotes from C. G. K. Reddy's *Baroda Dynamite Conspiracy: The Right to Rebel* (New Delhi: Vision Books, 1977).

98. The RSS chief's letters dated August 22 and November 10, 1975, to Mrs. Gandhi in Justice Demands: Letters of RSS Chief, undated, 1–10, quoted in Arvind Rajagopal, "Sangh's Role in the Emergency," *Economic & Political Weekly*, 38:27 (July 5, 2003), 2798.

99. Radha D'Souza, in her "Revolt and Reform in . . ." (65–66), likewise views the longer process in terms of a "dialectic of rebellion-repression-reform," and characterizes the relation of the nationalist elite with the colonial administration as fitting a "collaboration-confrontation model."

100. The poet Faiz Ahmed Faiz's memorable verse, ably translated by Victor Kiernan, that this chapter opened with.

101. Consider, for instance, the socialist intellectual C. G. K. Reddy who was part of the Emergency underground alongside his comrade George Fernandes, both of whom were later arrested and jailed as among the principal accused in the Baroda Dynamite Case. CGK, as he was called, a veteran of the struggles of 1946, forsook career, comfort, and security to devote himself to the just cause of freedom when the Emergency was imposed on the Indian people. I also remember Vikas (Arvind was his other alias), whom I met in the mid-1980s in the Gaya countryside in central Bihar, then a leader of the CPI(ML)(Party Unity), earlier a student-participant in the JP movement who became a Sarvodaya activist. As I observed him interacting with the villagers and the armed squads of the party, Vikas could really relate to the poor and landless peasants; he seemed to have earned their affection, loyalty, and respect by his deeds.

102. For one interested in understanding this strike from the perspective of the textile workers themselves, Hubert W. M. Van Wersch's *Bombay Textile Strike, 1982–83* (Bombay: Oxford University Press, 1992) is the most rewarding.

103. Radha D'Souza, "Revolt and Reform in South Asia . . ." 68, relying on Gurdev Singh Deol's *The Role of the Ghadar Party in the National Movement* (Delhi: Sterling Publishers, 1969), footnote 2 at 199.

104. David Hardiman, "Towards a History of Non-violent Resistance," *Economic & Political Weekly*, 48:23 (June 8, 2013), 47. Hardiman refers to Gandhi's "Fasting in Satyagraha," *Harijan* (October 13, 1940), in *Collected Works of Mahatma Gandhi* (New Delhi: Publications Division, Ministry of Information and Broadcasting, Government of India, 1958–84), Vol. 79, 295.

105. N. Venugopal, *Understanding Maoists: Notes on a Participant Observer from Andhra Pradesh* (Kolkata: Setu Prakashani, 2013), 86.

106. Harry W. Blair, "Mrs. Gandhi's Emergency," 255–57.

107. Atul Kohli, in his *The State and Poverty in India: The Politics of Reform* (Cambridge: Cambridge University Press, 1987), was very optimistic in those years about what parliamentary left parties like the CPM could achieve in terms of redistributive reforms from above, this mainly because of the then committed political leadership and a dedicated cadre. But I need to add that much of the groundwork was accomplished by the CPI(M) in the immediate aftermath of Naxalbari, in the period 1967–70, under the leadership of Hare Krishna Konar, when the party was forced to politically wean away the poor peasantry from the Naxalite movement. See D. Bandyopadhyay, "Land Reform in West Bengal: Remembering Hare Krishna Konar and Benoy Chaudhury," *Economic & Political Weekly*, 35:21/22, 1795–97.

3. UNEQUAL DEVELOPMENT AND EVOLUTION OF THE RULING BLOC

1. Cherabanda Raju, "Rebirth," in Sumanta Banerjee (edited and introduced), *Thema Book of Naxalite Poetry* (Calcutta: Thema, 1987), 105.

2.   In the Indian case, a hybrid of rich peasant, merchant and usurer, kulak is a Russian word for this particular rural stratum.

3.   I mainly draw on Irfan Habib's "Potentialities of Capitalistic Development in the Economy of Mughal India," *Journal of Economic History*, 29:1 (March 1969), 32–78. Habib however doesn't refer to seventeenth century Mughal society as a petty-commodity, tribute-paying social formation. That is my description, based on Samir Amin's theoretical discussion, "Modes of Production, History and Unequal Development," *Science & Society*, 49:2, Summer 1985, 194–207. I must also acknowledge the influence of Samir Amin's ideas on my thoughts as expressed by him in his book, *Unequal Development: An Essay on the Social Formations of Peripheral Capitalism* (New York: Monthly Review Press, 1976).

4.   Our account of the social, mainly class, forces underlying the rise and decline of the East India Company in India draws, not uncritically, from Ramakrishna Mukherjee's *The Rise and Fall of the East India Company: A Sociological Appraisal* (New York: Monthly Review Press, 1974), which was first published in German in 1955.

5.   For a good introduction to the colonial impact on the Indian economy up to the beginning of the twentieth century, one that demolishes the claims of a set of historians who study the colonial economy as if there was no exploitation and impoverishment under colonial rule, see Irfan Habib's "Studying a Colonial Economy—Without Perceiving Colonialism," *Modern Asian Studies*, 19:3 (April 1985), 355–381.

6.   *The Eighteenth Brumaire of Louis Bonaparte, 1848–1850* (1937 edition), 64, available online at: www.marxists.org/archive/marx/works/download/pdf/18th-Brumaire.pdf.

7.   In the Ryotwari Settlement, the individual *ryot* was responsible for payment of revenue directly to the state, in the Madras and then the Bombay presidencies.

8.   In the Mahalwari Settlement, the "village community" was collectively responsible for revenue payment, this in a large part of the Punjab, and in the United and Central provinces.

9.   B. R. Tomlinson, *The Economy of Modern India: From 1860 to the Twenty-First Century* (Delhi: Cambridge University Press, 2013), 85.

10. Raymond Williams, *Keywords: A Vocabulary of Culture and Society* (New York: Oxford University Press, 1983), 41.

11. Cited by Williams in *Keywords*, 155.

12. Paul A. Baran, *The Political Economy of Growth* (New York: Monthly Review Press, 1957), 145 and 148. Baran relies on the estimates of Indian economists K. T. Shah and K. J. Khambata as quoted in Rajni Palme Dutt's *India Today* (Bombay, 1949), 32. And he rightly reminds the reader that as a proportion of the economic surplus, if one could arrive at reliable estimates of the latter, the annual colonial drain would be much higher.

13. The expressions in single inverted commas are from Karl Marx and Friedrich Engels, *The German Ideology* (written in 1845-46; Moscow: Progress Publishers, 1968), in chapter 1 on Feuerbach, in the section "The Illusion of the Epoch," where they explain how ruling-class interests are made to appear as the general interest. www.marxists.org/archive/marx/works/1845/german-ideology/ch01b.htm.

14. "Minute by the Hon'ble T. B. Macaulay, dated the 2nd February 1835," reproduced at www.columbia.edu/itc/mealac/pritchett/00generallinks/macaulay/txt_minute_education_1835.html.

15. The economic surplus is the difference between what Indian society produced and what it consumed.

16. B. R. Tomlinson, *The Modern Economy of Modern India*, 10.

17. Marcello de Cecco, *Money and Empire: The International Gold Standard, 1890–1914* (Oxford: Basil Blackwell, 1975). Utsa Patnaik, "India and the World Economy, 1900 to 1935: The Inter-War Depression and Britain's Demise as a World Capitalist Leader," *Social Scientist*, 42:1/2 (January–February 2014), 13–35. Utsa Patnaik stresses, in particular, the "tribute" element, what I have called the colonial "drain" that contributed to Britain's large surplus on the current account of its balance of payments with India.

18. Hamza Alavi, "India: Transition to Colonial Capitalism," in Hamza Alavi, P. L. Burns, G. R. Knight, B. B. Mayer, and Doug McEarchern (eds.), *Capitalism and Colonial Production* (London and Sydney: Croom Helm, 1982), 40–42.

19. In this and the following two paragraphs, I draw on a thought-provoking essay by Suniti Kumar Ghosh, "Indian Bourgeoisie and Imperialism," *Economic & Political Weekly*, 23:45–47 (November 18, 1988), 2445–2458.

20. Over time, exports of some of these consumer goods (e.g., cotton cloth) or their intermediates (e.g., cotton yarn to Japan and China), besides, of course, jute textiles, provided the hard currency to pay for the capital goods imports.

21. Hamza Alavi, "State and Class Under Peripheral Capitalism," in Hamza Alavi and Teodor Shanin (eds.), *Introduction to the Sociology of 'Developing Societies'* (London: Macmillan, 1982), 297–298.

22. Amiya Kumar Bagchi, *Private Investment in India, 1900–1939* (Cambridge: Cambridge University Press, 1972).

23. Baran, *The Political Economy* . . .

24. Ibid., chapter 5, "On the Roots of Backwardness," Sections III and IV, 151–162.

25. Paul M. Sweezy and Harry Magdoff, "The Editors' Comment" on Aidan Foster-Carter's "Korea and Dependency Theory," *Monthly Review*, 37:5 (October 1985), 27–34, on 33.

26. Baran, *The Political Economy* . . ., 222.

27. Nirmal Kumar Chandra, "Monopoly Capital, Private Corporate Sector and the Indian Economy, 1931–76," in his book *The Retarded Economies: Foreign Domination and Class relations in India and Other Emerging Nations* (Bombay: Sameeksha Trust by Oxford University Press, Bombay, 1988), 253–303. The essay first appeared in *Economic & Political Weekly*, Special Number, 14:30–32 (August 1979), 1243–1272.

28. Chandra, "Monopoly Capital . . ." 298.

29. Indeed, Indian large business houses also grew by acquiring expatriate business-group companies. The Tatas, for instance, took over Forbes Forbes Campbell & Company (with four companies under it), Macneill and Barry (with a number of companies under it), Volkart Brothers (which became Voltas Ltd in 1954), and James Finlay & Co. The Birlas too acquired a number of companies of British expatriate business houses. Indeed, large business houses like those of Bangur, Thapar, and Dalmia–Sahu Jain focused on growth through such acquisitions. And, some relatively smaller business houses like Soorajmull Nagarmull, Goenka, and Khaitan, formerly big traders to British expatriate business groups, went on an acquisition spree to register unprecedented growth of assets. Brij Mohan Khaitan, for instance, acquired Williamson Magor in 1964 and went on to become one of the world's largest tea planters by the mid-1980s. See Dwijendra Tripathi and Jyoti Jumani, *The Oxford History of Contemporary Indian Business* (New Delhi: Oxford University Press, 2013), chapters 3 and 4.

30. The 1944 Bombay Plan—authored by Purshottamdas Thakurdas, J. R. D. Tata,

G. D. Birla, Ardeshir Dalal, Shri Ram, Kasturbhai Lalbhai, A D Shroff and John Mathai—was formally titled *A Brief Memorandum Outlining a Plan for Economic Development of India*. Thakurdas, Birla, Shri Ram, and Lalbhai were prominent among India's business tycoons at the time.

31. Paresh Chattopadhyay, "State Capitalism in India," *Monthly Review*, 21:10 (March 1970), 14–38.

32. Partha Ray, "Rise and Fall of Industrial Finance in India," *Economic & Political Weekly*, 50:5 (January 31, 2015), 61–68.

33. Reasonably priced steel and electricity required reasonably priced, good-quality coal, which, with better company management, it was possible to deliver, irrespective of wage increases and difficult mining conditions. K. V. Subrahmanyam, "Shades of Darkness: The Annals of the Coal Industry," *Economic & Political Weekly*, 3:40 (October 5, 1968), 1515–26. After all, the coal mines of the Tata Iron & Steel Company, better managed than the other private coal mines, were not nationalized.

34. The pricing policy of the oil MNCs in India was injurious not only to the private sector, but also to the government and the general public, and the government nationalized the three companies in the 1970s.

35. Sudip Chaudhuri, "Economic Reforms and Industrial Structure in India," *Economic & Political Weekly*, 37:2 (January 12, 2002), Table 4, 158.

36. This does not imply autarky—not all the products have to be produced in the economy—but it certainly calls for much stronger internal than external linkages.

37. Nirmal Kumar Chandra, "Long-Term Stagnation in the Indian Economy, 1900–75," in *The Retarded Economies . . ."* 168. This essay was first published in the *Economic & Political Weekly* in April 1982.

38. Vivek Chibber, *Locked in Place: State-Building and Late Industrialization in India* (Princeton: Princeton University Press, 2003), chapter 5.

39. Amiya K. Bagchi, "Long-Term Constraints in India's Industrial Growth," in E.A.G. Robinson and Michael Kidron (eds.), *Economic Development in South Asia* (London: Macmillan, 1970).

40. C. P. Chandrasekhar, "Aspects of Growth and Structural Change in Indian Industry," *Economic & Political Weekly*, 23:45–47, Special Number (November 1988), 2359–2370.

41. This paragraph, the previous one, and the one that follows, draws on a probing paper by Sudip Chaudhuri, "Public Enterprises and Private Purposes," *Economic & Political Weekly*, 29:22 (May 28, 1994), 1338–1347.

42. I drew on Norman Girvan's "The Approach to Technology Policy Studies" (*Social and Economic Studies*, 28:1 (March 1979), 1–53) for the concepts of technological dependence and technological underdevelopment.

43. Bernard D'Mello, "Innovation, Imitation and Dependence: Iron and Steel Technology in India, 1970–1990," *International Journal of Technology and Globalisation*, 5:1/2 (2010), 114–123.

44. Bernard D'Mello, "Some Recent Technology Imports: Approaching the New from the Perspective of the Old," Paper presented at a Seminar organized by the Working Group on Political Economy of India, Center for Studies in Social Sciences, Calcutta, February 28 and March 1, 1990. Sushil Khanna, "Transnational Corporations and Technology Transfer: Contours of dependence in India's Petrochemical Industry," and Biswajit Dhar, "Factors Influencing Technology Selection: Case Study of Thal Vaishet and Hazira Fertiliser Projects," *Economic & Political Weekly*, 19:31/33, Annual Number (August 1984), 1319–1340 and 1385–1395, respectively.

Sailendranath Ghosh, "Fertiliser Technology: Fractured Profile of Self-Reliance, *Economic & Political Weekly*, 21:16 (April 19, 1986), 698–705.

45. Amiya K. Bagchi, "Foreign Collaboration in Indian Industry," *Economic & Political Weekly*, 21:21 (May 24, 1986), 915–18. In this piece, Bagchi undertakes a thorough review of the Reserve Bank of India's fourth survey report on foreign collaboration in Indian industry.

46. The Indian large business houses and MNCs couldn't have been allowed, without any limits, to hollow out their smaller peers. With the MRTP Act and FERA in place, the government could claim to be protecting small and medium enterprises from both Indian and foreign monopolies and all Indian businesses from the latter. It must be added that FERA hastened the demise of the expatriate business houses. For instance, the third Lord Inchcape (K. J. W. Mackay) brought Brij Mohan Khaitan as a significant shareholder into Macneill and Barry, which was then merged with Khaitan's Williamson Magor, the merged company becoming Macneill and Magor. The latter eventually came to be controlled by Khaitan in 1982. Dwijendra Tripathi and Jyoti Jumani, *The Oxford History of . . .*, 112.

47. Sailendranath Ghosh, "Fertiliser Technology . . ."

48. "Grip of Technological Dependency," an editorial note, *Economic & Political Weekly*, 23:16 (April 16, 1988), 756. Also see Subhendu Dasgupta, "Structure of 'Interdependence' in Indian Industry: Electrical Equipment Industry," *Economic & Political Weekly*, 12:44 (October 29, 1977), 1857–65.

49. Bernard D'Mello, "Direct Foreign Investment Revisited," *Frontier*, 23:38 (May 4, 1991), 7.

50. Nirmal K. Chandra, "Growth of Foreign Capital and Its Importance in Indian Manufacturing," *Economic & Political Weekly*, 26:11/12, Annual Number (March 1991), Table 7, 685.

51. D'Mello, "Direct Foreign Investment . . ." 6.

52. Bernard D'Mello, "The Indian Model," *Frontier*, 21:13 (November 12, 1988), 6–7.

53. Dilip Subramanian, "Impact of Deregulation on a Public Sector Firm: Case Study of ITI," *Economic & Political Weekly*, 39:49 (December 4, 2009), 5233–5245.

54. Sudip Chaudhuri, "Premature Deindustrialization in India and Rethinking the Role of Government," Working Paper, FMSH-WP-2015-91 (April 2015).

55. D'Mello, "Direct Foreign Investment . . ." 5 and 9.

56. Sudip Chaudhuri, "Government and Transnationals: New Economic Policies since 1991," *Economic & Political Weekly*, 30:18/19 (May 6, 1995), 999–1011.

57. Ibid.

58. Jyoti Saraswati, *Dot.Compradors: Power and Policy in the Development of the Indian Software Industry* (London: Pluto Press, 2012).

59. K. S. Chalapati Rao, Biswajit Dhar, K. V. K. Ranganathan, Rahul N. Choudhury, and Vipin Negi, "FDI into India's Manufacturing Sector via M&A's: Trends and Composition," Institute for Studies in Industrial Development, Working Paper No. 161 (February 2014).

60. See K. S. Chalapati Rao and Biswajit Dhar, *India's FDI Inflows: Trends and Concepts* (New Delhi: Research and Information System for Developing Countries and Institute for Studies in Industrial Development, 2011).

61. Surajit Mazumdar, "Big Business and Economic Nationalism in India," Institute for Studies in Industrial Development Working Paper 2010/09 (September 2010), Table 8, 20. One must add that Indian big business has so far also dominated in upper-end tertiary healthcare (corporate hospitals), multi-brand retailing, civil aviation, and satellite television. Indeed, "medical tourism"—patients from abroad,

advised by medical insurers, availing of low-cost arbitraging of tertiary medical care in India—is seen by big businesses like the Apollo group of hospitals as a huge profit opportunity; they want to turn their five-star hospitals into a "global health-care destination."

62. Mazumdar, "Big Business and Economic Nationalism . . ." sections 4.3 and 4.4.
63. Whereas in the period before India's "1989," a large proportion of the total paid-up capital of companies registered under the Companies Act was in public-sector (i.e., government) companies, in the course of the "1989" period, this was reversed— private (i.e., non-government) corporations now account for most of such paid-up capital.
64. Sushil Khanna, "The Transformation of India's Public Sector: Political Economy of Growth and Change," *Economic & Political Weekly*, 50:5 (January 31, 2015), 47–60.
65. Baran, *The Political Economy* . . .., 174, 195.
66. At the levels of living then prevailing, net material product per capita was a better indicator of the well-being of an average Indian than net domestic product per capita, which includes the services sector that had grown much faster than the domestic economy as a whole. Nirmal Kumar Chandra, "Long-Term Stagnation in the Indian Economy, 1900–75," 157–252.
67. Alavi, "State and Class . . .," 302.
68. Ibid., 299–300.
69. Surajit Mazumdar, "Industry and Services in Growth and Structural Change in India: Some Unexplored Features," Institute for Studies in Industrial Development Working Paper No.: 2010/02 (January 2010).
70. I have estimated the sizes of the three different components of India's reserve army of labor with data drawn from the National Sample Survey Office's *Employment and Unemployment Situation in India, NSS 68th Round (July 2011–June 2012)*, Ministry of Statistics and Programme Implementation, Government of India (January 2014).
71. An explanation of why I take roughly 70 percent of the number of self-employed in 2011–12 to be petty commodity producers/service providers is given in my piece, "India's Labor-Market 'Pivot': Rough Estimates, Origins, and Implications" which can be found on sanhati-india.org/.
72. The two estimates of the reserve army of labor relative to the fully active army of labor, 2.1 in 1973 and 1.3 in 2011–12 are not comparable because, I think, my estimate of the stagnant "reserve" in 2011–12 doesn't fully capture the extent of intermittent unemployment among the casual wage laborers.
73. Oxford Poverty and Human Development Initiative, "Country Briefing: India— Multidimensional Poverty Index at a Glance" (July 2010), at www.ophi.org.uk.
74. Baran, *The Political Economy* . . . 144.
75. Alavi, "India: Transition to . . ." 64–65.
76. Charles Bettelheim's estimates of the average annual income per person of the families of the *mazdoors* and *kisans* in 1950–51 were 39 percent and 49 percent respectively of the national income per capita, itself very low, in that year. See Bettelheim, *India Independent* (Delhi: Khosla & Co, 1977), 25–26.
77. S. P. Shukla, "Globalisation: Agrarian Crisis in India," in K. B. Saxena and G. Haragopal (eds.), *Marginalization, Development and Resistance: Essays in Tribute to S. R. Sankaran, Vol. 1: The Crisis of Development* (Delhi: Aakar Books, 2014), 175–189.
78. Nirmal K. Chandra, "Industrialisation and the Question of Technology," Paper presented at a Symposium on the Third World and the International Economic Crisis, organized by the Association of Third World Economists at Algiers (October 1979), Table 1.

79. Nirmal K. Chandra, "The Concept of Development in the Context of the New International Economic Order," Paper presented to the ICSSR (Indian Council of Social Science Research) Seminar on the New International Economic Order, New Delhi (December 16–20, 1982).

80. Paul M. Sweezy, "Corporations, the State, and Imperialism," *Monthly Review*, 30:6 (November 1978), 2.

81. Indeed, the historian D. D. Kosambi seemed to have found that this was part of Magadhan statecraft—the Kautilian state, around 300 BC, fostered the ruling classes more than the other way around. D. D. Kosambi, *The Culture and Civilization of Ancient India in Historical Outline* (1964), chapter 6, "State and Religion in Greater Magadha, Section 6.2, "Magadhan Statecraft."

82. Rosa Luxemburg, *The Accumulation of Capital*, translated from the German by Agnes Schwarzschild (London: Routledge and Kegan Paul, 1951), 446.

83. Ibid., 365, 376, and 452.

4. Naxalite! "Spring Thunder," Phase II

1. Mao Zedong, "Be Concerned About the Well-being of the Masses, Pay Attention to Methods of Work" (January 27, 1934). Accessed at www.marxists.org/reference/archive/mao/selected-works/volume-1/mswv1_10.htm .

2. Varavara Rao, *Captive Imagination: Letters from Prison* (New Delhi: Penguin Books India, 2010), 102.

3. Norman Bethune, a surgeon, was a member of the Canadian Communist Party. He came to China in 1938—after serving the anti-fascist Spanish people in the civil war in Spain—to provide medical care to the Chinese people in the course of their war of resistance against Japan. Tragically, while operating on wounded soldiers he contracted blood poisoning and died on November 12, 1939. See the Notes in Mao's December 21, 1939, tribute, "In Memory of Norman Bethune," accessed at www.marxists.org/reference/archive/mao/selected-works/volume-2/mswv2_25.htm.

4. I draw on a telephonic conversation with the revolutionary Telugu poet Varavara Rao on June 27, 2011.

5. P. A. Sebastian, "Law: Suppression of Disturbances Act," *Economic & Political Weekly*, 15:33 (August 16, 1980), 1389–1390.

6. The other rivulet of the movement in Andhra Pradesh (AP) stemmed from the AP Coordination Committee of Communist Revolutionaries led mainly by Tarimela Nagi Reddy ("TN" as he was called, 1917–76, author of the acclaimed revolutionary tract, *India Mortgaged*) and Chandra Pulla Reddy (CP, 1917–84), who didn't join the CPI(ML) when it was formed in 1969. The two subsequently went their own way, with TN's followers (then led by D. V. Rao) in the Unity Centre of Communist Revolutionaries of India (ML) [UCCRI(ML)] and CP's supporters in CPI(ML)(Vimochana). Later, CP's followers and other revolutionaries came together to form CPI(ML)(Janashakti), which, also evolved to some extent into a force to reckon with in Andhra Pradesh. I will however focus on the evolution and growth of CPI(ML)(PW) because the "Naxalism" of the CPI(Maoist)—which the Indian state considers, in the words of Prime Minister Manmohan Singh in April 2006, as the "single biggest internal security challenge ever faced by our country"—basically stems from the CPI(ML)(PW).

7. Extension into the forests of Dandakaranya was crucial, for these forests were to constitute "the rear" for the guerrillas of North Telangana upon the formation of a guerrilla zone there.

8.   Arundhati Roy, "Walking with the Comrades," in her book, *Broken Republic: Three Essays* (New Delhi: Hamish Hamilton, 2010), 102–103. The essay first appeared in *Outlook* (March 29, 2010).

9.   However, I need to add a caveat here. The social anthropologist Verrier Elwin was attracted by the way the Gonds expressed their sexuality, openly, honestly and uninhibitedly, and seemed to be peeved by followers of M. K. Gandhi who were uptight and narrow-minded in these matters, even repressing their desires in a hypocritical manner. Ramachandra Guha, *Savaging the Civilized: Verrier Elwin, His Tribals, and India* (Chicago: University of Chicago Press, 1999), 89–90 and 95, in David Hardiman, *Gandhi: In His Own Times and Ours* (Delhi: Permanent Black, 2003), 148.

10. CPI (Maoist), "Strategy and Tactics of the Indian Revolution," Central Committee, Communist Party of India (Maoist), unpublished (January 27, 2007), chapter 12.

11. Mallarika Sinha Roy, *Gender and Radical Politics in India: Magic Moments of Naxalbari* (Abingdon: Routledge, 2011), and Srila Roy, *Remembering Revolution: Gender, Violence and Subjectivity in India's Naxalbari Movement* (Delhi: Oxford University Press, 2012).

12. The quotes from the internal rectification paper are as cited in Amit Bhattacharyya's book *Storming the Gates of Heaven: The Maoist Movement in India—A Critical Study, 1972–2014* (Kolkata: Setu Prakashani, 2016), 310.

13. Shoma Sen, "Class Struggle and Patriarchy: Women in the Maoist Movement," *Economic & Political Weekly*, 52:21 (May 27, 2017), 60. Also see Anuradha Ghandy, "The Revolutionary Women's Movement in India," in *Scripting the Change: Selected Writings of Anuradha Ghandy*, edited by Anand Teltumbde and Shoma Sen (Delhi: Daanish Books, 2011), 211–226.

14. In the following brief account of the mass-struggle phase of the Naxalite movement in north Telangana I draw upon K. Srinivasalu, "CPI(ML) and the Question of Caste: Dynamics of Social Mobilisation in Anti-feudal Struggles in Telangana," in Pradip Basu (ed.), *Discourses on Naxalite Movement, 1967–2009: Insights into Radical Left Politics* (Kolkata: Setu Prakashani, 2010), 222–237.

15. The extraordinarily committed civil liberties' activist K. Balagopal lamented the tragic loss of lives of "organic leaders" from among the most oppressed and doubted if, in the face of the repression, the Maoists will be able to retain the support of the next generation of the most oppressed. K. Balagopal, "Maoist Movement in Andhra Pradesh," *Economic & Political Weekly*, 41:29 (July 22, 2006), 3183–87.

16. I must remind the reader that in the post-independence period, the rural gentry, both the old and the new, besides being able to summon the state's repressive apparatus at the district and block levels, now unduly gained from access to a significant part of the state's expenditure allocated in the name of "development." This included funds for the various development programs, agricultural extension services, agricultural cooperatives, cheap credit from the rural banks, the various contracts (for example, road building, collection of forest produce, etc.) awarded. Later, they even gained political legitimacy through the panchayati raj institutions. See K. Srinivasulu, "CPI(ML) and the Question of Caste . . .," 228–29.

17. Translated from Telugu by K. Balagopal in K. Balagopal, "Physiognomy of Some Proscribed Poems," *Economic & Political Weekly*, 22:13 (March 28, 1987), 537–538.

18. K. Balagopal, "Chintapalli Again: One Eventful Day in a Lawless Life," *Economic & Political Weekly*, 23:5 (January 30, 1988), 182.

19. Ibid., 183.

20. Interview with K. S. in *Udayam* (March 24, 1988), a Telugu daily, as quoted in

G. Haragopal, "Abduction as a Method of Resistance: Negotiating Peace between Maoists and the Indian State," in K. B. Saxena and G. Haragopal (eds.), *Marginalisation, Development and Resistance: Essays in Tribute to S. R. Sankaran, Vol. 1: The Crisis of Development* (Delhi: Aakar Books, 2014), 286.

21. K. Balagopal, "Andhra Pradesh: The End of Spring?" *Economic & Political Weekly*, 25:34 (August 25, 1990), 1885.

22. People's Union for Democratic Rights, *Koel Ke Kinare: Agrarian Conflict in Palamu Plains* (Delhi: People's Union for Democratic Rights, April 1990).

23. Tilak D. Gupta, "Recent Developments in the Naxalite Movement," *Monthly Review*, 45:4 (September 1993), 18–19.

24. Bernard D'Mello, "Arwal Massacre: Report of People's Tribunal," *Economic & Political Weekly*, 22:35 (August 29, 1987), 1486–87. The double quotes indicate quotations from the report of the tribunal in the article cited.

25. Bela Bhatia, "The Naxalite Movement in Bihar," *Economic & Political Weekly*, 40:15 (April 9, 2005), 1536-1549.

26. Anand Chakravarti, *Social Power and Everyday Class Relations: Agrarian Transformation in North Bihar* (New Delhi: Sage Publications, 2001), 23.

27. Tilak D. Gupta, "Caste Complications in Agrarian Conflict," *Economic & Political Weekly*, 27:18 (May 2, 1992), 929.

28. George J. Kunnath, *Rebels from the Mud Houses: Dalits and the Making of the Maoist Revolution in Bihar* (New Delhi: Social Science Press, 2012), 138–141.

29. Dipankar Bhattacharya, "Bathani Tola II—Miscarriage of Justice," *Economic & Political Weekly*, 47:22 (June 2, 2012), web exclusive, accessed at www.epw.in/journal/2012/22/web-exclusives/bathani-tola-ii-miscarriage-justice.html.

30. People's Union for Democratic Rights, "Justice Delayed, and Denied Yet Again" (January 28, 2015), accessed at www.pudr.org/?q=content/justice-delayed-and-denied-yet-again-pudr-urges-supreme-court-suo-moto-intervene-shankarbigh.

31. Cobrapost, "Operation Black Rain: Revisiting the Killings of Dalits in Bihar and Confessions of Their Killers" (August 16, 2015), accessed at www.cobrapost.com/blog/operation-black-rain-revisiting-the-killings-of-dalits-of-bihar-and-confessions-of-their-killers/895.

32. (i) K. B., "The Karamchedu Killings: The Essence of the NTR Phenomenon," *Economic & Political Weekly*, 20:31, (August 3, 1985), 1298–1300; (ii) K. Balagopal, "Post-Chundur and Other Chundurs," *Economic & Political Weekly*, 26:42 (October 19, 1991), 2399–2405.

33. The CPI(ML)(Party Unity) and the CPI(ML)(PW) maintained close relations.

34. N. Venugopal, *Understanding Maoists: Notes of a Participant Observer from Andhra Pradesh* (Kolkata: Setu Prakashani, 2013), 96 and 167.

35. Haragopal, "Abduction as a Method of Resistance . . .," 301.

36. Venugopal, *Understanding Maoists . . .*, 171, 172.

37. Ibid., 164.

38. K. Balagopal, "Naxalite Terrorists and Benign Policemen," *Economic & Political Weekly*, 32:36 (September 6, 1997), 2254.

39. CPI (Maoist), "Strategy and Tactics of the Indian Revolution," chapter 11, in a section entitled "Mass Organization and Mass Movement," Central Committee, Communist Party of India (Maoist), unpublished (January 27, 2007). Although this document relates to a more recent period, and to the CPI (Maoist), it applies equally to the CPI(ML)(PW), one of the CPI (Maoist)'s predecessors.

40. CPI (Maoist), "Party Constitution," Chapter 12, Article 59 (Central Committee, Communist Party of India (Maoist), May 2007, unpublished). Although this con-

stitution relates to a more recent period, and to the CPI (Maoist), it applies equally to the CPI(ML)(PW), one of the CPI (Maoist)'s predecessors.

41. Mao Zedong, "Speech at the Assembly of Representatives of the Shensi-Kansu-Ningsia Border Region" (November 21, 1941), *Selected Works*, Vol. III (Peking: Foreign Languages Press, 1965), 33–34.

42. Mao Zedong, "Some Questions Concerning Methods of Leadership" (1943), *Selected Works*, Volume III (Peking: Foreign Languages Press, 1967), 119.

43. K. Balagopal, "Naxalite Terrorists . . .," 2253, 2257, 2259.

44. See "30 years of Naxalbari—An Epic of Heroic Struggle and Sacrifice" in Part 8 in the section on "Growing Armed Resistance" at www.naxalresistance.wordpress.com/2007/09/17/30-years-of-naxalbari/.

45. Mao Zedong, "The Problems of Guerrilla Warfare" (1937) in Mao's *On Guerrilla Warfare*, chapter 6, in *Selected Works of Mao Tse-tung*, Vol. 9, accessed at www.marxists.org/reference/archive/mao/works/1937/guerrilla-warfare/ch06.htm.

46. K. Balagopal, "People's War and the Government: Did the Police Have the Last Laugh?" *Economic & Political Weekly*, 38:6 (February 8, 2003), 514.

47. See Mao Zedong's "Why Is It that Red Political Power Can Exist in China" (October 5, 1928), and "The Struggle in the Chingkang Mountains" (November 25, 1928), *Selected Works*, Vol. I. I particularly draw the attention of the reader to the section "The Question of the Location of Our Independent Regime" in the second piece.

5. India's "1989"—"Financial Aristocracy" and Government
À Bon Marché

1.   Paul M. Sweezy, "What's New in the New World Order?" *Monthly Review*, 43:2 (June 1991), 4 and 2.

2.   We draw on a blunt, straightforward article by Nancy Holmstrom and Richard Smith, "The Necessity of Gangster Capitalism: Primitive Accumulation in Russia and China," *Monthly Review*, 51:9 (February 2000), 1–15.

3.   For the transition to capitalism in China, I draw on two edits, "Where Is China Going?" and "China at 60," drafted by me for the *Economic & Political Weekly*, and which appeared in its issues, 43:52 (December 27, 2008) and 44:43 (October 24, 2009), respectively.

4.   Nevertheless, China's political leadership does not allow capital to control the state, even as it uses the market to pursue what it deems to be the "public interest." Land is publicly owned and the state maintains control over it and over most financial institutions.

5.   Of course, elections can serve to spread progressive ideas as the Bernie Sanders campaign has demonstrated.

6.   WID.world Working Paper Series, No 2017/11 (September 7, 2017).

7.   Amit Bhaduri, "On Democracy, Corporations and Inequality," *Economic & Political Weekly*, 51:13 (March 26, 2016), 31–34.

8.   D. R. Gadgil, "The Economic Prospect for India," *Pacific Affairs*, 22:2 (June 1949), 120–122.

9.   Arun Kumar, *The Black Economy of India* (New Delhi, Penguin Books: 1999).

10. Arun Kumar, *Understanding the Black Economy and Black Money in India* (New Delhi: Aleph, 2017), 22.

11. *Black Money: White Paper* (New Delhi: Government of India, Ministry of Finance, Department of Revenue, Central Board of Direct Taxes, May 2012), Section 2.4.9.

12. Despite the tall talk of "bringing all the black money stashed abroad back home,"

Participatory Notes (PNs) that have Indian stocks as their underlying assets are still officially considered legitimate overseas derivative instruments for foreign portfolio investment in India.

13. "Captive of Hot Money," editorial, *Economic & Political Weekly*, 47:15 (April 14, 2012), 8.

14. Bertell Ollman, "Marxism," *Monthly Review*, 30:7 (December 1978), 36–37.

15. *Black Money: White. . .*, Section 2.1.1, 2.

16. Comptroller and Auditor-General of India, "Performance Audit—Report No. 19 of 2010–11." One does not, however, need to endorse the CAG's astronomical figure of the presumptive loss to the public exchequer.

17. *Abandoned: Development and Displacement* (Delhi: Perspectives, Revised, Second Edition, January 2008) and *Communities, Commons and Corporations* (Delhi: Perspectives, January 2012).

18. Karl Marx, *Class Struggles in France, 1848–1850*, "Part I: The Defeat of June, 1848," at www.marxists.org/archive/marx/works/1850/class-struggles-france/ch01.htm.

19. Comptroller and Auditor-General of India, "Report No. 5 of 2012-13—Performance Audit of Implementation of Public Private Partnership: Indira Gandhi International Airport."

20. Prabhat Patnaik, "An Aspect of Neo-Liberalism," *Macroscan* (19 December 2006), at www.macroscan.net.

21. Hamish McDonald, *The Polyester Prince: The Rise of Dhirubhai Ambani* (London: Allen & Unwin, 1998).

22. See chapter 6, "Findings in Respect of Panna-Mukta and Mid & South Tapti Fields" in the CAG's "Report No. 19 of 2011–12 for the period ended March 2011, Performance Audit of Hydrocarbon Production Sharing Contracts (Ministry of Petroleum and Natural Gas)," Government of India, New Delhi, 2012 at www.cag. gov.in/sites/default/files/audit_report_files/Union_Performance_Civil_Hydrocarbon_Production_Sharing_Contracts_Ministry_of_Petroleum_19_2011_chapter_6.pdf.

23. See "Reliance KG-D6 Reserves Est. Off 80 percent: Niko" at www.indianexpress. com/story-print/964902/. This figure is according to Niko Resources, RIL's Canadian partner in the venture.

24. See chapter 4, "Findings Relating to KG-DWN-98/3 Block," CAG's 2012 "Report No. 19 of 2011–12 . . .."

25. This was put on hold by the Election Commission, and the Narendra Modi-led government later found it to be too much of a bonanza to concede to RIL.

26. This brief is based on the complaint filed by former Cabinet Secretary T. S. R. Subramaniam, former Navy chief Admiral R. H. Tahiliani, former Secretary, Ministry of Power, E. A. S. Sarma, and Supreme Court lawyer Kamini Jaiswal to the Government of Delhi in February 2014, on the basis of which the Anti-Corruption Branch was directed by the then Chief Minister Arvind Kejriwal to register an FIR against the chairperson of RIL, Mukesh Ambani, union petroleum minister M. Veerappa Moily, former petroleum minister Murli Deora and former director general of hydrocarbons V. K. Sibal under various sections of the Prevention of Corruption Act. Also see E. A. S. Sarma's "Natural Gas Price Hike: Subsidising Producers' Profits?" *Economic & Political Weekly*, 48:28 (July 13, 2013), 12–15.

27. In this account of the accumulation process following the privatization of the telecom service function, we have drawn on the following three articles by C. P. Chandrasekhar: (i) "The Telecom Mess," *Macroscan* (January 25, 2000), at www.macroscan.org/fet/jan00/fet250100Telecom_Mess_1.htm; (ii) "The New Monopolists,"

Frontline (February 16, 2001), 102–103; and (iii) "Telecom Licensing: The End to the Mess?," *Macroscan* (November 12, 2003).

28.   Jason Miklian, "The Purification Hunt: The Salwa Judum Counterinsurgency in Chhattisgarh, India," *Dialectical Anthropology*, 33 (2009), 442.

29.   M. Bharati and R. S. Rao, "Linking Development and Displacement," *Economic & Political Weekly*, 34:22 (May 29, 1999), 1374–75.

30.   Aseem Shrivastava and Ashish Kothari, *Churning the Earth: The Making of Global India* (New Delhi: Penguin-Viking, 2012), chapter 7, "Crony Capitalism, Land Wars and Internal Colonialism," 193–230.

31.   POSCO pulled out of this steel project in March 2017.

32.   In the wake of the 2008 global financial crisis and the withdrawal of some of the fiscal incentives by the union government, the promoters no longer found the project viable.

33.   I draw on the draft of an editorial I penned for the *Economic & Political Weekly*, "Coal for a Song," that was published in its issue of 47:28 (July 14, 2012), 7–8.

34.   CAG, "Draft Performance Audit—Allocation of Coal Blocks and Augmentation of Coal Production by Coal India Ltd," unpublished (2012).

35.   Again, one does not need to endorse the CAG's estimate of the total presumptive "windfall gains" to private firms. Yet the real question as to why the government didn't take a timely decision on competitive bidding remains. All that was required to introduce competitive bidding was the framing of the required rules under the Coal Mines (Nationalisation) Act, 1973 read with the Mines and Minerals (Regulation and Development) Act, 1957, and the Mineral Concession Rules, 1960. This could have been done in 2006 itself but seems to have been deliberately delayed, which "rendered the existing process beneficial to a large number of private companies." See CAG, "Report No. 7 of 2012-13—Performance Audit of Allocation of Coal Blocks and Augmentation of Coal Production," chapter 4, "Allocation of Captive Coal Blocks," section 4.3, "Financial Gains to Private Parties."

36.   CAG, "Draft Performance Audit—Allocation of Coal Blocks. . .," Annexure 1B: Benefit Extended to Private Companies Year-wise as per Year of Allocation, 94–101.

37.   Part of the information on Sterlite Industries Ltd. is from Crocodyl Collaborative Research on Corporations. Besides this, there's a brilliant book by Felix Padel and Samarendra Das entitled *Out of This Earth: East India Adivasis and the Aluminium Cartel* (Hyderabad, Orient BlackSwan: 2010) that, among other things, is a deeply upsetting account of the impact of the mining and beneficiation of bauxite on the indigenous peoples of Odisha and their habitat.

38.   In an article "Meet the New Owners: The Billionaire Mittals" in makingsteel.com in 2005, Mark Reutter wrote:

> In 2001, Mittal made a £125,000 (about $235,000) contribution to the British Labour Party. A month later, Labour Party chief and UK Prime Minister Tony Blair interceded on Mittal's behalf to help him secure the purchase of Romania's state-owned steel works. Blair's personal letter to the Romanian Prime Minister argued that Mittal's bid could help Romania gain EU membership.
>   It has since come to light that the Blair government supported international loans worth hundreds of millions of dollars to assist Mittal's growing chain of steel mills.

39.   On plans for coal mining in and on the outskirts of Saranda forest in Paschim Singhbhum district, see Sayatan Bera's "Between Maoists and Mines," *Down to Earth* (April 30, 2012), at www.downtoearth.org.in/coverage/between-maoists-and-mines-37964.

40.   I am reminded of what the Australian journalist Hamish MacDonald wrote in his *The Polyester Prince: The Rise of Dhirubhai Ambani*, about Indian journalists reaping a pile with the issues of Reliance shares and debentures that they got at par or the gift vouchers they were given to pick up textile products at an "Only Vimal" retail outlet (p. 75). Truly, we have here journalists' à bon marché.

41.   "The Anna Hazare Scam" by *Analytical Monthly Review*, April 2011 at mronline. org/2011/04/15/the-anna-hazare-scam/.

42.   "Notes from the Editors," *Monthly Review*, 50:11 (April 1999).

43.   "The Anna Phenomenon," editorial, *Economic & Political Weekly*, 46:17 (April 23, 2011), 7–8.

44.   Arundhati Roy, "Capitalism: A Ghost Story," Anuradha Ghandy Memorial Lecture (January 20, 2012), St. Xavier's College, Mumbai; later published in *Outlook* (March 26, 2012), 18.

45.   Paul M. Sweezy, "The Triumph of Financial Capital," *Monthly Review*, 46:2 (June 1994), 1–11.

46.   It is not the market economy per se that transforms a non-capitalist region but significant entry of big business that brings this about, for big business comes with all the necessary political support to accomplish its mission.

47.   Rosa Luxemburg, *The Accumulation of Capital*, translated from the German by Agnes Schwarzschild (London: Routledge and Kegan Paul, 1951), 365, 376, and 452.

48.   In the process of advancing their power, their influence, and their mutual interests *beyond the country's borders*, the Indian state and big business, Indian and multinational, are dependent upon U.S. imperialism. I use the term "sub-imperialism" to designate this process. It is evident that I am also including the political expression of the "accumulation by dispossession" in the "non-capitalist areas" within the country as an integral part of this sub-imperialism.

49.   Rosa Luxemburg defined imperialism as "the political expression of the accumulation of capital in its competitive struggle for what remains still open for the non-capitalist environment" within a capitalist country's own borders and beyond, through militarism and war. *The Accumulation of Capital*, 446.

6. "The Near and the Far"—India's Rotten Liberal-Political Democracy

1.   K. Balagopal, "Obituary: Cherabanda Raju," *Economic & Political Weekly*, 17:30 (July 24, 1982), 1188–1189.

2.   Siddharth Varadarajan, "Time to Curb Unfettered Electoral Expenditure by Political Parties That Impacts Poll Outcomes," *Economic Times* (April 30, 2014), at http:// articles.economictimes.indiatimes.com/2014-04-30/news/49523708_1_election-expenditure-election-commission-election-rules.

3.   Even in states where the parliamentary left had addressed land reforms, albeit in a limited way, West Bengal and Kerala, the panchayati raj institutions (PRIs) didn't undermine the dominance of the rural rich, although the latter had to reach an accommodation with the ruling party, which called the shots. Nevertheless, in West Bengal, the Communist Party of India (Marxist) [CPM]-led Left Front government introduced the PRI system in 1978, much before the 73rd Constitutional Amendment of 1993, while the CPM-led Left Democratic Front government in Kerala activated it in 1991, again, before the constitutional amendment to that effect. But certainly, the introduction of the PRI system represented an expansion of liberal-political democracy in India.   Ratan Khasnabis, "Rules of Governance in Developing Rural India," in Ranabir Samaddar and Suhit K. Sen (eds.), *Political*

Transition and Development Imperatives in India (New Delhi: Routledge, 2012), 230–270.

4. Fali S. Nariman, "JMM Bribery Case," *India Today*, December 26, 2005, at http://indiatoday.intoday.in/story/jharkhand-mukti-morcha-bribery-scandal-in-1993-corruption-got-institutionalised-in-india/1/192408.html.

5. Prabhat Patnaik, "The First Communist Ministry," at www.firstministry.kerala.gov.in/ptnaik_art.htm. The imposition of Article 356 of the Constitution of India to dismiss a state government was quite common from the latter half of the 1960s until the Supreme Court's 1994 ruling in *Bommai vs. Union of India*, the most common pretext being the breakdown of civil order according to the state's governor, a central government appointee. The SC judgment in the Bommai case made it more difficult for central governments to arbitrarily impose central rule.

6. Michael Brecher, *Nehru: A Political Biography* (New York & London: Oxford University Press, 1959), 421, as quoted in Suniti Kumar Ghosh, *The Indian Constitution and Its Review* (Mumbai: Rajani X Desai for Research Unit for Political Economy, 2004), 8.

7. Quoted in Jonah Raskin's *The Mythology of Imperialism* (Delhi: Aakar Books, 2012), 252.

8. Surely such a paean for the Indian Constitution, this from an intellectual of the left, would have been music to the ears of the Indian ruling classes and their ideologists. See V. R. Krishna Iyer's "The Basic Structure of the Constitution and 'We, the People of India'," in *Towards Legal Literacy*, edited by Kamala Sankaran and Ujjwal Kumar Singh (New Delhi: Oxford University Press), 13.

9. Ibid., 11.

10. Meena Kandasamy, "No One Killed the Dalits," Text of the Seventh Anuradha Ghandy Memorial Lecture (October 30, 2015).

11. Suniti Kumar Ghosh, *The Indian Constitution . . .*, 10–11.

12. Coordination of Democratic Rights Organizations, *The Terror of Law: UAPA and the Myth of National Security* (CDRO, April 2012), 12.

13. Barrington Moore, Jr., *Social Origins of Dictatorship and Democracy* (Harmondsworth: Penguin Books, 1967), 414.

14. Ibid., 429.

15. Paul M. Sweezy, "Capitalism and Democracy," *Monthly Review*, 32:2 (June 1980), 27–32.

16. The economic "functions of the state are determined by the operation of the economy and not the other way around." The functioning of the capitalist economy is governed by "the mutual interaction of competing capitals on the one hand, and of capitalists and wage laborers on the other" (ibid., 27). I must, however, add that in an underdeveloped capitalist system, the economic sub-system is not as autonomous from the political superstructure as it is in a developed capitalist system.

17. Even the Supreme Court has forsaken the working class. See Ramapriya Gopalakrishnan, "Labour Jurisprudence of the Supreme Court: Recent Trends," in K. V. Ramaswamy (ed.), *Labour, Employment and Economic Growth* (Delhi: Cambridge University Press, 2015), 292–318.

18. Sitaram Yechury, Politburo member of the CPI(M) and Rajya Sabha member, in his column "LeftHand Drive" in *The Hindustan Times* (November 19, 2013).

19. J. C. B. Annavajhula and Surendra Pratap, "Worker Voices in an Auto Production Chain: Notes from the Pits of the Low Road," published in two parts in *Economic & Political Weekly*, 47:33 and 34 (August 18 and 25, 2012), 59 in part one, 49 in part two, and 59 in part one.

20. Our account of the Indian Slavery Act of 1843, bonded labor in independent India, and of protective laws and public policies concerning SCs and STs draws a lot from S. R. Sankaran's "Administration and the Poor," *The Administrator*, Vol. XLII (January–March 1997), 1–24.

21. "At War With Oneself: Constructing Naxalism as India's Biggest Security Threat," in Michael Kugelman (ed.), *India's Contemporary Security Challenges* (Washington DC: Woodrow Wilson International Centre for Scholars, Asian Program, 2011), 50.

22. The Constitution of India originally set aside 15 percent and 7.5 percent of government jobs and seats in public and government-aided higher educational institutions for Scheduled Castes and Scheduled Tribes respectively. In 1990 this was extended to include the OBCs, such that, together, 49.5 percent of all government jobs and seats in such higher educational institutions were reserved for SCs, STs, and OBCs. The OBC reservations were based on the recommendations of the Mandal Commission, which was set up in 1979 to identify the socially and educationally backward castes that would be eligible for such social-welfare benefits.

23. Ram Manohar Lohia, *The Caste System* (Hyderabad: Navahind, 1964), as quoted by Ajit Roy, "Caste and Class: An Interlinked View," *Economic & Political Weekly*, 14:7–8, Caste and Class in India, Annual Number (February 1979), 279–312.

24. Ramkrishna Mukherjee, "Caste in Itself, Class and Caste, or Caste in Class," *Economic & Political Weekly*, 34:27 (July 3, 1999), 1761.

25. Sumanta Banerjee, "Salvaging an Endangered Institution," *Economic & Political Weekly*, 41:36 (September 9, 2006), 3837–3841.

26. In this locks bit, I am merely paraphrasing what I heard Arundhati Roy, the novelist and writer of political prose, say at a public meeting in Delhi in December 2009.

27. Indivar Kamtekar, "The Fables of Nationalism," *India International Centre Quarterly* (Monsoon, 1999), 44–54.

28. The association of organized politics with the conduct of religious-communal riots/pogroms, set in motion in the 1920s, was institutionalized in the 1940s. The Congress, with its overwhelmingly Hindu leadership and cadre, in the Punjab Presidency, the United Provinces, and the Bengal Presidency, had failed to represent the interests of the increasingly vocal Muslim sections of middle-class employees and professionals and the peasantry, and they gravitated towards the Muslim League in the movement for Pakistan. The Muslim zamindars in the Punjab, until 1945 with the Unionist Party, joined the Muslim League in order to safeguard their landed class interests, while the Muslim peasantry of the Bengal was left with little choice but to opt for Pakistan when, toward the end of 1946, the Bengal Congress's bhadralok, absentee-zamindar leadership, having constructed the image of an imminent "Muslim tyranny," was bent upon the second partition of Bengal. For the latter, as also for Nehru and Vallabhbhai Patel, a united Bengal would have been a "Greater Pakistan." See Hamza Alavi's "Misreading Partition Road Signs" and "Social Forces and Ideology in the Making of Pakistan," *Economic & Political Weekly*, 37:44–45 and 51 (November 2 and December 21, 2002), 4515–23 and 5119–24 respectively, and Joya Chatterji's *Bengal Divided: Hindu Communalism and Partition, 1932–1947* (Cambridge: Cambridge University Press, 1994).

29. The latter, "based on a syncretic definition of Indian culture and the social-democratic aspirations of economically and socially oppressed Indians," as Dilip Simeon puts it. See his "Communalism in Modern India: A Theoretical Examination," *Mainstream* (December 13, 1986), South Asia Citizens Web at www.sacw.net/article2760.html.

30. Kamtekar, "The Fables . . .," 54.

31. "Toba Tek Singh" by Saadat Hasan Manto, translated from the Urdu by Francis W. Pritchett, at www.columbia.edu/itc/mealac/pritchett/00urdu/tobateksingh/translation.html.

32. Simeon, "Communalism in Modern India . . .."

33. Perry Anderson, "Gandhi Centre Stage," "Why Partition?" and "After Nehru," *London Review of Books* (July 5, July 19, and August 2, 2012) at www.lrb.co.uk.

34. Anuradha M. Chenoy and Kamal A. Mitra Chenoy, *Maoist and Other Armed Conflicts* (New Delhi: Penguin, 2010).

35. (i) *Buried Evidence*, International People's Tribunal on Human Rights and Justice in Indian Administered Kashmir (IPTK) (December 2009). (ii) *Alleged Perpetrators: Stories of Impunity in J&K*, IPKT and Association of Persons of Disappeared Persons (December 2012).

36. P. A. Sebastian, "Kashmir Behind the Propaganda Curtain," *Economic & Political Weekly*, 31:6 (February 10, 1996), 319–321. This is a review of a report, *Blood in the Valley—Kashmir Behind the Propaganda Curtain: A Report to the People of India*, written and published by a number of civil liberties and democratic rights organizations in 1995.

37. "Very difficult to move forward on amending AFSPA: PC," *Hindustan Times* (February 7, 2013), at www.hindustantimes.com/delhi-news/very-difficult-to-move-forward-on-amending-afspa-pc/story-Okg0ELAvCo5rWz3hkYvqxH.html.

7. Maoist! "Spring Thunder," Phase III

1. Paul M. Sweezy, "What Is Marxism?" *Monthly Review*, 36:10 (March 1985), 1–6.

2. A Scheduled Area comes under the purview of the Fifth Schedule of the Indian Constitution, which protects Adivasis residing in these areas. According to the Ministry of Tribal Affairs, government of India, the criteria followed for declaring an area as a Scheduled Area are "preponderance of tribal population; compactness and reasonable size of the area; underdeveloped nature of the area; and marked disparity in economic standard of the people." http://tribal.nic.in/Content/DefinitionofScheduledAreasProfiles.aspx

3. K. Balagopal, "Land Unrest in Andhra Pradesh—II: Impact of Grants to Industries" and "III: Illegal Acquisition in Andhra Pradesh," *Economic & Political Weekly*, 42:39 and 40 (September 29 and October 6, 2007), 3906–3911 and 4029–4034.

4. K. Balagopal, "Land Unrest in Andhra Pradesh—II: Impact of Grants to Industries," 3906, 3907.

5. "Attempts to Subvert 'Samatha' Judgment," *PUCL Bulletin* (2001), at www.pucl.org/reports/National/2001/samatha.htm.

6. The project apparently got stalled later on, in 2010, when the central government couldn't clear the mining project on legal grounds.

7. It is not the market economy per se that transforms a non-capitalist region but significant entry of big business that brings this about, for big business comes with all the necessary political support to accomplish the mission.

8. On these peace talks, see K. Balagopal, "Naxalites in Andhra Pradesh: Have We Heard the Last of the Peace Talks?" *Economic & Political Weekly*, 40:13 (March 26, 2005), 1323–1329.

9. See "Interview with Comrade Ganapathy," *The Worker*, No. 11 (July 2007).

10. In the process of advancing their power, their influence, and their mutual interests *beyond the country's borders*, the Indian state and big business, Indian and multina-

tional, are dependent upon U.S. imperialism. I use of the term "sub-imperialism" to designate this process. It is evident that I am also including the political expression of "accumulation by dispossession" in the "non-capitalist areas" within the country as an integral part of this sub-imperialism.

11. See Sudha Bharadwaj, "Gravest Displacement, Bravest Resistance: The Struggle of the Adivasis of Bastar, Chhattisgarh against Imperialist Corporate Land-Grab" (June 1, 2009), at http://sanhati.com/excerpted/1545/.

12. See Nandini Sundar, *Subalterns and Sovereigns: An Anthropological History of Bastar, 1854–1996* (New Delhi: Oxford University Press, 1997).

13. See the section "Involvement of Local Groups against the Naxalites" in *Annual Report, 2003–04, Union Ministry of Home Affairs* (New Delhi: Government of India, 2004), 44.

14. See *Annual Report, 2004–05, Union Ministry of Home Affairs* (New Delhi: Government of India, 2005), 47–48.

15. Jason Miklian, "The Purification Hunt: The Salwa Judum Counterinsurgency in Chhattisgarh, India," *Dialectical Anthropology*, 33 (2009), 442, 456. The reader wanting to get a feel for the mindsets of the officers manning the law-and-order apparatus at the district and state levels may see (i) Sudeep Chakravarti, *Red Sun: Travels in Naxalite Country* (New Delhi: Penguin, 2008), 27–94; (ii) Nandini Sundar, *The Burning Forest: India's War in Bastar* (New Delhi: Juggernaut Books, 2016), chapter 10. Sundar describes the majority of the regular police officers as "indifferent and careerist," who "try to convince themselves that the villagers support the Naxalites out of fear, and they need 'rescuing' by the police, though in their hearts they know otherwise. They find comfort in claiming that there is a vast conspiracy afoot by human rights activists to defame the nation, without caring that it is they who have destroyed the Constitution from within" (187). Some at the top of the police hierarchy, S. R. P. Kalluri, for instance, "like to see themselves as messiahs, saving the nation from the Naxalites, even if it means breaking several laws and every norm of the Constitution in the process" (207).

16. The extent of brutalization of the Salwa Judum, the Special Police Officers, and the central and state security forces in Chhattisgarh is evident from Human Rights Watch's report, *Being Neutral Is Our Biggest Crime: Government, Vigilante, and Naxalite Abuses in India's Chhattisgarh State* (New York: Human Rights Watch, July 2008). The Maoists and the victims responded with counter-violence, and this is also narrated and condemned. Of course, Human Rights Watch cannot be expected to look at the class war from the perspective of the oppressed and the Maoists who have organized the resistance. For this, see People's Union for Civil Liberties, *When the State Makes War on Its Own People: A Report on the Violation of People's Rights During the Salwa Judum Campaign in Dantewada* (Delhi: People's Union for Democratic Rights, 2006), a joint fact-finding report by several civil liberties and democratic rights organizations, including the People's Union for Democratic Rights, Delhi. Among other things, this report tells the reader about the sections of the society in Dantewada that support the Salwa Judum, the process of militarization that is tearing apart the whole social fabric, and the security forces acting like an occupation army. For a liberal-political democratic account, see the Independent Citizens' Initiative's report, *War in the Heart of India: An Enquiry into the Ground Situation in Dantewara District, Chhattisgarh* (No Place: Independent Citizen's Initiative, July 20, 2006) at http://sanhati.com/wp-content/uploads/2010/10/independentcitizensinitiative_dantewara_2006.pdf.

17. *Red Ant Dream* (2013), a documentary film directed by Sanjay Kak.

18.   Indeed, on July 5, 2011, the Supreme Court had declared the practice of the state of arming local tribal youth as Special Police Officers and of funding the recruitment of vigilante groups like Salwa Judum to fight the Maoists unconstitutional (Supreme Court of India, *Nandini Sundar & Others vs. State of Chhattisgarh* on July 5, 2010 at https://indiankanoon.org/doc/920448/), but the State of Chhattisgarh ignored the Supreme Court order.

19.   Satnam, *Jangalnama: Travels in a Maoist Guerrilla Zone* (New Delhi: Penguin, 2010).

20.   Gautam Navlakha, "Days and Nights in the Maoist Heartland," *Economic & Political Weekly*, 45:16 (April 17, 2010), 38–47 (quote on 41).

21.   Ibid., 38, 42–44.

22.   Ibid., 44–46. For a more elaborate coverage, see Gautam Navlakha's *Days and Nights in the Heartland of Rebellion* (New Delhi: Penguin, 2012).

23.   My account of the first year of the Lalgarh struggle draws mainly on excellent pieces by Partho Sarathi Ray, published by the website sanhati.com, especially "A Year of Lalgarh" (January 11, 2009).

24.   The Maoists investigated whether renegade factions had been behind the sabotage, but they found that this is not the case. See *Maoist Information Bulletin 20* (October–November, 2010).

25.   Partho Sarathi Ray, "Background of the Lalgarh Movement," *Sanhati.com* (November 13, 2008).

26.   *Letters from Lalgarh* by the People's Committee against Police Atrocities, edited and translated by Sanhati (Kolkata: Setu Prakashani in collaboration with www.sanhati.com, 2013).

27.   Ibid., 7, 140.

28.   Ibid., 106.

29.   "Condemn the Brutal Murder of Comrade Mallojula Koteswara Rao . . .," Press Release, Central Committee, CPI(Maoist) (November 25, 2011), www.bannedthought.net/India/CPI-Maoist-Docs/Statements-2011/111125-CC-KishenjiMartyrdom-Eng.doc

30.   Shiv Sahay Singh, "Kishenji's Body Handed Over to Niece," *The Hindu* (November 26, 2011), at www.thehindu.com/news/national/article2662217.ece?homepage=true

31.   Expert Group to the Planning Commission, *Development Challenges in Extremist Affected Areas: Report of an Expert Group to the Planning Commission* (New Delhi: Planning Commission, Government of India, 2008). The causes of discontent and the reasons for unrest and extremism, according to the Expert Group, are manifold—landlessness, the utter failure of land reform and the lack of payment of a minimum wage, the usurpation of common property resources by the powerful, the state's failure to fulfill the constitutional mandate of preventing the concentration of wealth in the hands of a few to the detriment of the many, the denial of justice and human dignity to the Dalits and Adivasis and their consequent alienation, the steady erosion of the rights of the latter and their command over forest resources, their political marginalization, mass displacement and the failure of resettlement and rehabilitation policy, and, indeed, the treatment of unrest arising out of all such factors as a mere law-and-order problem.

32.   Alpa Shah, "The Intimacy of Insurgency: Beyond Coercion, Greed or Grievance in Maoist India," *Economy and Society*, 42:3 (August 2013), 480–506.

33.   Bernard D'Mello, "What Is Maoism?" in a book introduced and edited by him, *What Is Maoism and Other Essays* (Kharagpur: Cornerstone Publications, 2010), 21–54. The essay can be accessed at http://monthlyreview.org/commentary/what-is-maoism/.

34. Shah, "The Intimacy of Insurgency. . .," 496.

35. Ibid., 496, 497.

36. Ibid., 499.

37. Juhi Tyagi, "Organizational Structure and Class: Examining Resilience in the Maoist Movement in India," Draft PhD Thesis in Sociology (New York: Stony Brook University, May 2016). I am grateful to Juhi Tyagi for sharing her draft thesis with me.

38. Robert Weil, *Is the Torch Passing? Resistance and Revolution in China and India* (Kolkata: Setu Prakashani, 2013), 223.

39. A "crisis in the affairs of the ruling order" occurs when the ruling classes are sharply divided over major policies and there are clear indications of bitter mass discontent among the oppressed.

8. "Rotten at the Heart"—the "Secular State"

1. "Text of PM's Address at the National Celebration of the Elevation to Sainthood of Kuriakose Elias Chavara and Mother Euphrasia" (New Delhi: Press Information Bureau, Government of India, February 17, 2015). http://pib.nic.in/newsite/PrintRelease.aspx?relid=115529.

2. P. K. Vijayan and Karen Gabriel, "Hindutva's Psychological Warfare: The Invidious Agendas of Ghar Wapsi," *Economic & Political Weekly*, 50:11 (March 14, 2015), 22–24.

3. "Memorandum on the Census of British India of 1871–72 Presented to Both Houses of Parliament by Command of Her Majesty" (George Edward Eyre and William Spottiswoode, Printers to Her Majesty's Stationery Office, 1875). http://arrow.latrobe.edu.au/store/3/4/5/5/2/public/page7f29.html?title=1871&action=next&record=1.

4. Mahatma Gandhi Foundation, *A Gandhi Anthology—Book 1* (The Official Mahatma Gandhi e-Archive & Reference Library, Mahatma Gandhi Foundation, India), 11–14, at www.mahatma.org.in/mahatma/books/showbook.jsp?id=15&link=bg&book=bg0013&lang=en&cat=books.

5. Moreover, a person intending to convert from Hinduism to Christianity or Islam has to endure a humiliating procedure to explain why he/she is converting, and it is up to the state to "determine" the "genuineness" of the conversion. But, when reconversion occurs, it is considered a homecoming (*ghar wapsi*), clearly indicating that the law is being applied in a discriminatory manner.

6. P. A. Sebastian, "Secularism and the Indian Judiciary," *Economic & Political Weekly*, 45:50 (December 11, 2010), 45.

7. Barbara D. Metcalf and Thomas R. Metcalf, *A Concise History of Modern India*, (New Delhi: Cambridge University Press, 2012), 150–53.

8. Meera Nanda, "Secularism without Secularization? Reflections on the Religious Right in America and India," in her *The Wrongs of the Religious Right: Reflections on Science, Secularism and Hindutva* (Gurgaon: Three Essays Collective, 2005), 44.

9. Following Professor Randhir Singh, I define communalism as oppression and discrimination of the Other based on religious identity. See his "Theorising Communalism: A Fragmentary Note in the Marxist Mode," *Economic & Political Weekly*, 23:30 (July 23, 1988), 1541–48. Communal-hate propaganda then relates to advocacy of oppression and/or discrimination of that Other. Communal-hate parties are authoritarian political organizations that conduct their politics on the premise that a shared religious faith makes for an aggressive assertion of identity based on religion and shared political interests.

10. Asghar Ali Engineer, "Communal Propaganda in Elections: A Landmark Judgment," *Economic & Political Weekly*, 24:24 (June 17, 1989), 1324.

11. Nanda, "Secularism without Secularization? . . .," 44–45.

12. Sebastian, "Secularism and the Indian Judiciary," 45.

13. Nanda, "Secularism without Secularization? . . .," 54–55.

14. Kannan Srinivasan, "A Subaltern Fascism?" in Jairus Banaji (ed.), *Fascism: Essays on Europe and India* (Gurgaon: Three Essays Collective, 2013), 99–134.

15. Mentor of K. B. Hedgewar (1889–1940), the founding Sarsanghachalak (supreme leader) of the Rashtriya Swayamsevak Sangh (RSS), and for many years the president of the Hindu Mahasabha until he handed over charge to V. D. Savarkar in 1937.

16. Marzia Casolari, "Hindutva's Foreign Tie-up in the 1930s: Archival Evidence," *Economic & Political Weekly*, 35:4 (January 22, 2000), 220 and 227.

17. Ibid., 223, 224.

18. Leena Gita Raghunath, "The Believer: Swami Aseemanand's Radical Service to the Sangh," *Caravan* (February 1, 2014), www.caravanmagazine.in/reportage/believer. After the Modi government assumed power at the center in May 2014, witnesses for the prosecution in the six Hindutvavadi terror cases being handled by the National Investigation Agency are turning "hostile," most likely because of fear of the repercussions of deposing against the Hindutvavadi terror accused when the NIA itself is now reporting to the BJP's Rajnath Singh as the Union Home Minister. See Rajesh Ahuja, "Asseemanand Acquittal Could Hit Other Saffron Terror Cases: In Limbo—Witnesses Turning Hostile and Slow Probes Have Plagued Most Cases Since the NDA Government Assumed Power in May 2014," *Hindustan Times* (March 10, 2017).

19. "The meaning very clearly was, don't get us favourable orders: Malegaon SPP Rohini Salian," Interviewed by Sunanda Mehta, *Indian Express* (June 25, 2015), http://indianexpress.com/article/india/india-others/the-meaning-very-clearly-was-dont-get-us-favourable-orders/. Sangik Chowdhury and Sunanda Mehta, "NIA 'asking' Salian to go soft: 'Am a criminal lawyer, not stupid to say this without proof'," *Indian Express* (July 10, 2015), http://indianexpress.com/article/india/india-others/nia-asking-salian-to-go-soft-i-am-a-criminal-lawyer-not-stupid-to-say-this-without-proof/.

20. An empirically rich account of the systematic bias and prejudice of the Intelligence and the police against Muslims can be found in Manisha Sethi's *Kafkaland: Prejudice, Law and Counterterrorism in India* (Gurgaon: Three Essays Collective, 2014).

21. Coordination of Democratic Rights Organizations, "Discharge of Sadhvi Pragya and Others in the Malegaon Blast Case—Saffronisation of Constitutional Agencies," Press Release (May 15, 2016).

22. There is the international context too, after the end of the Cold War, when US imperialism adopted the ideological doctrine of the "clash of civilizations," and not many years thereafter, the Indian state joined hands with it in the post-9/11 "war on terror" against specific enemies of the so-called "Islamic civilization."

23. "Operation Janmabhoomi: An Investigation into the Conspiracy Behind the Demolition of the Babri Masjid," *Cobrapost* (4 April 2014), www.cobrapost.com/index.php/news-detail?nid=5785&cid=23.

24. "No New Evidence in Cobrapost Sting: CBI Officials," *The Times of India* (5 April 2014), http://timesofindia.indiatimes.com/india/No-new-evidence-in-Cobrapost-sting-CBI-officials/articleshow/33256859.cms.

25. In the above paragraph, we have drawn upon a brilliant essay by Dilip Simeon, "The Law of Killing: A Brief History of Indian Fascism," in Banaji (ed.), *Fascism: Essays on Europe and India*, 153–213.

26. A copy of this report is available at www.deccanchronicle.com/131129/news-current-affairs/article/exclusive-sundarlal-report-police-action.

27. "Of a Massacre Untold," *Frontline*, 18:5 (March 3–15, 2001), at www.frontline.in/static/html/fl1805/18051130.htm.

28. PUDR–PUCL, *Who Are the Guilty?* (Delhi: People's Union for Democratic Rights and People's Union for Civil Liberties, December 1984). Dilip Simeon, "The Broken Middle," *Economic & Political Weekly*, 49:43 and 44, (November 1, 2014), 84–92. Amrita Kesselman and Mark Kesselman, "Class, Communalism, and Official Complicity: India after Indira," *Monthly Review*, 36:8 (January 1985), 13–21.

29. For Bombay, 1993, we draw on *The Bombay Riots: Myths and Realities — A Report* by Lokshahi Hakk Sanghatana and Committee for the Protection of Democratic Rights (Bombay: CPDR, March 1993).

30. For Gujarat, 2002, we draw on *When Justice Becomes the Victim: The Quest for Justice After the 2002 Violence in Gujarat*, authored by Stephan Sonnenberg (International Human Rights and Conflict Resolution Clinic, Stanford Law School, May 2014). http://humanrightsclinic.law.stanford.edu/project/the-quest-for-justice.

31. And, in the Lok Sabha elections that followed in late-December 1984, Congress wiped out the BJP—out of a total of 514 seats, it bagged 404 seats; the BJP, just two—as the *shuddha* Hindutva party; even the "Hindutva voters had switched to the Congress." Dilip Simeon, "The Broken Middle," 88.

32. Zakia Jafri is the widow of the Muslim ex-Member of Parliament, Ehsan Jafri, who was brutally hacked and then burnt to death on February 28, 2002. She has filed a case alleging criminal conspiracy and abetment in the 2002 Gujarat pogrom on the part of Narendra Modi and 59 other defendants. The case relies on circumstantial evidence to indicate that the pogrom was systematically planned. See Stephan Sonnenberg, *When Justice Becomes the Victim. . .* , 20–24.

33. Amicus Curiae Raju Ramachandran's report, cited in Stephan Sonnenberg, *When Justice Becomes the Victim. . .* , footnote 205 on page 103. Ramachandran insisted that "evidentiary questions [related to the Jafri case] should be decided in open court, rather than by the SIT [Special Investigation Team, which was asked to take over the investigatory functions of the police]. . ." (23).

34. D. E. Smith, *India as a Secular State* (Princeton, NJ: Princeton University Press, 1963), 4.

35. Article 26 provides that, within certain limits, every religious denomination has the right to manage its religious affairs. Article 27 makes it clear that the state cannot compel a person to pay taxes whose proceeds are specifically earmarked to pay for expenses related to promotion or maintenance of any particular religion or religious denomination, nor can the state use any tax revenue for such purposes. Article 28, with an exception, does not allow an educational institution wholly maintained out of state funds to provide religious instruction, nor can any person attending an educational institution which receives state funds be compelled to take part in the religious instruction imparted by it. As the distinguished judge, civil liberties activist, and radical humanist, V. M. Tarkunde has written: "The Indian Constitution neither encourages nor discourages the profession, practice or propagation of any religion or religious denomination." V. M. Tarkunde, "Secularism and the Indian Constitution," *Indian International Centre Quarterly*, 22:1 (Spring 1995), 143–152 (quote on 151).

36. The judiciary has the power to review or strike down an amendment of the Constitution by Parliament which is not in tune with or alters any of the basic, fundamental features of the Constitution.

37. Omar Khalidi, "Hinduising India: Secularism in Practice," *Third World Quarterly*, 29:8 (2008), 1557.
38. Utkarsh Anand, "Should Yakub Hang? SC Split, So Larger Bench to Hear Today," *Indian Express* (July 29, 2015).
39. The words in quotes are from the 1998 Srikrishna Commission Report, in the concluding part, and Justice B. N. Srikrishna's drawing on the testimony of the *Mahanagar* journalist Yuvraj Mohite.
40. Sebastian, "Secularism and the Indian Judiciary," 42–43, 44.
41. A. G. Noorani, "Impossible Agenda," *Frontline* (June 27, 2014), 39.
42. Anil Nauriya, "Relation between State and Religion: Antinomies of Passive Secularism," *Economic & Political Weekly*, 24:8 (February 25, 1989), 405–406.
43. Uma Chakravarti, "Long Road to Nowhere: Justice Nanavati on 1984," *Economic & Political Weekly*, 40:35 (August 27, 2005), 3795.

9. "Little Man, What Now?"—In the Wake of Semi-Fascist and Sub-Imperialist Tendencies

1. My attempt to understand historical fascism draws on the following works: (i) Paul M. Sweezy, *The Theory of Capitalist Development* (New York: Monthly Review Press, 1942, reprinted 1970), chapter 18, "Fascism"; (ii) Franz Neumann, *Behemoth: The Structure and Practice of National Socialism* (New York: Oxford University Press, 1942); (iii) Maxine Y. Sweezy, *The Structure of the Nazi Economy* (Cambridge, Mass.: Harvard University Press, 1941); (iv) Eric Hobsbawm, *The Age of Extremes: A History of the World, 1914–1991* (New York: Vintage Books, 1994), chapters 4 and 5; (v) Arthur Rosenberg (1934), "Fascism as a Mass Movement," translated and introduced by Jairus Banaji in Banaji (ed.), *Fascism: Essays on Europe and India* (Gurgaon: Three Essays Collective, 2013), 19–96; (vi) Jairus Banaji, "Introduction" to Rosenberg's essay, in Jairus Banaji (ed.), *Fascism: Essays on Europe and India*.
2. Benito Mussolini realized the significance of the volunteer corps retaking Fiume, and after 1921 he ensured that fascism became a mass movement in the March on Rome organized by the National Fascist Party in October 1922.
3. Germa Bel, "Against the Mainstream: Nazi Privatization in 1930s Germany," *Economic History Review*, 63:1 (February 2010), 34–55.
4. For the Marxist theory I am drawing upon, see Paul M. Sweezy, "Some Problems in the Theory of Capital Accumulation," *International Journal of Political Economy*, 17:2 (Summer 1987), 38–53.
5. For a succinct summary of the Marxist theory I am applying, albeit one that is more relevant to an economy where big business is in a commanding position, see Paul M. Sweezy, "Monopoly Capital," in John Eatwell, Murray Milgate, and Peter Newman (eds.), *Marxian Economics* (London: Macmillan, 1990), 297–303. The Indian economy, however, has a long way to go before it reaches "maturity" in the sense of tight oligopolistic market structures with excess capacity fulfilling mostly replacement demand, and with modern infrastructure (for example, urban infrastructural development, including the highway system) already in place, and therefore requiring very little large "Greenfield" investment. So, from the capitalist point of view, there isn't as much of a chronic deficiency of effective demand like there is in the developed capitalist economies.
6. In attempting to throw light on Indian capitalism's sub-imperialist tendency, albeit in desperate brevity, in this and the subsequent two sections, I need to emphasize that, as in the case of explaining imperialism, it would be erroneous to elucidate

everything—including the politics, the geo-politics, the social aspects, and the culture—in terms of economics. My conceptualization of sub-imperialism draws on two articles by the Brazilian scholar and activist Ruy Mauro Marini: (i) "Brazilian 'Interdependence' and Imperialist Integration," *Monthly Review*, 17:7 (December 1965), 10–23 and 26–29; (ii) "Brazilian Sub-imperialism," *Monthly Review*, 23:9 (February 1972), 14–24.

7. Deepak Nayyar, "The Internationalization of Firms from India: Investment, Mergers and Acquisitions," *Oxford Development Studies*, 36:1 (March 2008), 111–131.

8. Ministry of Corporate Affairs, *57th Annual Report on the Working and Administration of the Companies Act, 1956 for the Year Ended March 31, 2013* (Delhi: Government of India, Ministry of Corporate Affairs, 2014), 27, 29–30.

9. With financialization, the process of capital accumulation is increasingly a matter of adding to the stock of financial assets.

10. A considerable "sales effort" is now evident at the upper ends of the markets for consumer durables, including cars, and fast-moving consumer non-durables—in packaging, non-functional product-attributes, throwaways, and built-in product obsolescence.

11. For a deeper conceptual understanding, see Paul A. Baran, "The Theory of the Leisure Class," *Monthly Review*, 9:3 and 4 (July–August 1957), 83–91.

12. Matters concerning India's defense and defense production are shrouded in secrecy. The following pieces by Gautam Navlakha in the *Economic & Political Weekly* throw some light on the subject. "Internal Security: Cost of Repression," 34:20 (May 15, 1999), 1171–1174; "Whither People's Security," 36:23 (June 9, 2001), 2038–2043; "National Security: Prisoners of Rhetoric," 38:24 (June 14, 2003), 2356–2359; "Shrinking Horizon of an Expanding Economy: India's Military Spending," 41:14 (April 8, 2006), 1338–1340; "Military Budget 2013–14: Giant with Feet of Clay," 48:24 (June 15, 2013), 36–41. Also see C. Rammanohar Reddy, "Defence Expenditure," in Kaushik Basu (ed.), *The Oxford Companion to Economics in India* (New Delhi: Oxford University Press, 2008), 89–92.

13. "Joint Statement: The United States and India—Enduring Global Partners in the 21st Century," Office of the Press Secretary, The White House, June 7, 2016, at obamawhitehouse.archives.gov/the-press-office/2016/06/07/joint-statement-united-states-and-india-enduring-global-partners-21st.

14. In February 2017, the Anil Dhirubhai Ambani group's (ADAG) Reliance Defence and Engineering entered into a "Master Ship Repair Agreement" for repair and servicing of the Seventh Fleet's warships and other supporting vessels at the company's Pipavav shipyard. The contract will enable the company to rake in additional estimated revenue of around $1.5 billion over a period of five years. With the help and support of the central and Gujarat governments, the shipyard, which was acquired by ADAG in 2015, was rapidly upgraded and put in shape to be designated as an "approved contractor" of the US Navy.

15. Meera Nanda, "Hindu Triumphalism and the Clash of Civilisations," *Economic & Political Weekly*, 44:28 (July 11, 2009), 108.

16. Hindutvavadins take great pride in the supposed cultural imperialist past of India, its large-scale acculturation, especially in South-East Asia, including religious and spiritual tutelage there. In a recent interview in the *Hindustan Times* (July 17, 2014), Ashok Singhal, the main patron of the Vishwa Hindu Parishad, articulates the idea of building a "cultural commonwealth" of South and Southeast Asia.

17. India's 1950 Treaty of Peace and Friendship with Nepal, among other things, obliges Kathmandu to inform New Delhi of any planned armament purchases, and, in fact, makes it possible for India to determine Nepal's national security policy.

18. John Mage, "The Nepali Revolution and International Relations," *Economic & Political Weekly*, 42:20 (May 19, 2007), 1834–39.

19. Such religiosity, in its demonstration of power and wealth, exploits religious faith for political and pecuniary gains.

20. Meera Nanda, *The God Market: How Globalization Is Making India More Hindu* (New Delhi: Random House, 2009).

21. Tapan Basu, Pradip Datta, Sumit Sarkar, Tanika Sarkar, and Sambuddha Sen, *Khaki Shorts, Saffron Flags* (Hyderabad: Orient Longman, 1993), 8–9.

22. Romila Thapar, *The Past as Present: Forging Contemporary Identities through History* (New Delhi: Aleph, 2014), 115, 163, 143, 146, and 160.

23. Radhika Desai, "Forward March of Hindutva Halted?" *New Left Review*, 30 (November–December, 2004), 49–67.

24. Christophe Jaffrelot, "The Hindu Nationalists and Power," chapter 14, in Niraja Gopal Jayal and Pratap Bhanu Mehta (eds.), *Oxford Companion to Politics in India* (New Delhi: Oxford University Press, 2010), 205–218.

25. The Akhil Bharatiya Vidyarthi Parishad (since 1948), the Jana Sangh (founded in 1951), Vanavasi Kalyan Ashram (from 1952), the Saraswati Shishu Mandir network of schools (since 1952), the Bharatiya Mazdoor Sangh (since 1955), the Vishwa Hindu Parishad (since 1964), the Seva Bharati (from 1979 onward), and the Bharatiya Janata Party (after the 1980 split of the Janata Party), the Bajrang Dal (from 1984 onward), the Ram Janmabhoomi Nyas (1993 onward), etc.

26. The way in which politics influences caste is as important as the manner in which caste influences politics.

27. See the following two articles by Radhika Desai: (i) "The Cast(e) of Anti-Secularism," in Mushirul Hasan (ed.), *Will Secular India Survive?* (Gurgaon: Imprint One, 2004), 177–209; and (ii) "A Latter-day Fascism?," *Economic & Political Weekly*, 49:35 (August 30, 2014), 48–58.

28. As far as I know, Jairus Banaji has been the first scholar to suggest the use of this German term to designate the large section of society that has been passively complicit in the criminality of the regime and "morally indifferent to the fate of the regime's victims." See his article, "Trajectories of Fascism: Extreme-Right Movements in India and Elsewhere," in Jairus Banaji (ed.), *Fascism: Essays on Europe and India* (Gurgaon: Three Essays Collective, 2013), 215–230 (quote on 218).

29. After "a long and rambling interview" with Narendra Modi when the latter "was a nobody, a small-time RSS *pracharak*," the political psychologist and social theorist Ashis Nandy, a trained clinical psychologist, was left "in no doubt" that Modi was "a classic, clinical case of a fascist." See Ashis Nandy, "Obituary of a Culture," *Seminar*, Number 513 (May 2002), special issue on "Society under Siege: A Symposium on the Breakdown of Civil Society in Gujarat," edited by Harsh Sethi, at www.india-seminar.com/2002/513/513%20ashis%20nandy.htm.

30. The notion of "authoritarian democracy" was perhaps first formulated by Giovanni Gentile, one of the masterminds of the "fascistization" of Italian culture. For Gentile's political philosophy, see Gabriele Turi, "Giovanni Gentile: Oblivion, Remembrance, and Criticism," *The Journal of Modern History*, 70:4 (December 1998), 913–933.

31. Prabhat Patnaik, "The Goods and Services Tax," *People's Democracy* (June 15, 2016), at http://peoplesdemocracy.in/2016/0619_pd/goods-and-services-tax.

32. Quoted in "Pasolini: Murder of a Dissident" by Maria-Antonietta Macciocchi and Thomas Repensek, *October*, 13 (Summer 1980), 20.

33. I am drawing from a draft of an edit that I penned, which was published as "Harold

Pinter: Writer as Citizen," *Economic & Political Weekly*, 40:52 (December 24, 2005), 5440. The edit was based on Pinter's 2005 Nobel Lecture, "Art, Truth & Politics," at www.nobelprize.org/nobel_prizes/literature/laureates/2005/pinter-lecture-e.html.

10. History, Memory, and Dreams —Reimagining "New Democracy"

1. William Morris, *A Dream of John Ball* (Portland, Maine: Thomas B. Mosher, 1908), 32.
2. Karl Marx, *The Eighteenth Brumaire of Louis Bonaparte*, 1852 (Moscow: Progress Publishers, 1937), chapter 1, at www.marxists.org/archive/marx/works/1852/18th-brumaire/ch01.htm.
3. John Ball comes across as a practitioner of what we refer to today as liberation theology.
4. I am inspired by Hal Draper's "The Two Souls of Socialism," *New Politics*, 5:1 (Winter 1966), 57–84, at www.marxists.org/archive/draper/1966/twosouls/.
5. *Ashraf* refers to the Muslim descendents claiming foreign ancestry, elites of landowners, political leaders, religious heads, and professionals, compared to the *ajlaf*, indigenously converted Muslims who are ordinary people, mostly artisans, workers, and peasants.
6. When I think of all this, I tend to agree with the "world-systems" historian Immanuel Wallerstein that "capitalism has represented historically moral regression and for the vast majority of the world's population material regression. . ." See his essay, "Marx and Underdevelopment," S. Resnick and R. Wolff (eds.), *Rethinking Marxism: Struggles in Marxist Theory: Essays for Harry Magdoff and Paul Sweezy* (Brooklyn, New York: Autonomedia, 1985), 393.
7. Ranajit Guha, "Gramsci in India: Homage to a Teacher," unpublished lecture first read in absentia at a conference of the Gramsci Foundation in Rome, April 2007, in Ranajit Guha, *The Small Voice of History: Collected Essays*, edited and with an Introduction by Partha Chatterjee (Ranikhet: Permanent Black, 2009), 365, 368.
8. I have drawn on a fascinating account of the Gudem–Rampa uprisings by David Arnold, "Rebellious Hillmen: The Gudem–Rampa Risings, 1839–1924," in Ranajit Guha (ed.), *Subaltern Studies I* (Delhi: Oxford University Press, 1981), 88–142.
9. Sumanta Banerjee, *In the Wake of Naxalbari* (Kolkata: Sahitya Samsad, 2008), 112.
10. For Marx's ideas on the French Revolution, see Michael Lowy, " 'The Poetry of the Past': Marx and the French Revolution," *New Left Review*, I/177 (September–October, 1989), at http://newleftreview.org/I/177/michael-lowy-the-poetry-of-the-past-marx-and-the-french-revolution.
11. Mao Tse-tung, *On New Democracy*, January 1940, in *Selected Works of Mao Tse-tung*, Vol. II (Peking: Foreign Languages Press, 1967), 339–84.
12. I have drawn Mao's essential ideas on New Democracy from Stuart Schram, *The Thought of Mao Tse-Tung* (Cambridge: Cambridge University Press, 1989), 78–94 (Mao quote on page 94).
13. Hamza Alavi, "State and Class Under Peripheral Capitalism," in Hamza Alavi and Teodor Shanin (eds.), *Introduction to the Sociology of 'Developing Societies'* (London: Macmillan, 1982), 302.
14. Karl Polanyi, *The Great Transformation: The Political and Economic Origins of Our Time* (Boston: Beacon Press, 1944/1957).
15. Nirmal Kumar Chandra, "The Peasant Question from Marx to Lenin," *Economic & Political Weekly*, 37:20 (May 18, 2002), 1927.
16. I have liberally drawn from the experience of the Chinese land reform as recounted

in William Hinton, "Mao, Rural Development, and Two-Line Struggle," *Monthly Review*, 45:9 (February 1994), 1–15 (the quote is from pages 6–7).

17. Farshad Araghi, "The Great Global Enclosure of Our Times: Peasants and the Agrarian Question at the End of the Twentieth Century," in Fred Magdoff, John Bellamy Foster, and Frederick H Buttel (eds.), *Hungry for Profit: The Agribusiness Threat to Farmers, Food and the Environment* (New York: Monthly Review Press, 2000).

18. Utsa Patnaik, "The Republic of Hunger," *Social Scientist*, 32:9/10 (September 2004), 9–35 and "Poverty Trends in India, 2004–05 to 2009–10," *Economic & Political Weekly*, 48:40 (October 5, 2013), 43–58.

19. See, for instance, Jan Breman, "Agrarian Change and Class Conflict in Gujarat, India," *Population and Development Review*, 15, Supplement: Rural Development and Population: Institutions and Policy (1989), 301–323.

20. *Scripting the Change: Selected Writings of Anuradha Ghandy*, edited by Anand Teltumbde and Shoma Sen (Delhi: Daanish Books, 2011).

21. One of the world's most-accomplished macroeconomists, Amit Bhaduri, calls this "development with dignity." See his book, *Development with Dignity: A Case for Full Employment* (New Delhi, National Book Trust: 2005), which proposes a universal employment guarantee scheme and outlines the core requirements of the Keynesian macroeconomic policy regime that must be in place as a prerequisite to ensure its feasibility.

22. Hal Draper, "The Two Souls of Socialism," at www.marxists.org/archive/draper/1966/twosouls/.

23. "Marxism, the Capital System, and Social Revolution: An Interview with István Mészáros," *Science & Society, 63:3 (Fall 1999), 354–58.

24. "Victory" by Pier Paolo Pasolini, translated by Norman MacAfee with Luciano Matinengo—"A Hitherto Unpublished Pasolini Poem on the 30th Anniversary of the Poet's Death, A Direland Exclusive" (October 26, 2005), at http://direland.type-pad.com/direland/2005/10/a_hitherto_unpu.html

25. Jews, many of them forced refugees, did more than their bit, especially in France, where Armenian and Polish Jews even attacked German officers in Paris. And one must never forget the part played by women partisans.

26. Michael E. Tigar, "Terrorism and Human Rights," Commentary, *Monthly Review* (November 21, 2001), at http://monthlyreview.org/commentary/terrorism-and-human-rights. The rule of law based on the principle of equality before the law, to the extent that it is made to prevail, is certainly a means of protection of the weak, the victims of the anti-Muslim pogroms, and Muslims who are falsely accused of acts of terrorism.

27. Samir Amin, "In Defence of Humanity: Radicalisation of Popular Struggles," in Corinne Kumar (ed.), *Asking We Walk: The South as New Political Imaginary* (Bangalore: Streelekha, 2007), 160.

28. Karl Marx, in "On *The Jewish Question*," 1844, at www.marxists.org/archive/marx/works/1844/jewish-question/.

29. *Aufhebung* is the German word Hegel used, meaning overcoming and going beyond but nevertheless preserving the befitting core of what is overcome.

30. Karl Marx, in "A Contribution to the Critique of Hegel's *Philosophy of Right*" (1844), at www.marxists.org/archive/marx/works/1843/critique-hpr/intro.htm.

31. Dirk J. Struik, "People Are Important: A Mathematician's Faith," *Monthly Review*, 49:8 (January 1998), 49.

32. Barrington Moore, Jr., *Social Origins of Dictatorship and Democracy: Lord and*

Peasant in the Making of the Modern World (Harmondsworth: Penguin, 1966).

33. John Bellamy Foster, *Marx's Ecology: Materialism and Nature* (New York: Monthly Review Press, 2000).

34. Karl Marx, *Capital*, Volume I (Moscow: Foreign Languages Publishing House, 1954), a reproduction of the first English edition of 1887, edited by Frederick Engels, chapter 10, "The Working Day," 233.

APPENDIX: CASTE

1. See, for instance, Kumkum Roy, "Kosambi and Questions of Caste," *Economic & Political Weekly*, Special Issue on "D. D. Kosambi: The Man and His Work," 43:30 (July 26, 2008), 78–84, as also, Ajit Roy, "Caste and Class: An Interlinked View," *Economic & Political Weekly*, 14:7/8, Class and Caste in India, Annual Number (February 1979), 297–312. The Buddhist sources, texts, and inscriptions that throw light on caste *and* class in ancient India are more suggestive of the class evolution of caste. Unlike the Brahminical sources, they highlight the economic and political domains, not giving any importance to the ritual domain. See Uma Chakravarti, "Towards a Historical Sociology of Stratification in Ancient India: Evidence from Buddhist Sources," *Economic & Political Weekly*, 20:9 (March 2, 1985), 356–60.

2. Maurice Godelier, "Infrastructures, Societies and History," *New Left Review*, I/127 (May-June 1981), 3–17. I must emphasize that I do not subscribe to the *universal* theory of history derived by some latter-day "Marxists" from Marx's famous Preface to his 1859 book *A Contribution to the Critique of Political Economy*.

3. Uma Chakravarti, *Gendering Caste: Through a Feminist Lens* (Kolkata: Stree, 2002).

4. See, for instance, in relation to the province of Bihar, Anand Chakravarti's *Social Power and Everyday Class Relations: Agrarian Transformation in North Bihar* (New Delhi: Sage Publications, 2001).

5. M. N. Srinivas, *Caste in Modern India and Other Essays* (Bombay: Asia Publishing House, 1962).

6. Valerian Rodrigues, "Introduction" to *The Essential Writings of B. R. Ambedkar* (New Delhi: Oxford University Press, 2002), 7.

7. The Wikipedia entry on Debiprasad Chattopadhyaya is excellent as a brief introduction to the Marxist philosopher and his main works. https://en.wikipedia.org/wiki/Debiprasad_Chattopadhyaya.

8. Jayantanuja Bandyopadhyaya, *Class and Religion in Ancient India* (New Delhi: Anthem Press, 2007), 153, 204, 184–85. Incidentally, the *Manusmriti*, drafted by the lawgivers in the first century AD, assumed the name of the mythical Manu in order to impart divinity to its authorship.

9. Eleanor Zelliot, *Ambedkar's World: The Making of Babasaheb Ambedkar* (Bluemoon Books, 2004; New Delhi: Navayana, 2013).

10. Christophe Jaffrelot, "Caste and Political Parties in India: Do Indians Vote Their Caste—While Casting Their Vote," in *Routledge Handbook of Indian Politics*, edited by Atul Kohli and Prerna Singh (London and New York: Routledge, 2013), 107–118.

11. B. R. Ambedkar, "Untouchables or the Children of India's Ghetto," in Dr. Babasaheb Ambedkar, *Writings and Speeches*, Volume 5 (Bombay: Government of Maharashtra, 1989), 101–102.

12. Arundhati Roy, "The Doctor and the Saint: Ambedkar, Gandhi and the Battle Against Caste," *The Caravan* (March 1, 2014) at www.caravanmagazine.in/essay/doctor-and-saint.

Index

CPSIA information can be obtained
at www.ICGtesting.com
Printed in the USA
LVHW09s1358060918
589329LV00002BA/395/P